Compendium in Tourism and Hospitality Studies
Introduction To Tourism and Hospitality Service Systems

Maximino P. Zurbito, Jr.

Ukiyoto Publishing

All global publishing rights are held by

Ukiyoto Publishing

Published in 2023

Content Copyright © Maximino P. Zurbito, Jr.

ISBN 9789360169954

All rights reserved.

No part of this publication may be reproduced, transmitted, or stored in a retrieval system, in any form by any means, electronic, mechanical, photocopying, recording or otherwise, without the prior permission of the publisher.

The moral rights of the author have been asserted.

This is a work of fiction. Names, characters, businesses, places, events, locales, and incidents are either the products of the author's imagination or used in a fictitious manner. Any resemblance to actual persons, living or dead, or actual events is purely coincidental.

This book is sold subject to the condition that it shall not by way of trade or otherwise, be lent, resold, hired out or otherwise circulated, without the publisher's prior consent, in any form of binding or cover other than that in which it is published.

www.ukiyoto.com

PREFACE

Finally, the time has come for the fulfillment of this author's long-time dream to have this book published and fill the gap in the lack of a textbook and learning reference material in major subjects related to Tourism and Hospitality tertiary academic and training programs, that he personally experienced while teaching the course at the Polytechnic University of the Philippines sometime in the late 80's. The problem recurring until date of this writing. This is in addition to the fact that Tourism had become his passion ever since his first encounter of the industry system when he first landed a job in a travel agency while at the early age of only 18 years old, and rose from the lowest position of messenger to become a manager of the inbound/local tours division; and, lucky enough to have been awarded the International Tourism Scholarship by the WATA-World Association of Travel Agencies in 1980 together with a Swiss national. The first in Asia and the only one from the Philippines, the traveling scholarship catapulted him to have visited the 29 cities of 21 countries in Asia and Europe where he was mandated by the Scholarship to conduct an investigative research on tourism development in these areas as a part the traveling scholarship, after which his enclusion and enrollment to the 1987 Roll of Experts in Tourism Education and Training by the International Labour Office (ILO) Technical Cooperation for Developing Countries.

Additionally, what fortified the passion in tourism education of this author to have ultimately driven him to complete the final manuscript of this book is the adoption of NIPSC Northern Iloilo Polytechnic State College (now NISU Northern Iloilo State University) thru its Board of Trustees (BOT) in its academic system the Concept he formulated on Project TREASURE-Tourism Reinvented for Eco Agri Stimulus of the Unproductive to Rejuvenate Economy aimed at transforming the less if not unproductive local resources into potently income generating assets where the highly impoverished communities are given the opportunity to be a key player in the implementation of the major component programs on tourism-oriented 'Livelihood and Poverty Alleviation Development' to fairly share the tourism bounties for their every labor.. This is augmented by the fact that the same

Concept of Project TREASURE, more particularly the Component Program on 'Continuing Tourism Awareness-Key to the Institutionalization Culture of Tourism thru the Operationalization of CREATED Center for Rural Eco Agri Tourism Education and Development Training Center and Resort Theme Park had, in-fact accelerated the imperatives for the publication of this book to serve both as learning and funding sources to support the principal objectives of Project TREASURE's major component program. which was first adopted as a continuing flagship project of ANITOS- Association of Northern Iloilo Tourism Oriented Services, a local tourism oriented Non-Government Organization (NGO). This is likewise in consonance with the academic sector's requirement on the availability of authoritative textbook and reference learning material for the country's full compliance with the on-going implementation of the ASEAN Integration Mutual Recognition Arrangement for Tourism Professionals Common Competency Assessment Standards that took effect since 2016.

The realities on the ground, had given more strengths and became an impetus for this author to proceed and ultimately complete the book manuscript and work for its ultimate publication by the most trusted publishing company which terms and conditions are unquestionably most fair and equitable, if only to equip both the academic and local government sectors to truly understand Tourism and its importance to socio-economic development by using this book, in fact is the highest consideration transcending all others for this book ultimately come into being.

Maximino P. Zurbito, Jr., A.B.; J.D./Ph.D.
Author
Bgy. Bulaquenia, Estancia, Iloilo, Philippines

Acknowledgement

To WATA - World Association of Travel Agencies at www@wata.net/ www.wata.net thru its Secretary General Ms. Christine Fournier for her very kind FOREWORD; the ASEAN Association of South East Asian Nations's Website: www.asean.org. in expressly allowing the contents of the ASEAN MRAP TP Mututal Recognition Arrangement for Tourism Professionals recited in this book; and, Ukiyoto Publishing for being the most trusted and highly reliable publishing company to have accepted this book's publication under its most fair and equitable terms and conditions.

Colleagues in the tourism industry who have been both very vocal and straightforward with their thoughts on the early plans of this author to someday write a book in tourism studies as his humble contribution to the country's tourism development, particularly the late Willie Genciana, Bobby Laygo, Allan Brillantes, and foremost among them is Vidal C. Villaruz, Jr., who have sang so many songs to refresh the mind of this author while groping for words, phrases and terminologies that now find their permanent abode in the pages of this book; the late Hernani C. Coscolluela who mentored the author during his early years in the tourism industry being his direct superior, and afforded him every opportunity for career advancement and nomination in the WATA World Association Travel Agencies International Tourism Scholarship Award, as well as former Miss Universe Margarita Moran-Floirendo who was then the General Manager of House of Travel, Inc. that personally surprised her congratulations while handing to this author the WATA telex notice of scholarship grant in the first morning office hour; co-workers in companies with which this author had the opportunity to serve, particularly House of Travel, Inc., and Celebrity Travel and Tours where this author had the most productive and successful jouney in the most challenging highways and by-ways of travel and tourism systems from a fledgling industry worker; fellow early DOT Licensed Tour-Guides some of whom had already rested in peace, particularly the late Arthur Montaño a multi-lingual licensed tour guide who graciously shared and practically mentored this author on the basics of German and French languages; classmates and fraternal brothers at

Philippine Law School, professors particularly the late Dean Minerva Inocencio Peguing, Dominador Castro, Registrar and Simeon Rene Lacson, President that collectively allowed the author's absence from regular classes at Philippine Law School during his Traveling Scholarship; the Board of Trustees of the then NIPSC Northern Iloilo Polytechnic State College now NISU Northern Iloilo State University thru the intercession of Dr. Maria Teresa Gasapo-Palmares, Ph.D., that unanimously adopted in its system the major program components of Project TREASURE, specifically the 'Continuing Tourism Awareness-Key to the Institutionalization Culture of Tourism' thru the operationalization of CREATED Center for Rural Eco Agri Tourism Education and Development.Officers; and, finally the Members and Officers of ANITOS Association of Northern Iloilo Tourism Oriented Services under the leadership of Rogelio J. Arañador that adopted first the Concept of Project TREASURE Tourism Reinvented for Eco Agri Stimulus of the Unproductive to Rejuvenate Economy as its continuing flagship project which implementation it ultimately offered in partnership with NIPSC now NISU for which this book is a major support tool.

Dedication

To my wife Josephine Ciudad-de Angel, children Maximilian and wife Jhanissa with eldest son Maximilian II (Maxie Baby Bothchok), Karen Mae, and Mark Joseph with wife Alyssa all of whom served as the eternal flame that lights every path I take, and stand as the very ultimate source of inexhaustible strengths in every pigment of my mind and imagination to finally complete the manuscript up to its acceptance for publication, this humble work is eternally dedicated;

-and-

My elder sister Leonora Zurbito-Avelino; half-brothers Enrico Pancho Ling, Gaspar Pancho Ling (deceased), and Exzur Pancho Armada; Arturo Alavarez Zurbito, Sr., (deceased); Half-sisters Ana Pancho-Armada y Parcon and childlren; Monica Pancho Armada, Brenda Pancho ArmadaFunelas and childreh, and Amy Pancho Armada-Buensolido and childl; and finally to my mother (Nanay) Adelina Pancho Vda. De Zurbito and father Maximino A. Zurbito, Sr., who both have alrerady rested to eternal peace in the farthest beyond this humble work is soulfully dedicated."

The AUTHOR

 World Association of Travel Agencies
Office of Secretary General
Tranchepied 25 – 1278 LA RIPPE
Switzerland
Tel: +4179 239779 / wata@wata.net / www.wata.net

FOREWORD

Currently, there are countless of publications in the tourism sector both in hard and soft copies that are published and made available thru social media. These are considered to be the best sources of vital information in updating the knowledge of the tourism front-liners, key players, stakeholders, as well as industry professionals, practitioners, the academe and learners in the trade. However, few have authored and published books related to the complete overview of the whole tourism as a system, and that, should there be any, their respective author's views are very limited only to one specific component of the tourism sector. None among these published books had satisfactorily explained the peculiarities of the complicated and diverse nature of Tourism and Hospitality Industry as they are currently practiced globally.

Maximino Zurbito, as the First in Asia and the only Filipino awarded with the World Association of Travel Agencies (WATA) Daniel V. Dedina International Tourism Scholarship sometime in 1980, had indeed put to use what he experienced and learned during his traveling scholarship, and thus, meticulously explicated the variant views and understanding of Tourism translated into his dissertation conscripted in the pages of this book justifying on the process his chosen title "Compendium in Tourism & Hospitality Studies". His explication would certainly be an added value to the enrichment of the global understanding of Tourism not only as an ordinary industry but more so, a socio-economic development phenomenon and a system enjoyed by the world's population. Students, practitioners and stakeholders in the tourism sector will find in these pages the illumination that will facilitate their truest appreciation and in-depth comprehension and understanding of Tourism. The author's formidable notes will certainly enlighten and educate the reader about the origin, evolution, history; and, the most suited definition and meaning of Tourism, thus arming the reader with such erudition as will demystify the conduct and practice of any business or industry and profession related to Tourism as a system.

The finest dissertations propounded inevitably find their way in the pages and become authorities themselves, relied upon by the industry pillars who would craft future changes in their own publications, as the author's opus is a candidate for such distinction. This Edition of Compendium in Tourism and Hospitality Studies is thus, a worthy addition to the libraries of the academic institutions, government agencies, tourism authorities and private non-government organizations. A mastery of its contents absolutely offers the reader endless rewards in the field of tourism, travel and hospitality. It is indeed fortunate, that the author has embarked upon this endeavor, and has left a legacy that will be treasured in the annals of tourism learning and education, practice of business or industry and profession, for which WATA is proud to be a part.

La Rippe, Switzerland, January 4, 2017.

Christine FOURNIER,
Secretary General

Contents

Book – 1 Tourism Origin, Evolution and History 1
-and-.. 9
Discussion On The Origin And Interpretation Of Tourism 2

Book 2 - Brief Philippine Tourism History 12

The Early Tourism and First Recorded Foreign Visitors to the Philippines
.... 13
Philippine Modern Tourism History 18

Book 3 - Brief Philippine History 23

Pre-Historic Past 24
Early Spanish Expeditions and Conquests 30
World War II and Japanese Occupation 45
Independent Philippines and the Third Republic (1946–1975) 48
Fifth Republic (1986–Present) 63

Book 4 - Summary Of Current Philippine Tourism 70

Geography, Socio-Cultural and Economic Features 71

Book 5 - Tourism As A System-How It Works 83

The Tourism Service Systems 84
Tourism Development Planning 93
Tourism Destination Management 123
Facilities And Services 123
Travel Agency/Inbound-Local Tours Management And Operation 128
Fundamentals And Techniques In Tour Guiding 161

Book 6 (MICE)-Meetings, Incentives, Conventions And
Exhibits 172

Insights And Beginnings Of Conference Industry 173
Promotion Of A Destination 181
Contracts With Clients And Suppliers 188
Socials And Protocol 192
Standard Rules And Regulations On Exhibits 203

The Role Of Carrier/Transport..209
Mice Marketing Strategies..216
Languages, Interpretation And Translation A Necessity In International Congress 220
International Organizations 224
Standard Questionnaire For Professional Congress Organizers (PCOs)...224
Concerning Conditions Available For World Congress..............................224

Book 7 - Hospitality Service Systems..228

Introduction To Hospitality Service 229
Types And Categories Of Accommodation Facilities 244
Restaurant, Cocktail Lounge, Night Club, Training Center & Spa 265

Book 8 - Marketing Tourism & Travel..274

History And Evolution Of Modern Marketing..275
The Changing Needs And Priorities Of Affluent Society..........................281
Marketing Comes to Retailing 289
A Do-It-Yourself Approach To Marketing 296
Marketing In The 21st Century 305
Age Of Digital Information Technology 305

Book 9 - Asean Mutual Recognition Agreement For Tourism Professionals 314

Glossary of Words/Terms and Phrases 315
Executive Summary MRA-TP...318
The Mutual Recognition Agreement For Tourism Professionals...............321
ASEAN Common Competency Standards for Tourism Professionals 331
Common ASEAN Tourism Curriculum 338
Assessment of Competence 349
The Mechanisms Supporting MRA for Tourism Professionals..................373
Recognition of Tourism Professional Qualifications 381
Conclusion and Roadmap 389
ASEAN MRA-Mutual Recognition Agreement Guide Book for Tourism Education and Training Providers..394

Book 10 - ASEAN Mutual Recognition Agreement For Tourism Professionals (MRA-TP) 450

Guide Book for Assessors 451

Book 11 - Asean Mutual Recognition Agreement On Tourism Professionals 497

Preamble 498

About the Author..*507*

Book 1 - Tourism Origin, Evolution and History

Discussion On The Origin And Interpretation Of Tourism

I. The Etymological Study of the Origin and Evolution of Tourism

The Influence of Greece and Rome
In the old Greece (5th – 7th centuries AD) two types of social strata existed: the aristocrats and the slaves. The aristocrats enjoyed the privilege of the Scholé or leisure, the slaves the a-scholé. The Roman civilization applied similar parameters to make the distinction between the citizens and the non-citizens: the citizens had the opportunity to practice the otium (leisure) while the slaves practiced the neg-otium (negation of the leisure, business) (Guzmán, 1986:25)

During the 2nd century in Rome, the civis (citizen) were engaged in two activities: the occupation, (engagement in trade, handling administrative issues etc), and the otium, which was similar to the a-sholé who devoted their time to the otium iltteratum (arts and poetry etc.). All these activities were characteristic of the nobleman (nobilis) whose activities included active leisure (mutatio laboris), which were distinct from the athletic games, the hunt, the bathrooms of vapor, all characteristics of the profanum vulgus, or passive leisure.

The Romans created the Forum, the Coliseum and the Spas inside Rome, and similar to the Greeks, they gradually began to displace their centers of pleasure, toward places located outside the main cities (peripheries). Centumcellae and Hadriana were among the first villages established as pleasure peripheries. This resulted in building an entire chain of villages for leisure purposes in the outskirts of the big Roman cities, where patricians and noblemen would rest and seek pleasure (profanum vulgus).

After the fall of the empire, the renascimento (15th-17th centuries) introduced the concept of the "humanist trip", which was an attempt

to invigorate domestic culture with acquisition of customs and manners of other towns. The trip is conceived as a source of knowledge by a threatened monarchy. One such trip was the "grand tour" (England - France - 101 Italy - Germany and Low Countries), participants on this tour came from the noble and the bourgeoisie.
Getino has observed that "...in the old Europe, leisure was an ideal...practiced became widely adopted, almost at a similar time period, by the Latin European languages and Saxon.

Nevertheless, another school of thought - the Onomastic School - considers the origin of the concept not from a linguistic perspective but rather links it to the last name of the French aristocracy Della Tour. According to this school, after Carlos V signs a treaty with England in 1516, in celebration of this event, the future king gives the Della Tour family exclusive rights to conduct commercial transport and related businesses. Thus, Leiper (1983) states that this family organized the first trips of English merchants to continental Europe.

Theoretically, in this case tourism refers to an activity linked to commercial displacement (Jiménez Guzmán, 1986).

The Origin of the word TRAVEL
The origin of the word "travel" is even more controversial. In English, the term travel is derived from half travailen (from the verb to toil), which is originally from the French travailler. Similarly, the word "journey" is derived from the old French "jornee", which in turn originates from the Latin vulgar diurnata (diurnum), hence the term jour-ney-er (traveler). In Italian, the term "travel" is translated as viaggio, which is derived directly from the French word viatge that has its origin in old French veiage (voyage). The road finishes (finally) in the term Latin viaticum (with you in the trip). This way via that means road it is annexed to with you it passes to form the idea of provisions for the trip, or viático.

Thus, it is clear that the etymology of the term tourist and tourism is influenced by three classic languages. But considerable disagreement exists among scholars of tourism as to the origins of the concept and its interpretations.

Interpretation from an Economic Perspective

When analyzed from a purely sociological point of view, the displacement of people (trip, migration or diáspora) has an element in conjunction with tourism. The migrant leaves his/her place of habitual residence (home) in search of tangible or intangible resources which cannot be found in the home environment. In a similar way, the tourist is (self) displaced in search of finding something exotic (landscapes, customs, etc) that cannot be found in the home environment. However, this does not mean that an "epic adventure" can be considered in the same line with a tourist vacation. For this reason, it is necessary to examine the distinction between the "trip" and the "tour".

Historically, "trips" have arisen out of economic necessities. Jiménez Guzmán (1986,35-40) has proposed a conceptual history of the trip. This concept proposes five developmental phases. The first phase is the nomadismo (homo) phase, in which the by the cultured elites and people in power...conceived as a necessary time for the enjoyment of privileged few...lasted until the weakening monarchy in the 18th century." (Getino, 2002: 26). In this statement, we find a conceptual separation, i.e., to travel doesn't imply to be a tourist, and likewise tourism is associated with non-touristic activities. It won't be until 1841 that Thomas Cook offers the first trips for pleasure (in the modern sense of travel and recreation) for the elites. However, it was only in the middle of the 20th century that tourism took the form of mass pleasure trips. At this instance, both senses will have to fuse in one alone; the trip like synonym of pleasure or loisir.

In 1900, France reduced its daily labor to 10 hours, and in 1936, its labor law recognized the rights to earn paid vacations. Around 1960, legal reforms and technological revolutions made more free time available to laborers, and the notion of mass tourism gained strong support in contemporary society. (Houlot, 1961; Boyer, 1982; Lanquar, 1981; Jiménez Guzmán, 1986).

Etymological discussion

We can surmise that the roots of the word "tourism" comes from the old Saxon term Torn (England). This word extends to Torn-us (what gives turns) and Torn-are (to give turns). The meaning of the word "torn" can be roughly translated as a "departure with the intention of returning". In practice, it referred to the rest (vacation) trips taken by peasants during the 12th century (Fernández Fuster, 1967). By the middle of the 18th century, the English noblemen used the term "turn" to refer to the trips undertaken for education, search and culture exploration. In reality, the purpose of the noblemen's trip to the different parts of the kingdom was to acquire knowledge that was useful for governing these areas (e.g., asserting power, imposing rules and regulations, etc). The genesis of the "Grand Tour" lies in the early tours taken by the nobility. The term "turn" is abandoned in favor of the "tour", a French influence. In Saxon, the nouns of the original verbs are denominated with the suffix - er (writ-er, speak-er, etc). It is believed that during the 12th century a nobleman who goes on a trip and returns to his/her place of departure would be called a Torn-er. Centuries later, during the era of the bourgeoisie (18th and 19th centuries) the term er was substituted by Latin iste and Greek isme. During the 20th century the term "tour-ist" and the act of touring "tour-ism" are conceived. These terms are widely adopted in Spain. (Jiménez Guzmán, 1986:32) (Fernández Fuster, 1978) (Boyer, 1982)

But not all researchers agree with the above explanation, for example for the Semitic School whose main proponent is Arthur Houlot (1961), the term tourism doesn't derive from the Latin language but from the old Aramaic. According to Houlot, in old Aramic, the term Tur was used for the trip, exploration and movement of people. This word had been used, for the first time, when Moses begins his expedition to the lands of Canaán. Disagreeing with Fernández Fuster (1978), Houlot argues that the term Tur became widely adopted, almost at a similar time period, by the Latin European languages and Saxon.

Nevertheless, another school of thought - the Onomastic School - considers the origin of the concept not from a linguistic perspective but rather links it to the last name of the French aristocracy Della Tour. According to this school, after Carlos V signs a treaty with England in 1516, in celebration of this event, the future king gives the Della Tour family exclusive rights to conduct commercial transport and related businesses. Thus, Leiper (1983) states that this family organized the first trips of English merchants to continental Europe.

Theoretically, in this case tourism refers to an activity linked to commercial displacement (Jiménez Guzmán, 1986).

The Origin of the word TRAVEL

The origin of the word "travel" is even more controversial. In English, the term travel is derived from half travailen (from the verb to toil), which is originally from the French travailler. Similarly, the word "journey" is derived from the old French "jornee", which in turn originates from the Latin vulgar diurnata (diurnum), hence the term jour-ney-er (traveler). In Italian, the term "travel" is translated as viaggio, which is derived directly from the French word viatge that has its origin in old French veiage (voyage). The road finishes (finally) in the term Latin viaticum (with you in the trip). This way via that means road it is annexed to with you it passes to form the idea of provisions for the trip, or viático.

Thus, it is clear that the etymology of the term tourist and tourism is influenced by three classic languages. But considerable disagreement exists among scholars of tourism as to the origins of the concept and its interpretations.

Interpretation from an Economic Perspective

When analyzed from a purely sociological point of view, the displacement of people (trip, migration or diáspora) has an element in conjunction with tourism. The migrant leaves his/her place of habitual residence (home) in search of tangible or intangible resources which cannot be found in the home environment. In a similar way, the tourist is (self) displaced in search of finding something exotic (landscapes, customs, etc) that cannot be found in the home environment. However, this does not mean that an "epic adventure" can be considered in the same line with a tourist vacation. For this reason, it is necessary to examine the distinction between the "trip" and the "tour".

Historically, "trips" have arisen out of economic necessities. Jiménez Guzmán (1986,35-40) has proposed a conceptual history of the trip. This concept proposes five developmental phases. The first phase is the nomadismo (homo) phase, in which the man is yet to appropriate a (physical) space. He begins to perfect his hunting tools and techniques and gradually adopts cultivation, for which establishing a more permanent dwelling becomes a necessity. During this lapse of time, his trips had a very specific function, i.e., searching for food. As the main activities were associated with hunting, it was not convenient to establish a fixed territory; hunters pursued in the direction of their preys.

In the second stage, the homo pater families establish the division of work and specialization. The main activity of this group is agriculture, for which a social organization based on the clan and the exchange system is established. This organizational form begins to produce a surplus of goods and services. They enter into a period of crisis (or opportunity?), as they realize that some people have the opportunity to become rich, and to take either a part or whole of that surplus. This gives rise to entrepreneurship and commerce.

During the third phase - the artesanado (homo faber) period – a culture of servility begins to take hold (i.e., nobility vs. ordinary). The notion of "aristocratic rest" is gradually established. The social organization is founded based on a principle, where the "being" prevails. The organization takes a highly feudal character. The displacement for leisure for a privileged group starts to occur.

In the fourth phase, capital accumulation requires investments to extend the production (commodity) chain. The result is industrialism (homo proletarius) which introduces the ideas of work, bourgeoisie and of proletariat. This process not only creates a new social strata, it also breaks up the entire logic and social structures, which no longer rotate around the "being", but around "possessions".

The fifth stage - socialism (homo partner-turisticus) – is characterized by the conflicts between the privileged (bourgeoisie) and the laborers (proletariat). The struggles led to economic prosperity and leisure time for the masses, and a democratic form of recreation tourism begins to hold grounds in the society. This eventually turns leisure and travel into unprecedented levels of global movement and activities.

Jiménez Guzmán (1986:39) concludes that "…from these points of view we can assure then that there was a stage in the human being's life in that the word tourism didn't mean absolutely anything; it is a non-tourist stage whose social facts of displacement were tourist, but the history shows us that the social facts of displacement constitute the antecedents of tourism…today, we live at a time in which the social facts of displacement for recreation and rest are called tourist facts."

Conclusion

Today the term tourism is widely used in reports, research work, congresses, symposia and publications related to social sciences. No doubt, they have been lured by the phenomenon in the past decades. Mass media also uses this term on a daily basis. In some instances, tourism is so called "the no-stack industry." However, there is not yet a clear definition about what tourism is about and where to trace back its origins.

Etymologically, three schools intended to study the problem but even though they had plentiful evidence no consensus has been unfortunately reached. The Latin School believes the term tourism dates back to the Saxon term, torn – which result confronts it with the Semitic School which believes the term tourism is rooted in the old Aramaic term, turn. A third school is involved in this discussion; it is the Onomastic or British School where the root of the term goes back to an old pact between Charles V and the Dellatours'.

Beyond this debate on the etymological origin of the term, it is said that the ancestors of today tourists are the old travelers, emigrants, and conquerors of the past centuries. This assumption might be relatively enticing, but it is undoubtedly fake. The underlying motives of the old travelers followed dynamics and interests quite different from those of the modern tourists.

In this connection, the theoretical model of Jiménez de Guzmán has been used to set the scopes and limitations for defining the different evolution levels developed in mankind until the stage where tourism consolidates as a business and industrial activity.
Against this backdrop, it is worth underscoring that tourism is an activity including traveling, however not all traveling would be deemed a tourist fact. Some questions which need further research are immediately raised: Is tourism an industrial phenomenon? Which scientific bases and evidence lead to such statement?
(Maximiliano Karstanje, Etymological Study, e-Review of Tourism Research (eRTR), Vol. 5, No. 5, 2007 ,http://ertr.tamu.edu)

II. The Definitions and Meanings of Tourism

The unprecedented growth of Tourism sector becomes the world's acknowledged sustained economic activity employing the most number of workers across Five (5) continents, various studies have been conducted by scholars in different disciplines to ultimately establish the most responsive and justified meaning of the term.

Webster's Version
The Webster's Third New International Dictionary of the English Language Unabridged. Gove, Philip Bobcock. Ph.D. (Editor in Chief). MA: Meriam-Webster Inc., 1993 defines Tourism as:
"the practice of touring: traveling for recreation; the guidance or management of tourists as a business or government function: provision of itineraries, guidance, and accommodations for tourists: the economic activities associated with and dependent upon tourists".

The English Version
On the other hand the English definition of the term/word is: "tourism"
Syllabification: tour·ism, Pronunciation: /ˈto͝orˌizəm/
Definition of tourism in English: NOUN:

"The commercial organization and operation of vacations and visits to places of interest."

The UNWTO - United Nations World Tourism Organization
In order to prevent the disaccords in the understanding of the word, the UNWTO advanced a definition of " Tourism " , that says:
"Tourism comprises the activities of persons traveling to and staying in places outside their usual environment for not more than one consecutive year for leisure, business and other purposes."

It explained further that Tourism is different from travel. In order for tourism to happen, there must be a displacement: an individual has to travel, using any type of means of transportation (he might even travel on foot: nowadays, it is often the case for poorer societies, and happens even in more developed ones, and concerns pilgrims, hikers ...). But all travel is not tourism.

Three criteria are used simultaneously in order to characterize a trip as belonging to tourism. The displacement must be such that: It involves a displacement outside the usual environment:

-Type of purpose: the travel must occur for any purpose different from being remunerated from within the place visited: the previous limits, where tourism was restricted to recreation and visiting family and friends are now expanded to include a vast array of purposes; Duration: only a maximal duration is mentioned, not a minimal. Tourism displacement can be with or without an overnight stay. We shall discuss the particularity of in transit visits, from a conceptual and statistical point of view.

This AUTHOR's DEFINITION/MEANING & EXPLANATION/JUSTIFCATION

This author, however, is in the belief that all of the mentioned definitions run short of the real meaning of tourism as it is being practiced today. TOURISM in its strictest sense must be considered as a system. Tour'ism is like, and with similarity or in parallel with all other words, terminologies and subjects ending in a suffix "ism" in the likes of: Commun+ism=Communism; Federal+ism=Federalism; Marx+ism=Marxism; Feudal+ism=Feudalism;ocial+ism= Socialism; Shinto+ism=Shintoism; Buddha+ism=Buddhism; and, Capital+ism=Capitalism. All these words and all such others similarly situated connote of something that has to do with the systems in governance, religious beliefs or social, economic and political activities observed by a certain sector or sectors in human society.

Easily it can be concluded, therefore, that TOURISM is a term that can be interchangeably treated both as a noun or a verb. As a 'noun' Tourism is an organized service systems or activities that are made available for tourists or travelers seeking for respite or rest, relaxation and leisure; and, as a verb Tourism is simply any activity that entails movement to, from and within the destination that the tourists do and enjoy to satisfy his personal needs and wants.

Thus, based on this conclusion, it can be easily deduced that the most appropriate and justified meaning or definition of Tourism (Tour+ism), having parallelism or similarities with all the words suffixed by "ism" , and, as it is being practiced and observed today and in the future should be the:

"**T**otality of duly organized service systems required by tourists, with **O**bjective to experience and enjoy, the **U**niqueness of an undisturbed environment, in a **R**esting place complimented with activities, where **I**ncome is generated from infrastructure, and **S**ustained services rendered by persons, **M**otivated to nurture and preserve the natural resources, in order to pamper people of today and the future."

Book 2 - Brief Philippine Tourism History

The Early Tourism and First Recorded Foreign Visitors to the Philippines

I. Discovery by Magellan

Considering as the basis the assumption on the etymological origin of the term Tourism and Travel (Maximiliano Konstanje, e-Review of Tourism Research (eRTR), Vol. 5, No. 5, 2007), where it is said by the ancestors of today that tourists are the old travelers, emigrants, and conquerors of the past centuries that might be relatively enticing, and though the underlying motives of the old travelers followed dynamics and interests quite different from those of the modern tourists, it may be assumed that the beginning of Philippine Tourism maybe traced from the first recorded visit of a foreigners from the West led by Ferdinand Magellan, who sighted Samar Island on March 16, 1521 and landed on Homonhon Island (now part of Guiuan, Eastern Samar province) the next day. Homonhon Island is southeast of Samar Island.

Long before the arrival of Magellan, however, the Negrito tribes inhabited the isles, subsequently joined and largely supplanted by migrating groups of Austronesians. This population had stratified into hunter-gatherer tribes, warrior societies, petty plutocracies and maritime-oriented harbor principalities which eventually grew into kingdoms, rajahnates, principalities, confederations and sultanates. The Philippine islands were greatly influenced by Hindu religions, literature and philosophy from India in the early centuries of the Christian era. States included the Indianized Rajahnate of Butuan and Cebu, the dynasty of Tondo, the august kingdoms of Maysapan and Maynila, theConfederation of Madyaas, the signified Country of Mai, as well as the Muslim Sultanates and Maguindanao. These small maritime states flourished from the 1st millennium. These kingdoms trades with what is now called China, India, Japan, Thailand, Vitenam, and Indonesia. The remainder of the settlements were independent barangays allied with one of the larger states.

II. Spanish Colonization

Spanish colonization began with the arrival of Miguel López de Legazpi's expedition on February 13, 1565 who established the first permanent settlement of San Miguel on the island of Cebu, where they established a new town and thus began an era of Spanish colonization that lasted for more than three centuries. Much of the archipelago (previously occupied by independent kingdoms) gradually fell into Spanish rule, pushing back south the advancing Islamic forces and creating the first draft of the nation that was to be known as the Philippines. Spain also introduced Christianity, the code of law and the oldest modern Universities in Asia. The Spanish East Indies were ruled as part of the Viceroyalty of New Spain and administered from Mexico City from 1565 to 1821, and administered directly from Madrid, Spain from 1821 until the end of the Spanish–American War in 1898, except for a brief period of British rule from 1762 to 1764. They founded schools, a university, and some hospitals, principally in Manila and the largest Spanish fort settlements. Universal education was made free for all Filipino subjects in 1863 and remained so until the end of the Spanish colonial era. This measure was at the vanguard of contemporary Asian countries, and led to an important class of educated natives, like José Rizal.

III. The Coming of the Americans

In 1898, as conflicts continued in the Philippines, the USS Maine, having been sent to Cuba because of U.S. concerns for the safety of its citizens during an ongoing Cuban revolution, exploded and sank in Havana harbor. This event precipitated the Spanish–American War. After Commodore George Dewey defeated the Spanish squadron at Manila, a German squadron arrived in Manila and engaged in maneuvers which Dewey, seeing this as obstruction of his blockade, offered war— after which the Germans backed down. The German Emperor expected an American defeat, with Spain left in a sufficiently weak position for the revolutionaries to capture Manila—leaving the Philippines ripe for German picking.

The U.S. invited Aguinaldo to return to the Philippines in the hope he would rally Filipinos against the Spanish colonial government.

Aguinaldo arrived on May 19, 1898, via transport provided by Dewey. By the time U.S. land forces had arrived, the Filipinos had taken control of the entire island of Luzon, except for the walled city of Intramuros. On June 12, 1898, Aguinaldo declared the independence of the Philippines in Kawit, Cavite, establishing the First Philippine Republic under Asia's first democratic constitution.
In the Battle of Manila, the United States captured the city from the Spanish. This battle marked an end of Filipino-American collaboration, as Filipino forces were prevented from entering the captured city of Manila, an action deeply resented by the Filipinos. Spain and the United States sent commissioners to Paris to draw up the terms of the Treaty of Paris which ended the Spanish–American War. The Filipino representative, Felipe Agoncillo, was excluded from sessions as the revolutionary government was not recognized by the family of nations. Although there was substantial domestic opposition, the United States decided to annex the Philippines.

In addition to Guam and Puerto Rico, Spain was forced in the negotiations to hand over the Philippines to the U.S. in exchange for US$20,000,000.00. U.S. President McKinley justified the annexation of the Philippines by saying that it was "a gift from the gods" and that since "they were unfit for self-government, ... there was nothing left for us to do but to take them all, and to educate the Filipinos, and uplift and civilize and Christianize them", in spite of the Philippines having been already Christianized by the Spanish over the course of several centuries. The first Philippine Republic resisted the U.S. occupation, resulting in the Philippine– American War.

IV. Other Foreign Visitors (British, Chinese, Dutch and Portuguese)

While the Spaniards were the first recorded foreigners to have set foot in Philippine soil, there are other historical records showing that the Chinese were already in the country long before Magellan's troop landed in Limasawa, Eastern Samar. Then came the British few years after the Spanish Manila galleons linked Manila to Acapulco traveled once or twice a year between the 16th and 19th centuries. In fact the Spanish military have fought off various indigenous revolts and several external colonial challenges, especially from the British, Chinese pirates, Dutch, and Portuguese.

V. The Japanese Sojourn

The Japanese were already in the Philippines prior to the launched of a surprise attack of the Clark Air Base in Pampanga on the morning of December 8, 1941, just ten hours after the attack on Pearl Harbor. Aerial bombardment was followed by landings of ground troops on Luzon, while cannons installed in Corregidor Island purposely to defend Manila from the impending Japanese Naval attack, and instead the Japanese entered by air in the north. Not known to the US and even to the Philippine Governments, the Japanese were already monitoring the Corregidor Island fortification by the United States, while they were already in the country in the guise of propagating abaca (Manila Hemp) and Pineapple plantations Mindanao. The defending Philippine and United States troops were under the command of General Douglas MacArthur. Under the pressure of superior numbers, the defending forces withdrew to the Bataan Peninsula and to the island of Corregidor at the entrance to Manila Bay.

On January 2, 1942, General MacArthur declared the capital city, Manila, an open city to prevent its destruction. The Philippine defense continued until the final surrender of United States-Philippine forces on the Bataan Peninsula in April 1942 and on Corregidor in May of the same year. Most of the 80,000 prisoners of war captured by the Japanese at Bataan were forced to undertake the infamous Bataan Death March to a prison camp 105 kilometers to the north. About 10,000 Filipinos and 1,200 Americans died before reaching their destination.

President Quezon and Osmeña had accompanied the troops to Corregidor and later left for the United States, where they set up a government in exile. MacArthur was ordered to Australia, where he started to plan for a return to the Philippines.

The Japanese military authorities immediately began organizing a new government structure in the Philippines and established the Philippine

Executive Commission. They initially organized a Council of State, through which they directed civil affairs until October 1943, when they declared the Philippines an independent republic.

Philippine Modern Tourism History

I. Creation of the Department of Tourism

Prior the 70's tourism in the Philippines was never given the importance as matters thereunto appertaining in its governance was consigned in the Bureau of Tourism under the Department of Trade and Industry (DTI). It was only after the declaration of Martial Law by the late President Ferdinand E. Marcos, that tourism was given the importance, when the massive reorganization of the National Government Offices was effected as a result of the Martial Law declaration in 1972. President Marcos recognizing the imperatives of tourism development for the socio- economic development of the country, Presidential Decree No. 189 "AMENDING PART IX OF THE INTEGRATED REORGANIZATION PLAN BY RENAMING THE DEPARTMENT OF TRADE AND TOURISM AS THE DEPARTMENT OF TOURISM, AND CREATING THE DEPARTMENT OF TOURISM WITH A PHILIPPINE TOURIST AUTHORITY ATTACHED TO IT IN LIEU OF PHILIPPINE TOURIST COMMISSION" was issued and thus the birth of a duly organized tourism as a system in the country.

With the Department of Tourism became fully operational, all business activities and services of tourism orientation were under the control and supervision of the department that has the mandate to issue licenses, conduct trainings, promote and market the country as a destination for holiday seekers and international meetings, events and conventions.

The aftermath of all these efforts paved the way for the unprecedented demand for accommodation facilities for foreign tourists as arrivals of both groups and FITs most often exceeded the available rooms in Metro Manila, thus, Manila Hotel was renovated and more than a dozen high rise hotels constructed and thus, dominated the skyline of Metro Manila. Resorts were built in Cavite, Laguna, Batangas, Mindoro and other cities and provinces particularly Baguio, Banawe and Bontoc in the Cordilleras, Cebu-Mactan, Bohol, Leyte, Ilocos, Bicol, Davao, Zamboanga and Palawan.

This was the period when the Islands of Sicogon and Boracay in Panay Western Visayas rose into fame. Other facilities for conventions and international events in the likes of the Cultural Center of the Philippines, PICC-Philippine International Convention Center, Folk Arts Theatre, International Film Center, were likewise introduced making the Philippines one of the leading venues for international events, foremost of which were the United Nation International Development Organization (UNIDO) World Convention; Miss Universe Beauty Pageant; Muhamad Ali-Joe Frazier Heavyweight Boxing championship fight; the ASTA-American Society of Travel Agencies World Congress; the ASEAN Tourism Forum (ATF); and, the (WATA) World Association of Travel Agencies World Congress. The modern Manila International Airport, Mactan International Airport and Laoag International Airport were constructed and opened to accommodate international flights from the ASEAN Region; All the highways and road networks leading to tourist destinations and attractions were widened and concreted with travelers' rest areas along strategic locations. Corregidor Island War Memorial was rehabilitated with the audio-visuals installed. Cruise Ships regularly called at the Manila South Harbor including the Queen Elizabeth the biggest Luxury Cruise from England catering to the rich and famous cruising around the world.

Modern air-conditioned deluxe buses were operated including the double- deckers owned and operated by the government-owned Metro Manila Transit as well as Tourist buses, Self-Drive car rentals, and Chauffeur-Driven Limousines were aplenty. Tourism and Hospitality courses were then offered as a major course of studies when the Asian Institute of Tourism was opened, followed by other universities and colleges to prepare young Filipinos to the demands for professionals of the industry both locally and abroad

As a manifest of the undying commitment to the continuing growth of the country's tourism industry, President Marcos successively issued

Presidential Decrees in support of its development. These are the following:

II. Early Laws Related to Tourism

- PRESIDENTIAL DECREE No. 189 May 11, 1973, "AMENDING PART IX OF THE INTEGRATED REORGANIZATION PLAN BY RENAMING THE DEPARTMENT OF TRADE AND TOURISM AS THE DEPARTMENT OF TOURISM, AND CREATING THE DEPARTMENT OF TOURISM WITH A PHILIPPINE TOURIST AUTHORITY ATTACHED TO IT IN LIEU OF PHILIPPINE TOURIST COMMISSION"
- PRESIDENTIAL DECREE 1463 "REVISING PRESIDENTIAL DECREE NO. 189, DATED MAY 11, 1973, "AS AMENDED, CREATING THE DEPARTMENT OF TOURISM"
- PRESIDENTIAL DECREE No. 274 August 18, 1973 PERTAINING TO THE PRESERVATION, BEAUTIFICATION, IMPROVEMENT AND GAINFUL UTILIZATION OF THE PASIG RIVER, PROVIDING FOR THE REGULATION AND CONTROL OF POLLUTION OF THE RIVER AND ITS BANKS IN ORDER TO ENHANCE ITS DEVELOPMENT, THEREBY MAXIMIZING ITS UTILIZATION FOR SOCIO-ECONOMIC PURPOSES;
- PRESIDENTIAL DECREE No. 1616, August 18, 1973 CREATING THE "INTRAMUROS ADMINISTRATION" FOR PURPOSES OF RESTORING AND ADMINISTERING THE DEVELOPMENT OF INTRAMUROS;
- PRESIDENTIAL DECREE No. 1616, August 18, 1973 CREATING THE "INTRAMUROS ADMINISTRATION" FOR PURPOSES OF RESTORING AND ADMINISTERING THE DEVELOPMENT OF INTRAMUROS;
- REVISING PRESIDENTIAL DECREE NO. 189, DATED MAY 11, 1973, AS AMENDED, CREATING THE DEPARTMENT OF TOURISM;

- PRESIDENTIAL DECREE No. 499 June 28, 1974 "DECLARING PORTIONS OF THE ERMITA-MALATE AREA AS COMMERCIAL ZONES WITH CERTAIN RESTRICTIONS;
- PRESIDENTIAL DECREE No. 1448, June 11, 1978, "A DECREE RE- ENACTING PRESIDENTIAL DECREE NO. 867 AND AMENDING CERTAIN PROVISIONS THEREOF;
- PRESIDENTIAL DECREE No. 1463, August 18, 1973, "REVISING PRESIDENTIAL DECREE NO. 189, DATED MAY 11, 1973, AS AMENDED, CREATING THE DEPARTMENT OF TOURISM;
- PRESIDENTIAL DECREE No. 1193, September 6, 1977. "AUTHORIZING THE TOURIST DUTY-FREE SHOPS, INC. TO ESTABLISH AND OPERATE DUTY AND TAX FREE SHOPS AND REQUIRING IT TO PAY FRANCHISE TAX IN LIEU OF ALL OTHER TAXES.

III. The World Tourism Organization and Golden Years of Tourism

Aware of the ever growing tourism in the international travel and tourism market, and the imperatives of the sector to the nation's socio, economic progress, and to to pursue his vision to level up international awareness of the country's tourism treasures, the late President Ferdinand E. Marcos, issued:
PRESIDENTIAL DECREE No. 1407, June 8, 1978, "RATIFYING THE AGREEMENT BETWEEN THE WORLD TOURISM ORGANIZATION AND THE GOVERNMENT OF THE REPUBLIC OF THE PHILIPPINES CONCERNING THE LEGAL STATUS OF THE WORLD TOURISM ORGANIZATION AND ITS REGIONAL SECRETARIAT AT MANILA, PHILIPPINES.

The periods during the '70's up to the early 80's indeed was the golden era for Philippine Tourism as the country's Secretary of Tourism the Late Jose D. Aspiras was chosen the World's Tourism Golden Man, the title accorded by the UNWTO-United Nations World Tourism Organization during the 1980 ASTA- American Society of Travel

Agents World Convention at the Philippine International Convention Center. The convention, however, was abruptly cut-short due to the explosion of an improvised bomb that occurred at the opening ceremony timely when the documentary film was shown for the delegates immediately after President Marcos ended his Keynote/Opening Speech. The country's tourism promotion tagline then was "Where Asia wears a Smile" popularized by the country's flag carrier the Philippine Airlines.

Whatever President Marcos achieved and left that benefited the country's tourism sector, the Philippines and the Filipinos remain the living legacies that withstood the tests of times until Republic Act 9593, otherwise known as the "Tourism Act of 2009" authored by ex-senator Richard Gordon was finally approved, and currently governs the tourism sector of the country. It is noteworthy, however, that the same law still carries some very important features originally provided in the various Presidential Decrees related to tourism that President Ferdinand E. Marcos issued during his tenure as the President and Commander-in- Chief of the Republic of the Philippines.

Book 3 -Brief Philippine History

Pre-Historic Past

I. Archeological Basis and First Inhabitants

The earliest archeological evidence for man in the archipelago is the 67,000- year-old Callao Man of Cagayan and the Angono Petroglyphs in Rizal, both of whom appear to suggest the presence of human settlement prior to the arrival of the Negritos and Austronesian speaking people.

There are several opposing theories regarding the origins of ancient Filipinos.

F. Landa Jocano theorizes that the ancestors of the Filipinos evolved locally. Wilhelm Solheim's Island Origin Theory postulates that the peopling of the archipelago transpired via trade networks originating in the Sundaland area around 48,000 to 5000 BC rather than by wide-scale migration. The Austronesian Expansion Theory states that Malayo-Polynesians coming from Taiwan began migrating to the Philippines around 4000 BC, displacing earlier arrivals.

The Negritos were early settlers, but their appearance in the Philippines has not been reliably dated. They were followed by speakers of the Malayo-Polynesian languages, a branch of the Austronesian languages, who began to arrive in successive waves beginning about 4000 BC, displacing the earlier arrivals. Before the expansion out of Taiwan, recent archaeological, linguistic and genetic evidence has linked Austronesian speakers in Insular Southeast Asia to cultures such as the Hemudu and Dapenkeng in Neolithic China.

By 1000 BC the inhabitants of the Philippine archipelago had developed into four distinct kinds of peoples: tribal groups, such as the Aetas, Hanunoo, Ilongots and the Mangyan who depended on hunter- gathering and were concentrated in forests; warrior societies, such as the Isneg and Kalinga who practiced social ranking and ritualized warfare and roamed the plains; the petty plutocracy of the Ifugao Cordillera Highlanders, who occupied the mountain ranges of Luzon; and the harbor principalities of the estuarine civilizations that grew along rivers and seashores while participating in trans-island maritime trade.

Around 300–700 AD the seafaring peoples of the islands traveling in balangays began to trade with the Indianized kingdoms in the Malay Archipelago and the nearby East Asian principalities, adopting influences from both Buddhism and Hinduism.

During the period of the south Indian Pallava dynasty and the north Indian Gupta Empire Indian culture spread to Southeast Asia and the Philippines which led to the establishment of Indianized kingdoms. The end of Philippine prehistory is 900, the date inscribed in the oldest Philippine document found so far, the Laguna Copperplate Inscription. From the details of the document, written in Kawi script, the bearer of a debt, Namwaran, along with his children Lady Angkatan and Bukah, are cleared of a debt by the ruler of Tondo. From the various Sanskrit terms and titles seen in the document, the culture and society of Manila Bay was that of a Hindu–Old Malay amalgamation, similar to the cultures of Java, Peninsular Malaysia and Sumatra at the time. There are no other significant documents from this period of pre-Hispanic Philippine society and culture until the Doctrina Christiana of the late 16th century, written at the start of the Spanish period in both native Baybayin script and Spanish. Other artifacts with Kawi script and baybayin were found, such as an Ivory seal from Butuan dated to the early 11th century and the Calatagan pot with baybayin inscription, dated to the 13th century.

II. The Rajahnate of Butuan

In the years leading up to 1000, there were already several maritime societies existing in the islands but there was no unifying political state encompassing the entire Philippine archipelago. Instead, the region was dotted by numerous semi- autonomous barangays (settlements ranging in size from villages to city-states) under the sovereignty of competing thalassocracies ruled by datus, rajahs or sultans or by upland agricultural societies ruled by "petty plutocrats". States such as the Kingdom of Maynila, the Kingdom of

Taytay in Palawan (mentioned by Pigafetta to be where they resupplied when the remaining ships escaped Cebu after Magellan was slain), the Chieftaincy of Coron Island ruled by fierce warriors called Tagbanua as reported by Spanish missionaries mentioned by Nilo S. Ocampo, Namayan, the Dynasty of Tondo, the Confederation of Madyaas, the rajahnates of Butuan and Cebu and the sultanates of Maguindanao and Sulu existed alongside the highland societies of the Ifugao and Mangyan. Some of these regions were part of the Malayan empires of Srivijaya, Majapahit and Brunei.

Since at least the year 900, the thalassocracy centered in Manila Bay flourished via an active trade with Chinese, Japanese, Malays, and various other peoples in East Asia. Tondo thrived as the capital and the seat of power of this ancient kingdom, which was led by kings under the title "Lakan" and ruled a large part of what is now known as Luzon from or possibly before 900 AD to 1571. During its existence, it grew to become one of the most prominent and wealthy kingdom states in pre-colonial Philippines due to heavy trade and connections with several neighboring nations such as China and Japan. In 900 AD, the lord-minister Jayadewa presented a document of debt forgiveness to Lady Angkatan and her brother Bukah, the children of Namwaran. This is described in the Philippine's oldest known document, the Laguna Copperplate Inscription.

By year 1011 Rajah Sri Bata Shaja, the monarch of the Indianized Rajahnate of Butuan, a maritime-state famous for its goldwork[54] sent a trade envoy under ambassador Likan-shieh to the Chinese Imperial Court demanding equal diplomatic status with other states.[55] The request being approved, it opened up direct commercial links with the Rajahnate of Butuan and the Chinese Empire thereby diminishing the monopoly on Chinese trade previously enjoyed by their rivals the Dynasty of Tondo and the Champa civilization. Evidence of the existence of this rajahnate is given by the Butuan Silver Paleograph.

III.   The Rajahnate of Cebu

The Rajahnate of Cebu was a classical Philippine state which used to exist on Cebu island prior to the arrival of the Spanish. It was founded by Sri Lumay otherwise known as Rajamuda Lumaya, a minor prince of the Chola dynasty which happened to occupy Sumatra. He was sent by the maharajah to establish a base for expeditionary forces to subdue the local kingdoms but he rebelled and established his own independent Rajahnate instead. This rajahnate warred against the 'magalos' (Slavetraders)of Maguindanao and had an alliance with the Butuan Rajahnate before it was weakened by the insurrection of Datu (Lord) Lapulapu.

IV. The Confederation of Madja-as

During the 11th century several exiled datus of the collapsing empire of Srivijaya led by Datu Puti led a mass migration to the central islands of the Philippines, fleeing from Rajah Makatunao of the island of Borneo. Upon reaching the island of Panay and purchasing the island from Negrito chieftain Marikudo, they established a confederation of polities and named it the Confederation of Madja- ascentered in Aklan and they settled the surrounding islands of the Visayas. This confederation reached its peak under Datu Padojinog. During his reign the confederations' hegemony extended over most of the islands of Visayas. Its people consistently made piratical attacks against Chinese imperial shipping.

V. The Country of Mai

Around 1225, the Country of Mai, a Signified pre-Hispanic Philippine island-state centered in Mindoro, flourished as an entrepot, attracting traders & shipping from the Kingdom of Ryukyu to the Yamato Empire of Japan. Chao Jukua, a customs inspector in Fukien province, China wrote the Zhufan Zhi ("Description of the Barbarous Peoples"), which described trade with this pre-colonial Philippine state.

VI. The Sultanate of Lanao

The Sultanates of Lanao in Mindanao, Philippines were founded in the 16th century through the influence of Shariff Kabungsuan, who was enthroned as first Sultan of Maguindanao in 1520. The Maranaos of Lanao were acquainted with the sultanate system when Islam was introduced to the area by Muslim missionaries and traders from the Middle East, Indian and Malay regions who propagated Islam to Sulu and Maguindanao. Unlike in Sulu and Maguindanao, the Sultanate system in Lanao was uniquely decentralized. The area was divided into Four Principalities of Lanao or the Pat a Pangampong a Ranao which are composed of a number of royal houses (Sapolo ago Nem a Panoroganan or The Sixteen (16) Royal Houses) with specific territorial jurisdictions within mainland Mindanao. This decentralized structure of royal power in Lanao was adopted by the founders, and maintained up to the present day, in recognition of the shared power and prestige of the ruling clans in the area, emphasizing the values of unity of the nation (kaiisaisa o bangsa), patronage (kaseselai) and fraternity (kapapagaria).

VIII. The Sultanate of Sulu

In 1380, Karim ul' Makdum and Shari'ful Hashem Syed Abu Bakr, an Arab trader born in Johore, arrived in Sulu from Malacca and established the Sultanate of Sulu. This sultanate eventually gained great wealth due to its manufacture of fine pearls.

IX. The Sultanate of Maguindanao

At the end of the 15th century, Shariff Mohammed Kabungsuwan of Johor introduced Islam in the island of Mindanao and he subsequently married Paramisuli, an Iranun Princess from Mindanao, and established the Sultanate of Maguindanao. By the 16th century, Islam had spread to other parts of the Visayas and Luzon.

X. The Expansion of Islam

During the reign of Sultan Bolkiah in 1485 to 1521, the Bruneian Empire decided to break the Dynasty of Tondo's monopoly in the China trade by attacking Tondo and establishing the State of Selurong (now Manila) as a Bruneian satellite-state. A new dynasty under the Islamized Rajah Salalila was also stablished to challenge the House of Lakandula in Tondo. Islam was further strengthened by the arrival to the Philippines of traders and proselytizers from Malaysia and Indonesia. The multiple states competing over the limited territory and people of the islands simplified Spanish colonization by allowing its conquistadors to effectively employ a strategy of divide and conquer for rapid conquest.

Early Spanish Expeditions and Conquests

I. Beginning of Expeditions to and Conquest of the Philippines

European colonization began in earnest when Spanish explorer Miguel López de Legazpi arrived from Mexico in 1565 and formed the first European settlements in Cebu. Beginning with just five ships and five hundred men accompanied by Augustinian monks, and further strengthened in 1567 by two hundred soldiers, he was able to repel the Portuguese and create the foundations for the colonization of the Archipelago. In 1571, the Spanish occupied the kingdoms of Maynilad and Tondo and established Manila as the capital of the Spanish East Indies.

Legazpi built a fort in Maynila and made overtures of friendship to Lakan Dula, Rajah of Tondo, who accepted. However, Maynila's former ruler, Rajah Sulayman, refused to submit to Legazpi, but failed to get the support of Lakandula or of the Pampangan and Pangasinan settlements to the north. When Sulaiman and a force of Filipino warriors attacked the Spaniards in the battle of Bangcusay, he was finally defeated and killed.

In 1587, Magat Salamat, one of the children of Lakan Dula, along with Lakan Dula's nephew and lords of the neighboring areas of Tondo, Pandacan, Marikina, Candaba, Navotas and Bulacan, were executed when the Tondo Conspiracy of 1587–1588 failed] in which a planned grand alliance with the Japanese admiral Gayo, Butuan's last rajah and Brunei's Sultan Bolkiah, would have restored the old aristocracy. Its failure resulted in the hanging of Agustín de Legazpi (great grandson of Miguel Lopez de Legazpi and the initiator of the plot) and the execution of Magat Salamat (the crown-prince of Tondo).

Spanish power was further consolidated after Miguel López de Legazpi's conquest of the Confederation of Madya-as, his subjugation of Rajah Tupas, the King of Cebu and Juan de Salcedo's conquest of the provinces of Zambales, La Union, Ilocos, the coast of Cagayan, and the ransacking of the Chinese warlord Limahong's pirate kingdom in Pangasinan.

The Spanish and the Moros also waged many wars over hundreds of years in the Spanish-Moro Conflict, not until the 19th century did Spain succeed in defeating the Sulu Sultanate and taking Mindanao under nominal authority.

II. Spanish Settlement During the 16th and 17th Centuries

The "Memoria de las Encomiendas en las Islas" of 1591, just twenty years after the conquest of Luzon, reveals a remarkable progress in the work of colonization and the spread of Christianity. A cathedral was built in the city of Manila with an episcopal palace, Augustinian, Dominican and Franciscan monasteries and a Jesuit house. The king maintained a hospital for the Spanish settlers and there was another hospital for the natives run by the Franciscans. The garrison was composed of roughly two hundred soldiers. In the suburb of Tondo there was a convent run by Franciscan friars and another by the Dominicans that offered Christian education to the Chinese converted to Christianity. The same report reveals that in and around Manila were collected 9,410 tributes, indicating a population of about 30,640 who were under the instruction of thirteen missionaries (ministers of doctrine), apart from the monks in monasteries. In the former province of Pampanga the population estimate was 74,700 and 28 missionaries. In Pangasinan 2,400 people with eight missionaries. In Cagayan and islands Babuyanes 96,000 people but no missionaries. In La Laguna 48,400 people with 27 missionaries. In Bicol and Camarines Catanduanes islands 86,640 people with fifteen missionaries. The total was 667,612 people under the care of 140 missionaries, of which 79 were Augustinians, nine Dominicans and 42 Franciscans.

The fragmented nature of the islands made it easy for Spanish colonization. The Spanish then brought political unification to most of the Philippine archipelago via the conquest of the various states although they were unable to fully incorporate parts of the sultanates of Mindanao and the areas where tribes and highland plutocracy of the

Ifugao of Northern Luzon were established. The Spanish introduced elements of western civilization such as the code of law, western printing and the Gregorian calendar alongside new food resources such as maize, pineapple and chocolate from Latin America.

Education played a major role in the socio-economic transformation of the archipelago. The oldest universities, colleges, and vocational schools and the first modern public education system in Asia were all created during the Spanish colonial period, and by the time Spain was replaced by the United States as the colonial power, Filipinos were among the most educated subjects in all of Asia. The Jesuits founded the Colegio de Manila in 1590, which later became the Universidad de San Ignacio, a royal and pontifical university. They also founded the Colegio de San Ildefonso on August 1, 1595. After the expulsion of the Society of Jesus in 1768, the management of the Jesuit schools passed to other parties. On April 28, 1611, through the initiative of Bishop Miguel de Benavides, the University of Santo Tomas was founded in Manila. The Jesuits also founded the Colegio de San José (1601) and took over the Escuela Municipal, later to be called the Ateneo de Manila University (1859). All institutions offered courses included not only religious topics but also science subjects such as physics, chemistry, natural history and mathematics. The University of Santo Tomás, for example, started by teaching theology, philosophy and humanities and during the 18th century, the Faculty of Jurisprudence and Canonical Law, together with the schools of medicine and pharmacy were opened.

Outside the tertiary institutions, the efforts of missionaries were in no way limited to religious instruction but also geared towards promoting social and economic advancement of the islands. They cultivated into the natives their innate taste for music and taught Spanish language to children. They also introduced advances in rice agriculture, brought from America corn and cocoa and developed the farming of indigo, coffee and sugar cane. The only commercial plant introduced by a government agency was the plant of tobacco.

Church and state were inseparably linked in Spanish policy, with the state assuming responsibility for religious establishments. One of

Spain's objectives in colonizing the Philippines was the conversion of the local population to Roman Catholicism. The work of conversion was facilitated by the absence of other organized religions, except for Islam, which was still predominant in the southwest. The pageantry of the church had a wide appeal, reinforced by the incorporation of indigenous social customs into religious observances. The eventual outcome was a new Roman Catholic majority, from which the Muslims of western Mindanao and the upland tribal peoples of Luzon remained detached and alienated (such as the Ifugaos of the Cordillera region and the Mangyans of Mindoro).

At the lower levels of administration, the Spanish built on traditional village organization by co-opting local leaders. This system of indirect rule helped create an indigenous upper class, called the principalía, who had local wealth, high status, and other privileges. This perpetuated an oligarchic system of local control. Among the most significant changes under Spanish rule was that the indigenous idea of communal use and ownership of land was replaced with the concept of private ownership and the conferring of titles on members of the principalia.

Around 1608 William Adams, an English navigator contacted the interim governor of the Philippines, Rodrigo de Vivero y Velasco on behalf of Tokugawa Ieyasu, who wished to establish direct trade contacts with New Spain. Friendly letters were exchanged, officially starting relations between Japan and New Spain. From 1565 to 1821, the Philippines was governed as a territory of the Viceroyalty of New Spain from Mexico, via the Royal Audiencia of Manila, and administered directly from Spain from 1821 after the Mexican revolution, until 1898.

Many of the Aztec and Mayan warriors that López de Legazpi brought with him eventually settled in Mexico, Pampanga where traces of Aztec and Mayan influence can still be found in the many chico plantations in the area (chico is a fruit indigenous only to Mexico) and also by the name of the province itself.

The Manila galleons which linked Manila to Acapulco traveled once or twice a year between the 16th and 19th centuries. The Spanish military fought off various indigenous revolts and several external colonial challenges, especially from the British, Chinese pirates, Dutch, and Portuguese. Roman Catholic missionaries converted most of the lowland inhabitants to Christianity and founded schools, universities, and hospitals. In 1863 a Spanish decree introduced education, establishing public schooling in Spanish.

In 1646, a series of five naval actions known as the Battles of La Naval de Manila was fought between the forces of Spain and the Dutch Republic, as part of the Eighty Years' War. Although the Spanish forces consisted of just two Manila galleons and a galley with crews composed mainly of Filipino volunteers, against three separate Dutch squadrons, totaling eighteen ships, the Dutch squadrons were severely defeated in all fronts by the Spanish-Filipino forces, forcing the Dutch to abandon their plans for an invasion of the Philippines.

III. Spanish Rule During the 18th Century

Colonial income derived mainly from entrepôt trade: The Manila Galleons sailing from the Fort of Manila to the Fort of Acapulco on the west coast of Mexico brought shipments of silver bullion, and minted coin that were exchanged for return cargoes of Asian, and Pacific products. A total of 110 Manila galleons set sail in the 250 years of the Manila-Acapulco galleon trade (1565 to 1815). There was no direct trade with Spain until 1766.

The Philippines was never profitable as a colony during Spanish rule, and the long war against the Dutch in the 17th century together with the intermittent conflict with the Muslims in the South nearly bankrupted the colonial treasury. The Royal Fiscal of Manila wrote a letter to King Charles III of Spain, in which he advises to abandon the colony.

The Philippines survived on an annual subsidy paid by the Spanish Crown, and the 200-year-old fortifications at Manila had not been improved much since first built by the early Spanish colonizers. This was one of the circumstances that made possible the brief British occupation of Manila between 1762 and 1764.

IV. British invasion (1762–1764)

Britain declared war against Spain on January 4, 1762 and on September 24, 1762 a force of British Army regulars and British East India Company soldiers, supported by the ships and men of the East Indies Squadron of the British Royal Navy, sailed into Manila Bay from Madras, India. Manila fell to the British on October 4, 1762.

The British forces were confined to Manila and the nearby port of Cavite by the resistance organized by the provisional Spanish colonial government. Suffering a breakdown of command and troop desertions as a result of their failure to secure control of the Philippines, the British ended their occupation of Manila by sailing away in April 1764 as agreed to in the peace negotiations in Europe. The Spaniards then persecuted the Binondo Chinese community for its role in aiding the British.

V. Spanish Rule in the Second Part of the 18th Century

In 1766 was established direct communication with Spain and trade with Europe through a national ship based on Spain. Those expeditions were administered since 1785 by the Real Compañía Filipina, which was granted a monopoly of trade between Spain and the islands that lasted until 1834, when the company was terminated by the Spanish crown due to poor management and financial losses.
In 1781, Governor-General José Basco y Vargas established the Economic Society of the Friends of the Country. The Philippines was administered from the Viceroyalty of New Spain until the grant of independence to Mexico in 1821 necessitated the direct rule from Spain of the Philippines from that year.

VI. Spanish Rule During the 19th Century

During the 19th century Spain invested heavily in education and infrastructure. Through the Education Decree of December 20, 1863, Queen Isabella II of Spain decreed the establishment of a free public school system that used Spanish as the language of instruction, leading to increasing numbers of educated Filipinos. Additionally, the opening of the Suez Canal in 1869 cut travel time to Spain, which facilitated the rise of the ilustrados, an enlightened class of Filipinos that had been able to expand their studies in Spain and Europe.

A great deal of infrastructure projects were undertaken during the 19th century that put the Philippine economy and standard of living ahead of most of its Asian neighbors and even many European countries at that time. Among them were a railway system for Luzon, a tramcar network for Manila, and the Puente Colgante (now known as the Quezon Bridge), Asia's first steel suspension bridge. On August 1, 1851 the Banco Español-Filipino de Isabel II was established to attend the needs of the rapid economic boom, that had greatly increased its pace since 1840 as a result of a new economy based on a rational exploitation of the agricultural resources of the islands. The increase in textile fiber crops such as abacá, oil products derived from the coconut, indigo, that was growing in demand, etc., generated an increase in money supply that led to the creation of the bank. Banco Español-Filipino was also granted the power to print a Philippine-specific currency (the Philippine peso) for the first time (before 1851, many currencies were used, mostly the pieces of eight).

Spanish Manila was seen in the 19th century as a model of colonial governance that effectively put the interests of the original inhabitants of the islands before those of the colonial power. As John Crawfurd put it in its History of the Indian Archipelago, in all of Asia the "Philippines alone did improve in civilization, wealth, and population under the colonial rule" of a foreign power. John Bowring, Governor General of British Hong Kong from 1856 to 1860, wrote after his trip to Manila: "Credit is certainly due to Spain for having bettered the condition of a people who, though comparatively highly civilized, yet being continually distracted by petty wars, had sunk into a disordered and uncultivated state.

The inhabitants of these beautiful Islands upon the whole, may well be considered to have lived as comfortably during the last hundred years, protected from all external enemies and governed by mild laws vis-a-vis those from any other tropical country under native or European sway, owing in some measure, to the frequently discussed peculiar (Spanish) circumstances which protect the interests of the natives."

In The inhabitants of the Philippines, Frederick Henry Sawyer wrote: "Until an inept bureaucracy was substituted for the old paternal rule, and the revenue quadrupled by increased taxation, the Filipinos were as happy a community as could be found in any colony. The population greatly multiplied; they lived in competence, if not in affluence; cultivation was extended, and the exports steadily increased. Let us be just; what British, French, or Dutch colony, populated by natives can compare with the Philippines as they were until 1895?"

The first official census in the Philippines was carried out in 1878. The colony's population as of December 31, 1877, was recorded at 5,567,685 persons. This was followed by the 1887 census that yielded a count of 6,984,727, while that of 1898 yielded 7,832,719 inhabitants. The estimated GDP per capita for the Philippines in 1900, the year Spain left, was of $1,033.00. That made it the second richest place in all of Asia, just a little behind Japan ($1,135.00), and far ahead of China ($652.00) or India ($625.00).

VII. Philippine Revolution

Revolutionary sentiments arose in 1872 after three Filipino priests, Mariano Gómez, José Burgos, and Jacinto Zamora, known as Gomburza, were accused of sedition by colonial authorities and executed. This would inspire the Propaganda Movement in Spain, organized by Marcelo H. del Pilar, José Rizal, Graciano López Jaena, and Mariano Ponce, that clamored for adequate representation to the Spanish Cortes and later for independence. José Rizal, the most celebrated intellectual and radical ilustrado of the era, wrote the novels "Noli Me Tángere", and "El filibusterismo", which greatly inspired the movement for independence. The Katipunan, a secret society whose primary purpose was that of overthrowing Spanish rule in the Philippines, was founded by Andrés Bonifacio who became its Supremo (leader).

The Philippine Revolution began in 1896. Rizal was wrongly implicated in the outbreak of the revolution and executed for treason in 1896. The Katipunan inCavite split into two groups, Magdiwang, led by Mariano Álvarez (a relative of Bonifacio's by marriage), and Magdalo, led by Emilio Aguinaldo. Leadership conflicts between Bonifacio and Aguinaldo culminated in the execution or assassination of the former by the latter's soldiers. Aguinaldo agreed to a truce with the Pact of Biak-na-Bato and Aguinaldo and his fellow revolutionaries were exiled to Hong Kong. Not all the revolutionary generals complied with the agreement. One, General Francisco Makabulos, established a Central Executive Committee to serve as the interim government until a more suitable one was created. Armed conflicts resumed, this time coming from almost every province in Spanish-governed Philippines. In 1898, as conflicts continued in the Philippines, the USS Maine, having been sent to Cuba because of U.S. concerns for the safety of its citizens during an ongoing Cuban revolution, exploded and sank in Havana harbor. This event precipitated the Spanish–American War. After Commodore George Dewey defeated the Spanish squadron at Manila, a German squadron arrived in Manila and engaged in maneuvers which Dewey, seeing this as obstruction of his blockade, offered war— after which the Germans backed down. The German Emperor expected an American defeat, with Spain left in a sufficiently weak position for the revolutionaries to capture Manila—leaving the Philippines ripe for German picking.

The U.S. invited Aguinaldo to return to the Philippines in the hope he would rally Filipinos against the Spanish colonial government. Aguinaldo arrived on May 19, 1898, via transport provided by Dewey. By the time U.S. land forces had arrived, the Filipinos had taken control of the entire island of Luzon, except for the walled city of Intramuros. On June 12, 1898, Aguinaldo declared the independence of the Philippines in Kawit, Cavite, establishing the First Philippine Republic under Asia's first democratic constitution.

In the Battle of Manila, the United States captured the city from the Spanish. This battle marked an end of Filipino-American collaboration, as Filipino forces were prevented from entering the captured city of Manila, an action deeply resented by the Filipinos.

Spain and the United States sent commissioners to Paris to draw up the terms of the Treaty of Paris which ended the Spanish–American War. The Filipino representative, Felipe Agoncillo, was excluded from sessions as the revolutionary government was not recognized by the family of nations. Although there was substantial domestic opposition, the United States decided to annex the Philippines. In addition to Guam and Puerto Rico, Spain was forced in the negotiations to hand over the Philippines to the U.S. in exchange for US$20,000,000.00. U.S. President McKinley justified the annexation of the Philippines by saying that it was "a gift from the gods" and that since "they were unfit for self-government, ... there was nothing left for us to do but to take them all, and to educate the Filipinos, and uplift and civilize and Christianize them", in spite of the Philippines having been already Christianized by the Spanish overthe course of several centuries. The first Philippine Republic resisted the U.S. occupation, resulting in the Philippine–American War (1899–1913).

Filipinos initially saw their relationship with the United States as that of two nations joined in a common struggle against Spain. However, the United States later distanced itself from the interests of the Filipino insurgents. Emilio Aguinaldo was unhappy that the United States would not commit to paper a statement of support for Philippine independence. Relations deteriorated and tensions heightened as it became clear that the Americans were in the islands to stay.

VIII. Philippine–American War

Hostilities broke out on February 4, 1899, after two American privates on patrol killed three Filipino soldiers in San Juan, a Manila suburb. This incident sparked the Philippine–American War, which would cost far more money and take far more lives than the Spanish–American War. Some 126,000 American soldiers would be committed to the conflict; 4,234 Americans died, as did 12,000– 20,000 Philippine Republican Army soldiers who were part of a nationwide guerrilla movement of indeterminate numbers.

The general population, caught between Americans and rebels, suffered significantly. At least 200,000 Filipino civilians lost their lives as an indirect result of the war mostly as a result of the cholera epidemic at the war's end that took between 150,000 and 200,000 lives. Atrocities were committed by both sides.

The poorly equipped Filipino troops were easily overpowered by American troops in open combat, but they were formidable opponents in guerrilla warfare. Malolos, the revolutionary capital, was captured on March 31, 1899. Aguinaldo and his government escaped, however, establishing a new capital at San Isidro, Nueva Ecija. On June 5, 1899, Antonio Luna, Aguinaldo's most capable military commander, was killed by Aguinaldo's guards in an apparent assassination while visiting Cabanatuan, Nueva Ecija to meet with Aguinaldo. With his best commander dead and his troops suffering continued defeats as American forces pushed into northern Luzon, Aguinaldo dissolved the regular army on November 13 and ordered the establishment of decentralized guerrilla commands in each of several military zones. Another key general, Gregorio del Pilar, was killed on December 2, 1899 in the Battle of Tirad Pass—a rear guard action to delay the Americans while Aguinaldo made good his escape through the mountains.

Aguinaldo was captured at Palanan, Isabela on March 23, 1901 and was brought to Manila. Convinced of the futility of further resistance, he swore allegiance to the United States and issued a proclamation calling on his compatriots to lay down their arms, officially bringing an end to the war. However, sporadic insurgent resistance continued in various parts of the Philippines, especially in the Muslim south, until 1913.

In 1900, President McKinley sent the Taft Commission, to the Philippines, with a mandate to legislate laws and re-engineer the political system. On July 1, 1901, William Howard Taft, the head of the commission, was inaugurated as Civil Governor, with limited executive powers. The authority of the Military Governor was continued in those areas where the insurrection persisted. The Taft Commission passed laws to set up the fundamentals of the new government, including a judicial system, civil service, and local government. A Philippine Constabulary was organized to deal with the remnants of the insurgent movement and gradually assume the responsibilities of the United States Army.

IX. The Tagalog, Negros and Zamboanga Cantonal Republics

During the First Philippine Republic, three other insurgent republics were briefly formed: the Tagalog Republic in Luzon, under Macario Sakay, the Negros Republic in the Visayas under Aniceto Lacson, and the Republic of Zamboanga inMindanao under Mariano Arquiza. Despite resistance from these three republics ignored by Aguinaldo who included them in his gift to the USA, all three were eventually dissolved and the Philippines was ruled as a singular insular territory.

X. Insular Government (1901–1935)

The Philippine Organic Act was the basic law for the Insular Government, so called because civil administration was under the authority of the U.S. Bureau of Insular Affairs. This government saw its mission as one of tutelage, preparing the Philippines for eventual independence. On July 4, 1902 the office of military governor was abolished and full executive power passed from Adna Chaffee, the last military governor, to Taft, who became the first U.S. governor-general of the Philippines. United States policies towards the Philippines shifted with changing administrations. During the early years of territorial administration, the Americans were reluctant to delegate authority to the Filipinos, but an elected Philippine Assembly was inaugurated in 1907, as the lower house of a bicameral legislature, with the appointive Philippine Commission becoming the upper house. When Woodrow Wilson became U.S. president in 1913, a new policy was adopted to put into motion a process that would gradually lead to Philippine independence. The Jones Law, passed by the U.S. Congress in 1916 to serve as a new basic law, promised eventual independence. It provide for the election of both houses of the legislature.

In socio-economic terms, the Philippines made solid progress in this period. Foreign trade had amounted to 62 million pesos in 1895, 13% of which was with the United States. By 1920, it had increased to 601 million pesos, 66% of which was with the United States. A health care system was established which, by 1930, reduced the mortality rate from all causes, including various tropical diseases, to a level similar to that of the United States itself. The practices of slavery, piracy and head hunting were suppressed but not entirely extinguished. A new educational system was established with English as the medium of instruction, eventually becoming a lingua franca of the Islands. The 1920s saw alternating periods of cooperation and confrontation with American governors-general, depending on how intent the incumbent was on exercising his powers vis-à-vis the Philippine legislature. Members to the elected legislature lobbied for immediate and complete independence from the United States. Several independence missions were sent to Washington, D.C. A civil service was formed and was gradually taken over by Filipinos, who had effectively gained control by 1918.

Philippine politics during the American territorial era was dominated by the Nacionalista Party, which was founded in 1907. Although the party's platform called for "immediate independence", their policy toward the Americans was highly accommodating. Within the political establishment, the call for independence was spearheaded by Manuel L. Quezon, who served continuously as Senate president from 1916 until 1935.

World War I gave the Philippines the opportunity to pledge assistance to the US war effort. This took the form of an offer to supply a division of troops, as well as providing funding for the construction of two warships. A locally recruited national guard was created and significant numbers of Filipinos volunteered for service in the US Navy and army. Frank Murphy was the last Governor-General of the Philippines (1933-35), and the first U.S. High Commissioner of the Philippines (1935-36). The change in form was more than symbolic: it was intended as a manifestation of the transition to independence.

The Great Depression in the early thirties hastened the progress of the Philippines towards independence. In the United States it was mainly the sugar industry and labor unions that had a stake in loosening the U.S. ties to the Philippines since they could not compete with the

Philippine cheap sugar (and other commodities) which could freely enter the U.S. market. Therefore, they agitated in favor of granting independence to the Philippines so that its cheap products and labor could be shut out of the United States. In 1933, the United States Congress passed the Hare–Hawes–Cutting Act as a Philippine Independence Act over President Herbert Hoover's veto. Though the bill had been drafted with the aid of a commission from the Philippines, it was opposed by Philippine Senate President Manuel L. Quezon, partially because of provisions leaving the United States in control of naval bases. Under his influence, the Philippine legislature rejected the bill. The following year, a revised act known as the Tydings–McDuffie Act was finally passed. The act provided for the establishment of the Commonwealth of the Philippines with a ten-year period of peaceful transitions to full independence. The commonwealth would have its own constitution and be self-governing, though foreign policy would be the responsibility of the United States, and certain legislation required approval of the United States president. The Act stipulated that the date of independence would be on the July 4 following the tenth anniversary of the establishment of the Commonwealth.

A Constitutional Convention was convened in Manila on July 30, 1934. On February 8, 1935, the 1935 Constitution of the Republic of the Philippines was approved by the convention by a vote of 177 to 1. The constitution was approved by President Franklin D. Roosevelt on March 23, 1935 and ratified by popular vote on May 14, 1935.

On September 17, 1935, presidential elections were held. Candidates included former president Emilio Aguinaldo, the Iglesia Filipina Independiente leader Gregorio Aglipay, and others. Manuel L. Quezon and Sergio Osmeña of the Nacionalista Party were proclaimed the winners, winning the seats of president and vice-president, respectively.

The Commonwealth Government was inaugurated on the morning of November 15, 1935, in ceremonies held on the steps of the Legislative Building in Manila. The event was attended by a crowd of around 300,000 people. Under the Tydings–McDuffie Act this meant that the date of full independence for the Philippines was set for July 4, 1946, a timetable which was followed after the passage of almost eleven very eventful years.

World War II and Japanese Occupation

I. Japanese Military Attack

Japan launched a surprise attack on the Clark Air Base in Pampanga on the morning of December 8, 1941, just ten hours after the attack on Pearl Harbor. Aerial bombardment was followed by landings of ground troops on Luzon. The defending Philippine and United States troops were under the command of General Douglas MacArthur. Under the pressure of superior numbers, the defending forces withdrew to the Bataan Peninsula and to the island of Corregidor at the entrance to Manila Bay.

On January 2, 1942, General McArthur declared the capital city, Manila, an open city to prevent its destruction. The Philippine defense continued until the final surrender of United States-Philippine forces on the Bataan Peninsula in April 1942 and on Corregidor in May of the same year. Most of the 80,000 prisoners of war captured by the Japanese at Bataan were forced to undertake the infamous Bataan Death March to a prison camp 105 kilometers to the north. About 10,000 Filipinos and 1,200 Americans died before reaching their destination.

President Quezon and Osmeña had accompanied the troops to Corregidor and later left for the United States, where they set up a government in exile. MacArthur was ordered to Australia, where he started to plan for a return to the Philippines.

The Japanese military authorities immediately began organizing a new government structure in the Philippines and established the Philippine Executive Commission. They initially organized a Council of State, through which they directed civil affairs until October 1943, when they declared the Philippines an independent republic. The Japanese-sponsored republic headed by President José P. Laurel proved to be unpopular.

Japanese occupation of the Philippines was opposed by large-scale underground and guerrilla activity. The Philippine Army, as well as remnants of the U.S. Army Forces Far East, continued to fight the Japanese in a guerrilla war and was considered an auxiliary unit of the United States Army. Their effectiveness was such that by the end of the war, Japan controlled only twelve of the forty- eight provinces. One element of resistance in the Central Luzon area was furnished by the Hukbalahap, which armed some 30,000 people and extended their control over much of Luzon.

The occupation of the Philippines by Japan ended at the war's conclusion. The American army had been fighting the Philippines Campaign since October 1944, when MacArthur's Sixth United States Army landed on Leyte. Landings in other parts of the country had followed, and the Allies, with the Philippine Commonwealth troops, pushed toward Manila. However, fighting continued until Japan's formal surrender on September 2, 1945. Approximately 10,000 U.S. soldiers were missing in action in the Philippines when the war ended, more than in any other country in the Pacific or European Theaters. The Philippines suffered great loss of life and tremendous physical destruction, especially during the Battle of Manila. An estimated 1 million Filipinos had been killed, a large portion during the final months of the war, and Manila had been extensively damaged.

II.   Home Front

As in most occupied countries, crime, looting, corruption, and black markets were endemic. Japan in 1943 proposed independence on new terms, and some collaborators went along with the plan, but Japan was clearly losing the war and nothing became of it.

With a view of building up the economic base of the Greater East Asia Co- Prosperity Sphere, the Japanese Army envisioned using the islands as a source of agricultural products needed by its industry. For example Japan had a surplus of sugar from Taiwan, and a severe shortage of cotton, so they try to grow cotton in on sugar lands with disastrous results. They lacked the seeds, pesticides, and technical skills to grow cotton. Jobless farm workers flock to the cities, where there was minimal relief and few jobs. The Japanese Army also tried using cane sugar for fuel, castor beans and copra for oil, derris for quinine, cotton for uniforms, and abaca (hemp) for rope. The plans were very difficult to implement in the face of limited skills, collapsed international markets, bad weather, and transportation shortages. The program was a failure that gave very little help to Japanese industry, and diverted resources needed for food production. As Karnow reports, Filipinos "rapidly learned as well that 'co-prosperity' meant servitude to Japan's economic requirements."

Living conditions were bad throughout the Philippines during the war. Transportation between the islands was difficult because of lack of fuel. Food was in very short supply, with sporadic famines and epidemic diseases.

Independent Philippines and the Third Republic (1946–1975)

I. Administration of Manuel Roxas (1946–1948

Elections were held in April 1946, with Manuel Roxas becoming the first president of the independent Republic of the Philippines. The United States ceded its sovereignty over the Philippines on July 4, 1946, as scheduled. However, the Philippine economy remained highly dependent on United States markets– more dependent, according to United States high commissioner Paul McNutt, than any single U.S. state was dependent on the rest of the country. The Philippine Trade Act, passed as a precondition for receiving war rehabilitation grants from the United States, exacerbated the dependency with provisions further tying the economies of the two countries. A military assistance pact was signed in 1947 granting the United States a 99-year lease on designated military bases in the country.

II. Administration of Elpidio Quirino (1948–1953)

The Roxas administration granted general amnesty to those who had collaborated with the Japanese in World War II, except for those who had committed violent crimes. Roxas died suddenly of a heart attack in April 1948, and the vice president, Elpidio Quirino, was elevated to the presidency. He ran for president in his own right in 1949, defeating José P. Laurel and winning a four-year term.

World War II had left the Philippines demoralized and severely damaged. The task of reconstruction was complicated by the activities of the Communist- supported Hukbalahap guerrillas (known as "Huks"), who had evolved into a violent resistance force against the new Philippine government. Government policy towards the Huks alternated between gestures of negotiation and harsh suppression. Secretary of Defense Ramon Magsaysay initiated a campaign to defeat the insurgents militarily and at the same time win popular support for the government. The Huk movement had waned in the early 1950s, finally ending with the unconditional surrender of Huk leader Luis Taruc in May 1954.

III. Administration of Ramon Magsaysay (1953-1957)

Supported by the United States, Magsaysay was elected president in 1953 on a populist platform. He promised sweeping economic reform, and made progress inland reform by promoting the resettlement of poor people in the Catholic north into traditionally Muslim areas. Though this relieved population pressure in the north, it heightened religious hostilities. Nevertheless, he was extremely popular with the common people, and his death in an airplane crash in March 1957 dealt a serious blow to national morale.

IV. Administration of Carlos P. Garcia (1957-1961)

Carlos P. Garcia succeeded to the presidency after Magsaysay's death, and was elected to a four-year term in the election of November that same year. His administration emphasized the nationalist theme of "Filipino first", arguing that the Filipino people should be given the chances to improve the country's economy. Garcia successfully negotiated for the United States' relinquishment of large military land reservations. However, his administration lost popularity on issues of government corruption as his term advanced.

V. Administration of Diosdado Macapagal (1961-1965)

In the presidential elections held on November 14, 1961, Vice President Diosdado Macapagal defeated re-electionist President Carlos P. Garcia and Emmanuel Pelaez as a Vice President. President Macapagal was the President of the Philippines that changed the independence day of the Philippines from July 4 to June 12.

The Agricultural Land Reform Code (RA 3844) was a major Philippines land reform law enacted in 1963 under President Diosdado Macapagal.

The code declared that it was State policy:

- To establish owner-cultivatorship and the economic family-size farm as the basis of Philippine agriculture and, as a consequence, divert landlord capital in agriculture to industrial development;
- To achieve a dignified existence for the small farmers free from pernicious institutional restraints and practices;
- To create a truly viable social and economic structure in agriculture conducive to greater productivity and higher farm incomes;
- To apply all labor laws equally and without discrimination to both industrial and agricultural wage earners;
- To provide a more vigorous and systematic land resettlement program and public land distribution; and
- To make the small farmers more independent, self-reliant and responsible citizens, and a source of genuine strength in our democratic society.
- and, in pursuance of those policies, established the following,
- An agricultural leasehold system to replace all existing share tenancy systems in agriculture;
- A declaration of rights for agricultural labor;
- An authority for the acquisition and equitable distribution of agricultural land;
- An institution to finance the acquisition and distribution of agricultural land;
- A machinery to extend credit and similar assistance to agriculture;
- A machinery to provide marketing, management, and other technical services to agriculture;
- A unified administration for formulating and implementing projects of land reform;
- An expanded program of land capability survey, classification, and registration; and
- A judicial system to decide issues arising under this Code and other related laws and regulations.

MAPHILINDO

MaPhilIndo was a proposed non-political confederation of Malaya, the Philippines, and Indonesia. It was based on concepts developed during the Commonwealth government in the Philippines by Wenceslao Vinzons and by Eduardo L. Martelino in his 1959 book Someday, Malaysia".

In July 1963, President Diosdado Macapagal of the Philippines convened a summit meeting in Manila. Maphilindo was proposed as a realization of José Rizal's dream of bringing together the Malay peoples. However, this was perceived as a tactic on the parts of Jakarta and Manila to delay or prevent the formation of the Federation of Malaysia. The plan failed when Indonesian President Sukarno adopted his plan of Konfrontasi with Malaysia.

Marcos Era and Martial Law Period (1965–1986)

I. Marcos Election to the Presidency

Macapagal ran for re-election in 1965, but was defeated by his former party- mate, Senate President Ferdinand Marcos, who had switched to the Nacionalista Party. Early in his presidency, and assisted by the best Cabinet Secretaries manning the National Government Agencies, Marcos initiated ambitious public works projects and intensified tax collection which brought the country economic prosperity throughout the 1970s. His administration built more roads (including a substantial portion of the Pan-Philippine Highway) than all his predecessors combined, and more schools than any previous administration. Marcos was re- elected president in 1969, becoming the first president of the Philippines to achieve a second term. Opponents of Marcos, however, blocked the necessary legislation to further implement his expansive agenda. Because of this, optimism faded early in his second term and economic growth slowed. Crime and civil disobedience increased. The Communist Party of the Philippines formed the New People's Army in response to his shaky hold over the nation and the Moro National Liberation Front continued to fight for an independent Muslim nation in Mindanao. An explosion during the proclamation rally of the senatorial slate of the Liberal Party on August 21, 1971 prompted Marcos to suspend the writ of habeas corpus, which he restored on January 11, 1972 after public protests.

VI. NATIONAL POLICIES & PROGRAMS FOR SOCIO-ECONOMIC PROGRESS

A. Unprecedented Infrastructure Growth

The country's road network had improved from 55,778 kilometers in 1965 to 77,950 in five years (1970), and eventually reached 161,000 kilometers in 1985. Construction of irrigation facilities was also done that made 1.5 million hectares of land irrigated and increased the farmer's harvest and income.

In addition, nationwide telecommunication systems (telephone systems, telex exchange centers and interprovincial toll stations were also built.

PRESIDENT FERDINAND MARCOS's ACCOMPLISHMENTS ALL COMPLETED

Source: National Economic Development Authority (NEDA) Economic Development Projects 1965-86

1. Marcos completed Power plants in 20 years:
   a) Bataan Nuclear Power Plant, completed 1983
   b) Leyte Geothermal Power Plant, completed 1977
   c) Makiling-Banahaw Geothermal Power Plant, completed 1979
   d) Tiwi Geothermal Power Plant, completed 1980
   e) Angat Hydro Electric Power Plant, completed 1967
   f) Kalayaan Hydro Electric Power Plant, completed 1982
   g) Magat A Hydro Electric Power Plant, completed 1984
   h) Magat B Hydro Electric Power Plant, completed 1984
   i) Pantabangan Hydro Electric Power Plant, completed 1977
   j) Agus 2 Hydro Electric Power Plant, completed 1979
   k) Agus 4 Hydro Electric Power Plant, completed 1985
   l) Agus 5 Hydro Electric Power Plant, completed 1985
   m) Agus 7 Hydro Electric Power Plant, completed 1982
   n) Pulangi Hydro Electric Power Plant, completed 1985
   o) Agus 6 Hydro Electric Power plant, recommissioned in 1977
   p) Masiway Hydro Electric Power Plant, completed 1980
   q) Main Magat Hydro Electric Power Plant, completed 1983
   r) Calaca Coal Power Plant Completed in 1984
   s) Cebu Thermal Power Plant completed in 1981
   t) Palinpinon 1 Southern Negros Geothermal production Field completed in 1983.

Note: Not mentioned are diesel plants

Source: Department of Energy.

2. **Marcos completed Bridge projects in 20 years**
   a) Biliran Bridge 150 meters long of Leyte, completed 1975

b) Buntun Bridge 1369 meters long of Tuguegarao-Solana, Cagayan, completed 1974
c) Candaba Viaduct Pulilan 5000 meters long of Bulacan-San Simon, Pampanga, completed 1976
d) Mactan-Mandaue Bridge 864 meters long of Lapu-Lapu-Mandaue, Cebu 1972
e) Magapit Suspension Bridge 449 meters long of Lal-lo, Cagayan completed 1978
f) Mawo Bridge 280 meters long Victoria, Northern Samar completed 1970
g) Patapat Viaduct 1300 meters long Pagudpud, Ilocos Norte completed 1986
h) 9) San Juanico Bridge 2060 meters long Tacloban, Leyte-Santa Rita, Samar. Completed 1973

(Note: Not included in the list are the unnamed hundreds of bridges under 100 meters long.)
Source: Department of Public Works and Highways.
TOTAL LENGTH = 11,472 meters long

B. Food Sufficiency

1. Green Revolution

Production of rice was increased through promoting the cultivation of IR-8 hybrid rice. In 1968 the Philippines became self-sufficient in rice, the first time in history since the American period. It also exported rice worth US$7 million.

2. Blue Revolution

Marine species like prawn, mullet, milkfish, and golden tilapia were being produced and distributed to farmers at a minimum cost. Today, milkfish and prawns contribute substantially to foreign exchange income.

3. Liberalized Credit

More than one thousand rural banks spread all over the country resulting to the accessibility of credit to finance purchase of agricultural inputs, hired labor, and harvesting expenses at very low interest rate.

During 1981-1985, credit was available without interest and collateral arrangements.
Some of the credit programs were the following:
a) Biyayang Dagat (credit support for fishermen)
b) Bakahang Barangay —supported fattening of 40,000 head of cattle in farmer backyards
c) Masaganang Maisan, Maisagana, and Expanded Yellow Corn Program – supported 1.4 Million farmers through P4.7 Billion loans from 1975-1985
d) Gulayan sa Kalusugan and Pagkain ng Bayan Programs – provided grants and loans of P12.4 Million to encourage backyard and communal production of vegetables and improve nutrition of Filipino households
e) Kilusang Kabuhayan at Kaunlaran (KKK) - supported 25,000 entrepreneurial projects through P1.8 Billion and helping 500,000 beneficiaries

4. **Decontrol Program**
Price control policies were implemented on rice and corn to provide greater incentive to farmers to produce more. Deregulation of trading in commodities like sugar and coconut and agricultural inputs like fertilizer were done for more efficient marketing and trading arrangements.

5. **Education Reform**
   ➤ Access to free education widened during the Marcos Administration. The biggest portion of the budget was allotted for Educational Programs (P58.7 Billion in 20 years).
   ➤ The literacy rate climbed from 72% in 1965 to 93% in 1985 and almost 100% in Metro Manila on the same year.

A. **Marcos Established/Founded State Colleges/Universities**
   1) Don Mariano Marcos Memorial State University in La Union founded in 1981
   2) Mariano Marcos State University in Ilocos Norte founded in 1978
   3) Kalinga-Apayao State College in Tabuk Kalinga founded in 1970

4) Abra State Institute of Science and Technology in Abra founded in 1983
5) Pangasinan State University founded in 1979
6) University of Northern Philippines founded in 1965
7) Philippine State College of Aeronautics founded in 1969
8) Cagayan State University established in 1978
9) Quirino State University established 1976
10) Isabela State University established 1978
11) Pampanga Agricultural College established 1974
12) Mindoro State College of Agriculture and Technology- Calapan City established 1966
13) Occidental Mindoro State College established 1966
14) Palawan State University established 1965
15) Bicol University established 1969
16) Camarines Sur Polytechnic Colleges established 1983
17) Rizal Technological University established 1969
18) Technological University of the Philippines established 1971
19) Capiz State University 1980
20) Guimaras State College 1968
21) Northern Negros State College of Science and Technology established 1971
22) West Visayas State University became established as university in January 1986
23) Leyte Normal University 1976
24) SLSU- (Southern Leyte State University) - Sogod 1969
25) SLSU- Hinunangan 1975
26) SLSU- Tomas Oppus feb. 1 1986
27) SLSU- Bontoc 1983
28) SLSU- San Juan 1983
29) Basilan State College 1984
30) Western Mindanao State University became a university in 1978 followed with building the satellite campuses in:
    a) WMSU-Alicia campus, Zamboanga del Sur
    b) WMSU-Aurora campus, Zamboanga del Sur
    c) WMSU Curuan, Zamboanga City
    d) WMSU-Diplahan, Zamboanga Sibugay
    e) WMSU-Imelda, Zamboanga Sibugay
    f) WMSU-Ipil, Zamboanga Sibugay

g) WMSU-Mabuhay, Zamboanga Sibugay
h) WMSU-Malangas, Zamboanga Sibugay
i) WMSU-Molave, Zamboanga del Sur WMSU-Naga, Zamboanga Sibugay WMSUOlutanga, Zamboanga Sibugay
j) WMSU-Pagadian City, Zamboanga del Sur
k) WMSU-Pitogo, Zamboanga del Sur
l) WMSU-San Ramon, Zamboanga City WMSU-Siay, Zamboanga Sibugay
m) WMSU-Tungawan, Zamboanga Sibugay

31) Central Mindanao University established1965
32) Misamis Oriental State College of Agriculture and Technology established 1983
33) Northwestern Mindanao State College of Science and Technology established 1971
34) Davao del Norte School of Fisheries established 1969 (now known as Davao del Norte State College) Source: Depart
35) Mati Community College (MCC) founded in 1972 (now known as Davao Oriental State College of Science and Technology)
36) Malita Agri-Business and Marine and Aquatic School of Technology founded 1966 now known as:
37) Southern Philippines Agri-Business and Marine and Aquatic School of Technology
39) University of Southeastern Philippines established 1978Cotabato Foundation College of Science and Technology established 1967
40) Cotabato City State Polytechnic College established 1983
41) Mindanao state university- Iligan city founded 1968
42) Mindanao state university- Gensan city founded 1971
43) Surigao del Sur State University founded 1982
44) Surigao Del Norte School of Arts and Trades (Founded in 1969) now known as Surigao State College of Technology
45) Sulu State College founded in 1982
46) Tawi-Tawi Regional Agricultural College founded in 1975
47) Adiong Memorial Polytechnic State College founded in 1970's

48) Makati Polytechnic Community College-Technical High School founded in 1972

Note:
- o Not included are the state —owned institutions established/founded prior to 1965 that were improved and re-equipped to become colleges or universities between 1965 - 1985 these include among others all the Polytechnic State Colleges and Universities.
- o All others not included in the list are those either renamed after President Marcos was deposed, these include all the schools under the control and supervision of the TESDA which was formerly the NMYC-National Manpower and Youth Council.

B. **Secondary/High Schools Established/Built**
1) Amlan Municipal High School was established 1972
2) Amparo High School was established in 1979
3) Aplaya National High School was established 1969
4) Balayan National High School (BNHS) established 1985)
5) Balibago National High School established 1970
6) Bayugan National Comprehensive High School established 1980
7) Buenavista National High School established 1972
Dalupaon National High School established 1972
9) Don Emilio Macias Memorial National High School established 1982
10) Dona Francisca Lacsamana de Ortega Memorial National High School established 1972
11) Dr. Juan G. Nolasco High School established 1966
12) Eastern Samar National Comprehensive High School established 1969
13) Francisco P. Felix Memorial National High School (FPFMNHS) established 1973
14) Gen. T. de Leon National High School establsihed 1969
15) Ismael Mathay, Sr. High School, formerly called the GSIS Village High School established 1971

16) Jose Borromeo Legaspi Memorial National High School established 1981
17) Kaong National High School 1974
18) Lawang Bato National High School established 1967
19) Liloy National High School established 1974
20) Mag-aba National High School established 1977
21) Mandaluyong High School established 1977
22) Navotas National High School established 1983
23) Parañaque National High School (Main Campus) (Formerly known as Parañaque Municipal High School) established 1969
24) Pasay City North High School established in 1969
25) Pedro E. Diaz High School established 1977
26) Philippine High School for the Arts established 1977
27) Pinagtongulan National High School established 1967
28) Punta National High School established 1971
29) San Juan National High School established 1968
30) San Mateo National High School established 1985
31) San Pablo City National High School established 1969
32) San Pedro Relocation Center National High School established 1970
33) San Ramon National High School established 1967
34) Tabon M. Estrella National High School established 198135)
35. Makati Polytechnic Community College-Technical High School founded in 1972
36) Tomas Cabili National High school Iligan city 1971
37) Dasmarinas National high School 1971

6. Agrarian Reform

Tenant's Emancipation Act of 1972 or PD 27 was implemented without bloodshed. This was the first Land Reform Code our country. Since it was implemented until December 1985, 1.2 million farmers benefited, either they became the owner or leaseholder in more than 1.3 million hectares of rice and corn lands.

7. Primary Health Care

The Primary Health Care (PHC) Program made medical care accessible to millions of Filipinos in the remotest barrios of the country. This program was even awarded by United Nations as the most effective and most responsive health program among the third world countries. With PHC life expectancy increased from 53.7 years in 1965 to 65 years in 1985. Infant mortality rate also declined from 73 deaths per 1,000 live births in 1965 to 58 in 1984.

8. Mass Housing for the Masses

Bagong Lipunan Improvement of Sites and Services (BLISS) Housing project had expanded the government's housing program for the low-income group.

- Massive slum upgrading projects have improved to 14,000 lots in 1985 from 2,500 in 1976.
- The Tondo foreshore, for instance, is one of the biggest and most miserable slum colonies in Asia was transformed into a decent community.
- A total of 230,000 housing units were constructed from 1975-1985. The laws on socialized housing were conceptualized by President Marcos through a series of legal issuances from the funding, the lending, mortgaging and to the collection of the loans. These are governed by the Home Mutual Development Fund (Pag-Ibig Fund), the Housing and Land Use Regulatory Board (HLURB) and the National Home Mortgage Finance which remain intact up to the present

9. Energy Self-Reliance

Indigenous energy sources were developed like hydro, geothermal, dendrothermal, coal, biogas and biomass. The country became the first in Asia to use dendrothermal and in five years we became number two, next to US, in geothermal utilization. The extensive energy resource research and exploration and development resulted to reduction of oil imports from 100% in 1965 to 40% in 1985 and in the same year, more than 1,400 towns and cities were fully energized.

10. Export Development

During 1985 textile and textile products like garments and embroideries, furniture and rattan products, marine products like prawns and milkfish, raw silk, shoes, dehydrated and fresh fruits were exported aside from the traditional export products like coconut, sugar, logs, lumber and veneer. The maritime industry was also dominated by Filipinos wherein 50,000 seamen were employed by various world shipping companies.

22. Political Reform
The structure of government established by President Marcos remains substantially the same except the change of name, inclusive of superficial features in laws, to give a semblance of change from that of President Marcos regime.

The only significant department that was abolished after the departure of President Marcos was the Department of Ministry of Human Settlements under Imelda Romualdez Marcos. It was dismantled but the functions were distributed to different offices.

22. Fiscal Reform
Government finances were stabilized by higher revenue collections and loans from treasury bonds, foreign lending institutions and foreign governments.

The highest Exchange Rate for the USDollar is Php 14.00 in 1985.

23. Peace and Order
In 1966, more than 100 important smugglers were arrested; in three years 1966-68 they arrested a total of 5,000.
Military men involved in smuggling were forced to retire.

Peace and order significantly improved in most provinces however situations in Manila and some provinces continued to deteriorate until the imposition of martial law in 1972.

24. Tourism, Culture and Arts
Created and established the Department of Tourism under which are the adjunct agencies and bureaus i.e., the Philippine Convention

Bureau in-charge in the promotion of the country as the center for world congresses, congress, exhibits and meetings. It was during his administration that tourist facilities and infrastructure were developed to cater to the growing needs of the tourist markets from all over the world., thus, the Cultural Center of the Philippines (CCP), Philippine International Convention Center (PICC), Folk Arts Theatre and the International Film Center were constructed. Hotels and resorts of various categories were introduced in Metro Manila and other provinces and islands, together with support tourism services, i.e., airports, ports and harbors, tourism transports, etc.. Recognizing the tourism development programs of his administration, the UNWTO United Nation World Tourism Organization established its regional office in the country in 1978. It was during his period of administration that the country's tourism industry was accorded with highest recognition and respect.

Fifth Republic (1986–Present)

I. **Administration of Corazon Cojuangco Aquino (1986–1992)**

Corazon Aquino immediately formed a revolutionary government to normalize the situation, and provided for a transitional "Freedom Constitution". A new permanent constitution was ratified and enacted in February 1987. The constitution crippled presidential power to declare martial law, proposed the creation of autonomous regions in the Cordilleras and Muslim Mindanao, and restored the presidential form of government and the bicameral Congress. Progress was made in revitalizing democratic institutions and respect for civil liberties, but Aquino's administration was also viewed as weak and fractious. and a return to full political stability and economic development was hampered by several attempted coups staged by disaffected members of the Philippine military.

Economic growth was additionally hampered by a series of natural disasters, including the 1991 eruption of Mount Pinatubo that left 700 dead and 200,000 homeless. During the Aquino presidency, Manila witnessed six unsuccessful coup attempts, the most serious occurring in December 1989. In 1991, the Philippine Senate rejected a treaty that would have allowed a 10-year extension of the U.S. military bases in the country. The United States turned over Clark Air Base in Pampanga to the government in November, and Subic Bay Naval Base in Zambales in December 1992, ending almost a century of U.S. military presence in the Philippines.

Corazon Aquino immediately formed a revolutionary government to normalize the situation, and provided for a transitional "Freedom Constitution". A new permanent constitution was ratified and enacted in February 1987. The constitution crippled presidential power to declare martial law, proposed the creation of autonomous regions in the Cordilleras and Muslim Mindanao, and restored the presidential form of government and the bicameral Congress. Progress was made in revitalizing democratic institutions and respect for civil liberties, but Aquino's administration was also viewed as weak and fractious while the administration concentrated most of their times in running after the Marcos family's wealth that allegedly was ill-gotten. In addition instead of continuing the most beneficial programs left behind by President Marcos, Cory Aquino and her trusted relatives established their own political clique and gradually controlled all the most profitable and income earning corporations under the cloak of Sequestration Orders issued by the Philippine Commission on Good Government (PCGG) which creation was the first Executive Order issued under what they termed as the Revolutionary Government. Local Government Units (LGUs) elected officials, as well as the National Government Agencies incumbent officials were changed by inexperienced appointees that included well-known leftist who returned from their self-exile during the Marcos rule, that instead of helping the country's return to political and economic stability aggravated chaos in governance and thus, various attempted coups were staged by unsatisfied members of the Philippine Military, the same group that supported the People Power Revolution and the rise of Cory Aquino to the presidency.

Economic growth was additionally hampered by a series of natural disasters, including the 1991 eruption of Mount Pinatubo that left 700 dead and 200,000 homeless. During the Aquino presidency, Manila witnessed six unsuccessful coup attempts, the most serious occurring in December 1989. In 1991, the Philippine Senate rejected a treaty that would have allowed a 10-year extension of the U.S. military bases in the country. The United States turned over Clark Air Base in Pampanga to the government in November, and Subic Bay Naval Base in Zambales in December 1992, ending almost a century of U.S. military presence in the Philippines.

II. Administration of Fidel Valdez Ramos (1992–1998)

In the 1992 elections, Defense Secretary Fidel V. Ramos (a.k.a. Eddie), endorsed by Aquino, won the presidency with just 23.6% of the vote in a field of seven candidates. Early in his administration, Ramos declared "national reconciliation" his highest priority and worked at building a coalition to overcome the divisiveness of the Aquino years. He legalized theCommunist Party and laid the groundwork for talks with communist insurgents, Muslim separatists, and military rebels, attempting to convince them to cease their armed activities against the government. In June 1994, Ramos signed into law a general conditional amnesty covering all rebel groups, and Philippine military and police personnel accused of crimes committed while fighting the insurgents. In October 1995, the government signed an agreement bringing the military insurgency to an end. A peace agreement with the Moro National Liberation Front (MNLF), a major separatist group fighting for an independent homeland in Mindanao, was signed in 1996, ending the 24-year old struggle. However, an MNLF splinter group, the Moro Islamic Liberation Front continued the armed struggle for an Islamic state. Efforts by Ramos supporters to gain passage of an amendment that would allow him to run for a second term were met with large-scale protests, leading Ramos to declare he would not seek re-election. On his Presidency the death penalty was revived in the light of the Rape-slay case of Eileen Sarmienta and Allan Gomez in 1993 and the first person to be executed was Leo Echegaray in 1999.

III.   Administration of Joseph Ejercito Estrada (1998–2001)

Joseph Estrada, a former movie actor who had served as Ramos' vice president, was elected president by a landslide victory in 1998. His election campaign pledged to help the poor and develop the country's agricultural sector. He enjoyed widespread popularity, particularly among the poor.[168] Estrada assumed office amid the Asian Financial Crisis. The economy did, however, recover from a low −0.6% growth in 1998 to a moderate growth of 3.4% by 1999. Like his predecessor there was a similar attempt to change the 1987 constitution. The process is termed as CONCORD or Constitutional Correction for Development. Unlike Charter change under Ramos and Arroyo the CONCORD proposal, according to its proponents, would only amend the 'restrictive' economic provisions of the constitution that is considered as impeding the entry of more foreign investments in the Philippines. However it was not successful in amending the constitution.

On March 21, 2000 President Estrada declared an "all-out-war" against the Moro Islamic Liberation Front (MILF) after the worsening secessionist movement in Midanao The government later captured 46 MILF camps including the MILF's headquarters', Camp Abubakar. In October 2000, however, Estrada was accused of having accepted millions of pesos in payoffs from illegal gambling businesses. He was impeached by the House of Representatives, but his impeachment trial in the Senate broke down when the senate voted to block the examination of the president's bank records. In response, massive street protests erupted demanding Estrada's resignation. Faced with street protests, cabinet resignations, and a withdrawal of support from the armed forces, Estrada was forced out from office on January 20, 2001.

IV.   Administration of Gloria Macapagal-Arroyo (2001–2010)

Vice President Gloria Macapagal-Arroyo (the daughter of President Diosdado Macapagal) was sworn in as Estrada's successor on the day of his departure. Her accession to power was further legitimized by the mid-term congressional and local elections held four months later, when her coalition won an overwhelming victory.[158] Arroyo's initial term in office was marked by fractious coalition politics as well as a military mutiny in Manila in July 2003 that led her to declare a month-long nationwide state of rebellion.[158] Later on in December 2002 she said would not run in the May 2004 presidential election, but she reversed herself in October 2003 and decided to join the race anyways.

She was re-elected and sworn in for her own six-year term as president on June 30, 2004. In 2005, a tape of a wiretapped conversation surfaced bearing the voice of Arroyo apparently asking an election official if her margin of victory could be maintained. The tape sparked protests calling for Arroyo's resignation. Arroyo admitted to inappropriately speaking to an election official, but denied allegations of fraud and refused to step down. Attempts to impeach the president failed later that year. Halfway through her second term, Arroyo unsuccessfully attempted TP PUSH for an overhaul of the constitution to transform the present presidential-bicameral republic into a federal parliamentary-unicameral form of government, which critics describe would be a move that would allow her to stay in power as Prime Minister. Numerous other scandals (such as the Maguindanao massacre, wherein 58 people were killed, and the unsuccessful NBN-ZTE Broadband Deal) took place in the dawn of her administration. She formally ended her term as president in 2010 (wherein she was succeeded by Senator Benigno Aquino III) and ran for a seat in congress the same year (becoming the second president after Jose P. Laurel to run for lower office following the presidency).

V. Administration of Benigno Simeon Aquino III

Benigno Aquino III began his presidency on June 30, 2010, the fifteenth President of the Philippines. He is a bachelor and the son of former Philippines president Corazon C. Aquino. His administration claimed to be focused on major reforms that would bring greater transparency, reduced poverty, reduced corruption, and a booming market which will give birth to a newly industrialized nation. However, just as with his predecessor, Aquino's administration has been marked with a mix of success and scandal since his inauguration, beginning with the 2010 Manila hostage crisis that caused deeply strained relations between Manila and Hong Kong for a time. The Sultanate ofPanay, founded in 2011, was recognized by the Lanao Advisory Council in 2012. Tensions regarding Sabah due to the Sultanate of Sulu's claim gradually rose during the early years of his administration. Standoffs in Sabah between The Sultanate of Sulu's Royal Army and the Malaysian forces struck in 2013. In 2012 the Framework Agreement on the Bangsamoro was signed to create the Bangsamoro Government in Mindanao. In response, the Bangsamoro Islamic Freedom Fighters (BIFF) was assembled by religious extremists with the goal of seceding from the Philippines. In 2013, the Zamboanga City was attacked by a faction of Moro National Liberation Front (MNLF) under Prof. Nur Misuari, and in the same year, Typhoon Haiyan (Yolanda) struck the country, leading to massive rehabilitation efforts by foreign world powers sending aid, inevitably devolving into chaos following the revelations that the administration and that the government had not been properly handing out the aid packages and preference for political maneuvering over the safety of the people, leading to mass deterioration of food and medical supplies.

The Pork Barrel scam involving hundreds of billions pesos dominated the headlines and politicians involved in the misuse of these funds are now facing plunder cases in court resulting to the detention of leading opposition senators, congressmen and governors. However, those allied to the President Noy Aquino are spared.

Under his presidency, the Philippines has had controversial clashes with the People's Republic of China on a number of issues (such as the standoff in Scarborough Shoal in the South China Sea and the dispute over the Spratly islands), which the mainstream Philippine media has repeatedly been referring to as the West Philippine Sea. This resulted in the proceedings of the Philippines to file a sovereignty case against China in an global arbitration tribunal. Later on in 2014, the Aquino Administration then filed a memorial to the Arbitration Tribunal in The Hague which challenged Beijing's claim in the South China Sea after Chinese ships were accused of harassing a small Philippine vessel carrying goods for stationed military personnel in the South Thomas Shoal where an old Philippine ship had been stationed for many years. In 2014, the Comprehensive Agreement on the Bangsamoro was finally signed after 17 years of negotiation with the Moro Islamic Liberation Front (MILF), a move that is expected to bring peace in Mindanao and the Sulu. On April 28, 2014, when United States President Barack Obama visited the Philippines, the Enhanced Defense Cooperation Agreement (EDCA), between the United States of America and the Philippines, was signed.

On July 27, 2014, the Iglesia ni Cristo (INC) celebrates its 100 years in the Philippines, a big celebration was held in the largest indoor arena in the world, the Philippine Arena with an attendance of more than 2 million members. From January 15 to 19, 2015, Pope Francis stayed in the Philippines for a series of publicity tours and paid visits to the victims of Typhoon Haiyan (Yolanda). On January 25, 2015, 44 members of the Philippine National Police-Special Action Force (PNP-SAF) were killed during an encounter between MILF and BIFF in Mamasapano, Maguindanao. Findings of the as many investigative bodies that conducted in-depth investigations to the facts and circumstances surrounding the incident show that President Noy Aquino has committed culpable violations of the chain of command and many are of the conclusion that he must be held liable for the death of the 44 SAF officers and men together with the suspended PNP Director Purisima and SAF Commander Napeñas. President Benigno S. Aquina, III died unceremoniously by an unkown cause, as he was alone.

Book 4 - Summary Of Current Philippine Tourism

Geography, Socio-Cultural and Economic Features

I. The Philippines in the World

The Philippines is readily accessible from the travel capitals of the world. Traveling time to Manila from Hong Kong is 2 hours; from Singapore, 3 hours and 25 minutes; Bangkok, 3 hours and 15 minutes; Tokyo, 4 hours and 15 minutes;

Sydney, 9 hours and 35 minutes; London, 14 hours; Paris, 14 hour and 45 minutes; Frankfurt, 14 hours and 10 minutes; San Francisco, 11 hours and 50 minutes; Los Angeles, 12 hours and 35 minutes; and New York, 18 hours.

II. Geographic Features, Cultural Backdrop, Population and Languages

An archipelago of 7,107 islands, the Philippines stretches from the south of China to the northern tip of Borneo. The country has over a hundred ethnic groups and a mixture of foreign influences which have molded a unique Filipino culture.

English is the medium of learning and used in all official government and private business transactions, public signages and the mainstream media, making the country as the third largest English speaking country in the world. The Philippine population is currently at 82,000 spread in the 7,107 islands and islets composing the whole country. In addition Philippine has more than 87 local dialects with Tagalog as the National Language that every inhabitant is taught to speak and understand.

Philippines has fine facilities and services such as excellent accommodations, fine restaurants, modern shopping centers and communication services.

The country is divided into three geographical areas: Luzon, Visayas, Mindanao. It has 16 regions and 79 provinces. Its Capital is Manila.

III   Travel Tips Entry/Exit Regulations

Manila, Cebu, Davao, Clark and Laoag are the international gateways. The Ninoy Aquino International Airport (NAIA) in Manila is the premier gateway. It is served by more than 30 airlines which fly to different cities around the world. The Mactan International Airport (MIA) in Cebu is a host to regular flights from major travel capitals. Davao International Airport caters to regular flights from Indonesia and Singapore. The Diosdado Macapagal International Airport and Subic Airfield in Central Luzon service both chartered and cargo planes. Laoag International Airport in Ilocos Norte services regular flights to Taiwan and Macau.

Philippine Airlines, the country's flag carrier, linksManila to 14 cities in 8 countries. Major cruise liners call on the Port of Manila.

ENTRY REGULATIONS

Valid Passport passports for Foreign Nationals and Except for stateless persons and those from countries that do not have diplomatic relations with the Philippines, all visitors may enter the country without visas and may stay for 21 days, provided they have tickets for onward journey .Holders of Hongkong and Taiwan passports must have special permits. Visas and special permits may be obtained for Philippine embassies and consulates.

HEALTH REGULATIONS

A certificate of vaccination against yellow fever is required for travelers coming from an infected area.

AIRPORT INFORMATION

Airports and Facilities: Manila's Ninoy Aquino International Airport (NAIA) (formerly Manila International Airport MIA) is 7 kms., from the city center while the Manila Domestic Airport is one km., from the NAIA. The international airports have adequate traveler facilities: Duty-Free and Souvenir shops, tourist information and assistance counters, hotels and travel agency representatives, car rental services, banks and automated teller machines, postal service, national and international direct dial telephone booths, medical clinics and baggage deposit areas.

Facilities for the physically- handicapped: The airports are handicapped- friendly. Wheelchairs are available on request for airline ground staff.

Customs
Visitors are advised to fill in the Baggage Declaration Form before disembarking to facilitate Customs examination. The following are allowed inside the duty-free: reasonable quantity of clothes, jewelry, and toiletries; 400 sticks of cigarettes or two tins of tobacco; two bottles of wine or spirits of not more than one liter each.

Porterage:
Baggage carts are available for free. Poerter services are also free. Tipping is traditional.

Airport Transfers: Visitors are advised to avail of the accredited fixed rate or metered taxis at the NAIA's Arrival Area. At the Manila Domestic Airport, accredited transfer services are available on pre-paid coupon basis. Other airports are served by metered taxis. All airports have counters for hotel transport and car rental services.

Airport Fees:
Php750 for international departure and Php200 for local departure(paid in Philippine Peso only) Departing passengers for international destinations are advised to check with the tourist

information counters regarding departure fees. These fees are subject to change without prior notice.

Automated Teller Machine:
Duty-Free Shopping: Duty-Free Philippines near the NAIA is the country's largest duty-free outlet that carries quality imported items and selected Philippine products.

CLIMATE
March to May is hot and dry, June to October is rainy, November to February is cool. Average Temperatures: 78 F/32 C; humidity: 77%.

WHAT TO WEAR
Light casual clothes are recommended. Warmer garments are needed for mountain regions. When visiting churches and temples, propriety dictates that shorts and scanty clothing be avoided. For formal occasions require dinner jackets and ties (or Philippine barong tagalong) for men and cocktail dresses or long gowns for women.

CURRENCY UNIT
Unit currency: Peso (P) = 100 centavos, Bank Notes: P10, P20, P50, P100, P200, P500, P1000. Coins: 5c, 10c, 25c, P1, P5, P10.

TIPPING
Tipping is expected for many services. The standard practice is 10% of the total bill. Tipping is optional on bills that already include a 10% service charge.

LOCAL TRANSPORT
By Air:, Philippine Airlines, Air Philippines and Cebu Pacific provide daily services to major cities and towns, Asian Spirit (851-8888), Laoag International Airlines and Sea Air service the missionary routes. There are also scheduled flights served by smaller commuter planes to major destination, particularly the tourist destinations in Luzon, Visayas and Mindanao areas. These airlines also serve intra-regional and intra-provincial domestic routes on regular schedules.

By Sea: Fully air-conditioned vessels of Inter-Island shipping companies connect Manila to major ports in the country, and smaller fast ferries connect the smaller islands with major tourist destinations and attractions.

Inter-Modal Combination of Land and Sea - Ro-Ro (Roll On – Roll Off Ferries/Buses): Departs Regularly from Metro Manila to Visayas and Mindanao, passing the major cities and regional centers via the declared nautical highway.

By Land: Major cities in Luzon, Visayas and Mindanao are served by air- conditioned and non-air-conditioned public utility buses that operates 24 hours a day/7days a week. These buses operate with in the major cities with intra-provincial and intra-regional connectivity.

Metered and fixed rate taxis are widely available in key cities nationwide. Jeepneys and buses are the cheapest to getting around most places. In Metro Manila the fastest way of commuting is via the railway system. LRT connects the northern district of Monumento to the southern district of Baclaran, with stations situated in major intersections. MRT traverses the length of EDSA and connects North Avenue in Quezon City to Taft Avenue in Pasay City, passing through the major arteries of Makati's financial districts.

LANGUAGE
Filipino or Tagalog is the national language. English is the business language, spoken and understood all over the country. The Philippine is the third largest English speaking country in the world, closely following the United Kingdom and far ahead of Australia in terms of the number of inhabitants that speak, write and understand English.

ACCOMMODATIONS
In Metro Manila, key cities and towns throughout the country, a wide selection of deluxe, first class, standard economy and pension-type accommodations are available. In island destinations, there is a variety of resorts ranging from deluxe to special interest categories. The Department of Tourism has Homestay Program in several destinations

outside Manila. The program offers visitors the comfort of a modest home and an insight to into the Philippine life.

DINING OUT

Filipino food is an exotic, tasteful blend of Oriental, European and American culinary influences. There is a wide variety of fresh seafood and delectable fruits. First class restaurants offer gourmet specialties as well as Filipino cuisine.

CULTURE AND ENTERTAINMENT

Metro Manila is the center of entertainment and cultural activities. The premier venue for the performing arts, the Cultural Center of the Philippines, features world-class performances by local and international guest artists. Museums located in Manila and in some parts of the country, offer a glimpse of Philippine history and culture. Art galleries exhibit the works of the country's leading and promising visual artists.

Manila's nightlife is one of the most vibrant in Asia, reflecting the Filipino's love for music. The hubs of nightlife activities are the Remedios Circle Malata, Ayala Center and The Fort at Bonifacio Global City in Makati, Timog and Tomas Morato Avenues in Quezon City and Eastwood in Libis, Quezon City. Nightclubs, music lounges, pubs and sing-along bars feature Filipino bands and singers who are known for their great musical talent. De luxe hotels also offer a variety of live musical entertainment. Concerts and stage plays form part to the country's entertainment scene.

For visitors who want to try their luck at the gaming tables, there are casinos in Metro Manila, and the cities of Angeles, Olongapo, Tagaytay, Cebu, Davao, Bacolod and Laoag.

SHOPPING

Visitors can choose from an exciting selection of great buys in a country known for export-quality items at reasonable prices: south Sea pearls, hand-woven cloths, embroidered fineries, fashionable ready-to-wear and haute couture clothes, terra-cota, porcelain, coral and mother-of-pearl home accessories. Artifacts, pineapple fiber "Jusi" shirts, prehistoric jars, native handicrafts and footwear are interesting items, too. The Philippines also produces fine basketry, furniture, fresh and processed fruits, exquisitely crafted jewelry and gift items made of shell, wood and stone.

Big malls are located in Manila, Makati, Pasay and EDSA, while handicraft, antique and curio shops abound at the Ermita District, Manila.

TIME ZONE
GMT plus 8 hours

ELECTRICITY
220 volts, A.C. 60 cycles. Most hotels has 110-volt outlets.

WATER
Water in Metro Manila and in key cities and towns is potable and safe for drinking. Bottled water is available in almost all of the accommodation facilities, restaurants and groceries.

CONVENTION FACILITIES
Manila, the pioneer convention city in Asia, has played host to a number of prestigious international events. The Philippine International Convention Center is equipped with modern convention facilities and services. It can accommodate 4,000 delegates in Plenary Hall and 5,700 in its Reception Hall. The World Trade Center near the PICC can hold huge exhibitions and events. Smaller meetings can be held in hotels and other establishments. Out-of-town hotels and resorts are alternative convention sites.

MEDICAL SERVICES
Hospitals in the country are equipped with modern facilities to meet any medical need. In some remote towns and cities, clinics and health centers provide emergency medical attention. Most hotels and resorts provide medical assistance. Hospitals are listed in the "Yellow Pages" of the local telephone directory.

TOURS AND SPECIAL INTEREST ACTIVITIES

Tour packages, from day trips to five-day programs, are special ways of discovering the Philippines and its wealth of culture. Special interest activities include golfing, game-fishing, diving, white-water rafting and other aqua-sports, trekking, spelunking and safari trips.

BANKING AND BUSINESS HOURS

Private and government offices are open either from 0800H to 1700H or from 0900H to 1800H. Some private companies hold office on Saturdays from 0900H to 1200H. Most shopping malls, department stores and supermarkets are open from 1000H to 2000H daily. There are 24-hour convenience stores and drugstores.

Banks are open from 0900H to 1500h, Mondays to Fridays, with automated teller machines (ATM) that operate for 24 hours.

CREDIT CARDS

International credit cards such as Visa, Diners Club, Master Card and American Express Card are accepted in major establishments.

IV. THE GATEWAYS TO PHILIPPINES' WEALTH OF WONDERS

The country may be accessed through 7 international gateways. One explore other interesting destinations and venture out of these gateways by land, air or short sea travel.

THE MAJOR INTERNATIONAL TRAVEL GATEWAYS
MANILA

Offers may places of interests that are easily accessible for day excursions: Intra muros, he Walled City of Old Manila; Nayong Pilipino, a theme park that showcases in a small scale the country's famous landmarks; Rizal Park, a tribute to the country's national hero; museums and some of Asia's most modern and biggest shopping malls. From Manila, the country's premiere gateway, one can access the following destinations by land:

Cavite/Tagaytay City/Laguna/Barangay/Quezon Isabela/Cagayan
Banaue/Bontoc/Sagada
Baguio Bulacan/Pampanga

Visayas and Mindanao, and, accessible either by air or by sea, particularly:
Bohol
A favorite satellite destination from Cebu, may be accessed by fast seacraft is the home for the Tarsier believed to be the smallest primate in the world.
ILOILO
With its newly opened Cabatuan-Iloilo International Airport boasts of a number of historical attractions which includes churches and ancestral houses, as well as good beaches. Land and sea transportation connects Iloilo to Boracay, voted by travel writers one of the tropical island destinations which has the best beach in the world; and, the very recent discovery, the Islands of Gigantes in Northeastern tip of Panay Island, North of Iloilo Province, dubbed as the Enchanted Islands. Other serene and scenic places in the region includes:
Antique - the landing site of the Bornean Datus and the home of Datu Kalantiaw, author of the Kalantiaw Code.
Capiz - the seafood capital of the Philippines.
Aklan - the host of the famous "Ati-Atihan" Festival, dubbed as the mother of all festivals.
Guimaras - the Island Province of the world's sweetest mangoes.
Negros Occidental - which has in it's the town of Calatrava the home of the world's friendliest wild monkeys.
AKLAN
With Kalibo International Airport in its capital town that is a host to regular scheduled and chartered international flights from Taipeh, Taiwan; Inchon, South Korea; and Guang Zhou, China, it is known for its nerve rocking but colorful festival, the famous "Ati-Atihan" believed to be the mother of all festivals in the country. Within its jurisdiction is Boracay Island, voted as the one of the best tropical islandbeach destinations in the world, and other scenic places accessible by land and sea:
Iloilo
Capiz
Antique
Guimaras
Negros Island
Cebu

LAOAG
Situated in Ilocos Norte, it is the international gateway of the northern provinces in Luzon. Aside from offering a variety of destinations within the province, the city is also accessible to:
Ilocos Sur
La Union/Pangasinan
Baguio/Bontoc/Sagada/Banaue

SUBIC
The former US Naval Base that was transformed into an international seaport, and offers both rest and recreation and adventure. It serves as the gateway to: Bataan/Zambales/Pampanga/Tarlac

CEBU
The country's first capital and dubbed as the "Queen City of the South", offers diverse attractions and facilities to cater to every tourist preference. Due to its location in the Visayas, it also acts as the major hub to major cities in the Luzon, Visayas and Mindanao.

DAVAO
Offers an array of colors, shapes, tastes and textures that manifest a fusion of indigenous Filipino and Malay culture. In terms of land area, it is the biggest city in the world, part which is already the base of the country's highest peak, Mount Apo. It is popularly known for its pearl and banana export industries that made the industrial center of Mindanao, and the home to rare Philippine Eagle.

Situated in the eastern part of Mindanao, Davao acts as the international gateway to its neighboring provinces:
Davao Oriental Davao del Sur South Cotabato North Cotabato
Compostela Valley Bukidnon
Cagayan de Oro

THE SECONDARY TRAVEL GATEWAYS DOMESTIC TOURIST DESTINATIONS

To experience more of the country's wealth of wonders, the country is dotted with strategically located secondary gateways, which can afford the tourists more convenient travel connections to remote provinces and island destinations.

BATANGAS

Situated in the Tagalog Peninsula (Region IV-A), its is 3 hours south of Manila famous for its renowned heritage dive sites and beach resorts. From the city pier, fast ferries and other sea vessels may connect travelers to:
Mindoro Oriental and Occidental Romblon
Marinduque.

LEGASPI
Located right at the foot of, it is one's front seat to the spectacle of the Bicol region, the world renowned Mayon Volcano and jump-off point to eco-tourism sites.
Land and sea connections are available from this gateway to:
Camarines Norte and Sur
Sorsogon Catanduanes Masbate

TACLOBAN
The gateway to Eastern Visayas, which strategic location made it a perfect landing site for Gen. Douglas McArthur and the American troops that liberated the Philippines from the Japanese forces during World War II, from the city one can venture out to: Samar / Leyte

PUERTO PRINCESA
The capital of Palawan, known for its amazing species of wildlife and marine/underwater resources. The home of the Palawan Underground River, recently voted one of the world's Seven Wonders of Nature, it is the jump-off point to:
Northern Palawan Calamianes Group of Islands
Southern Palawan, Turtle Islands, the habitat for Sea Turtles the Endangered Specie

CAGAYAN DE ORO
Is another domestic travel gateway to picturesque Mindanao which offers five exotic destinations with an array of power-packed adventure activities such as while water rafting, kayaking, canopy walking and surfing:
Camiguin Island
Misamis Oriental/Lanao del Norte Agusan del Norte and Sur
Surigao Norte and sur Bukidnon

ZAMBOANGA
Known to be the country's city of flowers, Zamboanga offers a glimpse into the culture of five colorful tribal groups lining in harmony

with the Christian community. It is the gateway to the charming attractions and indigenous craft of the following exotic places:
Zamboanga del Norte
Zamboanga del Sur Basilan
Sulo
Tawi-Tawi

COTABATO

The center of the Autonomous Region of Muslim Mindanao (ARMM), it is another jump off point to Mt. Apo, this province is a playground of adventure. Among its popular and breathtaking sights are: Lake Sebu and its 7 falls, the soothing Sarangani Bay and numerous caves, rivers and beaches that will surely test your adveturism. It boasts of two airports: Cotabato Airport and General Santos City Airport.

Book 5 - Tourism As A System-How It Works

The Tourism Service Systems

I. TOURISM as a SYSTEM DEFINED

T - totality of duly organized services required by tourists, with
O - objective to experience and enjoy, the
U - uniqueness of an undisturbed environment, in a
R - resting place complimented with activities, where
I - income is generated from infrastructure, and
S - sustained services rendered by persons,
M - motivated to nurture and preserve the natural resources, in order to pamper people of today and the future.

II. The TOURISM SERVICE CYCLE

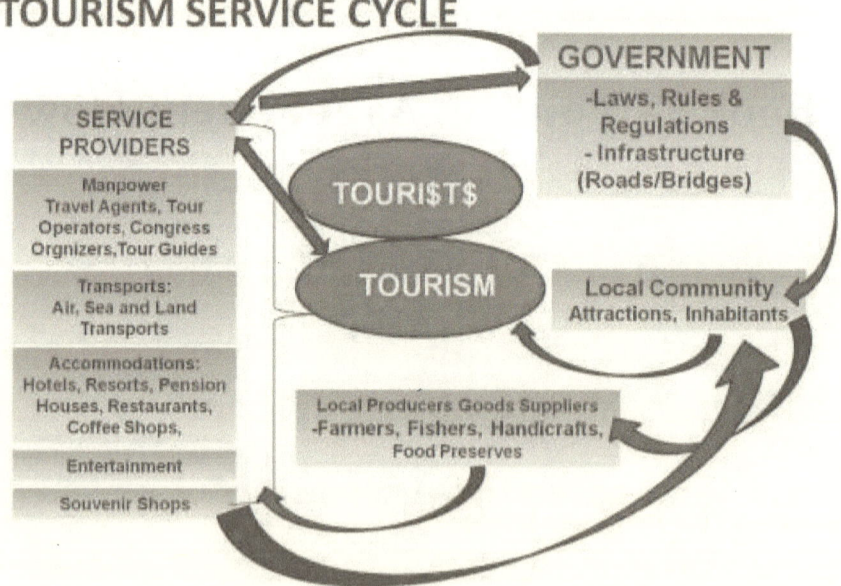

Figure I. Tourism System Service Cycle Tourism Service Cycle Explained

Figure No. 1., shows how the system of tourism service works. Tourist and Tourism are in the center of the diagram, however Tourists is over Tourism for without the tourist there is no tourism to speak of. On the upper right side is the government that is tasked to promulgate tourism laws, rules and regulations governing the tourism sector, as well as the local community including the local producers and suppliers of goods; the development of infrastructures that are necessary and required in the delivery of tourism related services by the service providers to the tourist-service users. Opposite to the left of the diagram are the Service Providers or Front-Liners that are directly involved in the delivery of tourism related services, and in contact with the Tourists. The service providers are fully explained in the succeeding chapter under Tourism Components. The arrows shown represent the interactions of the individual sector with each other that form the whole of the tourism system.

III. ELEMENTS for a TOURIST WORTHY DESTINATION

1. **Color** – in tourism is provided by the natural scenery and native way of life which, taken altogether, is known as the "Ambience", the uniqueness of which often determines its attractiveness. Color is the principal appeal of exotic places like Bali, Kyoto and Tahiti. The scenery, the impression of different ways of life, the strangeness that is palpable in faraway places with unfamiliar names, all combined to produce colorful picture that travelers more specifically the tourists look forward to, and look back afterwards. It is the element present in festivals and traditional events – the costumes, the settings, the rituals and ceremonies.

2. **Action** - in tourism refers to the organized activities offered to tourists, like entertainment and recreation. Entertainment is passive and includes the performing arts (Theatres, Floor Shows, and Stage Presentations), and visual arts (Museums, Exhibit collections). Recreation is participative and includes opportunities for Sports, both outdoor and indoor. Under this category maybe included are the opportunities for culture and education, art appreciation, folklore study, special interests for hobbyists, etc..

3. **Emotion** – in tourism is provide by history, legal, mythology, folklore, romance,tragedy, association with song and story, art and literature, health and wellness, religion, etc.. These are the things, material or otherwise, which stir human feelings, fire the imagination or in any way invite and provoke emotional reaction. Man-made monuments like forts, castles, palaces, churches and cathedrals, mosques and synagogues, specialty medical hospitals/clinics, are primarily attractive particularly if they are associated with personages or events of history, folklore, literature, myth and legend.

4. **Uniqueness** – in tourism maybe defined as the quality of being alone, unusual, exclusive or different. This fundamental element desired in tourist attraction and maybe found both in natural landscape or topography and man-made structures, and in artifacts and works of arts or as a product of history, legend or myth, etc. It may also be found in human activity like traditional events or festivals such as festivity rites, voodoo rites, black mass, witchcraft, historical, traditional cultural rites etc., celebrated periodically to commemorate very important events in the lives of the host country or community.

The presence of these elements in varying combinations and interdependence in tourist products provides the Tourism "Mix". The attractiveness of the product depends on the interrelation and diversity of elements found in the product. The ideal mixture in the tourist destination is one that may contain the broadest combination of all elements that appeal to the largest number of people. These are, therefore, a must and indispensably necessary in the sustainable tourism development.

IV.   Factors that Influence the Tourism Industry.

As compared to any other economic activities and industries, Demand is the major factor that influence the Tourism Industry. Demand increases for the following:
1. Reasons for the Increase of Tourism Industry Demand
2. Necessity
3. Employment
4. Inflation

5. Disposable income
6. Costs of goods and services
7. Opportunity costs Basic needs and wants
8. Marketing and promotions.

V. Meaning of Sustainable Tourism Development

The management of all resources that meet the needs of tourists and host regions while protecting the opportunities for the future, in such a way that economic, social and aesthetic needs can be fulfilled while maintaining cultural integrity, essential ecological processes, biological diversity and life support systems.

VI. Culture of Tourism Defined

Section 3.(d), R.A. 9593 defines the Culture of Tourism as "A sustainable tourism development principle that binds national and local governments, local communities, private sector and stakeholders to work together in creating pride of place and sustaining a tourist friendly destination.

VII. Resource Information Relating to Tourism Industry Statistics and Trends

1. Trade magazines
2. Hotel School Publications
3. Newsletters
4. Brochures
5. Advertisements
6. Reference books.

VIII. The Major Tourism Industry Statistics for Tourism Executives

There are endless statistics that can be researched, some of these include:
- ✓ Types of tourism businesses
- ✓ Types and demographics of customers
- ✓ Top destinations
- ✓ Hotel occupancy percentages
- ✓ Reasons for stays

- ✓ Current industry information
- ✓ Destination countries
- ✓ Departure months
- ✓ Length of stay
- ✓ Type of organization for the trip
- ✓ Transport mode
- ✓ Accommodation type
- ✓ Expenditure
- ✓ Popular tourist attractions.

IX. Components of Tourism System

Tourism System Components are categorized into the following:

1. **Tourist Destination** - is a certain place that has special features and extra- ordinary natural and man-made attractions of historic values uncommon in the and situated outside the place of residence of tourists, attracting the latter to visit and spend a vacation, holiday or other purpose including among others business activities, meetings, conferences, conventions, exhibits, study and research, sports, health and wellness. It is a place where tourism service providers and enterprises are properly in-place, and ready to deliver smoothly the organized tourism product and related services whenever required.

Under this component category, are the sub-components that include the following:

A. Tourist Attractions - A converging place with extra-ordinary features that is unfamiliar and uncommon to the places of tourist origin. Tourist attractions are often included in sightseeing, tours and day excursions. These component include both natural and man-made, itemized as follows:

1. Natural - a certain natural creation without the intervention of man. These are the following:
    - ➢ Beach Line in Coves, and Sandbars with Clear Waters and marine resources in the form of corals, fishes, sea grasses for swimming, and for snorkeling and scuba diving;
    - ➢ Islands and Islets of extra-ordinary shapes and formations;

- Forests and Caves with habitats for flora and fauna;
- Water Falls, Rivers, Lakes and Lagoons;
- Mountains and Hills with uncommon shapes, landscape and vegetation;
- Camp Sites;
- Natural Eco-Parks and Wildlife Centers;
- Cliffs and Canyons; and,
- Valleys and Planes.

2. Manmade - certain attractions that are created by the ingenuity of man these include among others the following:
   - Historical Landmarks;
   - Monuments for Local Heroes;
   - Theme Parks with Organized Activities and Entertainment;
   - Museums;
   - Old Aged Churches;
   - Olden Architectural Designed Buildings and Structures;
   - Theatres, Cultural and Centers for the Performing Arts;
   - Farms, Orchards and Cattle Ranches;
   - Sports Stadia and Coliseums;
   - Golf Courses;
   - Race Tracks;
   - Camp Sites.

B. Tourism Infrastructures - Public Utilities and Facilities that the government or private sector service provider introduce in tourists destinations and attractions. These include among others the following:
   - Ports, Airports and Bus Terminals;
   - Visitors' Information & Assistance Centers;
   - Access Roads and Bridges to Tourist Destinations and Tourist Attractions;
   - Rest and Comfort Areas;
   - Convention Centers;
   - Shopping Center for Handicrafts and Souvenir Items;
   - Mountain Trails and Stairways;
   - Water Supply System;

- Garbage Disposal Areas;
- Waste Water Treatment Facility;
- Emergency Clinics and Hospitals;
- Emergency Rescue Stations, Equipment & Machinery;
- Light Houses and Watch Towers;

C. Tourism Service Providers/Front Liners - These are the personalities that have direct contact with tourists, as they are the ones serving and delivering hands- on the services and products that the tourists may require in a given destination. This component include the following:

1. In Tourist Point of Origin:
A. Holiday/Vacation (Group and Individuals)
   a) Travel Agent/Tour Operator - A duly licensed service provider both wholesale or retailer selling organized package tours to certain tourist destinations with whom the tourists pre-book or pre-arrange their travel for a certain period of time. The package of services availed to the client include, acquisition of passport, visa/s, and vaccination where needed; and, airfare, hotel rooms for accommodation, transfers, sightseeing, tours and excursions.
   b) Air Transport /Airline Company - An air carrier that is either regularly or periodically used by the travel agent/tour operator as the official carrier of the Package Tour Programs sold to the touring public, that pre-books seats for tour group members.
   c) Ports and Airports - The government or privately owned facility with passenger terminal that serve both the outgoing and incoming airline passengers;
   d) Land Transport (Bus or Limousine Service) Operator - The agency that operates land transport (Limousine, Mini-Bus, Van, Bus/Motor-coach) used by the travel agency/tour operator in transporting the tourists from converging point of origin for departure from the point of exit.

2. In Tourist Point of Destination
   a) Inbound/Local Tour Operator - A duly licensed agency with which are pre- arranged by the outbound travel agency/tour

operator in point of origin all the services included in the package tours required by the tourist-client in the point of destination.
b) Land Tourist Transport Operator - (Bus/Motor-coach, Limousine) - The agency licensed to operate a land transport exclusively to serve the requirement of the tourist for transfers, sightseeing and excursions.
c) Sea Tourist Transport Operator - An agency licensed to operate sea tourist transport that caters to tourists for the tours, sightseeing and excursions within the area of the destination.
d) Tour Guide Services - The licensed professional assigned by inbound/local tour operator to assist the tourists during transfers on arrival and departure including the conduct of sightseeing, tours and/or excursions.
e) Hotels, Resorts, Pension and Lodging Houses - The enterprise that provides the room to accommodate the tourist in the point of destination.
f) Outdoor Activities Operators - These are local service providers of different outdoor activities, other than the basic sightseeing and transfer services included in the package tour program, i.e., rides, island hopping, snorkeling, spelunking that are normally taken in an optional basis by tour group members.
g) Disco House, Bars and Nightclub Operator - Normally these service providers are very commonly required by the younger group of tourists.
h) Grooming, Health and Wellness Clinic Operator - These include Spa and Massage Parlors, Masseuse/Masseurs, barbers, beauticians and manicurists.
i) Indoor Entertainment - Theatres, Performing Arts and Cultural Shows;
j) Local Public Utility - This includes public transports, i.e., Public Utility Bus/Mini-bus, trams, ferry boats, motorized bancas, jeepneys, taxis, tricycles, etc., communication systems (telephone, postal services, couriers, etc.), banks, money changer and transfer, that regularly operate in the destination.
k) Laundry Service - Normally required by long-staying tourists.

l) Fruit Stand Vendors - Selling locally grown and produced fruits that are not available in the places of tourist origins.
m) Entertainers - These are normally present in theatres, dining and drinking places, i.e., restaurants, cafes and bars.
n) The Local Inhabitants - These are the mainstay attraction for foreign tourists who are interested to know more of their tradition, culture , habit and idiosyncrasies.

Tourism Development Planning

I. INTRODUCTION

Tourism is one of many activities in a community or region that requires planning and coordination. This Chapter provides a simple structure and basic guidelines for comprehensive tourism planning at a community or regional level. Planning is the process of identifying objectives and defining and evaluating methods of achieving them. By comprehensive planning means, planning which considers all of the tourism resources, organizations, markets, and programs within a region. Comprehensive planning also considers economic, environmental, social, and institutional aspects of tourism development.

II. The NATIONAL and REGIONAL PLANNING

National and regional planning lays the foundation for tourism development of a country and its regions. It establishes the policies, physical and institutional structures and standards for development to proceed in a logical manner. It also provides the basis for the continuous and effective management of tourism which is so essential for the long-term success of tourism. This publication is divided into two parts. The first part briefly explains planning concepts and describes planning and marketing methodologies. Emphasis is placed on the integrated approach, balancing economic, environmental and socio-cultural factors, and achieving sustainable development.

Importance is also given to techniques that need to be used in implementing plans. Without adopting and applying these techniques, tourism plans cannot be realized.

III. The IMPORTANCE of PLANNING TOURISM

Planning tourism at all levels is essential for achieving successful tourism development and management. The experience of many tourism areas in the world has demonstrated that, on a long-term basis, the planned approach to developing tourism can bring benefits without significant problems, and maintain satisfied tourist markets. Places that have allowed tourism to develop without the benefit of planning are often suffering from environmental and social problems. These are detrimental to residents and unpleasant for many tourists, resulting in marketing difficulties and decreasing economic benefits. These uncontrolled tourism areas cannot effectively compete with planned tourist destinations elsewhere. They usually can be redeveloped, based on a planned approach, but that requires much time and financial investment.

Tourism is a rather complicated activity that overlaps several different sectors of the society and economy. Without planning, it may create unexpected and unwanted impacts. Tourism is also still a relatively new type of activity in many countries. Some governments and often the private sector have little or no experience in how to develop tourism properly. For countries that do not yet have much tourism, planning can provide the necessary guidance for its development. For those places that already have some tourism, planning is often needed to revitalize this sector and maintain its future viability.

First, tourism should be planned at the national and regional levels. At these levels, planning is concerned with tourism development policies, structure plans, facility standards, institutional factors and all the other elements necessary to develop and manage tourism. Then, within the framework of national and regional planning, more detailed plans for tourist attractions, resorts, urban, rural and other forms of tourism development can be prepared.

There are several important specific benefits of undertaking national and regional tourism planning. These advantages include:
- Establishing the overall tourism development objectives and policies - what is tourism aiming to accomplish and how can these aims be achieved.
- Developing tourism so that its natural and cultural resources are indefinitely maintained and conserved for future, as well as present, use.

IV. The TOURISM DEVELOPMENT PLAN DEFINED

A strategic framework that provides for the orderly and rational development of the tourism sector within a given area, providing the policy and approaches to develop, promote and integrate various programs and projects such as but not limited to accessibility, including infrastructure and transportation; investments and businesses; environment; cultural heritage; tourism products; marketing; human resources development; community development, among others.

- Integrating tourism into the overall development policies and patterns of the country or region, and establishing dose linkages between tourism and other economic sectors
- Providing a rational basis for decision-making by both the public and private sectors on tourism development.
- Making possible the coordinated development of all the many elements of the tourism sector. This includes inter-relating the tourist attractions, activities, facilities and services and the various and increasingly fragmented tourist markets.
- Optimizing and balancing the economic, environmental and social benefits of tourism, with equitable distribution of these benefits to the society, while minimizing possible problems of tourism.
- Providing a physical structure which guides the location, types and extent of tourism development of attractions, facilities, services and infrastructure.
- Establishing the guidelines and standards for preparing detailed plans of specific tourism development areas that are consistent with, and reinforce, one another, and for the appropriate design of tourist facilities.
- Laying the foundation for effective implementation of the tourism development policy and plan and continuous management of the tourism sector, by providing the necessary organizational and other institutional framework.
- Providing the framework for effective coordination of the public and private sector efforts and investment in developing tourism.
- Offering a baseline for the continuous monitoring of the progress of tourism development and keeping it on track.

The planned approach to developing tourism at the national and regional levels is now widely adopted as a principle, although implementation of the policies and plans is still weak in some places. Many countries and regions of countries have had tourism plans prepared. Other places do not yet have plans, but should consider undertaking planning in the near future. In some countries, plans had previously been prepared but these are now outdated. They need to be revised based on present day circumstances and likely future trends. Founded on accumulated experience, the approaches and techniques of tourism planning are now reasonably well understood. There is considerable assurance that, if implemented, planning will bring substantial benefits to an area.

V. Approaches to Tourism Planning

It is important to understand the basic approaches to planning and managing tourism development.

A. PLANNING TOURISM AS AN INTEGRATED SYSTEM

An underlying concept in planning tourism is that tourism should be viewed as an inter-related system of demand and supply factors. The demand factors are international and domestic tourist markets and local `residents who use the tourist attractions, facilities and services. The supply factors comprise tourist attractions and activities, accommodation and other tourist facilities and services. Attractions include natural, cultural and special types of features - such as theme parks, zoos, botanic gardens and aquariums - and the activities related to these attractions. Accommodation includes hotels, motels, guest houses and other types of places where tourists stay overnight. The category of other tourist facilities and services includes tour and travel operations, restaurants, shopping, banking and money exchange, and medical and postal facilities and services. These supply factors are called the tourism product. Other elements also relate to supply factors. In order to make the facilities and services usable, infrastructure is required. Tourism infrastructure particularly includes transportation (air, road, rail, water, etc.), water supply, electric power, sewage and solid waste disposal, and telecommunications.

DEMAND and SUPPLY FACTORS
- International tourist markets
- Attractions and activities

- Domestic tourist markets
- Accommodation
- Residents' use of tourist attractions,
- Other tourist facilities and services facilities and services
- Transportation
- Other infrastructure
- Institutional elements
- Provision of adequate infrastructure is also important to protect the environment. It helps maintain a high level of environmental quality that is so necessary for successful tourism and desirable for residents. The effective development, operation and management of tourism requires certain institutional elements. These elements include:
- Organizational structures, especially government tourism offices and private sector tourism associations such as hotel associations.
- Tourism-related legislation and regulations, such as standards and licensing requirements for hotels and tour and travel agencies.
- Education and training programs, and training institutions to prepare professionals and technical persons to work effectively in tourism.
- Availability of financial capital to develop tourist attractions, facilities, services and infrastructure, and mechanisms to attract capital investment.
- Marketing strategies and promotion programs to inform tourists about the country or region, and induce them to visit it, and tourist information facilities and services in the destination areas.
- Travel facilitation of immigration (including visa arrangements), customs and other facilities and services at the entry and exit points of tourists.

The institutional elements also include consideration of how to enhance and distribute the economic benefits of tourism, environmental protection measures, reducing adverse social impacts, and conservation of the cultural heritage of people living in the tourism areas.

As an inter-related system, it is important that tourism planning aim for integrated development of all these parts of the system, both the demand and supply factors and the physical and institutional elements. The system will function much more effectively and bring the desired benefits if it is planned in an integrated manner, with coordinated development of all the components of the system. Sometimes, this integrated system approach is also called the comprehensive approach to tourism planning because all the elements of tourism are considered in the planning and development process.

Just as important as planning for integration within the tourism system is planning for integration of tourism into the overall development policies, plans and patterns of a country or region. Planning for this overall integration will, for example, resolve any potential conflicts over use of certain resources or locations for various types of development. It also provides for the multiuse of expensive infrastructure to serve general community needs as well as tourism.

Emphasis is given to formulating and adopting tourism development policies and plans for an area in order to guide decision-making on development actions. The planning of tourism, however, should also be recognized as a continuous and flexible process. Within the framework of the policy and plan recommendations, there must be flexibility to allow for adapting to changing circumstances. Planning that is too rigid may not allow development to be responsive to changes. There may be advancements in transportation technology, evolution of new forms of tourism and changes in market trends. Even though allowed to be flexible, the basic objectives of the plan should not be abrogated although the specific development patterns may be changed. Sustainable development must still be maintained.

Planning for tourism development should make recommendations that are imaginative and innovative, but they must also be feasible to implement.

The various techniques of implementation should be considered throughout the planning process. This approach ensures that the recommendations can be accomplished, and provides the basis for specifying the implementation techniques that should be applied. Implementation techniques can also be imaginative and not only rely on established approaches. It is common practice for a tourism plan to include specification of implementation techniques, and sometimes a separate manual on how to achieve the plan recommendations.

B. PLANNING FOR SUSTAINABLE DEVELOPMENT

The underlying approach now applied to tourism planning, as well as to other types of development, is that of achieving sustainable development. The sustainable development approach implies that the natural, cultural and other resources of tourism are conserved for continuous use in the future, while still bringing benefits to the present society. The concept of sustainable development has received much emphasis internationally since the early 1980s, although tourism plans prepared even before that period often were concerned with conservation of tourism resources. The sustainable development approach to planning tourism is acutely important because most tourism development depends on attractions and activities related to the natural environment, historic heritage and cultural patterns of areas. If these resources are degraded or destroyed, then the tourism areas cannot attract tourists and tourism will not be successful. More generally, most tourists seek destinations that have a high level of environmental quality - they like to visit places that are attractive, clean and neither polluted nor congested. It is also essential that residents of the tourism area should not have to suffer from a deteriorated environment and social problems. One of the important benefits of tourism is that, if it is properly developed based on the concept of sustainability, tourism can greatly help justify and pay for conservation of an area's natural and cultural resources. Thus, tourism can be an important means of achieving conservation in areas that otherwise have limited capability to accomplish environmental protection and conservation objectives.

A basic technique in achieving sustainable development is the environmental planning approach. Environmental planning requires that all elements of the environment be carefully surveyed, analyzed and considered in determining the most appropriate type and location of development. This approach would not allow, for example, intensive development in flood plain and steep hillside areas.

An important aspect of sustainable development is emphasizing community- based tourism. This approach to tourism focuses on community involvement in the planning and development process, and developing the types of tourism which generate benefits to local communities. It applies techniques to ensure that most of the benefits of tourism development accrue to local residents and not to outsiders. Maximizing benefits to local residents typically results in tourism being better accepted by them and their actively supporting conservation of local tourism resources.

The community based tourism approach is applied at the local or more detailed levels of planning, but it can be set forth as a policy approach at the national and regional levels. The benefits accruing to local communities are also beneficial to the country, through the income and foreign exchange earned, employment generated and support that local communities give to national tourism development and conservation policies. Also related to sustainable development is the concept of quality tourism. This approach is being increasingly adopted for two fundamental reasons – it can achieve successful tourism from the marketing standpoint and it brings benefits to local residents and their environment. Quality tourism does not necessarily mean expensive tourism. Rather, it refers to tourist attractions, facilities and services that offer 'good value for money', protect tourism resources, and attract the kinds of tourists who will respect the local environment and society. Quality tourism development can compete more effectively in attracting discriminating tourists. It is also more environmentally and socially self-sustaining. Achieving quality tourism is the responsibility of both the public and private sectors. This concept should be built into the tourism planning, development and management process.

C. LONG-RANGE and STRATEGIC PLANNING

Long-range comprehensive planning is concerned with specifying goals and objectives and determining preferred future development patterns. Tourism development policies and plans should be prepared for relatively long-term periodsusually for 10 to 15 and sometimes 20 years - depending on the predictability of future events in the country or region. These may seem to be long planning periods, but it commonly requires this length of time to implement basic policy and structure plans. Even development of specific projects, such as major resorts or national park- based tourism, can require a long time. A planning approach which has received considerable attention in recent years, and is applicable to some tourism areas, is strategic planning.

While the Long-range and strategic planning outcomes of strategic and long- range comprehensive planning may be very similar, strategic planning is somewhat different. It focuses more on identification and resolution of immediate issues. Strategic planning typically is more oriented to rapidly changing future situations and how to cope with changes organizationally. It is more action oriented and concerned with handling unexpected events. Applied only by itself, strategic planning can be less comprehensive in its approach. By focusing on immediate issues, it may deviate from achieving such long-term objectives as sustainable development. But if used within the framework of integrated long-range policy and planning, the strategic planning approach can be very appropriate. The relationship between long-range and strategic planning is illustrated, in a simple manner, in

VI. PUBLIC INVOLVEMENT in PLANNING

Planning is for the benefit of people, and they should be involved in the planning and development of tourism in their areas. Through this involvement, tourism development will reflect a consensus of what the people want. Also, if residents are involved in planning and development decisions - and if they understand the benefits the tourism can bring – they will more likely support it. At the national and regional levels of preparing tourism plans, the common approach to obtaining public involvement is to appoint a steering committee. This committee offers guidance to the planning team and reviews its work, especially the draft reports and policy and planning recommendations that are made. A planning study steering committee is typically composed of representatives of the relevant government agencies involved in tourism, the private sector, and community, religious and other relevant organizations.

Also, open public hearings can be held on the plan. These hearings provide the opportunity for anybody to learn about the plan and express their opinions. Another common approach, when the plan is completed, is to organize a national or regional tourism seminar. This meeting informs participants and the general public about the importance of controlled tourism development and the recommendations of the plan. Such seminars often receive wide publicity in the communications media.

In a large country or region, the usual procedure is for the tourism plan to be prepared by the central authority with public involvement as described above. This can be termed the `top-down' approach. Another procedure sometimes used is the `bottom-up' approach. This involves holding meetings with local districts or communities to determine what type of development they would like to have. These local objectives and ideas are then fitted together into a national or regional plan. This approach achieves greater local public involvement in the planning process. But it is more time consuming and may lead to conflicting objectives, policies and development recommendations among the local areas. These conflicts need to be reconciled at the national and regional levels in order to form a consistent plan. It is important that the development patterns of the local areas complement and reinforce one another, but also reflect the needs and desires of local communities. Often a combination of the `top-down' and `bottom-up' approaches achieves the best results.

VII. The TOURISM PLANNING PROCESS

The process for preparing tourism plans at the national and regional levels - based on the sustainable, integrated and implementable approaches described in Chapter 2- can be described as a step-by-step procedure. This procedure, which is applicable to any national and regional planning situations.

A. STUDY PREPARATION

The first step in the planning process is careful preparation of the study so that it provides the type of development guidance that is needed.

Study preparation involves formulating the project terms of reference, selecting the technical team to carry out the study, appointing a steering committee, and organizing the study activities.

The terms of reference (TOR) for the planning study should be carefully formulated so that the study achieves its desired results and outputs. The TOR for a national or regional plan indicates the outputs and activities that are necessary to prepare the development policy and plan. The special considerations to be made in planning - such as economic, environmental or social issues and the critical institutional elements -should be specified in the TOR. Identification of implementation techniques are also specified. The TOR format typically follows the planning process explained here, but it is tailored to the specific characteristics and needs of the planning area.

Many places already have some limited tourism development, and these existing patterns must be considered in formulating the TOR. Other countries or regions will have considerable existing tourism development, but it may be declining or not be in a form that generates optimum benefits. The TOR will therefore emphasize how to rejuvenate and improve existing development, along with how to provide guidance on the future expansion of tourism.

It is common for a single study include various levels of tourism planning, such as national and regional plans along with detailed planning for priority development areas and projects. The planning for all these levels will need to be specified in the TOR.

B. TWO SIDES of TOURISM PLANNING

Tourism planning has evolved from two related but distinct sets of planning philosophies and methods.

1. On the one hand, tourism is one of many activities in an area that must be considered as part of physical, environmental, social, and economic planning. Therefore, it is common to find tourism addressed, at least partially, in a regional land use, transportation, recreation, economic development, or comprehensive plan. The degree to which tourism is addressed in such plans depends upon the relative importance of tourism to the community or region and how sensitive the planning authority is to tourism activities; and,

2. Tourism may also be viewed as a business in which a community or region chooses to engage. Individual tourism businesses conduct a variety of planning activities including feasibility, marketing, product development, promotion, forecasting, and strategic planning. If tourism is a significant component of an area's economy or development plans, regional or community-wide marketing plans are needed to coordinate the development and marketing activities of different tourism interests in the community.

A comprehensive approach integrates a strategic marketing plan with more traditional public planning activities. This ensures a balance between serving the needs and wants of the tourists versus the needs and wants of local residents. A formal tourism plan provides a vehicle for the various interests within a community to coordinate their activities and work toward common goals. It also is a means of coordinating tourism with other community activities.

C.   STEPS in the PLANNING PROCESS

Like any planning, tourism planning is goal-oriented, striving to achieve certain objectives by matching available resources and programs with the needs and wants of people. Comprehensive planning requires a systematic approach, usually involving a series of steps.

The process is best viewed as an interactive and on-going one, with each step subject to modification and refinement at any stage of the planning process.

There are six steps in the planning process:

1. Define goals and objectives.
2. Identify the tourism system.
a) Resources
b) Organizations
c) Markets
3. Generate alternatives.
4. Evaluate alternatives.

5. Select and implement.
6. Monitor and evaluate.

STEP ONE: Defining Goals and objectives.
Obtaining clear statements of goals and objectives is difficult, but important. Ideally, tourism development goals should flow from more general community goals and objectives. It is important to understand how a tourism plan serves these broader purposes. Is the community seeking a broader tax base, increased employment opportunities, expanded recreation facilities, better educational programs, a higher quality of life? How can tourism contribute to these objectives? If tourism is identified as a means of serving broader community goals, it makes sense to develop plans with more specific tourism development objectives. These are generally defined through a continuing process in which various groups and organizations in a community work together toward common goals. A local planning authority, chamber of commerce, visitors bureau, or similar group should assume a leadership role to develop an initial plan and obtain broad involvement of tourism interests in the community. Public support for the planning process and plan is also important.

Having a good understanding of tourism and the tourism system in your community is the first step toward defining goals and objectives for tourism development. The types of goals that are appropriate and the precision with which you are able to define them will depend upon how long your community has been involved in tourism and tourism planning.

In the early stages of tourism development, goals may involve establishing organizational structures and collecting information to better identify the tourism system in the community. Later, more precise objectives can be formulated and more specific development and marketing strategies evaluated.

STEP TWO: Identifying Your Tourism System
When planning for any type of activity, it is important to first define its scope and characteristics. Be clear about exactly what your plan

encompasses. A good initial question is, "What do you mean by tourism?" Tourism is defined in many ways. Generally, tourism involves people traveling outside of their community for pleasure. Definitions differ on the specifics of how far people must travel, whether or not they must stay overnight, for how long, and what exactly is included under traveling for "pleasure". Do you want your tourism plan to include day visitors, conventioneers, business travelers, people visiting friends and relatives, people passing through, or seasonal residents? Which community resources and organizations serve tourists or could serve tourists?

Generally, tourists share community resources with local residents and businesses. Many organizations serve both tourists and locals. This complicates tourism planning and argues for a clear idea of what your tourism plan entails.

You can begin to clarify the tourism system by breaking it down into three subsystems:
(1)   tourism resources;
(2)   tourism organizations; and
(3)   tourism markets.

An initial task in developing a tourism plan is to identify, inventory, and classify the objects within each of these subsystems.

TOURISM RESOURCES are any of the following:
1)   natural,
2)   cultural,
3)   human, or
4)   capital resources that either are used or can be used to attract or serve tourists. A tourism resource inventory identifies and classifies the resources available that provide opportunities for tourism development. Conduct an objective and realistic assessment of the quality and quantity.

(Table I provides a suggested classification to help obtain a broad and organized picture of your tourism resources.)

TOURISM ORGANIZATIONS combine resources in various proportions to provide products and services for the tourist. Table 2 is a partial list and classification of organizations that manage or coordinate tourism-related activities. It is important to recognize the diverse array of public and private organizations involved with tourism. The most difficult part of tourism planning is to get these groups to work toward common goals. You should develop a list of these organizations within your own community and obtain their input and cooperation in your tourism planning efforts. Setting up appropriate communication systems and institutional arrangements is a key part of community tourism planning.

TABLE 1. TOURISM RESOURCES
Natural Resources
- ✓ Climate-seasons
- ✓ Water resources-lakes, streams, waterfalls
- ✓ Flora-forests, flowers, shrubs, wild edibles
- ✓ Fauna-fish & wildlife
- ✓ Geological resources-topography, soils, sand dunes, beaches, caves, rocks & minerals, fossils
- ✓ Scenery-combinations of all of the above
- ✓ **Cultural Resources**
- ✓ Historic buildings, sites Monuments, shrines
- ✓ Cuisine
- ✓ Ethnic cultures
- ✓ Industry, government, religion, etc. Anthropological resources
- ✓ Local celebrities

Human Resources
- ✓ Hospitality skills Management skills Seasonal labor force
- ✓ Performing artists-music, drama, art, storytellers, etc. Craftsman and artisans
- ✓ Other labor skills from chefs to lawyers to researchers Local populations

Capital

- ✓ Availability of capital, financing
- ✓ Infrastructure-transportation roads, airports, railroads, harbors & marinas, trails & walkways
- ✓ Infrastructure: utilities water, power, waste treatment, communications

TABLE 2. TOURISM MANAGEMENT ORGANIZATIONS AND SERVICES

Off-Site:
- ✓ Coordination, planning, technical assistance, research, regulation: National Government Agencies & departments of tourism and commerce, transportation, & natural resources;
- ✓ National, Regional, Provincial & local tourism associations;
- ✓ Educational organizations & consultants, e.g., Travel & Tourism Research Association;
- ✓ Department of Tourism Research Office Travel information & reservation services

On-Site:

Development, promotion and management, of tourism resources:

*   **National Government Agencies:**
Department of Tourism; Departments of Trade & Industry; Department of Transportation;
Department of Public Works and Highways;
Department of Environment & Natural Resources, Land management agencies

*   **Regional agencies:**
Departments of Trade and Industry;
Department of Transportation, & land/facility management agencies

* **Local Government Units and Organizations:** Visitors Information;
Chamber of Commerce;
Convention & visitor bureaus, parks managers;

* **Businesses/Enterprises: Accommodations:**
Hotels, motels, Lodges, resorts, bed & breakfast cabins & cottages, Condominiums, second homes, Campgrounds/Campsites

* **Food & Beverage:**
Restaurants, Grocery, Bars, nightclubs, Fast food, Catering services ;

* **Transportation:**
Air, rail, bus; Local transportation: taxi, limo, Auto, bicycle, boat rental; Local tour services.

* **Information:**
Travel agencies, Information and reservation services, Automobile clubs.

* **Recreation Facilities & Services:**
Golf courses, miniature golf; Swimming pools, water slides, beaches; tennis, handball, racquetball courts, bowling alleys; Athletic clubs, health spas; Marinas, boat rentals and charters; hunting & fishing guides; Horseback enterprises; Sporting goods sales & rentals; gyms; scuba diving gears and sites.

* **Entertainment:**
Nightclubs, amusement parks, spectator sport facilities; Gambling facilities: casinos, horse racing, bingo; video arcades; art galleries and studios, craft shops, studios, demonstrations; performing arts: theater, dance, music, film; historic & prehistoric sites; museums: art, history, science, technology; arboreta, zoos, eco-parks and nature centers,

* **Special festivals and events Support services:**
Auto repair, gasoline service stations; boat & recreation vehicle dealers and service; retail shops: sporting goods, specialties, souvenirs, clothing; health services: hospitals, clinics, pharmacies; laundry and dry

cleaning; beauty & barber shops; babysitting services; pet care; communications: newspaper, telephone; banking and financial services.

* **TOURISM MARKETS:**

Tourists makeup the third, and perhaps most important subsystem. Successful tourism programs require a strong market orientation.

The needs and wants of the tourists you choose to attract and serve must be the focus of much of your marketing and development activity. Therefore, it is important to clearly understand which tourism market segments you wish to attract and serve. Tourists fall into a very diverse set of categories with quite distinct needs and wants. You should identify the different types of tourists, or market segments that you presently serve or would like to serve. This may involve one or more tourism market surveys.

A visitor survey identifies the size and nature of the existing market and asks the following questions:
* What are the primary market segments you presently attract?
* Where do they come from?
* What local businesses and facilities do they use?
* What attracted them to the community?
* How did they find out about your community?
* How satisfied are they with your offerings?

A market survey (usually a telephone survey) also can be conducted among households in regions from which you wish to attract tourists. This type of study helps identify potential markets, and means of attracting tourists to your area.

Tourism market segments in a general tourism plan, some clear target tourism market segments should be identified (See Table 3). You might begin by defining the market area from which you will draw most of your visitors. The size of your market area depends upon the uniqueness and quality of your "product", transportation systems, tastes and preferences of surrounding populations, and your competition. Identifying the market area will help target information and promotion and define transportation routes and modes, competition, and characteristics of your market.

Next, divide your travel market into the following trip length categories:

* day trips from a 50 mile radius,
* day trips from 50 to 200 miles away,
* pass-through travelers,
* overnight trips of 1 or 2 nights (most likely weekends), and
* extended overnight vacation trips.

After you have an idea of your market area and kinds of trips you will be serving, begin defining more specific market segments like vehicle campers, sightseers, family vacationers, single weekenders, and the like. These segments can be more clearly tied to particular resources, businesses, and facilities in your community.

What kinds of products and services are likely to attract each of these Groups? Tourist needs as well as their impact on the local community are quite different for day tourists versus overnight tourists. Areas catering primarily to weekend traffic will experience large fluctuations in use. In deciding the relative importance of these different segments, communities need to assess both their ability to provide required services (do you have enough rooms?), as well as the demand for different types of trips relative to the supply and your competition.

D. The ENVIRONMENT:

A tourism plan is significantly affected by many factors in the broader environment. Indeed, one of the complexities of tourism planning is the number of variables that are outside of the control of an individual tourism business or community. These include such things as tourism offerings and prices at competing destinations, national and provincial/municipal policy and legislation, currency exchange rates, the state of the economy, and weather. These factors are parts of the market environment analysis.

Local populations also must be considered in tourism planning. As they compete with tourists for resources, they can be significantly affected by tourism activity, and they are an important source of support in getting tourism plans implemented. A survey of local residents can be conducted to assess community attitudes toward tourism development, identify impacts of tourism on the community, and obtain local input into tourism plans. Public hearings, workshops, and advisory boards are other ways to obtain public involvement in tourism planning.

Local support and cooperation is important to the success of tourism programs and should not be overlooked.

TABLE 3. TOURISM MARKET SEGMENTS

I. **Geographic market areas** (International (Foreign), National, Intra-Regional, Intra-Provincial and Inter-Municipal (Local/Domestic)

2. **Trip categories**

Day Trips: * short-within 50 miles
* long-up to 200 miles

Pass through traffic:
* day visitors
* overnight stays

Overnight Trips:
* weekend
* vacation

3. **Activity or trip purpose**
Outdoor Recreation:
* Water-based Activity:
-Boating: sail, power, cruise, row, canoe, water ski
-Swimming: pool, beach, sunbathing, scuba
-Fishing: charter, sport, from pier, boat, shore,

* Land-based Activity:

- Camping: backpacking, primitive, developed
- Hiking: climbing, beachcombing, spelunking
- Hunting
- Bicycling
- Horseback riding
- Picnicking

* Air-based Activity:
-Airplane rides, hang gliding, ballooning, parachuting
* General:
- Nature study
- Photography or landscape painting
- Viewing natural scenery

Sightseeing & Entertainment:
* Visiting particular sites or areas:
  - historic or pre-historic
  - cultural - amusements
  - scenic

Attending particular events, shows, or demonstrations:
- ethnic festivals
- sporting events
- performances
- agricultural fair or festival
- boat show
- shopping

Other Primary Purpose for Trip:
* Visiting Friends & Relatives
* Convention & Business/Pleasure

STEP THREE: Generating Alternatives.
Generating alternative development and marketing options to meet your goals requires some creative thinking and brainstorming. The errors made at this stage are usually thinking too narrowly or screening out alternatives prematurely. It is wise to solicit a wide range of options from a diverse group of people. If tourism expertise is lacking in your community, seek help and advice outside the community.

Tourism planning involves a wide range of interrelated development and marketing decisions. The following development questions will get you started:

* How much importance should be assigned to tourism within a community or region?
* Which general community goals is tourism development designed to serve?
* Which organization/s will provide the leadership and coordination necessary for community tourism planning?
* What are the relative roles of public and private sectors?

Tourism marketing decision questions include:
* **Segments:** Which market segments should be pursued; geographic markets, trip types, activity or demographic subgroups?
* **Product:** What kinds of tourism products and services should be provided? Who should provide what?
* **Place:** Where should tourism facilities be located?
* **Promotion:** What kinds of promotion should be used, by whom, in which media, how much, when? What community tourism theme or image should be established?
* **Price:** What prices should be charged for which products and services. Who should capture the revenue?

STEP FOUR: Evaluating Alternatives.
Tourism development and marketing options are evaluated by assessing the degree to which each option will be able to meet the stated goals and objectives. There are usually two parts to a systematic evaluation of tourism development and marketing alternatives: (1) Feasibility analysis, and (2) Impact assessment. These two tasks are interrelated, but think of them as trying to answer two basic questions: (1) Can it be done?, and (2) What are the consequences? A decision to take a specific action must be based both on feasibility and desirability.

E. FEASIBILITY ANALYSIS:
First, screen alternatives and eliminate those that are not feasible due to economic, environmental, political, legal, or other factors. Evaluate

the remaining set of alternatives in more detail, paying particular attention to the market potential and financial plan.

Second, Make a realistic assessment of your community's ability to attract and serve a market segment or segments. This requires a clear understanding of the tourism market in your area and how this market is changing. Also carefully identify your competition and evaluate your Advantages and disadvantages compared to the competition.

Third, Plan toward the future because it takes time to implement decisions and for your actions to take effect. Therefore, look at the likely market and competition for several years to come. Review forecasts for the travel market in your area, if available. Careful tracking of tourism trends in your own community can help identify changes in the market that you will have to adapt to.

F. IMPACT ASSESSMENT

When evaluating alternative development and marketing strategies it is important to understand the impacts, both positive and negative, of proposed actions.

The types of impacts and their importance vary across different communities and proposed actions. Generally, the size, extent, and nature of tourism impacts depend upon:

* volume of tourist activity relative to local activity;
* length and nature of tourist contacts with the community;
* degree of concentration/dispersal of tourist activity in the area;
* similarities or differences between local populations and tourists;
* stability/sensitivity of local economy, environment, and social structure; and,
* how well tourism is planned, controlled, and managed.

Look at both the benefits and costs of any proposed actions. While tourism development can increase income, revenues, and employment, it also involves costs. Evaluate benefits and costs of tourism development from the perspectives of local government, businesses, and residents.

TABLE 4. IMPACTS OF TOURISM
Economic Impacts:
* Sales, revenue, and income
* Employment
* Fiscal impact-taxes, infrastructure costs
* Prices
* Economic base & structure

Environmental Impacts:
* Lands
* Waters
* Air
* Infrastructure
* Flora & fauna

Social Impacts:
* Population structure & distribution
* Values & attitudes
* Education
* Occupations
* Safety & security
* Congestion & crowding
* Community spirit & cohesion
* Quality of life

1. Impacts on Local Government

Local government provides most of the infrastructure and many of the services essential to tourism development, including highways, public parks, law enforcement, water and sewer, garbage collection and disposal. Evaluate tourism decisions with a clear understanding of the capacity of the local infrastructure and services relative to anticipated needs, and take into account both the needs of local populations and tourists.

A fiscal impact analysis evaluates the impact of tourism on the community's tax base and local government costs. It entails predicting the additional infrastructure and service requirements of tourism development, estimating their costs, deciding who will pay for/provide them, and how. Will tourism generate increased local government revenue through fees and charges, local sales or use taxes, increased property values or property tax rates, or larger local shares of National and Local tax revenues?

2. Impacts on Business and Industry

Businesses that are directly serving tourists benefit from sales to tourists. Through secondary impacts, tourism activity also benefits a wide range of businesses in a community. For example, a local textile industry may sell to a linen supply firm that serves hotels and motels catering primarily to tourists. A local forest products industry sells to a lumberyard where local woodcarvers or furniture makers buy their supplies. They in turn sell to tourists through various retail outlets. All of these businesses benefit from tourism.

If most products and services for tourists are bought outside of the local area, much of the tourist spending "leaks" out of the local economy. The more a community is "self-sufficient" in serving tourists, the larger the local impact.

3. Impacts on Residents

Local residents may experience a broad range of both positive and negative impacts from tourism development. Tourism development may provide increased employment and income for the community. Although tourism jobs are primarily in the service sectors and are often seasonal, part time, and low-paying, these characteristics are neither universal nor always undesirable. Residents may value opportunities for part time and seasonal work. In particular, employment opportunities and work experiences for students or retirees may be desired.

Residents may also benefit from local services that otherwise would not be available. Tourism development may mean a wider variety of retailers and restaurants, or a better community library. It may also mean more traffic, higher prices, and increases in property values and local taxes. The general quality of the environment and life in the community may go up or down due to tourism development. This depends on the nature of tourism development, the preferences and desires of local residents, and how well tourism is planned and managed.

STEPS FIVE AND SIX: Implementation, Monitoring and Evaluation.
We will not attempt a complete discussion of decision making, plan implementation, and monitoring, but these are critical steps in the success of a tourism plan. A set of specific actions should be prescribed with clearly defined responsibilities and timetables. Monitor progress in implementing the plan and evaluate the success of the plan in meeting its goals and objectives on a regular basis. Plans generally need to be adjusted over time due to changing goals, changing market conditions, and unanticipated impacts. It is a good idea to build monitoring and evaluation systems into your planning efforts.

VIII. IMPORTANT NOTES TO REMEMBER

Successful tourism planning and development means serving both tourists and local residents. The bulletins in this series stress the importance of a market orientation for attracting and serving tourists. This market orientation must be balanced with a clear view of how tourism serves the broader community interest and an understanding of the positive and negative impacts of tourism development.

Remember, tourism should serve the community first and the tourist second. Tourism development must be compatible with other activities in the area and be supported by the local population. Therefore, the tourism plan should be closely coordinated with other local and regional planning efforts, if not an integral part of them.

IX. The THREE QUESTIONS The TOURISM DEVELOPMENT MASTER PLAN must ANSWER

1. Where are we?
After you have identified an area prime for destination development, one of the next steps should be conducting a destination tourism assessment. This assessment will provide an analysis of the competition in your region as a tourist destination and help implement the steps you need to take for your tourism planning.

The market ultimately decides the boundaries of a destination as well as it's physical and cultural limits, which is why you should keep in mind the following:

- ✓ Attractions: What draws people to this destination? The culture, the biodiversity, landscapes, architecture, history, agriculture, festivals etc.
- ✓ The Environment: The climate, safety, what are the cultures, religions, infrastructure, resources, facilities, services, etc.
- ✓ The Policies: Government type, laws, you need to know what you can and can't do when developing a tourism plan.
- ✓ The Competitors: What is being implemented in your destination already? What are neighboring destinations offering?
- ✓ Key Stakeholders: Who will be involved in tourism activities in this destination? How should they be involved in the planning stage?
- ✓ Potential & Opportunities: In what areas can further development be useful? Is there untapped potential in the destination?

2. Where do we want to go?

After assessing the destination, you can move toward the planning stage. One of the most important aspects of planning is visioning. You need to have an ultimate vision for the destination. This vision will help you set goals and determine how your destination can achieve the desired outcomes. These goals should be attainable and feasible, some examples are:

Increased visitation Higher sales
Increase awareness of destination among target markets
Increase awareness of vision (eg: ecotourism, community-based tourism, protect natural resources, improve water quality, help local economy) among target markets
More tourism products offered

3. How do we get there?

After creating a vision for your destination, the real work begins. How do you get where you want to go? In order to reach your vision and meet your goals, you need to create strategies and tactics that will engage community members & key tourism stakeholders while raising

awareness among your target markets to drive sales & visitation. Here are a few initiatives you might need to reach your goals:
- ✓ Get community involvement from key tourism stakeholders
- ✓ Focus on the creation or improvement of tours, lodging, attractions, events, and visitor services that can enhance the visitor experience. This in turn can increase your opportunity to attract investments.
- ✓ Set up social media platforms & integrated marketing efforts Implement marketing contests and campaigns.
- ✓ Create partnerships with investors, government agencies, etc.

X. The Deliverables in Tourism Development Planning Objective

Formulated long-term development framework for tourism (10-20 years) with emphasis on policy and strategy, planning, institutional strengthening, legislation and regulation, product development and diversification, marketing and promotion, tourism infrastructure and superstructure, economic impact of tourism and tourism investment, human resource development, and socio-cultural and environmental impacts of tourism. It includes a short term (three-year) action plan for priority actions to be undertaken to kick-start sustainable tourism development, and preparation of several demonstration projects for pilot areas.

Objective:
Duration: 4-12 months

Indicative budget
To be supplied by the Proponents Target Beneficiaries.

Target beneficiaries
Target beneficiaries:
Destination Management Organizations National Tourism Administration Provincial Governments
Municipal Governments

Outputs / deliverables
A Tourism Development Master Plan which provides an organized and structured framework for tourism development and promotion.

Methodology:
Three phase approach:
Phase 1
Project formulation mission which analyses the current tourism scenario and prepares a project document (detailed terms of reference) for the formulation of a Tourism Development Master Plan.

Phase II
Formulation of a Tourism Development Master Plan which focuses on the following sectors:
- transport;
- accommodation;
- tourist activities;
- product development;
- tourism zoning;
- marketing and promotion;
- institutional framework;
- statistics and research;
- legislation and regulation; and
- quality standards of tourism services.

The Plan prioritizes actions for each sector and includes an Action Plan defining roles and responsibilities of various stakeholders, timelines, indicative budgets, monitoring guidelines, and, success criteria.

Phase III:
Implementation of the Master Plan by providing technical assistance to the Government in implementing the priority recommendations of the Master Plan.

Note: Tourism Development Master Plans can be formulated at a national or local level. Furthermore, they can also be thematic in nature:
- rural tourism;
- community-based tourism;

- mountain tourism;
- coastal tourism;
- ecotourism; and
- spa tourism, etc.

Tourism Destination Management Facilities And Services

I. Introduction

Tourism destination is one of the major elements of the tourism system. Without the destination there could be no tourism to speak of. It is in this context that the management of a tourism destination is most crucial in the delivery of tourism products and services to the consuming public, particularly the tourists both of domestic or overseas origins.

Basically, tourism destination is collectively managed by both the front-liners and stakeholders/key players in the tourism systems. A failure of one to perform its role shall mean a failure of the whole system, thus, a degeneration of the industry that ultimately diminishes its contribution to the economic development opportunities intertwined with the system.

This chapter, therefore, provides the tourism industry learners the answers to the whats, hows, and wherefores related to tourism destination management, taking into account the role of every sector in the tourism system.

II. Composition of the Destination Management Team

In order for a destination to achieve its objective in getting more interests from both the domestic and international tourist markets, it is imperative that its development, administration and management must be cohesively performed as a shared responsibility of all sectors that compose the entire tourism service systems. For this purpose the need to institutionalize the culture of tourism in the destination (community) must be given emphasis and highest priority, and, at all times put in place and functional. The mechanics for the institutionalization of the culture of tourism should be established with each sector's role and parameter of duties and responsibilities clearly defined for them to be guided in every disposition of their legal obligations and social responsibilities.

A. Composition
1. Stakeholders and Key Players
The key players in destination management are classified as follows:
Government Sector
1. **The National Government Agencies (NGAs):**
a) The Governing Agency Department of Tourism (DOT); and,
b) Support Agencies:
   1. Department of Transportation and Communications;
   2. Department of Trade and Industry (DTI);
   3. Department of Public Works and Highways (DPWH);
   4. Department of Interior and Local Government (DILG); (Police Authorities for Security and Maintenance of Peace)
   5. Commission on Higher Education (CHED); and,
   6. The respective Regional Offices.

2. **The Local Government Units (LGUs) include the following:**
a) Community/Village Officials (Barangay);
b) Municipality/Town Officials, particularly the officers charged with the responsibility related to tourism development, i.e., Municipal Tourism Officer; and, Chairman-Committee on Tourism, the Municipal Legislative Council;
c) Province, particularly the officers tasked/charged with the responsibility related to tourism development, i.e., Provincial Tourism Officer; and the Chairman-Committee on Tourism, the Provincial Legislative Council;

3. **Private Sector** - Registered and Accredited Tourism Business/Enterprise Owners.
Non-Government Organization - The duly organized and recognized tourism industry related organization advocating tourism development in the locality, e.g., Association of Service Providers

(Hotels, Restaurants, Pension and Lodging Houses; Transport Operators; Travel Agencies and Tour Operators; Socio-Civic Organizations directly or indirectly involved in tourism related activities);

B. The Front Liners
This sector includes all the service providers' work-force and human resources, including the government authorities field workers who are directly in contact with the tourists while in a given tourism destination, as follows:
1) Travel Agents/Tour Operators, i.e., Reservations Staff, Tour Guides, Tour Conductors, Coordinators and Drivers;
2) Transport (Air, Sea and Land) Operating Personnel; Port/Airport Personnel
3) Personnel/Staff of Hotels, Resorts, Pension/Lodging Houses, i.e., Front Office Staffs, Concierge Service Staff, Waiters/Waitresses; Housekeeping Personnel; Bar Tenders, etc.;
4) Souvenir Shops/Handicraft Store Sales Persons; Restaurant, Coffee Shop Food Servers;

C. The Academe/Training Centers
This sector includes all educational institutions of higher/technical education as well as training centers both government and privately owned offering tourism and hospitality service related courses.

III. The Basic Roles of Tourism System Components
A. Stakeholders and Key Players
   Government Sector
   1. Promulgation of Laws, Rules and Regulations and enforcement and implementation of these laws, rules and regulations without fear or favor;
   2. Introduction of the basic infrastructures and public utilities, i.e., access roads, ports, airport, passenger terminals and other support services, i.e., waste disposal, sewerage system, water and power supply in the tourism destinations;
   3. Repair and maintenance of these infrastructures and public utilities;

    4. Maintenance of Peace and Order;
    5. Security and Safety of tourists; and,
    6. Marketing and Promotion of the Destination.

   The Private Sector
    1. Compliance with the laws, rules and regulations, particularly accreditation of establishments with the accrediting agencies and Department of Tourism;
    2. Continuing training and retraining program for its personnel and staff;
    3. Safety and security of clients/customers;
    4. Timely delivery of products and services to clients;
    5. Fair and reasonable pricing of products and services;
    6. Availability of facilities and services when required;
    7. Preservation of the environment; and,
    8. Proper disposal of solid and liquid waste materials

B. **The Front Liners Service Providers**
    1. Tourism Product Development;
    2. Tourism Product Packaging and Costing;
    3. Marketing and Promotion;
    4. Tourism Product and Service Delivery;
    5. Participation in the Continuing Education Program, Seminars and Workshops for the improvement or upgrading of services;

    Non-Government Organization
    1. Conduct of continuing education and information drives for the general membership of the organization in regards issues and concerns involving their common and individual objective, interests, prerogatives and social obligations;
    2. Proper coordination with the government sector on the programs and activities geared towards the improvement of the tourism system;
    3. Advocacy to institutionalize the culture of tourism in the community;
    4. Collective efforts in the promotion and marketing of tourism products;

5. Improvement and Upgrading of facilities and services of the member business enterprises; and,
6. Control in costing/pricing of products and services.;
7. Organization of, and Participation in meetings, conventions, congresses and exhibits

The Academe and Training Centers
1. Full compliance with the declared National Policy for the tourism sector, clearly pronounced in Republic Act 9593, as well as international bodies agencies with which the national government is by agreements a part of;
2. Adopting the most responsive course curriculum with subjects related to tourism and hospitality services in elementary and secondary educations;
3. Continuous offer of tourism and hospitality related courses;
4. Improvement of Course Syllabi and Teaching Methodology;
5. Upgrading of learning tools (audio visuals, text books, etc.) and methodologies;
6. Employment of tourism professors and instructors with hands-on experience in tourism and hospitality service related enterprises;
7. Training and retraining of tourism instructors to update their knowledge of the current trend in the tourism sector;
8. Elimination of subjects that are irrelevant and not substantially related to tourism and hospitality services;
9. Participation in tourism congresses, conventions and exhibits;
10. Comprehensive on-the-job training or practicum service program for students; and ,
11. Keeping updated with the international standard requirements in tourism education and training.

Travel Agency/Inbound-Local Tours Management And Operation

I. Introduction the Travel Agency Business

Origin of Travel Agency Business Discussed

Most of the Jewish and Christians particularly in the Roman Catholic faith believe that the business of travel agency was started by the Jewish people of Israel. This belief is based on the biblical accounts about the travel of Virgin Mary and Joseph who found no room in Bethlehem when both visited the synagogue to worship. The Bible being the officially acknowledged and recognized to be the repository of the oldest recorded events even before the birth of Christ certainly overshadows all other writings in terms of age. The theories and other epitaphs written in other forms after it, certainly could never disturb those scribbled in the Bible. On that fateful day of December 24, Virgin Mary riding over the donkey that Joseph was towing escort started from Nazareth for their journey to the town of Bethlehem to visit the synagogue for the purpose of worship. The town of Bethlehem is the traditional worship place for the Jewish during that time. Due to the distance between Nazareth and Bethlehem, Joseph and Virgin Mary arrived at the start of dusk when worshipers were already crowding Bethlehem. Virgin Mary then was pregnant with a baby conceived by the Holy Spirit, and was to deliver the child anytime of that fateful night. Concerned of the physical condition of Virgin Mary, Joseph was all around town looking for a room where Virgin Mary could rest and wait for her delivery of the child. However, on that fateful day the couple arrive too late, and all rooms in pension and lodging houses were already occupied by the early visitors that directly checked-in.

Without any vacant room found, the couple decided to occupy a space in the sheep's shelter where both decided to stay and rest for the night. It was in the midnight of that day when Virgin Mary delivered a baby to be known as the Holy Infant Jesus Christ. Absence of the comforts and other amenities, the newly borne Holy infant was wrapped with Virgin Mary's over-coat and placed in a manger. The birth of the Holy Infant became known to the three kings Gaspar, Melchor and

Baltazar who were already aware that when the king of kings is borne there will be a sign to appear in the sky, which in that instance was a shining comet with its rays pointing to the direction of the birthplace that is the town of Bethlehem. These comet rays then serving as the guide, the three kings took a camel ride that was the novelty transport in a desert at that time and journeyed towards Bethlehem to deliver their gifts to the newly borne Holy Infant whom they believed is the King of all Kings.

The Jewish have never known of the story on how Virgin Mary delivered Jesus Christ until a news spread in town, that indeed the king of all kings was really borne in Bethlehem. The Jewish King of Israel who refused to recognize someone more powerful than he is, then ordered his soldiers to look for the infant Jesus Christ. However, it took the soldiers more than three decades to finally have captured Jesus Christ while curing the sick in Jerusalem.

In the meantime, unknown to other communities in Israel, Jewish entrepreneurs in the Kibbutz (Community Cooperative) of Nazareth, the hometown for Joseph and Mary, after having learned the experience of the couple during that midnight of December 24, started to organize the system on how worshipers and outbound travelers could avoid the same fate in Bethlehem that was then the famous converging place.

Thus, it is the conclusion of the Jewish that the system of a travel agency business started in the Kibbutz (village commune) of Nazareth where the villagers were informed that whenever they travel to places outside of Nazareth, it is necessary for them to make arrangements ahead of time so that their accommodation is pre- arranged and paid in advance with the lodging and pension house operators in their destination. Thus, the Jewish believed this is how the business of travel agency started, and they were the same people who were considered the first recorded travelers even before the birth of Christ and were known as the 'Wandering Jews'..

II. Definitions of Words and Phrases Commonly Used in Travel and Tour Operations

A la Carte - A menu from which items are chosen and paid for individually. This type of meal arrangement is hardly ever included in any tour.

American Plan - Hotel accommodation with three meals daily included in the price of the room. Meals are usually "table de' Ho'te". Sometimes referred to as "full pension".

Assistance - Services rendered by an interpreter who gives clients any help they need at any place (railway or bus stations, airport or air terminal, pier, hotel.)

Carrier - A public transportation company such as air or sea-going vessels (steamship line), railroad, etc.

Charter Flight - A certain airline flight booked exclusively for the use of a specific group of people who generally belong to the same organization. Charter flights are generally cheaper than regularly scheduled line services, but are not open for sale to the general public. They may be carried out by regularly scheduled or supplemental carriers.

Conducted Tour - A certain prepaid pre-arranged vacation for a group of people travelling together under the guidance of tour leader who stays with them from the beginning to end of trip.

Continental Breakfast - This generally consists of a beverage (coffee, tea, cocoa or milk), plus rolls, butter and jam or marmalade. In Holland and Norway, cheese, cold cuts or fish are generally also provided.

Couchettes - Sleeping accommodation provided on some European railroads, consisting of a day compartment which may be converted into bunks for 4 (1st Class) or 6 (2nd Class) passengers. Pillow and blankets are provided. Since sexes are not segregated, passengers may not disrobe at night. Slight additional charge above railroad fare.

Coupons (Vouchers) - Documents issued by tour operator in exchange for which travelers receive prepaid accommodation, meals, sightseeing trips, excursions, etc. also referred to as Vouchers or Exchange Orders.
Courier (Tour Escort, Tour Leader, Tour Manager) - A professional travel escort.
Cruise - An all expenses pre-paid, pre-arranged tour by ship to specific ports.
Driver-Guide - A driver who is authorized to act as a guide on sightseeing, excursions or tours.
English Breakfast - This type of breakfast is generally served in Great Britain. It usually includes hot or cold cereal, bacon, or ham and eggs, toast, butter, jam or marmalade and a beverage. (though not a juice)
Entrance Fees - The amount of money paid to have a right of visiting a museum, a monument, a park, an exhibition, etc.
Escorted Tour - See conducted tour.
European Plan - Hotel accommodations with no meals whatsoever included in the cost of the room.
Exchange Orders - Same as Coupons.
Excursion - A tour outside the limits, but however in the vicinity of the town where the organizing agency is located. Such a tour may last from half-day to three days according to the rule adopted by the organizing agency. It comprises accommodation, meals and transportation from departure to return to the given town or city.
Flight Sightseeing - sightseeing by air.
Full Pension - See American Plan.
Garni - When appended to the name of the hotel, this means that the establishment does not have a restaurant or dining room. Such hotels usually have a breakfast room.
Ground Arrangement - All services provided to the clients after they have reached their first foreign destination.
Guide (official) - Someone who is licensed to take paying guests on local sightseeing and excursions. In countries where an official license does not exist for guides, the services usually supplied by a guide may be supplied by a travel agency's clerk.
Half-Pension (Modified American Plan) - Hotel accommodation which includes continental breakfast and either table d' hòte lunch or dinner in the price of the room.

Modified American Plan - See "Half-Pension"

Motor-coach Hire - A motor-coach hired to a party. The basic conditions of hire are usually the same as private cars, but of course take into consideration the seating capacity of the vehicle.

Optional Tour - Means that clients have a choice of taking or not taking the service mentioned. It they take it, there is always an additional charge which is not included in the basic tour price.

Pension - A French word widely used in Europe meaning guest house or boarding house.

Porterage - The amount of money paid to have one or several pieces of luggage handled at airports, city air terminals, railway stations, piers and hotels.

Private Car Hire with Driver - A car hired to clients who will pay, according to the agencies, a rental based either on mileage or on an hourly or daily basis. Each agency will indicate all that are included in the rates given, such as fuel (gasoline) insurance, excess mileage, tips, etc.

Self-Drive - Car hired to clients without driver. Conditions of hire vary from agency to agency, they may be based either on mileage or on an hourly or daily basis.

Sightseeing - A tour within the city/town limits showing to clients the main particularities of the place: avenues, churches, monuments, parks, etc.

Sleepers - Sleeping cars consisting of a private bedroom with accommodation for one or two persons. Pillow, sheets and blankets are included.

Table de' Hòte - A complete menu form which deviations involve additional charges. This is the type of meal which will generally be provided when meals have been included in the price of the tour. In Europe, table de' hòte means hardly ever include coffee or tea after the meal (these are considered "extra").

Tips - Gratuities to hotel employees, porters, guides, drivers, etc. In a very few countries tipping is not allowed.

Tour - A long distance circuit of more than 3 days organized by a travel agency in a given and comprising of sightseeing in several other places or towns, either within or outside the country of origin.

Tour-Basing Fare - A reduced round-trip fare available on specified dates, and between specified times, only to those passengers who purchase pre-planned, pre- paid tour arrangements prior to their departure.

Tour Escort - See "Courier"

Transfer - Service provided for the travelers when they arrive and leave a given city, which takes them from the airport, air terminal, pier or railway station to their hotel and vice-versa, accompanied by a representative of the local agency. The cost depends on whether transfers are carried out by private car or taxi, and also on the distance between airport, or air terminal, or station and hotel. Porterage of two pieces of hand luggage is included.

U-Drive - See Self-Drive.

Vouchers - See Coupons.

Wagons-Lits - Sleeping carts on the European continental railroads, consisting of a private bedroom with accommodation for one, two or more persons depending on the class of travel. Pillow, blankets and a sink are included.

III.   Travel Agency Defined

Travel Agency is a primary tourism enterprise duly licensed and accredited by the Department of Tourism authorized to conduct the business of travel documentation for outbound travelers and booking of seats with public or chartered carriers, particularly air, sea and land transports from one place to the other both in domestic and international routes; packaging of tourism related services of specially contracted tourism related service providers that include room of hotels, resorts inns, pension and lodging houses for accommodations, land or sea transport for transfers on arrival and departure, and, sightseeing, tours of, or excursions to the attractions in point of destinations for a fee.

A travel agency can also operate both the outbound travel as well as inbound/local tourism service for foreign/overseas and domestic clients.

(Note: In the Philippines, most of the Travel Agencies are doing purely the sales or booking/reservation business for airlines for domestic and international travels and passenger shipping lines for local/domestic journeys.)

IV. Organization of Travel Agency or Local Tour Operation

The travel agency may be organized as a single proprietorship, partnership or corporation in accordance with the applicable laws, rules and regulations particularly the Corporation Code of the Philippines, and Department of Trade and Industry. It may be owned fully or majority by Filipino citizen with the foreign nationals to own not more than forty per centum (40%) of its capital or shares of stocks in case of a corporation. A travel agency may operate both outbound travel business or inbound tourism service or both.

A. Travel Agency Differentiated from Inbound/Local Tour Operator and Tourist Transport Operator

The Travel Agency normally is engaged in airline ticketing for both international and domestic travel and Travel Documentation (acquisition of passport, visas, and inoculations) of outbound traveling clients. It may also package, sell and operate package tours for domestic and international/overseas destinations;

The Inbound/Local Tour Operator is engaged purely in the packaging of tours that may or may not include hotel accommodations, and the conduct of these tours including sightseeing or excursions covering the tourist attractions in the local tourist destination.

The Tourist Transport Operator is mainly engaged in the business of operating duly licensed and accredited tourist transports chartered by the travel agency or inbound/local tour operator that include land (buses, mini-buses, limousine), aircrafts, and sea crafts.

In many cases however, the bigger travel agencies simultaneously operate the businesses of Inbound/Local tours as well as Tourist Transport, by creating a division and acquiring a license for each line of service.

B. Requirements for Travel Agency Operation

Requirements for Travel Agency Operation are as follows:

a. It shall be located in a commercial district and not in a residential area.
b. It shall be used exclusively for the travel agency business.
c. It shall be easily identifiable.
Note: The travel agency should present an annual in-bound and out-bound tour programs for submission to the Municipal Tourism Promotion Board (PTPB) and its implementation schedule for the whole year.

C. Travel Agency Basic Organizational Structure

The basic travel agency Organizational Structure is found in Figure: II.

Figure II. Travel Agency with Inbound/Local Tours

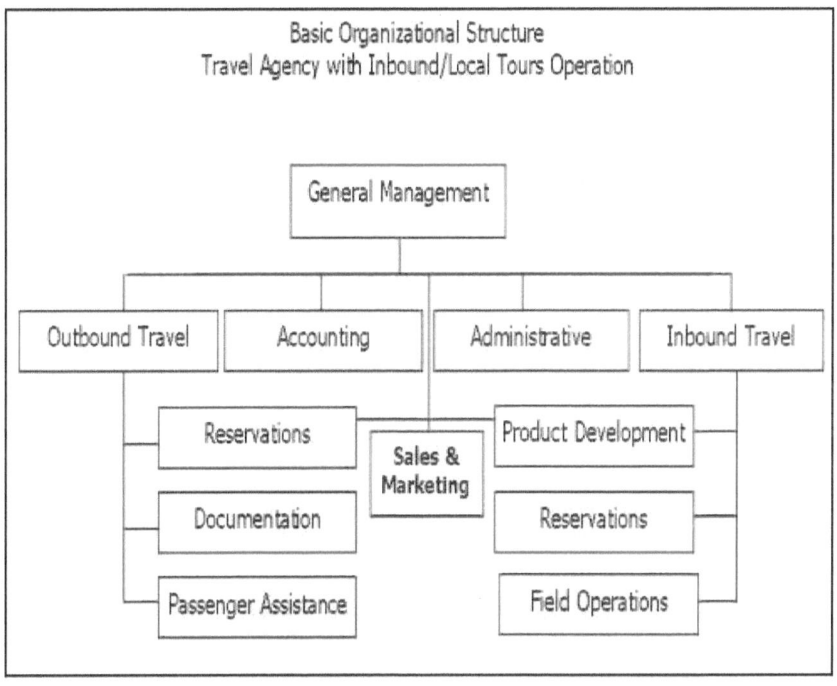

Figure II. Organizational Structure

D. Travel Agency Service Sections, Duties and Responsibilities

1. General Management Section

The General Manager - holds the highest position in the office as head of the General Management of the day to day operations. He/she is assisted by the Managers of Outbound and Inbound/Local Tours operations, the Chief Accountant who heads the Accounting Section and the Administrative Officer, head of the administrative section.

2. Accounting Section

The Chief Accountant —Holds the highest position in the accounting section and responsible for the maintenance of accounting books of accounts including receivables and payables and the preparation of financial statements.

3. Administrative Section

The administrative officer - is holds the highest position in the administrative section, and assists the General Manager in all aspects of the administrative functions.

4. Outbound Travel Section

A. Scope/Coverage of Service

The outbound travel section is responsible for the delivery of services required by the outbound travel passengers. The personnel and staff required in the organizational structure vary upon the size of the agency operation and volume of passengers that it handles. For the basic operational requirement reference, hereunder is the recommended by the author.

B. Personnel/Staff Requirements

The staff/personnel required in the operation of outbound travel section are:

Manager - holds the highest position and the over-all in-charged of the day to day functions of the outbound travel section. He/she is the supervising head of all the staff and personnel in the section, closely coordinates with accounting and administrative section for internal concerns, and acts as the contact point of outbound travel service providers, i.e., air and shipping lines, overseas hotels, resorts, etc.. In most cases, the outbound travel manager concurrently does the sales and marketing of the outbound travel services, and reports directly to the general manager. Under his/her section are the following:

a) *Marketing and Sales Staff* - the function of the staff is to conduct research and develop a certain market to which the product and services of the travel agency are linked and offered. These product and services may cover both the outbound and inbound/local travel and tours for a travel agency operating both services.

b) *Reservation staff* - the main function is to do the bookings/reservations of seats/space with passenger carriers i.e., air and shipping lines, and other services in that the passenger clients require in their point of destinations, i.e., arrival/departure transfers, rooms for hotels/resorts, sightseeing and excursions, and sees to it that all the required travel documents, i.e., passport, visa, inoculations where needed, confirmed reservations vouchers for all the required services in the point of passenger destinations are intact and given to, and the passenger is fully briefed and oriented of what to do and expect in the destination ahead of time prior to the date of departure.

c) *Documentation Staff* - are personnel in the documentation section whose main responsibility is assisting the passenger-clients in the processing of the required travel documents, i.e., passport, visas, inoculations where needed, including preparation of application and submission of pre-requisite documents for their issuance by the agencies concerned. These agencies include among others, the Department of Foreign Affairs for the Passport, Foreign Embassies and Consular Offices for the Visa, Department of Health for the inoculation/vaccination where needed, Department of Tourism for the Travel Tax, etc., and the Bureau of Internal Revenue for Tax Exemption Certificates.

d) *Passenger/Client Assistance Staff* - Field personnel assigned to assist the outbound passengers during departure, seeing to it that the passenger-clients smoothly checks-in the specific airline counter and finally enters the pre- departure airport terminal departure area.

5. *Inbound Travel/Local Tours Section*
A. Scope/Coverage of Service

The inbound travel/local tours section is basically involved in all of the services that maybe require by the inbound travel/local tours passenger-clients or guests in a given tourist destination. These services include among others the following:

- a) Hotel/Resort Rooms for accommodations and meals as required; Land Transport for transfers on arrival and departure; Sightseeing, tours and excursions;
- b) Passenger tickets for domestic travel (air, sea and land); Tour Guide/Escort Services; and,
- c) Entertainments and other activities.

B. Personnel/Staff Requirements

The basic required staff/personnel in the operation of the Inbound Travel/Local Tours section are as follows:

1. Management Section

Manager - holds he highest position and over-all in-charge of the day to day operations of the inbound travel/local tours section. He/she is the supervising head of all the staff/personnel in the section, closely coordinates with the administrative and accounting sections for the internal concerns, and acts as the direct contact point of overseas wholesale travel agencies that organize/operate package tours to the local/domestic tourist destinations within its territorial coverage. He/she is likewise the main linkage of the agency with local service providers, i.e., hotel, resort, restaurant, transport, and local tour operators in the local/domestic destinations outside the area of the agency's coverage. He/she may concurrently act as the sales person for the agency's local or domestic tours services. The personnel/staff under his/her supervision are the following:

2. Product Development Section

Product Development Staff - Responsible for developing tour products and services by way packaging and costing these package services, including preparation of promotional materials, i.e., brochures, flyers and leaflets for these products and services, subject to the approval of the manager. The product development staff/personnel are likewise in-charge in contracting for special rates with the service suppliers/providers.

3. Bookings and Reservation Section

Booking and Reservation Staff - Responsible for making bookings and reservations the service requirements of the inbound passengers/guests with the service providers, i.e., specific category and number of rooms for hotels/resort accommodation including meals that maybe taken in hotel , number of seats/space for domestic carriers (air, sea and land transports), as well as other activities that maybe required by passengers/guests in the destination, including transfers, tours, sightseeing, excursions and entertainments that maybe included in the packaged services, and sees to it that documents for these bookings and reservations are obtained and delivered to the tour guide/coordinator who they shall fully briefed and oriented prior to the arrival of the inbound guests in the destination.

4. Field Operations Section

Tour Coordinator - is responsible in the proper coordination with the service providers, and sees to it that the required services are in place and ready prior to the departure in case of the transports as there may be required for transfers, tours, sightseeing, excursions and other activities that require the same are in place and available prior the movement of passenger/client; and, rooms for accommodation in the hotels/resorts are made-up and available; and, tables/seats in restaurants are in place and foods are prepared prior to the time of guests arrival.

Tour Guide - is a professional licensed person employed by the travel agency/tour operator with the main responsibility to meet on arrival, accompany and lead the tourist client in all their movements, i.e., transfers from and to the point of entry/exit on arrival and departure, brief and orient the guests of all the arrangements of activities/movements as confirmed, and deliver commentaries of the sights and attractions, including what the guests may expect along the routes towards, and the tourist destination per se.

Tour Conductor/Tour Escorts- The tour conductor/escort is a person employed either regularly or temporarily by the travel tour agency with the responsibility to conduct or escort a tour group taking a packaged tour to the destination other than the main entry point of offered by the agency. A Tour Guide may likewise act as tour conductor in the absence of the latter whenever the tourist group is bound to another domestic destination outside the tour guide's local coverage.

V. The Travel Agency/Tour Operator Service Cycle

The travel agency/tour operator Service Cycle is presented in Figure III.

Figure III. Travel Agency-Outbound/Inbound Operation Cycle

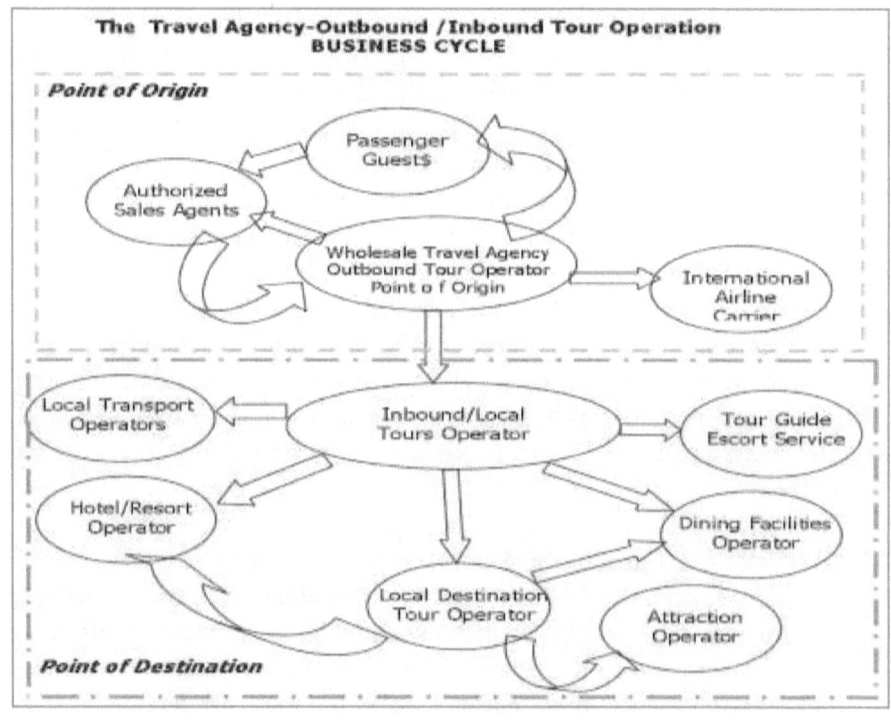

VI. Travel Agency-Outbound/Inbound Tour Operation Cycle Explained

The travel agency business cycle starts from the passenger/guests shown in the upper most bracket of the cycle system. The upper small dotted line represents the Outbound Travel /Tour operational cycle and the bigger dotted line below it is the Inbound/Local Tour service operations in the tourist destination. Following the presentation in Figure III., the pattern and flow of travel agency business operation is hereunder presented.

1. Passenger-Client Consideration

The passenger-client is the highest consideration as it makes up the ultimate market for the travel agency outbound service business. The market then is categorized into various market segments by the travel agency and tour operator, for which is based what destinations and services should be considered in the packaging and costing to determine what is most likely fitted and desirable to each and every market segment.

2. Price Contracting and Booking with Service Providers

The travel agency-outbound/inbound tour operator starts its business transaction cycle by way of establishing a contact with:

A. Service Providers in Point of Origin - these are the air and shipping lines serving the routes to and from the chosen destinations as defined in the tour itinerary that may offer the best viable contracted rates; and,

B. Service Providers in Point of Destinations - these include local/inbound tour operators that maybe contracted to supply and actually deliver the full package of services that are included in the tour program, particularly local transport operator (land, air and sea) for transfers, sightseeing, tours, excursions and guide services with specific language as there maybe required; and hotel rooms for accommodations. There are instances, however, that some of the overseas wholesale tour operators normally contract and book their room requirements directly with hotels.

3. Tour Packaging and Costing

After having gathered and finalized the cost/rates for every service component that maybe required from local service providers, the wholesale travel agent/tour operator packaging the tour shall make the costing and formulate the Prices, including the incentives for the sales agents/outlets. The Published Rates for the package tours shall always secure a mark-up for the income of the travel agency- tour operator on top of the sales agency/outlet commissions that most hotels and other service providers normally observe.

The same manner of costing is observed by the Inbound/Local Tour Operator in the formulation of costs for their services in the destination.

4. Different Types of Tour Packaging The different types of Package Tours that the travel agency/tour operator normally organized are as follows:

A. Regular Package to Traditional and Non-Traditional Destinations
Packaging of these tours is purely based on the assumption that the program could easily appeal to the interests of the general traveling public. The tours has particularly schedule for the series of departures during a certain period of the year. This schedule then is transmitted via the fastest way of communication to the Local/Inbound tour operator in the destination for reference and proper confirmation of booking/reservation and coordination with the contracted service providers.

B. Special Package to a Chosen/Off-Beat Destination
Packaging of these tours is purely based on the pre-arranged destination by the passenger-clients themselves. This is normally for a one- time travel and custom-tailored for the specific client requirements, they be individual (FITs) or in groups (GITs). This type of tour packaging includes sports activities, heritage, religious, special studies, nature trekking and explorations (spelunking, mountain climbing, scuba diving. This special package may also include sentimental journeys of war veterans, graduates of certain educational institutions for home coming and reunions, etc..

C. Special Package for MICE (Meetings, Incentives, Convention and Exhibits)
This type of packaging requires a relatively long period of time considering the required organization of the various services included and the specific market segment targeted, that normally involves a specific professional and business groups.

D. Special Package for Health and Wellness Tourism
This type of packaging is on a case to case basis with the highest consideration to the availability of highly skilled service providers that basically involve health and wellness specialists, specialty hospitals and clinics; and the physical conditions of the targeted market segment
In any of the cases preceding, this package tours are published in the tour magazine or brochure or flyers that the travel agency prints out and distributes to the authorized sales agents and outlets. The details of the package tours are included in the publication particularly the day to day tour itinerary and program of activities for the duration of the tour, from point of origin to points of destination and return to point of origin with the costs.

5. Advance Booking/Reservation
It is a common practice for overseas and foreign wholesale travel agents/tour operators to prepare the package tours at least a year before it is offered to the market. In the same way, that bookings and reservations for rooms in the contracted hotels/resorts in point of destination are likewise blocked corresponding to the scheduled series of arrivals. The same is true for the arrangements of the local transport requirements for transfers, sightseeing, tours and excursions as arranged by the inbound/local tour operator.

6. Pre-payment/Advance Deposit
The practice of pre-payment of advance deposit is the normal requirement by hotels, in order to confirm the rooms as required in the scheduled dates. It is therefore, necessary that the local/inbound tour operator making all the arrangements in the destination shall require the pre-payment for the advance deposit, which is not less than the equivalent of the payment for one room night stay of the

passenger- guests, or fifty per cent (50%) of the total package cost of the Inbound/local tour operator. The justification for the deposit of confirmed reservation is to insure the income of hotels in case sudden cancellation occurs, and the hotel is unable to dispose of the reserved and duly confirmed rooms for the particular dates.

7. Tour Package Documents

Overseas/Foreign Wholesale Travel Agents/Tour Operators is obligated to prepares issues the documents that are required by the service providers in the destination. These documents are given for safekeeping by the Tour Escort/Conductor or Tour Leader assigned to accompany the group of passenger- guests taking the package tour and presented to the service provider upon arrival in the point of destination. These documents are necessary in order to assure that all arrangements are required, booked and confirmed are secured by the service providers in the destination. These documents are as follows:

a) Airline Tickets of Tour Group Members;
b) Computer Generated Airline Seat Confirmation Documents;
c) Hotel Reservation Vouchers/Exchange Order for room accommodations; Transfers and Tours Voucher/Exchange Order for Inbound/Local Tour Operator in the destination:
d) Final Rooming List of Tour Members for Tour Group Members Room Assignments;
e) Final Detailed Tour Itinerary/Tour Program; and,
f) Copies of communications confirming all the required services from the local service provider;
g) The inbound/local tour operator and the hotel shall be furnished with all the information appearing in the above documents ahead of time or at lest 15 days prior to arrival of the tour group to the destination, particularly copy of the Rooming List and the Vouchers for each respectively.

VII. The Basic Forms in Travel Agency Operations
A. Outbound Travel Section
1. Booking/Reservation Card (Air, Sea or Land) for Individual Passengers

This form is the quick reference on all the information as to the travel requirement of the client. It is where recorded the details on:

- ✓ Coded Name of Carrier (Air, Sea or Land (Bus/Train);
- ✓ Date and Time of Flights/Trips;
- ✓ Code for Airport of Origin (Exit) and Airport of Destination/Entry;
- ✓ Flight Number and Class/Category of Space/Seat reserve and confirmed;
- ✓ Visa/s and Inoculations Required;
- ✓ Name and Address of Hotels for confirmed Rooms;
- ✓ Land arrangements (i.e., Airport Meeting Assistance, Transfers/Tours);
- ✓ Name, Address and Contact Information of Service Providers in the destinations; and,
- ✓ Travel/Trip Itinerary with details of Activity and Guide of What to Do.

2. Travel Itinerary Form - In this document contains the travel routes and activities of the guest/client in points of destination from day of departure to day of return. Please refer to Sample Illustration No. 1;

3. Service Voucher/Exchange Order - This document contains the confirmed services that the guest/client require in points of destination and serves as a medium of exchange for the confirmed services to be supplied by the service provider in points of destination.

B. Inbound/Local Tour Operations

1. Tour Costing Form - This is the document used as a guide in the computation of tour package cost and serves as a reference of the accounting section for purposes of cross-checking the income of the agency.

2. Tour Itinerary Form - This document defines the day to day activities of the guest from the day of arrival and day of departure from the destination.

3. Booking Order Form - The document that contains the required services of the guests/clients issued by the inbound/local tour operator to service providers, particularly, space in hotels for rooms; seats and tables for restaurants; ticket for entrance to parks and museums; and units and type of transport facility for overland travel. It serves as a reference for the confirmation of the services as pre-arranged, booked and reserved for specific time and date.

4. Service Voucher/Exchange Order – this document is issued by the inbound/local tour operator in favor of the service provider as a medium in exchange of the services to be availed by the guests/clients in the establishment, i.e.,
hotels/resorts for rooms; foods and beverage for restaurants; type and units of transport equipment and facility for transport operator, etc.. The same document serves as the basis for the payment by the agency of the services provided by the supplier to the guest/clients.

1. Tour Package Costing

Tour Cost
Tour Cost is the total amount of accommodations and services included in the package tours that the tourist shall pay to the travel agency or tour operator that operates and conducts the tour in a given tourist destination.

2. Formula in Obtaining the Tour Component Costs

In obtaining the cost for every component of the tour services follows the hereunder formula as follows:

A. For Individual/Independent Travelers (FIT's)

Room Cost= Contracted Room Rate divided by the number of persons in a room times the number of nights plus mark up; (CRR/NP x NN equals Room Rate for costing consideration);
Transfers, Sightseeing/Tours or Excursions = Contracted Transport Rate on a per Trip Basis divided by Number of Paying Persons plus Entrance Fees and Other Charges, plus Guide Fees, plus Meals or Drinks if required, plus Mark Up; or (CTR ÷ NPP + EF & Ocs + GF + MU = Cost for Costing Consideration)

B. For Group International Travelers (GITs) with Free of Charge (FOCs)
1) Room Cost = Contracted Rate times the Number of Rooms required, divided by the Number of Paying

Guests, times the Number of Nights required in the destination plus Mark Up; or (CRR x NR ÷ NPGs x NNs + MU).

2) Transfers, Sightseeing/Tours or Excursions = Contracted Transport Rate on a per Trip Basis divided by Number of Paying Persons plus Entrance Fees and OtherCharges, plus Guide Fees, plus Meals or Drinks if required, plus Mark Up; or (CTR ÷ NPP + EF & Ocs + GF + MU = Cost for Costing Consideration).

3. Types of Tour Package Costing

The tour package costing is categorized into different types. These are:

1. Custom-Tailored for Individuals (FITs-Foreign Independent Travelers) – This type of costing is entirely dependent on the choice of the customer that has the option to choose a certain place or places to be visited and the services.

2. Package Tours for Groups (GITs – Group International Travel) – This type of tour costing is dependent on the travel agency's regularly operated tour programs. The tour itinerary is ready-made, and the costing is basically based on a minimum number of persons in a group traveling together for the given schedule of departure.

4. Fundamental Steps in Package Tour Costing

Tour costing is the most important component of the tour package. It is the main factor being considered in the profitability of the travel agency/tour operation business. It involves a meticulous research on the viability of the tour package that could attract most the specific segments of the tourist market being targeted as the would-be takers of the package tours being offered. It involves the price of services as contracted with the service providers, i.e., hotels/resorts for accommodations, restaurants, destination local/inbound tour operator for transfers, sightseeing and excursions, airfare for outbound travel from point of origin and return, travel documentations for the acquisition of passport, visas and inoculations if needed. The fundamental steps are as follows:

Step One – Prepare the Tour Itinerary from point of origin based on the final number of days duration of the tour, and finalize the number of nights stay in the destination. If the tour package has multi-destination, see to it that the number of nights in each destination is determined first prior to the encoding of the prices of rooms and the cost of other services for the land arrangements for each destination. Always remember that it is much better to contract only one official inbound/local tour operator in the destination to package all the services to include hotel rooms and land arrangements in order to simplify the costing. Normally, it is given that local tour operators in the destination has the better working relationship with the hotels/resorts so that they are expected to have the lower contracted rates with hotels.

Step Two – Reserve and block-book the maximum number of seats with the airline of choice with which an arrangement for special air fare had been contracted, and, reconfirmed the rates/prices with the service providers in the destination.

Step Three – Gather all the costs included, particularly the ones covered by the contract with the airline for airfare; hotels for rooms and meals; Inbound/Local Tour Operator in the destination for transfers and sightseeing/excursions; and, Travel Documents acquisition for passports, visa and inoculations if necessary;
(Note: Should there be no contracted rates, it is necessary that the outbound travel agency must communicate first with the local/inbound tour operator in the destination to request for the rates of services as there maybe required for the package tours intended to be operated. Confirmation of the rates as requested from and submitted by the local/inbound tour operator in the tour destination must be confirmed and reconfirmed in writing.)

Step Four – Having gathered and confirmed all the prices as supplied by the service providers, encode the same in the costing form. See to it that the figures so encoded are reviewed to make sure that the same are correctly extracted and the same as the ones supplied and confirmed by the service suppliers.

Step Five – After encoding all the prices individually in the spaces provided in the Costing Format, add the mark up and obtain the total for each service incorporated in the package tour. (Please see ILLUSTRATION No. I)

5. **Tour Costing Illustrations**

A. **For FITs (Foreign Independent/Individual Tourists)**
Illustration No. 1

Sample No. 1
    Travel Agency/Tour Operator at Point of Origin

Name of Party : Mr. & Mrs John Doe x Party of 2 Pax
Tour Duration : 3 Days/2 Nights
Destination   : Island Resort in Western Visayas
Point of Origin : Singapore
Accommodation : First Class Hotel/Resort
Room Requirement : One Double Bed Room
Land Arrangements :

In this example, the travel agent/tour operator in point of origin shall:
1) Prepare the Tour Itinerary for 3days and 2Nights illustrated in the form, as the recommended tour itinerary and present the same to the client. Sample Tour Itinerary is found the next page Illustration Illustration No. 1.

Illustration No. 1
Sample Tour Itinerary for FIT
3 Days/ 2 Nights Western Visayas Island Resort

	RECOMMENDED TOUR ITINERARY FOR:	
	Name of Client/s: Mr. & Mrs. John Doe x 2 Pax	
Day	Time	Tour Activity/ies Description
01	0700 H	Departure from the designated point of origin and assisted check-in at the airport airline counter;
	1000H 1350H	Departure to Airport Flight ; Estimated Time of Arrival in Manila. Representative of the Inbound Travel Agency/Tour Operator shall meet and assist for transfer to hotel of choice;
	1530 H	Estimated Time of Arrival at the Hotel for assisted Check-in. Welcome Drink is served. Rest of the time FREE for rest and Overnight at the Hotel
02	0700H 0900H	Breakfast at the hotel. Depart hotel for a guided City Sightseeing of Metro Manila. (InboundTravel Agency/Tour Operator shall insert the description of the City's Special Features and Attractions.
		Sightseeing to include all places to be visited)
	1200 H	Estimated Time of return to the hotel. Balance of the Day FREE for rest.
	0700 H	Breakfast at the hotel.
	0830 H	Departure from Hotel to airport for flight to Caticlan via___.
	0915 H	Estimated Time of Arrival in Caticlan. Local Tour Operator shall meet and assist for your transfer to Caticlan Jetty port where you will be assisted in boarding a ferry-boat to Cagban Jetty Port, Boracay Island which is less than 10-minute cruise across channel. Then, you will be assisted for your transfer by land to your resort.
	1035 H	Estimated Time of Arrival at the resort in Boracay Island for your immediate check-in. Balance of the day is free for you to explore the island or simply while away in the beach for swimming. Overnight at the resort.
03	0900 H	-In Boracay Island (Your breakfast is served in the hotel in the duration of your stay);
	1030 H	Departure of your Island Hopping Tour of Boracay Island with lunch. Rest of the day and Evening free for more optional activities of your choice not included in your package.
	1115 H	Departure from your resort for transfer to Caticlan Airport for your return flight to Manila.
	1800 H	Estimated Time of Arrival in Manila International Airport.
	2150 H	Estimated Time of Departure for Singapore. Estimated Time of Arrival in Singapore.

2) After the client accepts your recommended Tour Itinerary, ask the client the indicative dates of travel and having obtained the information, communicate with the service providers as follows:
   a) Airline – for the seat reservation and airfare;
   b) Inbound Travel Agency/Local Tour Operator in the point of destinations for rooms required as well as the land arrangements for transfers, sightseeing and excursions and ask confirmation of rates;
   c) After receipt of the confirmation of space from airline, hotel/resort, and services, i.e., transfers and sightseeing/excursions arrangements start the costing of the tour package following the formula as presented. For Illustration see sample of tour cost computation in Illustration No. I., based on Sample No. 1.

Illustration No. I.
Tour Cost Computation For FITs (Foreign Independent Traveler)

Destination	Manila						

1. Accommodation: First Class Hotel

Type of rooms	Units	Net Cost	Nights	Total Cost	No. of Pax	Cost/Pax
DWB	1	58.00	5	290.00	2	145.00

Meals	Net Cost	Units/Pax	Net Total	Mark Up	Total Cost	Cost/Pax
Breakfast	US$4.00	2	US$8.00	0.80	US$8.80	$4.40
Lunch						
Dinner						

2. Land Arrangements

Services	Net Cost	No. of Pax	Cost/Pax	Mark-Up	Total Cost	Cost/Pax
Transfers	US$ 25.00	2	25.00	2.50	27.50	13.75
Sightseeing	30.00	2	30.00	2.50	32.50	16.25
Excursions						

Destination	Boracay Island						

3. Local Transport Fare: (Airfare Round Trip) 175.00 17.50 192.50

4.
Type of rooms	Units	Net Cost	Nights	Total Cost	No. of Pax	Cost/Pax
DWB	1	58.00	5	290.00	2	145.00

Meals	Net Cost	No. of Pax	Net Total	Mark Up	Total Cost	Cost/Pax
Breakfast	US$4.00	2	US$8.00	0.80	US$8.80	US$4.20
Lunch						
Dinner						
Transfers	15.00	2	30.00	3.00	15.50	15.50
Tours	28.00	2	56.00	5.60	61.60	30.80

	Total Cost of Package Per Pax	US$374.90

Having obtained the total net costs in the destination, add the airfare from point of origin, thus;

Cost of Land Arrangements in Point of Destination = US$ 374.00 Airfare: Singapore/Manila/Singapore = 175.00
Total Cost of Package = US$ 549.00 per pax.
Please refer to the Costing Form in Illustration No. 2

The preparation of tour costing for group package follows the same pattern with that of the Individuals as illustrated. The only difference is when the travel agency/tour operator in point of origin requires for the Free of Charge (FOC) for tour escorts or group organizers. In cases of this kind, the Inbound Travel Agency/Local Tour Operator has to secure FREE OF CHARGE accommodation with all the service providers so that the cost for the paying group members is not disturbed. However, in cases where any of the service providers is unable to extend free of charge then the inbound travel agency/local tour operator has no choice but to factor-in such cost to the package price of the tour that the customer shall pay. Please see Illustration No. 3.

Illustration No. 2

Name	: Far East Adventure Group
Group No.	: 26
of Pax Tour Duration	: 4 Nights/5 Days with American Breakfast(2 Nights –Manila and 2 Nights Boracay)
Hotel Required	: First Class
Rooms Required	: 12 Twins and 1 Single

In this example the formula as explained is followed except that the cost for the complementary service of the Tour Escort is factored into the package price that shall be distributed to the paying members of the group, thus, the whole costs are summed up and divided by the number of paying members. The computation is shown in Sample No. 2.

Illustration No. 2
Sample Costing for Group (GITs)

A. In Manila: 2 Nights (Overnight on Arrival and Overnight Before Departure)

1. Rooms:
12 Twins at US$55.00 x 2 nights = US$ 1,320.00 1 Single at   45.00 x 2 nights =   90.00
Sub-Total   = US$ 1,410.00
2. Breakfast   : 25 pax at US$ 3.50   =   87.50
Sub-Total for Rooms and Breakfast =   1,497.50
14. Round Trip Transfers:
On Arrival   US$ 12.00 x 2 x 25 pax = US$ 600.00
City Sightseeing 18.00 x 25 pax =   450.00
Sub-Total   = US$1,137.50
15. Boracay Overnight Excursion:
16. Airfare, Transfers and Excursions:
Round Trip Airfare   = US$ 178.85 x 25 pax =   4,471.25 Round Trip Transfers =   35.00 x 25 pax =   875.00
Island Hopping Excursion w/ Lunch = 36.00 x 25   =   900.00
Sub-Total   = US$ 6,246.25

17. Resort Rooms and Meals:
12 Twins at US$ 48.00 x 2 nights   = US$ 1,152.00
1 Single at US$ 43.00 x 2 nights =   86.00
Breakfast at US$ 2.80 x 2 x 25 pax   =   140.00
Sub-Total   = US$ 1,378.00
Total Net Cost   = US$10,259.25 Plus Mark-up 10% 1,025.95
Total Gross   = US$11,285.20 ÷25
Cost per Person US   451.40

Note: Cost for Transfers and Sightseeing/Excursions already include the Guide Fees for Guide Services. Please refer to the TOUR COSTING FORMS in the succeeding pages.

Outbound Travel/Tour Operator in Point of Origin
Sample Copy of Coting Form

For Outbound Travel Agency/Tour Operator (Point of Origin)

Destination: _____

Accommodation:

Type of Room	No. of Units	Net Cost	Total	Mark Up	Total

Destination: _____

Land Arrangements

Type Services	Cost/Person	Mark Up	Total

3. Airfare Computation:

	Gross	Net	Total

4. Other Services:

Total Cost of Package	

Tour Costing Form 2
Inbound/Local Tour Operator

Destination					
1. Accommodation:					
Type of Rooms	No. of Units	Net Cost	Mark Up	Total Cost	

Destination					
2. Land Arrangements					
Bus/Car Hire	Net Cost	No. of Pax	Cost/Pax	Mark-Up	Cost/Pax
Transfers					
Sightseeing					
Excursions					
3. Local Transport Fare:					
4. Other Fees and Charges:					
		Total Cost of Package			

XI. Tour Tariff Costing (Inbound/Local Tour Operator)

Tour Tariff is the quick reference for rates/prices of services availed by the Inbound/Local Tour Operator, particularly to foreign outbound wholesale travel agencies/tour operators organizing tour movements to points of tour destinations. Tour Tariff is an indispensable component of the Tour Brochure. It contains the prices for every service that varies based on the number of customers.

A.   Types of Tariff Costing

There are two types of Tour Tariff Costing that is normally prepared by the Inbound/Local Tour Operator. These are the following:

1.   Component Services (Transfers, Sightseeing, Tours & Excursions)

Tariff for this kind of service is prepared based on the assumption that the service users shall have the option to choose the individual service that they will avail while in the destination, and/or for the wholesale foreign outbound travel agency/tour operator to have the ready reference in the preparation of their own outbound package tours without the hassle of having to research and communicate with the inbound/local tour operator in the point of destination; and,

2.   Package Services (Combination of two or more component services)

Tariff for this kind of service is prepared with consideration to discount privilege in taking two or more services. Oftentimes, cost for this type may include accommodation, meals and other extra services available in the destination that are not included in the component tours services.

B.   The Basic Procedure in Tariff Preparation
1. Obtain the Special Rates from Service Suppliers, particularly the:
   a.) Land Transport Operators for Limousine, Van, Bus/Motor-coach;

b.) Attractions in the places of stop-over and destination that maybe included in the service, i.e., Parks, Museums, Forts and Resorts for their individual fees and charges for entrance and rides;

c.) Restaurants for the meals (foods and beverage) that maybe included in the component tour service;

XII. Basic Forms in Travel Agency Tours Operation

A. Booking Reference Card

This is a basic form for travel agency/tour operator serving as the quick reference for the information and details of the transaction with the client, particularly on the flight schedule and hotel accommodations in points of destination. This is a handy tool for the reservation staff/personnel for easy access to the information that may from time is inquired by the client and a practical substitute in case the computer bogs down.

Sample Copy 1 Booking Reference Form

BOOKING REFERENCE CARD

Name of Pax:
Address:
Contact Tel.

Flight Details							Hotel Reservations				
Route	Date	Carrier	Flt. No.	Class	Status	Ref.	Name of Hotel	Type of Room	From	To	Status	Ref.

LAND ARRANGEMENTS

Date	Place/Location	Services Required	Service Provider/Agency	Status

B. Booking Order Form

This form is normally used for reservation/booking of rooms/space in a hotel/resorts as required by the clients. It is a documentary reference to cross check the records of a travel agency/Tour operator as against the ones being held by the hotel/resort or any other service providers including land transports, restaurants, etc..

Sample Copy 2 Booking/Reservation Order Form

(COMPANY NAME & LOGO)		
To:	Date	Booking Order No. 000001
Name of Client/s:	Exclusive Date: From: _____ To: _____	
Please book/reserve and CONFIRM the hereunder accommodation and services as follows:		
Description of Accommodation & Services Required		
Reserved By: _____ Date of Issue: _____	Confirmed By: _____ Signature Over Printed Name Date: _____	

This form is printed with at least three (3) copies, one original and two duplicates. The original copy is received and kept by the service provider/supplier to which it is addressed and from which the services are booked/reserved. The received duplicate copy is kept by the issuing agency and the third copy is normally kept by the accounting section as reference for any disbursement related to payment of the services as described therein.

C. Service Voucher/Exchange Order

The Service Voucher or Exchange Order is an accountable form that serves as the basis of the service supplier to provide the services to the client as required by the travel agency/tour operator. It likewise serves as the documentary reference in the collection of payment for the service/s rendered by the service provider from the travel agency/tour operator that issues the same. This form serves as a medium of payment guarantee of the travel agency/tour operator issued for the service provider.

Sample Copy 3 - Service Voucher/Exchange Order Form

```
┌─────────────────────────────────────────────────────────────┐
│                    (COMPANY NAME & LOGO)                     │
│              SERVICE VOUCHER/EXHANGE ORDER                   │
├──────────────────────────┬──────────────┬───────────────────┤
│ To:                      │ Date         │     SV/EO         │
│                          │              │     No. 000001    │
├──────────────────────────┴──────────────┴───────────────────┤
│ In EXCHANGE of this ORDER please PROVINDE the hereunder      │
│ named clients with accommodation and services as described   │
│ in the service requirement box, as per confirmed             │
│ booking/reservation. Kindly ATTACH ORIGINAL COPY of this     │
│ form in your Statement of Account when collecting payment.   │
├──────────────────────────┬──────────────────────────────────┤
│ Name of Client/s:        │ Exclusive Date:                  │
│                          │ From: _____ To: _____      │
├──────────────────────────┴──────────────────────────────────┤
│                   SERVICE REQUIREMENT BOX                    │
│                                                              │
│                                                              │
│                                                              │
├──────────────────────────┬──────────────────────────────────┤
│ Reserved By: _____  │ Confirmed By: _____   │
│ Date of Issue: _____  │         Signature Over Printed Name│
│                          │ Date : _____          │
└──────────────────────────┴──────────────────────────────────┘
```

The Service Voucher/Exchange Order is printed in four (4) copies the original of which is submitted to the service supplier i.e., (hotel, resort, restaurant, etc.) upon actual delivery of the services and accommodation to the clients for which the same is issued.

Fundamentals And Techniques In Tour Guiding

I. Introduction

The story of TOURISM as well as GUIDING started way back during the period prior to the birth of Jesus Christ in Bethlehem. This was during the eve of Christmas, when Joseph an ordinary carpenter in Nazareth with Virgin Mary who was pregnant as unto her womb was a baby conceived by the Holy Spirit, traveled to Bethlehem in order to worship together with other Jews who did the same. Due to non-existence of travel agents and tour operators during that time, Joseph and Mary made their journey from Nazareth and entered Bethlehem as walk-in visitor, without anybody doing room reservation for them, thus, both arrived in Bethlehem with all the rooms taken as they are already fully booked. Joseph and Mary then found no room to stay for even an overnight, resulting as it did for the couple to sleep in a manger, where Jesus was unexpectedly borne. Then the three great KINGS Gaspar, Melchor and Baltazar were notified by the Holy Spirit through the shining comet that appeared over the horizon, symbolizing the birth of the Son of God in Bethlehem to where the comet rays were pointing. The same rays served as the guide for the three kings' journey towards Bethlehem to deliver their gift and presents to Jesus Christ the King of all Kings.

The significance of the story in so far as tourism and tour guiding is concerned is the lesson that the Jewish learned the necessity of a tour operator that could have arranged a reservation for Joseph and Mary prior to their journey to Bethlehem, and a licensed local tour guide to have met and ushered them to the hotel for their accommodation.

II. Tour Guide Defined

In order to arrive at the exact definition of the word Tour Guide, the author belabors to first present the meaning of the word Tour, being the root in the phrase Tour Guide.

TOUR Defined:
According to Webster, TOUR means "a journey for sightseeing, business or education ending at a place from which one started out." Therefore, it simply means any movement of person with the purpose and mission to enjoy and accomplish that purpose, from a place of origin to a certain place necessary to do the purpose of his movement or journey that ends up in the same point of his origin or from where he comes. It is not specifically referring to a foreigner or person of whatever nationality, religion, color or political ideology. The meaning Webster advanced as it is asserted, is generic in form in so far as the person is concerned and the purpose it intends to achieve.

Then, lets go further to the word TOURIST. It is necessary to understand this word because without a TOUR and TOURISTS, TOUR GUIDING is of no necessity.

TOURIST - The word TOURIST is defined as "a person visiting or staying for period of time certain in a place on holiday outside his place of residence."

Holiday - means, a break from the day to day works for unhampered enjoyment of that specific time for rest and recreation.

Then, let's go to the word GUIDE.
GUIDE - Webster defines a Guide as, "A person who shows the way to the stranger, to tourist or mountaineers, book of information for visitors to a place, an adviser, a book for beginners, the principle governing behavior of choice. To control, direct or influence."

The World Association of Travel Agencies, WATA, a cooperative non-government organization of independent tour and travel agencies with exclusive membership of only one per city or state or country with 10 Million traveling population, in its book the WATA-MASTER KEY made as reference for WORDS, TERMS and PHRASES officially used by travel agents, tour operator, airline and shipping companies, hotels resorts and such other providers of tourism related services defines a TOUR GUIDE as, "*Someone who is licensed to take paying guests on a local sightseeing and excursions, while explaining the special features and significance of sights along the route, and places of historic value and economic importance.*" Therefore, a licensed tour guide, is not only what as Webster defines "as someone showing the way", but most importantly imparting information of the locality's tourism attractions for the tourist to experience and enjoy.

III. The Effective Tour Guide

To be most effective in satisfying a client/customer tourist or visitor a LOCAL TOUR GUIDE, in tourism parlance while conducting a tour, must have something of everything. His principal duty and obligation is to:

1. GUIDE and NEVER to MIS-GUIDE;
2. INFORM and never to MIS-INFORM;
3. He/she is the person show-casing the natural as well as man-made assets of tourism value of the locality.
4. He is the epitome of a person with well-rounded personality.
5. He must have the first hand information by way of personal experience of the places to be visited, the test of every service component, and the know-how of the outstanding features of the sights and sounds peculiar in the place.

IV. Qualities of an Effective Tour Guide

The TOUR GUIDE to be most effective must substantially possess the level of qualities for:

Teacher or Mentor/Educator, and must have the mastery of the basic information including history, personages associated to landmarks, monuments and structures, so the delivery of the same information to tourists under his/her care must be with fullest clarity and complete authority. For whatever he says and describes, the tourist have no choice but to believe. It should be noted, however, that most of the tourists before going to a place for sightseeing, may have already gained some information that convinced them to come and visit the place. So, that, once the tour guide fails to properly deliver the right and correct information about the place or attraction, natural or manmade, dissatisfaction on the part of client is expected; complaints shall flow in to the management of the tour or travel agency that shall ultimately mean losses on the part of the latter, and the locality as the same negative impression may easily spread in the tourism community where the dissatisfied client originate, thus, others who are would-be visitors may shy away and recall its intention to visit the same place, and divert to other destinations which they believe having the efficient service by local tour guides.

Public Speaker, Commentator, Announcer or Desk Jockey – A Tour Guide must speak in a well-modulated voice with fullest clarity extemporaneously and delivered spontaneous and in timely fashion with the passing through, or upon sight of the spot, structures and objects of tourism importance and value.

Leader or Shepherd – A tour guide leads the way; it is on him/her that the visitor solely depends on where to go and what to do, while within his turf or area of responsibility.

Program Host and Entertainer – A tour guide entertains and eliminates boredom of tourists under his/her care. For which purpose, he/she must be equipped with a talent to entertain, in whatever form. These can be in the likes of music or singing, instrument playing, cracking a joke or humor, and mastery of lines in famous poems, adages and dictums that could be of interest to and stir feelings of-the guests.

Ambassador of Goodwill and Diplomat – for he/she is expected to speak only the best that the place could ever offer to tourists, and squarely answer every question of, and deliver the assistance needed by tourists/visitors with diplomacy. He/she is expected to never say NO, to any lawful and moral request, or I don't know, to any query poised on him/her by. Any reaction to the request or answer to a query must be delivered in a subtle way and clarity. It is the duty of a Tour Guide to learn the country of origin, nationality, tradition, language and religious belief of the tourists, so that, when the tourists arrive, the tour guide shall have the readiness to inter-act and bond easily with them. Delivering a welcome note, greetings and gestures of respect from English translated to the language or dialect of the tourists shall be appreciated by and the feeling of trust established as a means to facilitate the bonding process between the guide and the tourists.

Salesperson – for he/she is expected to convince his customers/clients to spend more money in the locality by way of extending his/her stay, and taking tours or other activities i.e., shopping, dinner with show, night club visits, etc., in addition to what is pre-paid and included in original itinerary. For in doing so, the tour-guide earns extra income by way of commissions in addition to the professional fees for his services on the pre-paid tour arrangements.

Innovator – for he is expected to introduce innovative ideas and put them into motion complimentary to his principal obligation to inform, sell or market and entertain. The best example for an innovative idea is looking into the date of birthday, wedding anniversary of a customer, then announcing on board the same with the expression of the best wishes and greetings. Offering a bouquet of flower or a token symbolizing the greetings and wishes could be very much appreciated by the customer. Such other innovative ideas in little things for the tourists to enjoy is something that the latter shall always treasure.

Student – for he/she is expected to continually conduct research, studies and readings of current events, new facilities, utilities, products and services of tourism orientation offered and are available. It is his/her bounden duty to learn, familiarize and educate himself/herself first before educating others.

V. The Service Component for Tour Guide

Tour Guide is indispensable as the service of tour guiding is required and necessary in the following:

Transfer Services - This service component required particularly on organized packaged tours availed by tourists on arrival in, and departure from transport terminals (Airport, Sea Port, Bus and Train Terminals). This is where tour guide acts to welcome and usher the guests to the hotel. This is classified into:

- ✓ Transfer In – for Incoming guests; and,

- ✓ Transfer Out - for Departing to their onward destination;
- ✓ Sightseeing – a short trip within the city locale visiting historical landmarks, monuments museums and parks, olden churches and institutions of higher learning significantly related to famous personalities who contributed outstanding works and achievements enriching the cultural heritage and history of the locality;
- ✓ Tour/Excursion – a journey outside of the city or town center to a certain attraction that lasts for a day or overnight.

VI. Dynamics in Tour Guiding (Responsibilities and Duties of the Tour Guide)

The performance of the responsibilities, obligations and duties of the TOUR GUIDE begins upon receipt of the written assignment from the TOUR AGENCY, with the complete TOUR ITINERARY, ROOMING LIST and such other documents given out for the purpose, i.e., Service Vouchers/Exchange Orders for service suppliers, i.e., hotels, restaurants, transportation, etc., that maybe included in the package of services, when and where the TOUR GUIDE has the working basis, in looking into the program or activities, accommodation requirement and location of the hotel, restaurant for dining, shops for shopping and places for sightseeing and excursion. However, the actual conduct of his TOUR-GUIDING service starts upon reporting for duty to handle the conduct of a tour classified into two categories, as follows:

A. REGULAR RUN or REGULARLY OPERATED SIGHT SEEING TOURS/EXCURSIONS – While tourists are boarding the transport unit, i.e., Car, Bus or Motor Coach for overland sightseeing or excursion, Boat for Island Hopping, Cruising, Snorkeling and Plane for Air Sightseeing. After tourist joining this component service are settled in their seat, the TOUR GUIDE, then delivers the BRIEF COMMENTARY on the overview of the destination and the expected point for stops over with exact period of time allotted to stay, and, what are the services expected while in the same point/area.

B. CUSTOM TAILORED PRE–ARRANGED LOCAL GROUND SERVICES -Upon meeting of tourists in their arrival point (airport, sea-port or Bus/Train Terminals) for which the hereunder services may be included in the pre-arranged ground services.

1. *Transfer In* - Upon Boarding the land or sea transport exclusively chartered for the purpose.

   In this component service, the tour guide's duty are to:
   a. Ask for the FINAL ROOMING LIST of the guests if traveling together in a group;
   b. After Boarding and tourists are seated, deliver the WELCOME NOTE;
   c. Then distribute the Comment Form together with the Tour Itinerary containing the schedules with precise timings; and briefings and orientation of the guest on the following:
      1) Name, Description of Facilities and Location of the Hotel and the inclusions on Accommodation (Meals, Bed and Breakfast);
      2) The Estimated Travel Time (ETT);
      3) Overview of the City, Province and Country that includes:
      4) History;
      5) Socio Economic Profile including Population based on latest census and statistics
      6) Currency and Exchange Rates of US Dollar to Local Currency;

   If time permits, the tour guide may orient/brief ahead the tourist in regards the succeeding activities, particularly the schedule that includes time of assembly at the hotel lobby and time of departure to the place included in the tour program;

   Upon arrival at the hotel:
   a) -Assist the Tour Coordinator in the registration of the tourists for check-in purposes;

b) -Assist the distribution of keys in accordance with the Rooming List, (Note: Normally, hotels are serving welcome drinks while rooms are assigned and keys are individually distributed)
c) -The tour guide then is expected to assist the hotel's tour coordinator in serving the welcome drinks.

2. *Sightseeing and Excursions*

Tour Guide is expected to be at the hotel at least One (1) hour before scheduled time of departure, and see to it that:
  a) The unit of transport required for the trip is ready with all the necessary gadgets and amenities are at hand and working particularly the air- conditioning and public address system;
  b) Tourists are duly reminded of the Time of Departure;
  c) Tourists are assembled in the hotel lobby at least 30 Mins, prior to the scheduled time of departure;
  d) Tour Guide shall assist guests in boarding the transport unit;
  e) Do the headcount prior to taking off for the sightseeing/excursion;
  d. Start the commentaries by way of delivering the WELCOME NOTE and the expected component services as they are included in the tour program and/or Tour itinerary;
  e. Brief or Orient the tourists/guests on the place, and period of time allowed for stops over, the place and their amenities as expected by them.
  f. Deliver the information on landmarks special feature in relation to History and Importance together with personages attached to it, particularly streets, monuments, shrines, museums, etc;

3. Transfer Out:

Tour Guide is expected to:

a. Be at the hotel at least two (2) hours before scheduled time of departure by the guests from the hotel to the terminal point of departure for onward journey;
b. See to it that guests have already cleared of their personal charges and checks-out of hotel smoothly;
c. transport equipment is at hand and ready;
d. See to it that luggage are collected from their respective room and duly accounted for loading;
e. See to it that guests are boarded in the bus or coach on time of the scheduled departure from the hotel;
f. Collect the COMMENT FORM if it is the practice by the tour company;
g. While on board and while cruising on the way to the terminal for departure to onward destination, the guide shall deliver the orientation on the important reminders of what to do at, and the facilities of the terminal, i.e., availability of souvenir shops, restaurants money changing counter, duty free shop, etc., thence the FAREWELL NOTE must be delivered;

VII. Tour Guiding - A Profession

Unlike traditional courses, tour guiding has its own peculiarities. It is a profession or calling that requires no specific college degree, except the innate talent with comprehensive grasp of information delivered with ease and authority, complemented with patience, perseverance and innovative ideas. Tour Guide being the front-liner in the delivery of the major services to the tourists is an indispensable component of the tourism system. The services of a tour guide may make or unmake the long term development of the industry in any given locality. Tour Guide is the mouth piece of stakeholders and key players in tourism. On him, dependent are the tourists and visitors who may promote the place not only for recreation/holiday destination, but perhaps, a haven for investments.

In countries where tourism had thrived to be the major economic activity, Tour Guides are being looked upon with high respects. Through a tour guide, tourism service oriented establishments earn the interests and confidence of tourist-clients and guests, for they are the personalities that the tourist customers ask, and from whom are expected only the most trustworthy answers and first hand information for the destination. Tour Guides earn more than just the Regular Professional Guide Fees, but likewise Commissions and Rebates on sales of extra services for optional tours, souvenir items, and finally token or gifts from most satisfied clients.

VIII. Opportunities in the Field of Tour Guiding

The Tour Guiding field is very much wide open specially outside Metro Manila particularly in North, Central and South Luzon, Visayas and Mindanao areas. As per records of the Department of Tourism, there are less than a dozen Licensed Tour Guide listed in the rolls particularly in Western Visayas. Of this number less than five are actively practicing the profession. With the Island of Boracay as the anchor destination, Western Visayas is the host and ranked almost second to Metro Manila in both the number of hotel rooms and the number of recorded tourist/visitor arrivals in the country. It is in these region that the biggest tourism investment had been poured in during the past two decades, particularly in the island of Boracay, where the tourism expenditure is estimated to be more or less 16 Billion Pesos annually. Sadly, however, nowhere in Boracay Island and other leading destinations in the country or even in the Regional Capitals, particularly in the City of Iloilo and other Provincial Capitals in the likes of Kalibo, San Jose and Bacolod, Licensed Professional Tour Guides are organized as they are available to serve the conduct of sightseeing, tours and excursions for tourists and visitors.

The reason is obvious. Except for the few Local Government Units or LGUs in the region, no one seem to extend priority to the TOURISM SECTOR. Almost all of the LGU officials do not seem to fully understand the importance of tourism to the people and local economy. Almost all do not have even a single piece document containing the plan for tourism development in their respective locality. In short TOURISM in this part of the country is to each his own. Without any Tourism Development Plan, there could never be sustained efforts for tourism development; without tourism development, there could never be an organized tourism service delivery; without organized tourism service delivery there could never be any organized tourist movement; without an organized tourist movement, there could never be an organized tour guiding service.

However, all is not LOST. Today, Republic Act 9593 otherwise known as the National Tourism Policy Act of 2009 and its Implementing Rules and Regulation have been approved and now ready for full implementation. The declared National Policy under this Law is to INSTITUTIONALIZE the CULTURE of TOURISM in all sectors of society, including the education sector. This had been awaited by those who are worth his salt and in the mainstream for the advocacy of tourism development during the last four (4) decades. And, finally it comes. This law now gives birth to the most promising life of tourism, and lucky you are the students who are graduating for after your graduation, hopefully this law is in its fullest implementation, that will afford you with all the opportunities. The profession of TOUR GUIDING is considered one of the best opportunities. All what you need to do are:
-Know by heart the Importance of TOURISM and its COMPONENT SERVICES
-Learn the rudiments of TOUR GUIDING; Read and Enhance Knowledge in Local History and the Places of Tourism Importance; Develop Self-Confidence
-Research, Research and Conduct More Research.

Book 6 (MICE)-Meetings, Incentives, Conventions And Exhibits

Insights And Beginnings Of Conference Industry

I. INTRODUCTION

Conferences, meetings, conventions, training sessions, and product launches have become a way of life of business and professional people. And, as you open this chapter, consider you are in the month of January the year 1990 which is a typical convention period recognized all over the world

As you sit down in the comfortable set in the classroom, people around the world will be the same but in a more formal manner in a well-equipped convention center in famous convention venues. Brief cases will be opened, papers shuffled, neighbors greeted, around the conference tables of the world. In hotels, Palais de Congress and university lecture rooms, in hi-tech conference centers and remote country houses; in specially designed meeting rooms on ships, evey; participants, delegates and speakers will be getting ready to talk about their problems, opportunities, ideas, hopes and fears and the brave new world everyone always hopes for.

You or They are Having a Conference
On the morning such as today, as you are in this classroom Rotary International is meeting in Singapore; Mobility International is in Utrecht; Cardiologists are getting together in Panama; Consumers are uniting in Berlin; the Applied Geologists are in Uppsala; there's an International Pediatric Nutrition Congress in Sau Paulo; and an International meeting of Pigeon Fanciers all a flutter.

The Importance of Meetings
Conference an Everyday Part of Communication Process

In every sizeable town in Europe and most other continents, people meet every day for small or large meetings. It's a major, high-spending industry directly or indirectly employing thousands.
Meetings breakdown into several segments. Most are conferences of either professional associations, or of business corporations.

The associations maybe local, national or international. The business meetings may be for stockholders, sales staff, training sessions, new product Launches; they may be in an exotic vacation resort as a form as a form of incentive award for topping a sales target or for some other forms of corporate achievement.

Where did it all start?
The Conference Beginnings
The Austrians insist it began in 1815 with the Congress of Vienna; this is a tradition carried on today, not just in the Viennese capital, but in other ancient cities such as Innsbruck, Salzburg, Graz and scores of smaller centers and hotels throughout the pleasant Austrian countryside.

Many feel, however, that the modern habit of stems, from the United States, where meetings have become a way of life, representing an annual investment, of over $35 billion yearly.

Over 150 years ago the French historian and observer of the social scene, Alexis de Tocqueville, remarked that Americans had an unusual affinity for getting together in associations and holding meetings. They liked, as they now do, to do it some style and comfort. One of the grudges of the Founding Fathers against George III was that he had called meetings "at places unusual, uncomfortable and distant . .
. . for the sole purpose of fatiguing them . . . "

In Europe, where London visitor and Convention Bureau, which offers an invaluable free service in finding facilities and services and generally providing a helping hand to anyone planning an event in the capital, estimates its value at around 800 million pounds per annum, the statistics are less easy to come by. There is no doubt however that going to meetings is an important aspect of business and professional life. Some people say, indeed say they never seem to be doing much else.

Whether in small meetings, medium sized conferences and big conventions, brief cases will be opened, papers shuffled, neighbors greeted, around the conference tables of the world. In hotels, Palais de Congress and university lecture rooms, in hi- tech conference centers and remote country houses; in specially designed meeting rooms on ships, even; participants, delegates and speakers will be getting ready to talk about their problems, opportunities, ideas, hopes and fears and the brave new world everyone always hopes for.

Conferences have become an everyday part of the communication process. In every sizeable town in Europe and most other continents, people meet every day for small or large meetings. It's a major, high-spending industry, directly or in- directly employing thousands.

Meetings break down into several segments. Most are conferences of either professional associations or trade associations, or of business corporations. The associations may be local, national or international. The business meetings may be for stockholders, sales staff, training sessions, new product launches; they may be in an exotic vacation resort as a form of incentive award for topping a sales target or for some other form of corporate achievement.

II. Basic Rules in Conference Management

A. Define Objectives
1. Continuing education: experts lecturing to general practitioners;
2. Exchange of knowledge: experts such as researchers talking to other experts;
3. Consumer-producer contacts: trade exhibition main or secondary aim;
4. Promotion to public: to attract attention to a theme, a declaration;
5. Social contacts: many or few social events planned in advance;

6. Association politics: Are business meetings of Councils, General Assemblies etc. an important part of the program?

B.   Define Participants
1.   Categories and numbers
-     Different categories may have different rights and pay different fees.
-     Estimated numbers per category times enrollment fees essential for calculation of income budget.
-     Differences in some congresses between early, lote and on site enrollment fees.
-     Differences in rights may influence space requirements.

Terminology is confusing, so that a clear definition of the following is absolutely necessary:

Active or full participant is the person for whom the main programme is organized, in English sometimes called delegate.

A delegate is a participant, appointed by a country or association to participate in an Assembly

A member is sometimes used instead of the term participant. It should be used in such congresses where participants have to be members to attend or where non- members pay a higher enrollment fees.

Associate participants may be participants in related occupations for whom special programmes may be included.

2.   Composition.

Initial analysis of one, sex, social status and income as well as proportions between local and overseas participants is very important for the planning of many facilities and activities in a congress. It is dangerous to base the planning on generalizations about presumed standard of different occupations.

C.   Define Framework

Some clients have only vague ideas about how their congress should be organized, others may have bed home used to a set pattern, which may not necessarily be the only possible.

By knowing thoroughly the facilities available and when they offer the best conditions for a congress, you may be able to suggest a mix of attractions which suit his basic ideas better than his original plans.

- Under Room requirements, add university which increasingly offer facilities for smaller conferences, or certain times of the year also for bigger ones.

- A majority of clients wish to organize their congresses during September- November. They compete therefore not only with each other about the same participants but also with big business about conference centers and hotel rooms.

You may help them to better deals if you can get them to consider other times of the year.

D. Congress Language
1. If printed material in several languages is desired
- make every clear with the client who shall be responsible for producing the translations and guarantee that they are correct. Few things make such a bad advance impression of a congress as amateurish translations of promotion material.
- Remember also to make allowance for the extra time needed to produce the translations when setting up the timetable for promotion.

2. Because of the high costs, simultaneous interpretation is an increasingly debated issue.
- The temptation to look primarily at the cost is great.
- Bad interpretation is more irritating than none.
- The quality of the interpreters must match the complexity of the message to be interpreted:
- The simplest case: two languages, presentation of material from manuscript or comprehensive summaries, including vocabulary which the interpreter can study in advance.
- Often possible to use local, non-AIC interpreters.
- Three or more languages, pre-written material available.
- Necessary for most of the interpreters to have two active and one passive language.

Active: the interpreter can translate both from and into the language.
Passive: the interpreter can translate from the language.

If the interpreters do not have two active languages interpretation must be relayed through his or her passive language. This causes delay, which make the interpretation difficult to follow, and also increases the number of errors.

Still, if the availability of local interpreters with relevant active languages is good, and most material is available for study in advance, it should be all right to rely mostly on local interpreters.

- The most difficult case: three or more languages, many sessions consisting primarily of discussions in all the languages without the benefit of pre-written material for study in advance. The majority of interpreters must have full AIC- competence and may have to be recruited from overseas, primarily on the basis of their language-combinations.

- Most important of all: to find a reliable and experienced organizer of the teams of interpretation and give him or her wide authority to make preliminary bookings of suitable interpreters.

Beware of experts on the subject matter of the congress offering to act as interpreters. It very rarely works well. Interpreter is a very highly skilled profession in its own right.

E.   PRINTED MATTER

1. For administration
   - stationery, envelopes, stickers, paper clips
   - badges
   - tickets, invitation cards, menus, place cards

2. For promotion
   - 1st announcements
   - preliminary program
   - enrollment forms
   - posters

3. Final Program
   - one or several books, such as separate books for scientific programme; and trade exhibition?
   - separate languages or combinations? Note differences in number of copies between different languages.

F. **SOCIAL EVENTS**
- A policy matter: all included in the budget, all self-financed or a mixture of both;
- If accompanying people pay enrollment fee: What do they perceive that they get for the money?
- Another policy matter: Should privately sponsored social events be allowed/encouraged? What responsibility, if any should the organizer of the congress take for co-ordination of those events with the congress social events proper? Timing, guest lists, distribution of invitations.

III. Languages, Interpretation and Translation

A. Introduction

It is of common knowledge that while English is considered the universal language, not all professionals and business persons worldwide may know how to speak and understand English. This is so, because some other countries do not use English as a medium of instructions in schools and thus in communications for the local practice of their profession, conduct of their business or exercise of their vocation.

Thus, in events where participants expected to participate are of different nationalities, it is an acknowledged tradition that documents covering the minutes of official proceedings in working sessions require translations and interpretations in different languages for the full understanding and comprehension of participants. Interpretation and translations are of paramount concern to any international gathering to encourage more participants who may feel the confidence to get their money's worth in attending the international event, specially meeting, convention or congress.

B. Factors in the Choice of Language

The decisive factors in the choice of languages used at an international congress are the following:
Participation from different language areas; Regulations of the Association;
Politics; Prestige; and, Finance.

C. Translation and Interpretation

Interpretation – verbal reproduction to another language.
Translation – refers to written work

Types of Interpretation:

Consecutive: the interpreter takes notes and interprets when the speaker has finished. This system is precise, but slow.
Simultaneous: interpreters work in soundproof booths, while the speaker is talking., with the help of electronic equipment.
Whispered: the interpreter whispers the interpretation (simultaneously) to one or two participants.

D. Technical Support

The International Standardization Organization (ISO) has established standards with the minimum requirements for permanent interpreters' booths and equipment (ISO/DIS 2603-1983) and for portable booths (ISO/DIS 4043).

Simultaneously interpretation equipment can be permanently installed or portable; it can be wired or wireless.

The following must be determined before renting simultaneous interpretation equipment:
- Is the equipment up-to-date, practical, and, above all, dependable?
- Are the receiving sets and earphones comfortable for the delegates?
- Is the reception free from inter-channel interference (cross-talk) or can the other channels be heard as back-ground noise?
- Is the wireless receiver sufficiently powerful to be received in any position it is held? The reception maybe too weak in certain areas in the meeting hall.
- Is the transmitter powerful enough to prevent outside noise from interfering with the reception?
- Is the quality of the sound satisfactory for the interpreters?
- Are the booths for the interpreters in accordance with the minimum requirements of the International Standardization

Organization (ISO)? Are they for example, sufficiently soundproof, air-conditioned, and illuminated?
☐ If the discussions are confidential, can the transmission be received outside the meeting room?
☐ Is the rental company reliable? Are the technicians experienced in international meetings and will they provide first class service for the meeting organizers, the delegates, and the interpreters?
☐ Is the meeting room available sufficiently in advance to allow for the installation and testing of the equipment?

E. Interpreters

Interpreters must be experienced and thoroughly professional.
The International Association of Professional Conference Interpreters (AICC), which is the association which groups he majority of the professional conference interpreters, has set regulations for minimum size of teams, minimum rates and regulations for the salary, per diem, travel expenses, contracts, etc.
For meetings with more than two working languages and/or more than two concurrent meetings with simultaneous interpretation, it is advisable to engage a coordinating interpreter to recruit, coordinate and supervise the team.
The interpreters must receive sufficient documentation in advance (abstracts, manuscripts, terminology, etc.) in order to be able to prepare their work. A briefing session or a briefing day befoe the Congress is most useful and necessary.

Promotion Of A Destination

I. Elements for Consideration in the Promotion of Destination

A. The Convention Bureau

Status – this will show if the Convention Bureau is: Under the administration and control of the city; Private or semi-official institution;
Department of Tourism Office, which can as well be official or private;
Activities – the specific functions of the Convention Bureau

Political and technical stimulation for infrastructure and development;
Marketing for conventions and fairs (selling a destination);
sultancy for organizer;
Act as "Honest Broker" between potential clients and potential suppliers of facilities and services;
Contacts to, cooperation with suppliers, officials, media, sponsors, etc. (Industry Managements);
Research and maintenance of databank on: Product
Target group (direct clients) Bidding for conference.

Financial Resources
Part of the city budget Public and private subsidies Membership fees
Overnight tax
Commercial revenue by selling services

B. The Product
Total Conference Package Parts of Package
- ✓ Physical Product Meeting facilities
- ✓ Exhibition space Technical service Decoration, signposts, etc.
- ✓ Translations, interpreters Construction (booths, stages, etc.) Accommodations, food, and beverage Social events
- ✓ Touristic programs, transportation Technical Visits
- ✓ Pre and Post tours
- ✓ Administration, secretariat, accounts, prints Media, publicity, photographs
- ✓ Other services
- ✓ Non-Physical product (product relating to subject matter of potential conferences)
- ✓ Industry
- ✓ Universities and other academic institutions Hospitals
- ✓ Local, regional, national and international headquarters in your destinations
- ✓ Spokesman
- ✓ The convention bureau speaks on behalf of or assures contacts to the local suppliers.

Competition

How is your destination compared to other destinations? If badly, what steps can be taken to improve the product?

C. The Market

Segmentation
No promotion is possible without knowing the market and defining the target groups within the market segments., Pattern is shown in the next page.

Market Segments (Example shown in the next page is the pattern used by IAPCO in Stockholm, Sweden 1984)

Market Segments Pattern

Sex	Age	Country of Residence	Profession Professional Status	% Congress Participation	Headquarters of Int'l. Ass. Total Participants
Male				82%	
Female				18%	
	1-16			0%	
	17-24			2%	
	25-40			48%	
	41-64			47%	
	65 Plus			3%	
		Europe		88%	15,000
		North America		5%	2,500
		Latin America		2%	1,300
		Asia		3%	1,200
		Africa		1%	850
		Australia/Pacific		1%	200
			Civil Service	43%	
			Private Ind.	32%	
			Independents	12%	
			Professors	8%	
			Students	3%	
			Others (Retired, Housewives	2%	

D. Target Groups
Direct Clients
Presidents of local and national chapters of international associations
Incentive houses, travel agents, airlines
Decision makers of associations and business Congress organizers, professional and others

Indirect Clients
Participants of previous events Participants of future events

Reference people influencing decisions (being consulted for advise at site selection)

II. Promotion
1. Message
The message bring the right information: In an adequate basket, On a safe vehicle, To the target client

The message starts the communication between convention bureau and client. It must therefore, stimulate a reaction.
The message must be adapted to the profile of the receiver to grant an effective impact. (Language, standard, style)
The goal of the message is making the receiver consider a specific place in his site selection for a conference.
Information must be true but not necessarily complete from the beginning. It is rational and must be understood.
The basket is the package of the message. It must be adapted to the personal profile of the receiver. It must be mainly rational and must be liked.

2. Vehicle
The message vehicle must:
Find the way to the target receiver Arrive safely
Be cost effective
- The choice of the vehicle depends on The kind of message
The profile of the receiver group
- The most common vehicle is the tourist promotion board of the destination.

Other vehicles are:
- Presentation prospect In other cities
In home city
At previous event (before voting for the next venue)
- Direct mail
- Ads in
Magazines of the conference industry
Daily newspapers of a geographical target group Publications of a profession target group.

- Fairs, exhibitions, congress, marts,
- PR (articles in the press),
- Personal calls, letters, phone calls,
- Joint actions with competitors,
- Joint actions with suppliers,
- Through national carrier, travel agents, hotel chains, national tourist offices, embassies, export council
- Local publicity for community awareness
- Education seminars: Ambassadors Officials

Export companies
- Films, videos, slide shows

3. Promotion Material

- By producing promotional material we must consider
  o Size
  o Colors
  o Weight
  o Paper quality
  o Front page
  o Picture quality
  o Print
  o Text
  o Subdivision
  o Clear headline
  o Comprehensive style
  o Correct language (translators)
  o Knowing well also the weakness of the product must be from the beginning – soften probable objections by emphasizing counterpoints.
- Promotional material must appear

Attractive enough to make the receiver start reading Informative enough to make the reader continue

- Impressive enough to make the reader positively.

III. Criteria for the Site Selection to be Considered

- Objective feasibility (facilities, services, prices)
- Conference goals
- Prestige and policy of association or business

- Personal prestige, interests and feelings of the decision maker
- Attractiveness and appeal to participants

INTERNATIONAL SURVEY ON THE FACTORS CHOICE of MEETING SITE

Factor	Associations	Business
Hotels and facilities	86%	70%
Accessibility	52%	62%
Travel Distance for Participants	30%	42%
Transport Costs	25%	38%
Climate	29%	32%
Leisure activities	26%	23%
Excursions and Culture	20%	9%
Image of destination	14%	8%

DIAGRAM Elemental Concerns MICE Product Promotion

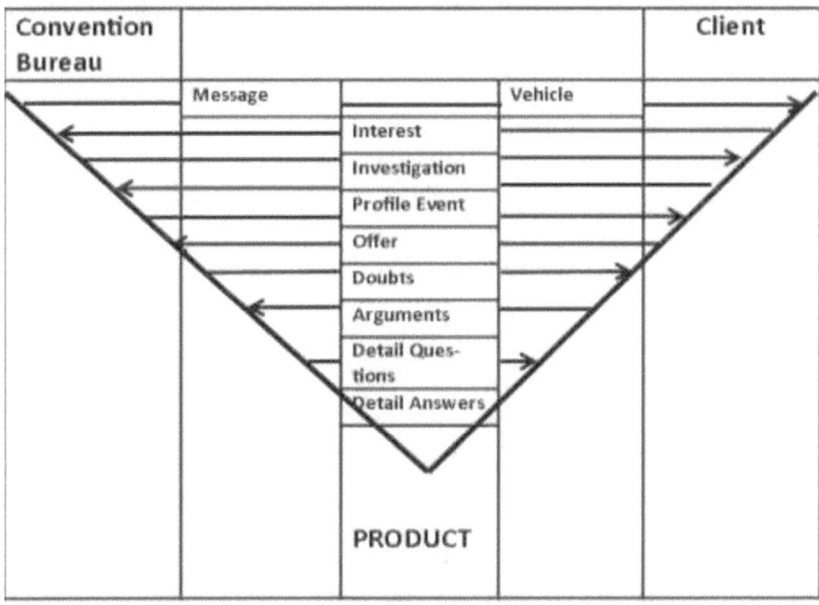

Contracts With Clients And Suppliers

In whatever capacity you work, you will be involved in the supplying or in the placing of orders and contracts:

- The PCO contract with the client
- The PCO contract with the supplier
- The Hotel contracts
- The Exhibition contracts
- The Delegates contracts

I.   The PCO Contract with Client

In order to prepare the contract between the PCO and client, various factors need to be established. These will vary with each contract, but in principal they cover the need to establish:

A.   The areas of responsibility ; the role of agent or principal
B.   The fees and payments
C.   The total anticipated income for cancellation clause

It is necessary to establish whether the PcO is the agent or the principal; simply: as an agent a fee is received by the PCO, and the profits, losses and responsibility rest with the client; i.e., the risk. As a principal, the profits are received by the PCO who also takes full responsibility for any losses or liability.

Fees and payments come from a variety of sources;

1.   Congress administration fees
2.   Exhibition administration fees
3.   Per capita registration fees
4.   Accommodation commission
5.   a/p; pre/post tours, when you are acting as a principal
6.   miscellaneous commission

It is necessary to establish hos and when these payments are going to be made; this will vary with the policy with the policy of individual companies. The ability of the client to pay fees in advance before income form registrations or the exhibition is available must be taken into account and a correct calculation can make a great deal of difference to your proposal.

Cancellation clauses are up to individual companies. Divide the total anticipated income not just the fees into equal monthly installments and that is the charge for cancellation.

II. The Three Types of Contract

1. Formal Contract

A Formal Contract is often a problem and not very constructive, as it is generally drawn up by lawyers who are not involved with conference.

2. Standard Contract

A Standard Contract covering the legal requirements substantiated by the proposal, is the ideal situation, and for this purpose IAPCO created a "standard" contract which meets all the contractual needs of both PCO and client.

When wishing to us the contract to cover both an exhibition and a conference, a few minor adjustments need to be made to the IAPCO contract.

3. Exchange of Letters

An Exchange of Letters is little better than a 'Gentleman's Agreement', and will never stand up in dispute.

III. Contracts with Suppliers

Three types of contract are involved:

1. Formal Contract with Suppliers

In general the only formal contracts relate to the AICC contracts with simultaneous interpreters and the Hire Agreements with certain conference centers and venues.

2. Contract with Regular Suppliers

It is all too easy to handle the regular suppliers with telephone calls, messages left, face to face discussion. Always confirm conversations and meetings in writing when relating to a financial purchase or a service required, thereby instigating a contract.

3.   Contract with New Supplier

A new supplier will probably make some attempt to contract his own position. Avoid this by informing him of your financial arrangements and thus drawing up your contract terms.

All need client authorization as the client is the Principal and this takes two stages, firs, by formal acceptance of minutes of meetings which have outlined action, and secondly, by signing a commitment authorization, a copy of which included.

IV.   Hotel Contracting

Hotel contracting is one of the more tricky aspects of contracting. The main issue here is to determine as accurately as possible your bed requirements. One has of course to sympathize with the hoteliers – too often large blocks of rooms are reserved and then cancelled at the last minute because of overbooking.

Having established the room requirements, the contract must then be examined in detail. While dates and prices are negotiable the small print is fairly standard. The main point to note is what these conditions are and to ensure that the are applied to the administration. At this stage it is a formal written and signed contract.

V.   Exhibition

The entire exhibition prospectus forms a contract in itself. It is divided into three sections: the event information, rules and regulations and the booking form.

The event information provides the exhibitor with all the details of the event. However, this is not a finite part of the contract and details can be amended should the event particulars change.

The booking form is the agreement whereby the exhibitor contracts to take the space. Once signed the exhibitor is committed and absolutely considered under contract.

VI.   Registration

Conference contracts are not as binding; however, the registration and hotel form is the nearest thing to a formal contract between the PCO and the delegate.

In order to attempt any form of binding contract, it is essential that full details relating to the 'Contract' are available within the programme containing the registration form, such as cancellation clauses, and insurance arrangements.

Full contractual details of hotel bookings also need to be contained with the documentation.

V. Defaulting

When something has gone wrong it is necessary to resort to the contract: There are Three Golden Rules;
1. Do not be afraid to use your contract
2. Know your facts
3. Know what is it you want to achieve

Remember, contracts are there to help, take good care with them, and make good use of them when necessary. A contract well drawn up, and well understood, will always provide the required support.

Socials And Protocol

I. Introduction

Why People Attend the Congress

Attending the congress is not only to be informed and updated on new developments in one's field but also for the pleasure of travelling, meeting colleagues from other countries and building or strengthening relationships and friendships.

Why there are Social Activities

The basic objective of the all congresses is the communication and interrelating of participants. Social activities are an excellent way of achieving this while simultaneously giving the participants their share of time to mingle and bond together in a very special gathering that does not happen every day but perhaps to one its once in-a-lifetime. The program must be balanced though.

II. General Information on Protocol and Ceremony

Ceremony - A word of Latin origin meaning the external action or act arranged by law, statute or customs to worship things divine or to honor or revere things providential.

Protocol - From the Latin word "protocollum", or formalities observed through the establish propriety in certain ceremony.

Etiquette – Ceremony of styles, uses and customs to be observed and guarded by royalty and in solemn public acts and, by extension, ceremony for dealing with specific persons or in acts in private life, contrary to uses dictated by intimacy or familiarity.

The terms ceremony, protocol and etiquette are actually synonymous, the difference among them being the period in which one or the other is used.

There are those who do not appreciate the harmony and order provided by ceremony nor its value as a means of interrelating persons in our modern society.

The individuals who are responsible for ceremony are not guided by rigid norms. To the contrary, they are often faced with exceptions to the established rules and must resolve situations on the basis of deduction or analogy.

The existence of multiple international organizations including the United Nations, NATO and the OAS has contributed to the greater use and practice of ceremonial norms since otherwise harmony in the events carried out by these organizations would be lost.

It is not enough to know ceremonial rules. What matters most is to know when and how exceptions can be made since, as mentioned before, these situations arise more often than imagined. And experiences, both good and bad, are valuable and should be taken into account.

Modern times require dynamic and active ceremony; the pomp of the past has been set aside in favor of a more practical approach.

According to an author of the book "Practical Guide to Protocol": Ceremony creates the right atmosphere for holding meetings pacifically The function of protocol is to code the rules governing ceremony, giving
each participant the privileges and immunities he is due
Ceremony and protocol guarantee equal rights and impose the courtesy that should exist among gentlemen.

III.   General Rules for Social Events

Head Table at an Opening Ceremony:

The Head Table must have an odd number of seats: 3, 5, 7, 9. This permits the person who presides at the Opening Ceremony to be seated just in the middle of the table. The seat should be numbered from "0" on, considering the most important place will be at the right of the number "0", the second at his left, and so on:

Right Side: The right side is always the most important one: the

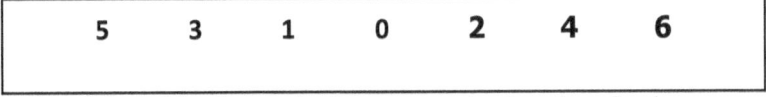

example of the table shown is the same as in the place in the car, etc.

The Flags: To be placed at the back of the stage. If there are flags of all the countries represented at the congress, these will be placed according to the alphabetical order of the countries. Should there be only a flag of the host country it will be placed at the stage, at the left side of its (because it is the right of the persons seated at the head Table)

Speeches at Opening Ceremony: The speeches will be given in the order of importance of the speakers, e.g. the las one will be the person who presides and who will officially inaugurate the congress.

IV. Relationship Between the Program and Budget

The social program must be analyzed taking into account the available economic resources. It is easy to organize social activities when the budget is unlimited. On the other hand, the smaller the budget for this item is, the greater is the challenge for the PCO, who must use all of its creative ability.

Statistics show that no more than 25% of the total budget should be applied to this item.

According to the type of congress or association organizing entity, the social activities can be:

o   Covered entirely by the fee for the congress
o   Partially covered by the fee; that is, some can be included and others can be optional
o   Entirely optional

Another alternative for social activities is to have "sponsors".

The most recent trends point to use of the second choice, that is, that not all social events be included in the fee for the congress.

In the first case in which all social events are included in the congress fee, certain statistics show that a great number of the participants, as well as special guests and the press attend the opening cocktail party while a much smaller number attends

 the closing banquet. When making up the budget for the social events, this fact must be kept in mind. If, for example, the participant must pay for the closing banquet, the PCO has a clear idea ahead of time of the number to plan for at that event. In addition, it will create a better impression with the Organizing Committee since it will allow the Committee to save money as well as avoid empty tables in the room chosen which always leaves the impression of poor or bad organization.

V. Basic Social Program
General

When putting together the social program of a congress, the following must be kept in mind:
- Location of congress and available space
and profile of participants, taking into account their socio-economic level
- Study of the congress' traditions
- Budget.

It should be pointed out that the study of the congress's traditions is used only as a reference point. It is believed that there is often nothing better than breaking the traditions since that can bring to the congress a distinctive quality which may well be carried on. It also allows the advantages and characteristics of each country to be taken into account.

For example, it may be a tradition to have a concert of classical music at the opening ceremony of a certain congress. If this congress is held in Mexico, however, a "mariachi" concert would be more fun and appropriate and in Buenos Aires, a tango concert.

In addition, an analysis of the location is essential since it must not only be attractive and appealing but must also be comfortable and have certain basic installations. It is wonderful, unique experience to go to a gala dinner at a medieval palace but, if may be an unpleasant experience if the palace has few bathrooms and one has to wait in line for "15 minutes" to relieve his discomfort.

Examples of the Basic Social Programs for a Five Day Congress in which included is the Program for Accompanying persons and Optional Events.

Day 01
2:00 - 6:00 pmRegistration of participants and accompanying persons
5:00 - 6:30 pmOpening Ceremony
6:30 - 8:00 pmWelcome Cocktail Party (Included in the registration fee; open to all participants and accompanying persons)

Day 02 Delegates   Accompanying Persons

09:00 – 10:30 am	Working Session	Morning; City Tour
10:30 – 11:00 am	Coffee Break
11:00 – 12:30 nn	Working Sessions
12:30 - 2:00 pm	Lunch
2:00 - 4:00 pm	Working Sessions	Afternoon: a. Museum Tour or
4:00 - 4:30 pm	Coffee Break b. Handicrafts Tour
4:30 - 6:00 pm	Working Sessions
8:00 - 8:00 pm	Typical Local Evening
Buffet Dinner or Cocktail (Included in the Registration Fee)

Day 03
09:00 - 10:30 am	Working Sessions	Full-day Tour 10:30 - 11:00 am	Coffee Break
11:00 - 12:30 nn	Working Sessions
12:30 - 2:00 pm	Lunch
2:00 - 4:00 pm Working Sessions
4:00 - 4:30 pm Coffee Break
4:30 - 6:30 pm Working Sessions EVENING FREE

Day 04
9:00 - 10:30 am Working Sessions	Morning:

10:30 - 11:00 am	Coffee Break a. Organized shopping, or
11:00 - 12:30 nn	Working Sessions b. Half-day tour
12:00 - 2:00 pm	Lunch
2:00 - 4:00 pm	Working Sessions
4:00 - 4:30 pm	Coffee Break Afternoon: FREE
4:00 - 6:00 pm	Working Sessions
8:00 pm	Closing Dinner-Dance
(Included in registration fee or optional)

Day 05
9:00 - 10:30 am Working Sessions	FREE 10:30 - 11:00 am	Coffee Break
11:30 - 12:00 am	Working Session
12:00 - 12:30 nn	Closing Ceremony

Analysis of the Program

An analysis of this program shows that:
- It is important to offer a night with typical entertainment from the seat country
- Full-day tours for accompanying persons should coincide with the day the night is free
- The afternoon of the Closing Dinner-Dance has been left free for the accompanying persons to go shopping, go to the beauty shop or rest.
- The fifth day ends at noon because many participants go on tours after the congress.
- There is one night free for participants to make plans with friends or to rest.
- The entire program for accompanying persons is included in the congress because it is self-financing.

VI.   Opening Ceremony

This is very important event since it determines the participants first impression of the organization of the congress.

It is recommended to hold the opening ceremony in the same place where the scientific session will take place for reasons of space and cost. When choosing the location, it is important to remember that 95% of the participants will attend as well as special guests and the press.

Likewise, the following points should be taken into account:

1. Entertainment to be offered: symphony, chorus, audiovisual, folk dances, etc.;
2. Signs and decoration of the room: for example, a sign with the congress:
3. Logo, flower arrangements, flags of participating countries, etc.;
4. Equipment needed   such as projectors, screens, video equipment, simultaneous interpretations, etc.;
5. Lighting;

6. Printed material such as invitations, programs for the opening ceremony which can be included in the total program or printed separately, floor plans to seat participants, etc.;
7. Transportation of delegates to the event;
8. Analysis of staging and programming of events.

Regarding the protocol for this ceremony, the following should be noted:

1. Special invitations to authorities: once the list of guests is made up, in accordance with the protocol and style of each country, the invitations will be mailed. Once a response is received, it is advisable to reconfirm the attendance of the main authorities 48 hours before, and notify guests of their assigned seats.;
2. Reserved areas: the room should be divided with colors or signs to make it easier for delegates to find their set. This also allows for sections for special guests, diplomats, the press, etc. to be defined.
3. VIP room and stage: due to the great flow of people on the first day, VIP's to be seated in the first row or on the stage should be informed that they are not join ahead of time in special room where introductions will be made before going into the main room where the ceremony will be held. This way the main room can be opened 30 minutes before the ceremony and delegates are seated before the authorities enter.
4. Regarding the stage, it is traditional to use a head table on the stage. Day by day this is giving way around the world since it is becoming more and more common to present some type of show.

VII.   Opening Cocktail

This event normally follows the opening ceremony and can take place at the same location or at some place nearby.

It should not go on for over 3 hours and should be held in a place big enough for delegates to mingle freely since this is their first informal contact.

The number of people should be taken into account when contracting the service. For it to be really good, there should be a bar for every 250 persons and 10 meters of narrow buffet tables for every 200 persons. Both should be refurbished constantly.

As much as possible, speeches should be avoided while if music is desired, it should be very soft. It is recommended that the President of the Congress greet the guests at the door.

VIII. Typical Local Evening

An event of 3-4 hours, this is the evening of local traditions, music, dances and folklore. The environment and location should be in keeping with those traditions and the event to take place.

As a consequence of its duration and its inherent informality, it is advisable to have a meal which allows people to choose their own seating at the tables. The entertainment should not last too long. On the other hand, some comments about the history and traditions of the country should be made.

OPTION: BALLET
This event should not last more than 2 or 3 hours. A glass of champagne is normally served during the intermission or at the end.

IX. Free Night

In all congresses there is a stand for the official travel agency which should make available optional tours and outings such as dinner shows, theaters, discotheques, etc. to interested participants at corresponding cost.

In addition, small dinners can be organized in local homes or cocktail parties at the embassies of the participating delegations.

X. Closing Dinner

This event should not last more than 3 or more hours. An extremely important occasion, it closes the congress and is the last social contact among participants until the next congress.

The planning of the room is important since it must hold tables, a dance floor and a stage in case there is an orchestra or a show in addition to the more traditional disc jockey. The orchestra and disk jockey should be able to play both local and light international music so that participants are entertained and can dance.

Round table for 10 to 12 persons allow people to see each other and talk among themselves.

To make the entrance and seating more fluid, delegates should be given the opportunity to select their tables. To this end, 2 days before a floor plan with the tables numbered will be exhibited and participants may sign up for the tables. This will also avoid confusion.

Protocol should not be forgotten and some centrally located tables should be reserved for congress officials.

Entrance to the room should be marked in such a way as to help delegates to find their tables.

XI. Others

A. Working Lunches

The decisions to hold working lunches depends on certain variables which must be taken into account. These include the availability of space, the proximity of restaurants, the interest of participants in such events and the participation estimated.

These lunches can be included in the general fee or they can be optional. Nowadays the trend is towards light.

B. Coffee Breaks

Coffee breaks are normally included in the congress fee since they can be handled as food-tasting events or have sponsors. Lasting ½ an hour, there should be one in the morning and one in the afternoon. The place should be planned carefully snce it has to be big enough to allow delegates to circulate freely. In the case of parallel sessions held in rooms which do not open onto the same central hall, it is advisable to locate the coffee service outside each room. When there is a simultaneous commercial exhibition, it normally contains an area where food-tasting takes place or coffee is served. This usually attracts large numbers of people and satisfies the demands of exhibitors whose primary interest is the visit of delegates to the exhibition area.

C. Programs for Accompanying Persons

All accompanying persons attend the social program., aside from this, a special program should be organized for them for those hours that their spouses are in the scientific sessions.

If space and budget allow, it is advisable to have a "hospitality suite" for information relaxing or as a meeting place.
When making this program, places and activities must not overlap with   the general social program.
The fee for accompanying persons includes both this special program and the congress's social program. Optional tours or events may also be included.

D. Transportation

The planning nd organization of this item varies according to the location of the congress in relation to the hotels and the location of the social events. It also depends on the efficiency and safety of the local public transportation. If the congress is held far from the hotels where delegates are staying, not only must transportation for social events be supplied but there must be a "shuttle-service" to the sessions as well.

In cities where the location of the congress is relatively close to the hotels and public transportation is efficient, certain services can be overlooked.

Nowadays, there are few cities in the world where bus service for evening events is not essential since the streets are not particularly safe even when the distance is not great.

Once the decision to supply transportation is made, it is important to notify delegates through posters displayed in the hotels and congress, including the pick-up points for the service.
When there are few passengers in a hotel, pick-up points strategically located to serve several hotels can be set.

E. Invitations – Vouchers

The social program with the accompanying persons program is one of the elements in the decision to participate in a congress. A PCO must therefore try t be as detailed as possible in the description of different events in the invitation program. As it is a preliminary program, it is subject to change. There is one thing that must never change: the first appointment time and place, such as registration and opening ceremony. It would be difficult to advise the registrants of last minute arrivals or a change in location or scheduling.

All the optional events have been prepaid and also guaranteed, both financially and numerically. The tickets for these activities are delivered to participants when they check in at the registration desk. Of course, you must provide some additional tickets for these events for sale during the congress, for new registrants and for those already registered participants who change their minds at the last minute.

For the events included in the registration fee, there are two possible alternatives:
- ✓ Deliver the invitations to all registered participants entitled to them.
- ✓ Deliver only the coupons or vouchers which the participants must exchange for invitations or tickets at the social program desk.
- ✓ This second system enables one to keep the situation under control and avoid useless expense in catering and transportation.

Information Voucher Should Contain
- ✓ Who extends the invitation
- ✓ Date
- ✓ Location and address
- ✓ Map if necessary
- ✓ Cost, if any
- ✓ In the case where there is a cost, number and stub
- ✓ R.S.V.P.
- ✓ Color, if there are seating areas
- ✓ Meeting place if there is transportation

Standard Rules And Regulations On Exhibits
for
PROFESSIONAL CONGRESS ORGANIZER

I. Definition

In these Regulations the term 'Exhibition' in all cases refers to the aforesaid Trade and Exhibition being held in conjunction with the aforesaid conference. The term 'Exhibitor' includes any person, firm, company or corporation and its employees and agents to whom space(s) has been allocated for the purpose of exhibiting at the Exhibition. The term 'Organizers' means (Name of PCO) on behalf of the Organizing Committee. The term 'Premises' refers to those portions of the stated venue licensed to the Organizers.

II. Installation and Removal of Exhibits

Exhibitors will be advised of when they may commence fitting up and arrangement of exhibits. Exhibitors are prohibited from commencing such fitting up until the time nominated to them.

III. Stand Construction and Services

The Organizers will appoint official contractors for all construction, all electrical work and all furniture supplies. No other contractors will be permitted to undertake any of the work.

IV. Application

The Organizers reserve the right to refuse any application or prohibit any exhibit without assigning any reason for such refusal or prohibition.

An exhibitor may not, except by express written permission of the Organizers, display directly or indirectly, advertise or give credits to any products other than his own or his named principal's. The display of acknowledgement or credit indicating membership or organizations or Trade Associations is not allowed except by express written permission of the Organizers. The Organizers reserve the right to have masked or removed from the Premises any product or sign violating the regulation.

V.   Cancellation

An Exhibitor cancelling or reducing his stand space after his application has been accepted by the Organizers is liable for the total charge of the booking unless the stand space can be relet. In the event of an application for stand space being refused by the Organizers previous deposits will be returned to the applicant in full.

VI.   Bankruptcy and Liquidation

In the event of Exhibitor becoming bankrupt or entering into liquidation (other than voluntary liquidation for the purpose of amalgamation or reconstruction) or having Receiver appointed, the contract with the such an Exhibitor will terminate forthwith, the allotment of stand space will be cancelled.

VII.   Occupation of Stand Space

The Exhibitor, his servants, agents, employees and contractors may enter the building at a time which will be nominated to them for the purpose of stand dressing and fitting. In the event of an Exhibitor falling to take possession of his stand the Organizers, have the right to re-allocate the stand and all monies paid shall be forfeit.

All exhibits, displays, stand fittings and materials must be removed from the Premises by the time and date stated by the Organizers. Removal of exhibits and dismantling may not commence until after the official closing time unless prior approval has been obtained from the Organizers.

VIII. Obstruction of Gangways and Open Spaces

Exhibitors will not be allowed to display exhibits in such a manner as to obstruct the light or impede or project over gangways or affect the displays of neighboring exhibitors. Gangways must at all times be kept clear and free for passage. Any Exhibitor who continues to cause obstruction or nuisance after notice has been given will be liable to have his stand closed by the Organizers.at the Exhibitors expense and risk.

IX. Trade Union and Labor

All stand fitting, construction or display work should be carried out by members of the appropriate Trade Unions recognized by the Exhibitions Industry at the rates of pay and overtime and conditions in accordance with the Terms of the Working Rules Agreement currently in force.

X. Electrical Requirements

Full lighting and power services will be available to the Exhibitor through the official electrical contractor. A schedule of these services will be available once application has been made. Exhibitors may provide their own electrical fittings where such fittings are in the form of made up units, showcases and/or signs complete and ready for connection to the main supply.

XI. Dangerous Materials and Exhibits

The Exhibitor must conform to the conditions concerning explosives and dangerous combustible materials as laid down by the appropriate authority and all other statutory bodies. Any material or exhibit not approved by the appropriate authority or the Organizers must be removed from the building.

XII. Fire Precautions

In accordance with requirement of the appropriate authority, all material used in construction work display materials etc. must be effectively fire-proofed or made of non-flammable materials in accordance with the standards of every appropriate authority. Drapes and curtains must be at least 150mm (6") clear from the floor. Fire extinguishers will be provided by the Organizers in the display areas and placed as regulations require. The Exhibitors must comply with any reasonable instructions given by the appropriate authority or the Organizers to avoid the risk of fire.

XIII. Damage to the Premises

No nails, screws or other fixtures may be driven into any part of the Premises including floors. Nor may any part of the Premises be damaged or disfigured in any way. Should any such damage occur, the Exhibitor responsible will be invoiced for any reparation charges incurred.

XIV. Cleaning
The Organizers will arrange for the daily cleaning of the aisles outside Exhibition open hours.

XV. Security Services
The Organizers will arrange a site security service during the period of the Exhibition but will accept no liability for loss or damage.

XVI. Storage
There are no storage facilities available within Exhibition area and Exhibitors are advised to make their own arrangements for removal and storage of packing cases etc. Under no circumstances may packing materials of any kind be left in the aisles or on the stands.

XVII. Freight and Transport
The Organizers will appoint official forwarding agents for temporary importation of goods for the Exhibition. Overseas Exhibitors wishing to bring in goods or materials for temporary importation MUST contact the Organizers for details of the official contractor and new regulations which apply.

XVIII. Liability
While the Organizers will endeavor to protect exhibition property while on display at the Exhibition, it must be clearly understood that the management of the Premises, the Organizing Committee and the Organizers cannot accept liability for any loss or damage sustained or occasioned from any cause whatsoever.

Exhibitors will be responsible for all the damage to property and for any loss or injury caused by them or their agents or employees and will indemnify the Organizers against all claims and expenses arising therefrom.

In the event of it being necessary for any reason whatsoever for the Exhibition to be abandoned, postponed or altered in any way in whole or in part, or if the Organizers find it necessary to change the dates of the Exhibition, the Organizers shall not be liable for any expenditure, damage or loss incurred in connection with the Exhibition. The Organizers shall further not be liable for any loss which the Exhibition or exhibition contractors may incur owing to the intervention of any authority which prevents or restricts the use of the Premises or any part thereof in any manger whatsoever.

XIX.   Insurance
Exhibitors are reminded of the need to consult their Insurance Company or Insurance Brokers to cover themselves fully against all risks at the Exhibition. Particular attention is drawn to the need for the following:
- ✓ Abandonment Insurance. Exhibitors will have seen from paragraph 18 above that the organizers are not obliged to return any monies paid for space in the event of cancellation or restriction of Exhibition.
- ✓ Stands, Fixtures and Similar Insurance. All Risks on loss or damage to Exhibitor's property, fixtures, fittings and all other property of a similar nature such as personal effect of directors, principals and employees while on the Premises and transit risks from the Exhibitor's premises to the Exhibition and return.
- ✓ Public Liability. Liability to the public may arise out of the Exhibitor's activities and should be covered by insurance.
- ✓ Insurance should be effected with minimum delay.

XX.   General Conditions
The Organizers are responsible for the control of the Exhibition area. Exhibitors are responsible for the control and supervision of their own stands. The decision of the Organizers is final and decisive on any question not covered in the foregoing regulations.

Exhibitors must comply in all respects with the requirement of every appropriate authority, with the Terms of Agreement by which the Organizers may occupy the Premises and with the policies of insurance effected by the Organizers. Copies of the Agreements and policies of insurance may be inspected at the Exhibition Office 30 days prior to the opening of the Exhibition.

The Role Of Carrier/Transport
(Air, Land, Sea)

I. Definition of Terms & Phrases Commonly Used

Chartered Carrier – refers to any mode of transport that operates on specially contracted service on specific date and time between the point of origin and destination that is dictated by the charterer.

Carrier – refers to any type of transport i.e., air, land and sea duly licensed and permitted to operate on both regular basis or by charter in order to transport the traveling public and goods within a specific franchise route as defined it its Certificate of Public Convenience issued by the concerned authorities of its home port.

Domestic Carrier – refers to any type or mode of transport which license to operate is with specific areas within a certain country. It is not allowed to transport passengers and goods from its country home port to the other.

Franchise Route – refers to the places within which the carrier is licensed to operate from a definite point of origin and destination defined in a Certificate of Public Convenience (CPC).

International Carrier – refers to any mode of transport that is licensed to operate between two or more countries as its point of origin and destination.

Regular Carrier – refers to any mode of transport that operates and catering to both paying passenger and cargo within its franchise route on specific schedule of departure from its point of origin to point of destination. This is likewise normally referred to as Public Utility Transport;

Official Carrier – refers to any mode of transport either regular or chartered that is under contract to transport passenger and cargo for a specific purpose, particularly on packaged tour programs, MICE (Meetings, Incentives, Conventions and Exhibits) or any other special events.

Public Transport – refers to any mode of transport duly licensed to cater and carry paying passengers or travelling public in its franchised routes, also known as Regular Carrier.

Tourist Transport – refers to any mode of transport duly licensed exclusively to carry and transport tourists to and from any tourist attractions and destinations.

II. Introduction

Carrier or the transport system serves as the front-line component among the duly organized service systems that functions as the major artery distributing energies to, and ignites as it keeps the flame of other tourism components burning. By the term burning, it means functional, healthy and active. Carrier/Transport System is the source of life for any tourist destination. It is the very ultimate means that keep tourists mobile to achieve their objective in reaching places of touristic value-their dreamed destination. Without a duly organized carrier or transport system, tourism is a myth.

In the current practice, carrier of the transport system, particularly the airline is always the most active and major contributor in promoting places with tourist attractions to eventually become a destination.

III. The Role of Carriers/Transport System in Tourism Related Activities

Mobility is the keyword that makes the carrier/transport system an indispensable component of any tourism related activity. Tourism entails movement of people, particularly tourists from their homes to places they wish to, or with the necessity for them to visit for rest, recreation, holiday and business or professional concerns. Carrier/Transport system also is very much vital for the movement/delivery of different kinds of goods and supplies in the form of cargoes that are needed as they are required for an organized and systematic delivery of tourism products and services to the both the tourists and residence of that place.

IV. Modes of Carrier/Transport System

Carrier/Transport Systems are classified into the following;

A. Stand-Alone Carrier/Transport System – is any mode of carrier/transport (air, sea, land or air) operating only by its own without any other mode complementing its service to passenger and cargo in their point of origin, in- between to their final destination. This mode of transport system is classified into:
  1. Domestic/Inter–Island is the type of carrier/transport with license to operate only within its franchise rout in the territorial limits of the country where it is registered.
  2. Regional/Continental is the type of carrier/transport with license to operate within its franchise route in the region of a certain continent.
  3. Intercontinental/International is the type of carrier/transport licensed to operate within its franchise route between international ports of countries of two or more continents.

B. Intermodal – is system of two or more modes both land-sea or air-land-sea transport in unified service system catering to passenger and cargo from point of origin to point of final destination. The example of this system is the Ro-Ro or Roll-On/Roll-Off a combination of land-sea-land. This system is normally operating in archipelagic countries with different islands within its territorial jurisdiction where passengers and cargo are traveling from their point of origin first by land, then then the land transport is loaded or rolled on to the sea transport (vessel/ferry) to the next island where the land transport are disembarked or rolled-off the port to continue its travel towards their final destination. This transport system is normally covered with unified fare system, meaning fares are paid by passengers in one time with the major carrier from point of origin.

V. The Necessity of Official Carrier in MICE and Tourism Activities

In any tourism related activity either for domestic or international purpose designating an official carrier for such an activity is necessary as it is most vital for its success. The official carrier can certainly benefit the tourism product/service providers, e.g., travel agents/tour operators, and professional congress organizers as well as all the service users (tourists) and participants in the activity.

VI. The Benefits
In General Terms

For the Principal
The designation or appointment of an official carrier particularly a national airline or flag-carrier has the best benefits for international tourism requirement.

A. The national carrier has a strong name in its home country, and its appointment or designation simply means all gains for being associated with such company, because:
B. They know the local circumstances
C. They have the local connections, influence and buying power
D. Airlines have their own worldwide communications network that is made available to serve the needs of the program.
E. Airlines may easily share the cost of promotion and marketing for the either the international tour package, convention, exhibits or any other special events that could easily drum-up interest of all targeted market segments.
F. The nominated air carrier is there to extend assistance with setting up a presentation as a "candidate" for the transportation of material and possibly participants.
G. For Meetings, Incentives, Conventions and Exhibits organizers, airline is ready to assist in the following:

1) Transportation needs (air, land) for site inspection arrangements.
2) Transportation of conference papers to destination and back.
3) Bulk transportation of congress literature.
4) As local representative on behalf of the congress, convention or exhibits Organizers.
5) Assistance to local committee in marketing and promotion.
6) Together with the local organization and travel agent, carry out reasonable sales and marketing campaign.
7) Worldwide the same partner with its own communications and internal mail network.

For the Participant/Passenger
1. Use the airline as the local expert and information office about the congress destination.
2. Possibility of group flights to the congress.
3. Through the involvement of the airline in mailings etc., their own organization (International Association) has lower costs. This may result in lower congress fees.
4. Since its own association has a working agreement with the airline, the participant may confidently use and rely on the carriers services.

The Business Deal
The airline may provide:
1. Assistance at destination airports upon arrival and departure, especially for groups:
2. Arrival handling (baggage handling, customs and transfer assistance).
3. Convention Desk (message relay, etc.).
4. Directional signals and Welcome Signs.
. Arrival information (access to reservation computer).
6. Departure (baggage check-in, seat assignments, departure formalities.
7. Possibility of an airline ticket office (with computerized reservation system) at the conference center.
8. To put at the airline's disposal names of already registered or potential participants, membership rosters, address material, etc.
9. Advertisements in advance and main programs, call-for-papers.
10. Statistics on participants (how did they travel, to/from the congress country of origin).
11. Nomination as Official Carrier and mentioning as such in all pertaining congress-literature.

VII. Steps to Nominate an Airline as "Official Carrier"
A simple appointment won't do; It must be preceded an in-depth discussion and possibility by a contract agreement or simply term of reference. Therefore, it is a must for MICE organizer to:

- ✓ Make a list of the services needed from the airline;
- ✓ List of Information and Actions that can be offered to the airline as a compensation;
- ✓ Approach the airline and ask to be put in contract with the "MICE Manager" or "ICCA contact person" (usually to be found in an airline office).
- ✓ Another useful contact is the national or local tourist board of the country concerned.
- ✓ Do all the above at the earliest possible moment. The first contact should be before the idea about is presented to an international audience.

VIII. Sample of Barter Agreement

BARTER AGREEMENT
BARTER AGREEMENT
Between:
-and-
_____

_____

We,_____
_____(Contractor/Principal) willperform for_____
_____Air
the following services, to be completed on or before_____;

1) Nomination of_____Air as Official Carrier for (Name ofEvent);
2) Supply the airline with the statistical data as the travel of participants to/from thecongress; country of origin statistics;
3) Put at the carriers disposal one free ad (size A4) in a Call-for-Papers, the Pre andFinal Programs.

As a remuneration for the above services,
_____
_____
air will issuea Barter Credit for the equivalent of
_____
(currency andamount);
Such credit shall be evidenced by special forms exchangeable for flight tickets, subject to the conditions to be found on the reverse side of this agreement.
This Barter Credit shall be the sole remuneration for all services to be rendered hereunder, including casts and expenses and similar items and the partner
, .

Mice Marketing Strategies

I. Data Gathering of Facts and Figures on:

How and Why People Come to Meetings
Information gathered, shall serve as the concrete basis for a PCO start the first step on the planning of a marketing activity for a product. All the information shall be the guiding parameter of the strategies that the PCO shall employ on the process of selling its MICE products and services.

II. Sources of Information
It is an established fact that 35% of people come to meetings because of mail publicity which they have personally received. Previous meetings are the second most important source of information – 27% of people rely on friends and co-workers to give them information about meetings. This information caused the change of strategy completely, and develop mechanisms to reach people, e.g. the cohort form.

Professional Journals and posters together account for 15% of people, which makes these less important sources of information than the preceding.

III. When Decision is Reached
Studies have shown that 73% of the time, the decision to attend an international meeting is made 6 months to 1 year prior to the meeting. This helps the committee to develop strategies to induce the delegate to attend.

In order to find out if there is a significant difference between the decision time for, say Canadian and that for people of other countries, the responses were broken down and discovered that Canadians will make the decision closer to the date of the meeting than will delegates from other countries.

70% of those from countries other than Canada will make the decision between 6 months and 1 year prior to the meeting.

IV.   Principal Reason for Attending
Site: Because Montreal is such an appealing city, "site" is selected by 26% of delegates as the main reason for attending. It is indeed curious to understand how many of those considered access important and how many considered the touristic appeal of Montreal as their principal reason for deciding to attend the meeting.

Participant: 25% of the delegates attend because they are actually presenting a paper. This poses a special challenge; it is encouraged to accept as many papers as possible each paper represents a delegate.
Program: 23% of the delegates are attracted by the program.
"Always Attend: 16% of delegates fall into this category, which means that special attention should be given to prioritizing carefully the lists of delegates from other meetings.
Other Reasons: 10% cited other reasons, such as job search or interviews.

V.   Duration of Stay
The collective results of surveys conducted by tourism departments on the length of stay of the delegates show that 35% stay for the duration of the meeting and a surprising 35% again stay 1-3 days longer than the meeting.

VI.   Accompanying Persons
67% of delegates do not bring accompanying persons. 25% bring one person and 8% two or more.

VII.   Marketing Options

A.   Direct Mail
To prepare for your direct mailing campaign, a mailing list has to be developed.
- ✓ As many names and mailing lists as possible of people in the field are collected;
- ✓ A list of lists is created;

- ✓ A Master Computer List is prepared with source codes for each list, so that it is possible to see where each name came from;
- ✓ A Master Alphabetical List is then prepared and duplicates are removed. The two primary tools used in direct mail include the 1st Announcement and Registration package and call for papers.
- ✓ The 1st Announcement is designed to be a very simple piece, stating date, time, place, theme and – a very important – containing two reply cards.

B. Previous Conference

It is imperative to have a major previous presence at previous conferences in the field, i.e., if you are running the 4th International Conference on X, it is important to have a significant representation at the 3rd. Model of display – if the conference will agree to give the space distribute the 1st announcement.

C. Journals

- There are two ways of using journals to market a meeting:
- Include a notice in the list of coming events – this is free;
- A paid advertisement

D. Newsletters and Press Releases

Press releases about the meeting can be sent to world media in the field and to specialized newsletters in various countries.

E. Posters

Posters can be created, publicizing the meeting. The PCO must make certain that these posters are placed in display areas where potential delegates can see them.

F. Congress Calendars

Notices about the meeting should be sent to all World Congress Calendars in sufficient time to be sure they are published in the next issue.

G. Official Carriers and Travel Agents

A bulk supply of notices is sent to official carriers and all travel agents affiliated with the conference.

H. Government Offices of Tourism
These offices must receive appropriate notices.

I. Speaker's Aid Kit
This is a slide show with script, which is prepared for the client to take to meetings in the field. It gives an update on the meeting, names of speakers who have agreed to present work, etc.

J. Embassies and Consulates
These should be contacted once the speakers have been selected, so that they can use their channels to promote the meeting.

K. Result Analysis
It is imperative for the strategic planners to analyze results of all communications.

Languages, Interpretation And Translation A Necessity In International Congress

I. Introduction

It is of common knowledge that while English is considered the universal language, not all professionals and business persons worldwide may know how to speak and understand English. This is so, because some other countries do not use English as a medium of instructions in schools and thus in communications for the local practice of their profession, conduct of their business or exercise of their vocation.

Thus, in events where participants expected to participate are of different nationalities, it is an acknowledged tradition that documents covering the minutes of official proceedings in working sessions require translations and interpretations in different languages for the full understanding and comprehension of participants. Interpretation and translations are of paramount concern to any international gathering to encourage more participants of whatever nationality to attend knowing that they are assured to easily understand the proceedings during the working sessions though they may not be adept in the official language of the conference that is normally in English. In this case, they are highly confident to get their money's worth in attending an international event.

II. Factors in the Choice of Language

The decisive factors in the choice of languages used at an international congress are the following:

o Participation from different language areas;
o Regulations of the Association;
o Politics;
o Prestige; and,
o Finance.

III. Translation and Interpretation Meaning and Types

Interpretation – verbal reproduction to another language.
Translation – refers to written work

Types of Interpretation:

Consecutive: the interpreter takes notes and interprets when the speaker has finished. This system is precise, but slow.
Simultaneous: interpreters work in soundproof booths, while the speaker is talking., with the help of electronic equipment.
Whispered: the interpreter whispers the interpretation (simultaneously) to one or two participants.

IV. Technical Support

The International Standardization Organization (ISO) has established standards with the minimum requirements for permanent interpreters' booths and equipment (ISO/DIS 2603-1983) and for portable booths (ISO/DIS 4043)

Simultaneously interpretation equipment can be permanently installed or portable; it can be wired or wireless.
The following must be determined before renting simultaneous interpretation equipment:

- ✓ Is the equipment up-to-date, practical, and, above all, dependable? Are the receiving sets and earphones comfortable for the delegates?
- ✓ Is the reception free from inter-channel interference (cross-talk) or can the other channels be heard as back-ground noise?
- ✓ Is the wireless receiver sufficiently powerful to be received in any position it is held? The reception maybe too weak in certain areas in the meeting hall.
- ✓ Is the transmitter powerful enough to prevent outside noise from interfering with the reception?
- ✓ Is the quality of the sound satisfactory for the interpreters?
- ✓ Are the booths for the interpreters in accordance with the minimum requirements of the International Standardization Organization

(ISO)? Are they for example, sufficiently soundproof, air-conditioned, and illuminated?
- ✓ If the discussions are confidential, can the transmission be received outside the meeting room?
- ✓ Is the rental company reliable? Are the technicians experienced in international meetings and will they provide first class service for the meeting organizers, the delegates, and the interpreters?
- ✓ Is the meeting room available sufficiently in advance to allow for the installation and testing of the equipment?

V.   Interpreters

Interpreters must be experienced and thoroughly professional.

The International Association of Professional Conference Interpreters (AICC), which is the association which groups he majority of the professional conference interpreters, has set regulations for minimum size of teams, minimum rates and regulations for the salary, per diem, travel expenses, contracts, etc.

For meetings with more than two working languages and/or more than two concurrent meetings with simultaneous interpretation, it is advisable to engage a coordinating interpreter to recruit, coordinate and supervise the team.

The interpreters must receive sufficient documentation in advance (abstracts, manuscripts, terminology, etc.) in order to be able to prepare their work. A briefing session or a briefing day befoe the Congress is most useful and necessary.

VI.   Instructions

The speakers must be instructed in advance about the interpretation service and advised of the best way to present their papers (maximum 100 words per minute) for the most accurate interpretation.

Poor interpretation due to unsatisfactory equipment, unqualified interpreters or technicians may be worse than no interpretation at all.

VII.   Translation

Decisions must be made regarding the translation of:Administrative documents (Preliminary and Final Programs, Registration Forms, etc.).
Scientific documentation (Abstracts, papers, proceedings).
The cost of translation and printing is a major factor and may influence the number of printed languages.

VIII. Secretariat

The Congress Secretariat (registration, information desk, etc.) and other services (bank, post office, restaurants, etc.) should be staffed by competent people who are proficient in the principal languages of the congress.

In working conferences, a large staff of multilingual verbatim reporters, minute writers, secretaries, typists, messengers, and distribution clerks are often required.

International Organizations
Standard Questionnaire For Professional Congress Organizers (PCOs)
Concerning Conditions Available For World Congress

Preamble

The implementation of an Annual World Dental Congress is a major undertaking which requires many facilities, made available by many different bodies who must cooperate correctly with the local organizing committee and the FDI. Many other organizers of congresses and trade fairs also tend to compare for the same facilities. It is therefore becoming increasingly necessary and in the interest of all parties concerned to confirm what facilities will be available as early as possible and definitely prior to the FDI acceptance of the invitation. The questions below serve the above purposes. Please take care to give us complete and correct answer as possible in each case. The answers will be presented to the finance committee and Council of the FDI and taken as a binding confirmation that your Association guarantees the facilities offered in accordance with your replies.

1. Proposed Venue:

	YES	NO
2. Government attitude and regulations		
Has the Health Authorities (equivalent) expressed support for the congress?	( )	( )
-Do restrictions exist for the entry of participants fromAny country beyond the routine granting of visas for the congress period?	( )	( )
-Are there any restrictions on the transfer of funds abroad, such as FDI Revenue in the form of subscriptions or share of enrolment fees?	( )	( )

If your answer to 2.2. or 2.3. is yeas, what restrictions apply

3. Accommodation Requirements:

A large hall with stage seating 4,000 – 5,000 or more people?	( )	( )
A large room seating 1,000 – 2,000 people	( )	( )

	YES	NO
3.1. A room seating 500 people?	( )	( )
Which of the halls have permanent equipment for simultaneous interpretation?	( )	( )

Please specify number of languages per hall
Three room seating 500 people	( )	( )
Additional meeting rooms suitable for table clinics?	( )	( )

Two office for President and President-Elect and six roomsprovidingTwo workplaces each for office purposes	( )	( )

Six larger rooms for (1) delegates files and information
2 Duplication and collation of documents
(3) Editor's briefings
(4) Commission officers
(5) Interpreters' briefing
(6) Scientific Program Committee   ( ) ( )

An area for trade exhibition providing a minimum
net space available for letting 5,000 square meters   ( ) ( )

3.10 If your answer to any of the above question is negative, please explain below what alternative arrangements, if any, you propose. Please refer to the relevant numbers above:

_____

_____

N.B. Please enclose plans and leaflets illustrating the facilities offered under Section 3.

4. Hotel Accommodation:

Please list the number of hotel rooms available at the congress venue in each category
Deluxe (5 Star)
First Class (4 Star)
Second Class (3 Star)
Tourist Class (2 Star)

What hotel(s), guaranteeing at least 300 rooms (Single and Double) and some suites for Congress do you propose as headquarters hotel(s)?
*Please enclose brochure(s) and current rate cards.

4.3. What percentage discount off the normal rack rate will the hotels grant to congress Participants?

4.4. What percentage do the hotels grant to travel agents which regularly bring them groups?

4.5. The FDI requests two complimentary suites and 35 ordinary hotel rooms for the period

4.6. Congress to be provided by the organizing committee, which may negotiate for the Hotels to absorb part of/or total cost.

    YES   NO

4.7. Is your association prepared to give a guarantee to provide this complimentary Accommodation?   ( ) ( )

5. Air Travel:

5.1. Does the congress venue have access to an international airport that can handle several thousand participants arriving from and departing for all world during a period of two/three days at the beginning and end of the congress ( ) ( )

5.2. The FDI requires 35 complimentary return airfares, economy class, for its Officers and staff to be provided by organizing committee, which may negotiate for the costs to be absorbed by one or more airlines appointed as official carrier ( ) ( )

6. Finance:

6.1. Sections 5 and 9 of the Memorandum on Annual World Dental Congresses set out the financial responsibilities of the host association represented by the organizing committee, and of the FDI respectively. .Please confirm that you have studied and accepted those commitments.   ( ) ( )

                                                                                     YES NO

6.2.   Enrolment fees form a major part of the congress income. How may dentists do you expect participate in the congress from our country ( ) ( )

6.3.   What approximate enrolment fee would they expect to pay at today's price? ( ) ( )

6.4.   Is there a notable number of dental or dentistry related companies or subsidiaries of international dental companies in your country? ( ) ( )

6.5.   Have you received preliminary confirmation of their interest in a dental trade exhibit in the congress ( ) ( )

Do you intend to plan and organize the trade exhibition in close collaboration with a local dental trade association or equivalent? ( ) ( )

7.   Any additional comments:

If you have any additional comment please make them in the space provided below:

_____
_____
_____
_____
_____

Book 7 - Hospitality Service Systems
Accommodation, Foods and Beverage
(Hotel, Resorts, Restaurant, Training, Spa and Wellness Centers Management Fundamentals)

Introduction To Hospitality Service
(Hotel/Resort and Restaurant)

I. **Hospitality Defined and Explained**

Webster defines Hospitality (n.) a friendly and liberal reception of strangers or guest. On the other hand Rodget's 21st Thesaurus in Dictionary Form gives Hospitality (n) synonymous to: neighborliness; accommodation, affability, amiability, cheer, companionship, comradeship, consideration, conviviality, cordiality, entertainment, friendliness, generosity, geniality, good cheer, heartiness, hospitableness, obligingness, reception, sociability, warmth, welcome. It is the attitude, habit and an act present between the host and the guest/visitor. This is main reason that in the accommodation/hotel business, customers/clients are addressed as they are considered guests.

As observed today, Hospitality is considered a major component of Tourism Service System covering: Accommodation, Convention, Exhibit and Training, Health and Wellness Centers, Cruise Ships, Entertainment (Bars, Night Clubs), Restaurants and other facilities offering food and beverage products and services.

II. **Definition of Terms and Phrases Commonly used in Hotel and Restaurant and Entertainment Service Business Operations**

Accommodation - a room offered by hotels, resort, inns, apartel (apartment- hotel) lodging and boarding houses availed by the visitors, tourists and transients as sleeping and resting facility during their stay in the tourist destination.

Adjoining Rooms - two separate rooms in the same floor which doors are facing each other.

A la Carte - a certain meal which is served to the choice of and as ordered by the customer and priced individually.

American Breakfast - a type of breakfast served with toasted bread, butter and jam or marmalade, egg cooked to guest's choice; choice of bacon or ham, sliced fruit; and a choice of coffee or tea.

American Plan - Hotel accommodation with three meals daily included in the price of the room. Meals are usually "table de' Ho'te". Sometimes referred to as "full pension".

Apartment - a type of accommodation that offers complete facilities in every unit or room that includes, living room, dining room, bedroom, kitchen, comfort/shower room and walk-in closets.

Apartel - an accommodation facility that offers a room with kitchen and cooking facilities. It is a combination of an apartment and a hotel.

Bars, (KTV/ Video-ke Bar), Cocktail Lounge, Night or Day Clubs/Super Clubs - any establishment engaged in entertainment and selling/serving intoxicating and fermented liquors or malt and other liquid concoctions with alcoholic substance in addition to cooked food. It may also feature videoke entertainment or live bands. Night or Day Club includes any place frequented at night-time or day-time, as the case may be, where patrons are served food and drinks and are allowed to dance with their partners or with professional dance instructors. Super Club includes any establishment where food and drinks are served to its patrons, with musicians or jukeboxes/ record players installed within its premises, and where patrons may dance with their companions.

Bed and Breakfast - a package of accommodation offered by the hotel that includes bed for sleeping during the night and a morning meal.

Breakfast - a set of meal taken in the morning.

Buffet Meal - a kind of meal which food items are displayed in a buffet table from which the guests may choose and eat all he can at a fixed price.

Brunch - a type of meal as a combination of breakfast and lunch serve late in morning after breakfast time but before lunch time

Coffee Shop - a facility in a hotel that serves foods and beverage open from breakfast and dinner times. It serves as the in-house restaurant for a hotel, resort and pension and lodging houses.

Continental Breakfast - a type of breakfast served with slices of bread, butter and marmalade or jam; and a choice of coffee or tea.

Connecting Rooms - two rooms next to and connected with a common inside door.
Dinner - a meal served in the evening.
Double Bed Room - type of accommodation in a room with One (1) bed for two (2) persons abbreviated as DWB or Double with Bath;
European Plan - a type of accommodation package offered by the hotel no meals whatsoever included in the cost of the room.
Full Board - a type of accommodation package offered by the hotel that include room and all meals.
Guest Folio - A custom-built envelope containing documents supporting the accountabilities of the guest with the accommodation facility. There are two kinds of Guest Folios: 1) Individual– normally prepared for FITs/Individual Guest; and 2) Group - for a Tour Group records of accountabilities that normally cover the accommodation and meals reserved for the group by the handling travel agency/tour operator.
Hotel - any building, edifice or premises which offers venue for receptions, functions, seminars/ conventions/ forums, accommodations or lodging of travelers or tourist for a fee.
Motorist Hotel (Motel) -- any structure with several units, primarily located along the highway with individual or common parking space at which motorists may obtain lodging, and, in some instances, meals for a fee.
Pension House - a private or family-oriented tourist boarding house or tourist lodging house, employing non-professional domestic helpers, regularly catering to tourist and/or travelers. Containing several independent lettable rooms, providing common facilities such as toilets, bathrooms/ showers, living and dining rooms and/ or kitchen and where a combination of board and lodging may be provided.
Resort - any place or places with a pleasant environment and atmosphere conducive to a comfortable, healthful relaxation, offering food, sleeping accommodations and recreational facilities to the public for a fee. It could be inland, mountain, or beach resort.
Restaurant – a business establishment licensed and permitted to sell and serve foods of any kind, both alcoholic and non-alcoholic drinks and beverages to the tourists/visitors and the general public for a fee.

Rooming List -- a duly certified list of guests actually accommodated by the resort or hotel with their name, period of stay, point of origin and nationality.

Special Interest Resort -- refers to resorts providing the facilities and equipment for the conduct of special interest activities, wildlife observation and bird watching, backpacking, camping, trail riding (either motorized or horseback), target shooting and hunting, and theme parks.

Set or Plated Meal - a certain meal with complete combination of food items altogether placed in a single plate and priced on a per plate basis.

Suite - type of room with space for space for guest reception, dining table and a divider separating the bed/s from the reception area mini-bar a toilet and bath tub/shower in the bath room.

Triple Accommodation - type of accommodation for three (3) persons staying together in a room.

Twin Bed Room - type of room accommodation with two (2) single beds and a bath room.

Valet - a service section assisting guest in parking safely of motor vehicle ;

Wash-Up Room - type of room availed to short staying (not overnight stay) of guest to freshen up.

Walk-in Guest - a kind of guest that walks-in to the hotel counter to seek accommodation but without any confirmed room reservation and whose accommodation is purely dependent on the availability of the room during his intended period of stay.

III. Basic Organizational Structure and Service Cycle

A. Organizational Structure

Figure 5. shows the basic organizational structure for accommodation facility. Figure 5

Figure 5

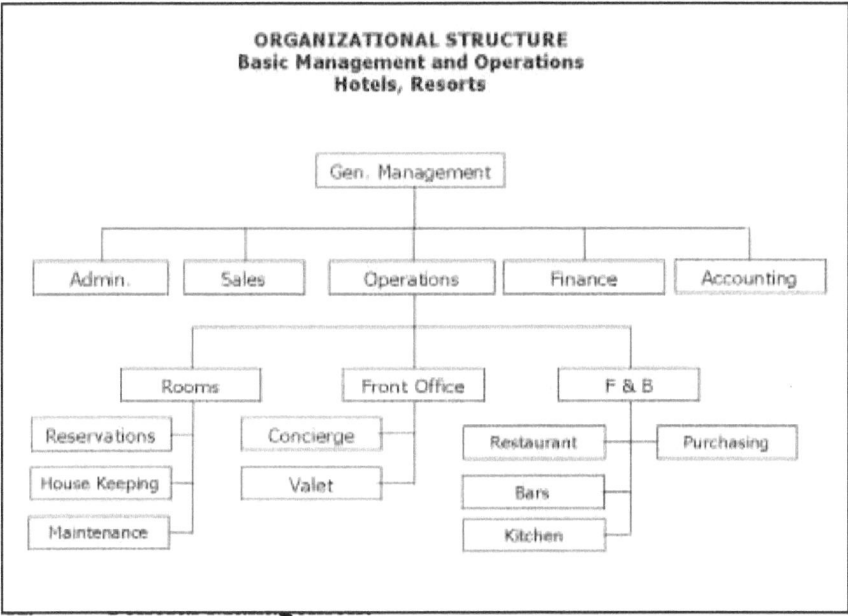

The General Management is the highest position which position is occupied by the General Manager. The position requires experienced professional who is adept in the delivery of every service system of the accommodation facility. Immediately underneath the General Management are the different executive departments as follows:

1. Administration or Administrative Department/Section. This department is responsible for administrative functions of the establishment and has over-all jurisdiction of the following:
   a. Human Resource Development:
      This department/section although immediately under the General Management, it has exclusive responsibility for:
      1. It has the control of all matters concerning information on Labor Relations;
      2. Hiring and Firing of Personnel and Staff;
      3. Training and Skill Development of hired personnel including the trainees under apprenticeship;
      4. Promotion/Demotion of personnel/staff;

b. Over-all responsible in proper use and utilization of all the assets of the accommodation facility and directly has the control and supervision over:
   - Repairs, Maintenance; and,
   - Security/Protection of all the properties and assets of the accommodation facility;

2. Sales Department/Section. This department/section is in-charge of the over- all sales, marketing and promotion of the product and services of the accommodation facility, including the formulation of the most effective marketing, sales and promotional tools for the accommodation facility covering all of the service sections, i.e., Rooms, Banquet, Meetings and Conventions.

3. Operations. This department or section has jurisdiction over the over-all service operations of the accommodation facility. This is the reason why it has direct access with the three service sections that are considered the front- liners and are in contact with the guest/customer of an accommodation facility. Its main function is to see to it that the services are at all times delivered with quality and timely passion. Immediately under its supervision are the following:

a. Rooms Section which in turn takes care of:
   o Reservations - Although this section should be likewise under the Sales, Marketing and Promotion, when it pertains to the upkeep of reserved rooms.
   o House Keeping - The primary function is to make-up the rooms reserved in their proper hygiene and see to it that all gadgets and fixtures are properly functional and ready to use at all times.
   o Maintenance, that includes engineering personnel for day to day check up of the lighting, air-conditioning units, water-heating gadget and other equipment, fixtures and furniture;

b. Front Office/Reception.
   This department/section serves in the front line of the accommodation facilities. Its functions include among others the following:
   1. To receive the incoming guests and see to it that the rooms with all its gadgets and amenities are ready and functional before the guests are ushered in.
   2. Under its area of service are the:
      o Concierge. In-charge in ushering and taking care of the personal belongings of the Guests for the proper handling and delivery in and out of the room; and,
      o Valet. In-Charge in assisting Guest from the Entrance up to the Front Desk for registration and taking care for the parking service of the guest's vehicles.

c. Food and Beverage
   This department/section has jurisdiction over service outlets related to the preparation and delivery of food and beverage to the guests. It is headed by a Director that has the over-all control over all service outlets directly under this department/division that include among others the following:

   1. Coffee Shop and Restaurant - the service outlet that serves as the main dining area for guests, where breakfast, lunch and dinner are served to both the in-house and walk-in guests. Normally it is open twenty four hours a day for hotels from first to upper classes, and ready to take orders from in-house guests anytime of the day. The staff and personnel under its jurisdiction are:

      a) Restaurant Duty Manager/Supervisor - that oversee the operation of the restaurant and always

in the frontline in case there are complaints from guests. The Duty Manager/Supervisor has the over-all responsibility in the preparation of the daily sales report to the Accounting Department. Under its direct control and supervision are the service staff/personnel as follows:
Captain/Supervising/Senior Waiters/Waitresses

Bar Tender/Barista for the preparation and service delivery of drinks and beverages required by guests; and, Bash Boys responsible for the clearing and cleaning of dining tables immediately after guest finishes taking their served food and drink, and see to it that the dining table is cleared and cleaned as well as the dining area are always free of any litters.

V. Accommodation Service Cycle and Inter-action with Guest

Figue I

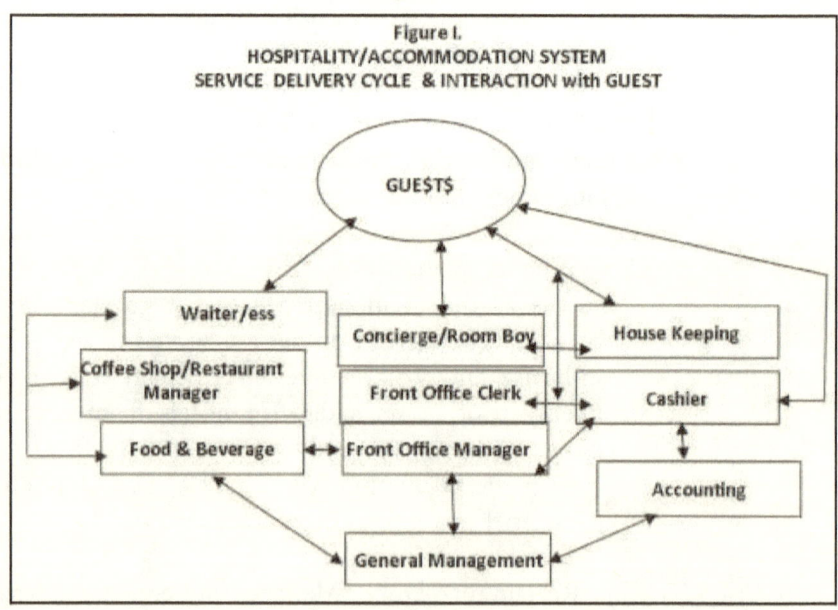

Figure I. shows that the Guest is in the top and all the service sections of the accommodation are placed below. This is because the highest consideration for the system is the interest of the Guest when he/she comes in to the establishment (Hotel, Resort, etc.). Right in the middle immediately below the Guest is Concierge/Room Boy who has the duty to usher the Guest towards the Front Office for check-in/registration where the Front Office Clerk shall take care for the formalities. On the check-in process the Front Office clerk is connected to House Keeping and the Cashier, for the purpose of:

a) House Keeping to see to it that the room is ready; and,
b) Cashier to take note of the fees, i.e., deposit and the mode of settlement of account when the Guest checks out. If the Guest will settle his/her account by Credit Card, it would then be noted by the Cashier that gets the Credit Card for examination and verification after which the Credit Card Number is recorded in the Guest Folio.

In the left side of the Figure shows the Food and Beverage Section with which the first line of service is the food server or waiter/ess that is connected with arrows representing interaction with the Manager; to the right side of the Figure is the House Keeping that takes care of the room requirements in making-up of the room i.e., cleaning, and replenishment of personal amenities, i.e., toiletries, bath soap, shampoo, toothpaste, sanitary tissues, etc..

Both the Food and Beverage and Housekeeping Sections are interconnected with the Front Office and the Cashier for proper coordination in the smooth delivery of service as well as the process of check- in up to the time of check-out so that proper coordination over the delivery of services needed by the guest is duly complied, and all accountabilities are updated and fully settled.

VI.   Start/End of Hospitality Service with the Guest/Client

The accommodation service to the guest/client starts at the point and time of contact by the guest with the duly authorized representative of the hospitality service provider, particularly hotel, resort, inn, pension house and,/or apartel. This means that the host/guest relationship arises from the point and time when the guest arrived at the destination where they are meet by the representative of accommodation facility.

VII. The Frontline Positions and Area of Service Coverage and Guest-related Functions

The service coverage of the accommodation facility starts from the first point of contact by its representative with, and ends at the time of check out of the guest from the accommodation facility. These services are performed and delivered by;

A. Front Office/Reception

The Front Office/Reception is considered the mirror of any accommodation facility for it is the first and last contact of the guest. It sets the tone of the impression of the guest of the accommodation facility. It is therefore, of utmost importance that this service section must be manned by the amiable, courteous, respectful and accommodating personnel and staff. The guest related function of this section are as follows:

1)   When the guest has a confirmed booking/room reservation, the obligation and duty of the front desk/reception starts from the time of the first contact of the Front Office personnel assigned to meet and assist the guest on the day of the confirmed date of guest's arrival at his/her entry point. This is where the front office staff, particularly the concierge-transfer service of the accommodation facility shall meet the guest at the passenger terminal (airport, port or bus), and from there the guest shall be assisted in his/transfer to the accommodation facility (Hotel or Resort).

2)   Upon arrival at of the guest in the accommodation facility, the concierge personnel at the main entrance door shall then usher the guest to the Reception Counter where the receptionist/front-desk clerk shall be at hand for the check-in formalities including among others the following:

1. **Guest Time of Arrival**
A..   For FIT/Individual Guest
Check-In Procedure;
   ✓ Assist the guest to Fill-up of the Registration Card;
   ✓ Preparation of Guest Folio;

- ✓ Verification and Validation of Credit Card in case the guest opts to settle his/her account at the time of check-out;
- ✓ Briefly orient the guest on the special features of the facilities and services of the hotel/resort;
- ✓ Advice the House Keeping to check the readiness of the room reserved including the amenities that are included, i.e., toiletries, etc.;
- ✓ Courteously hand-in to the guest the Meal Coupon for the meals included in the reservation (mostly breakfast), informative brochure of the hotel that contains the information on the locales directional map, tours, shops, dining and entertainment center; and,
- ✓ Call the concierge staff to usher/guide the guest to his/her assigned room.

2. **Guest Time of Departure**
Check-Out Procedure
Unless the guest has his/her own schedule earlier than 12:00 noon which the international standard check-out time is observed, it is the duty of the Front Desk personnel to:
- ✓ Advise the House Keeping section (Room Boys/Girls) to see to it that the rooms are checked/inspected at least one hour before the check-out time. This is for the purpose of conducting inventory and preparation of report of all the chargeable non-consumable and consumable items specially when there is a mini-bar in the room for reporting to the Front Office' Cashier.
- ✓ Front Office Cashier then prepares the Guest Folio for the accountabilities of the Guests and make sure that is ready immediately after the receipt of the inventory report by the House Keeping personnel assigned. This is order to record all the chargeable items that are included in the inventory report;
- ✓ Concierge then takes out the guest's luggage and assist him/her towards the Front Desk Cashier for clearing and full settlement of all accountabilities;

✓ If the guest settles his/her accounts with the credit card, the Cashier then hands in to the guest the Statement of Account for signature.

B.   For Group

Check-In Procedure
Every Tour Group has a Tour Group Conductor or Leader and mostly are handled by a Local/Inbound Tour Operator. In this instance it is the duty of the Rooms Section to coordinate closely with the Local/Inbound Tour Operator in regard the: 1) Final Rooming List; and 2) Actual Group Room and Meal Requirements.

The normal practice observed by the accommodation facility is to require the Final Rooming List prior to the group's arrival so to effect the pre-check in room assignment subject to changes or amendments upon arrival of the group based on the Final Rooming List for the group members:

1)   actual names;
2)   number; and,
3)   actual room requirement.

In this case, the groups' check-in procedure is a bit different from that of the FITs. The accommodation facility assigns a certain area normally a vacant function room where the group is ushered by the Front Office's Group Coordinator to first settle down, so that:

1)   'Welcome Drink' is served to individual group members;
2)   Reserved rooms are assigned in accordance with the Final Rooming List; and,
3)   Brief Orientation is conducted in regards the special features of the facility, including the schedule of activities included in the service package for the group.

The group luggage are orderly lined-up for easy identification and marking of room number by the concierge or room boy immediately after rooms are assigned to the individual group members. This procedure is necessary to avoid crowding of the front desk and allow smooth check-in for FITs/Individuals. The Room Keys then are distributed to individual group members, after which they are ushered by the Room Boys, while their luggage are delivered to their respective rooms.

The Final Rooming List with the corresponding rooms of the guest are then submitted to the Front Office Cashier for the preparation of: 1) Group's Folio to contain the records of accounts chargeable to the group and payable by local handling Local/Inbound Tour Operator; and. 2) Individual Guest Folio for the each Room of Group Members to which personal accounts (not included in the Group's Account) are recorded.

Check Out Procedure
The same procedure is observed for the FITs/Individuals.

B. Housekeeping

House Keeping section is jointly under the direct supervision by the Rooms Division in coordination with the Maintenance Section of the accommodation facility. It is the service section that takes care of the daily upkeep of the rooms that includes among others the following:

1. Cleaning of rooms and hallways;
2. Making Up of he bed and beddings;
3. Replenishment of consumable items included the cost of the room, i.e., toiletries (bath soap, toothpaste, shampoos, tissue papers, etc.), as well as non-consumables (Bath Towels, Face Towels, linen, blanket, and pillow covers;
4. Reporting to the Maintenance Section any concern on the functionality of room service utilities, fixtures and furniture;
5. Laundry servicing of guest apparels.

C. Dining Area/Coffee Shop, Bar and Cocktail Lounge

This Service Outlets is directly under the Food and Beverage department/section and manned by the following:
 1. Manager who is responsible for the day to day operation of the service outlet;
 2. Cashier that takes care for the proper recording and handling of sales income of the restaurant and bar;

3. Supervisor that directly supervises the functions of the waiters/waitresses and bash boys;
4. Captain Waiter that oversees and monitor the movements of customers and the first to coordinate with the service crew the orders and requirement of the guest, particularly in table settings, taking of orders, etc.;
5. Usher and Usherettes responsible in assisting the guest/customers to their tables and see to it that their needs are immediately attended to by the service crew;
6. Bar Tender responsible for the functions of the bar counter covering drinks and beverage;
7. Barista in-charge of the preparation of beverage concoctions that maybe ordered by the guest;
8. Bash Boys responsible for the clearing and cleaning of dining tables and the perimeters of the restaurant, particularly the dining area that at all times must be kept free from any trash/garbage.

D.   Banquet and Special Events

This service outlet area is designed for functions of exclusive guests, particularly dining receptions and meetings and convention. It is entirely distinct and separate from the operation of the restaurant, bar and cocktail lounge. Normally it is operational on case to case basis and its functions is dependent and tailor-made on the requirement of the customer.

The personnel and staff manning this service outlet are:
1. Manager that has the over-all responsibility for the proper and smooth delivery of the services required;
2. Supervisor that acts as the head of all the service crews assigned to the banquet reception to include the following:
    a. Banquet Event Coordinator whose main function is to coordinate between the concerned service outlets (i.e., kitchen, restaurant, front office and the customer as to the preparation and actual delivery of the service requirement of the latter;

b. Food Servers whose main function is to serve the foods and beverage included in the banquet service package and if not take care of other extra orders from the individual guest.

Types And Categories Of Accommodation Facilities

I. Overview on Accommodation Facilities

While accommodation facilities in their generic sense offer rooms to pass a night or two, there are types and categories that requires further elaboration and detailed explanation in order to avoid confusion in their respective interpretation so to escape misunderstanding with the tourists and guests. It is therefore, necessary to draw boundary lines to differentiate these facilities from each other.

II. Definition and Classifications
A. Hotels

Hotel is an accommodation facility that offers a room with sleeping beds ranging from single, double/twin occupancy with toilet and shower /bath room within a room. It may also offer a Suite that has wider space and additional amenities i.e., receiving room/sala apart from the sleeping room, dining table, refrigerator food heater, safety deposit box in addition to the other normal fixtures and gadgets. Hotels are classified in based on their special features in accordance with the requirements of the concerned authorities.

1. Classes of Hotels

Hotels are classified in different types and categories for the purpose of accreditation and pricing as follows:

1. De Luxe Class;
2. First Class;
3. Standard Class; and
4. Economy Class.

2. Required Facilities and Services for Hotels

A. De Luxe Class:

The following that are minimum requirements for the establishment, operation and maintenance of a De Luxe Class Hotel.

1. Location

The locality and environs including approaches shall be suitable for a luxury hotel of international standard. The façade, architectural features and general construction of the building shall have the distinctive qualities of a luxury hotel.

2. Bedroom Facilities and Furnishings

Size – All single and double rooms shall have a floor area not less than twenty five (25) square meters, inclusive of bathrooms.

Suite -There shall be one (1) suite per thirty (30) guest rooms.

Bathrooms – All rooms shall have bathrooms which shall be equipped with fittings of the highest quality befitting a luxury hotel with twenty-four (24) hour service of hot and cold running water. Bathrooms shall be provided with bathtubs and showers. Floor and walls shall be covered with impervious material of elegant design and high quality workmanship.

Telephones – There shall be a telephone in each guest room and an extension line in each guest room.

Radio/Television – There shall be a radio, a television and relayed or piped-in music in each guest room.

Cold Drinking Water -- There shall be cold drinking water and glasses in each bedroom.

Refrigerator/Mini Bar -- There shall be a small refrigerator and a well-stocked bar in each guest room.

Room Service -- There shall be a twenty-four (24 hour room service (including provision for snacks and light refreshments).

Furnishing and Lightings – All guest rooms shall have adequate furniture of the highest standard and elegant design; floors shall have superior quality wall-to-wall carpeting; walls shall be well furnished with well-tailored draperies of rich materials. Lighting arrangements and fixtures in the rooms and bathrooms shall be so designed as to ensure aesthetic as well as functional excellence.

Information Materials – Room tariffs shall be prominently displayed in each bedroom including notices for services offered by the hotel, fire exit guidelines, house rulers for guests, including food and beverage outlets and hours of operation.

3.   Front Office/Reception

There shall be a reception, information counter and guest relations office providing a twenty-four (24) hour service and attended by highly qualified, trained and experienced staff.

Lounge - There shall be a well-appointed lounge with seating facilities, the size of which is commensurate with the size of the hotel.

Porter Service - There shall be available 24 hour porter service.

Long Distance/Overseas Call – Long distance and overseas telephone calls shall be made available in the establishment.

E-mail Facilities - There shall be telex-transceiver facilities in the establishment.

Reception Amenities - There shall be a left luggage room and safety deposit boxes in the establishment.

4.   Housekeeping shall be of the highest possible standard.

Linen - There shall be plentiful supply of all linen, blanket, and towels, etc., which shall be of the highest quality and shall be spotlessly clean. These shall be changed every day.

Laundry/Dry Cleaning – Laundry and dry cleaning services shall be available in the establishment.

Carpeting – All public and private rooms shall have superior quality carpeting which shall be well-kept at all times.

5. Food and Beverage

Dining Room - There shall be a coffee shop and at least one specially dining room which are well-equipped, well-furnished and well-maintained, serving high quality cuisine and providing entertainment.

Bar – Wherever permissible by law, there shall be an elegant and well-stocked bar with an atmosphere of comfort and luxury.

Kitchen - The kitchen, pantry and cold storage shall be professionals designed to ensure efficiency of operation and shall be well-equipped, well- maintained, clean and hygienic. The kitchen shall have an adequate floor area with -slip flooring and tiled walls and adequate light and ventilation

Crockery -The crockery shall be of elegant design and superior quality. There shall be ample supply of it. No piece of crockery in-use shall be chipped, cracked or grazed. The silverware shall be kept well-plated and polished at all times.

6. Recreational Facilities

Swimming Pool – There shall be a well-designed and properly equipped swimming pool.

Tennis/Golf/Squash/Gym Facilities - There shall be at least one recreational facility to tie-up with one within the vicinity of the hotel.

7. Entertainment. – Live entertainment shall be provided.

8. Engineering and Maintenance.

Maintenance – Maintenance of all sections of the hotel (i.e., building. furniture, fixture, etc.) shall be of superior standard.

Air-Conditioning - There shall be centralized air-conditioning for the entire building (except in areas which are at a minimum of 3,000 feet above sea level)

Ventilation - There shall be technologically advanced, efficient and adequate ventilation in all areas of the toilet.

Emergency Power - There shall be a high-powered generator capable of providing sufficient lighting for all guest rooms, hallways, public areas/rooms, operating elevators, food refrigeration and water services.

Fire Prevention Facilities – The fire prevention facilities shall conform with the requirements of the Fire Code of the Philippines.

9. General Facilities:
Outdoor Area – The hotel premises shall have a common outdoor area for guest (example: a roof garden or a spacious common terrace).

Parking/Valet - There shall be an adequate parking space and valet service. Function/Conference Facilities -- There shall be one or more of each of the following: conference rooms, banquet halls (with a capacity of not less than 200 people seated) and private dining rooms. Shops - There shall be a barber shop, recognized travel agency/tour counter, beauty parlor and sundries shop.

Security - Adequate security on a 24-hour basis shall be provided in all entrances and exits of the hotel premises.

Medical Service – A medical clinic to service guests and employees shall have a registered nurse on a 24-hour basis and a doctor on-call.

9. Service and Staff. – Professionally qualified, highly trained, experienced, efficient and courteous staff shall be employed. The staff shall be in smart and clean uniforms.

10. Special Facilities. – Business Center, limousine service and airport transfers shall be provided.

12. Insurance Coverage. – There shall be an adequate insurance against accident for all guests.

B. First Class Hotel.

The following are the minimum requirements for the establishment, operation and maintenance of a first class hotel:

(a) Location. – The location and environs including approaches shall be suitable for a first class hotel of international standard. The façade, architectural features and general construction of the building shall have the distinctive qualifies of a first class hotel.

(b) Bedroom Facilities and Furnishing. –

Size – All single and double rooms shall have a floor area of not less than twenty-five (25) square meters, inclusive of bathrooms.

Suite – There shall be one (1) suite forty (40) guest rooms.

Bathrooms – All rooms shall have bathrooms which shall be equipped with fittings of the highest quality befitting a first class hotel with a 24-hour service of hot and cold-running water. Bathrooms shall be provided with showers and/or bathtubs. Floors and walls shall be covered with impervious material of aesthetic design and high quality workmanship.

Telephone – There shall be a telephone in each guest room.

Radio/Television -- There shall be a radio, television and relayed or piped-in music in each guest room.

Cold Drinking Water -- There shall be a cold drinking water and glasses in each bedroom.

Room Service -- There shall be a 24-hour room service including provision for snacks and light refreshment.

Furnishing and Lighting – All guest rooms shall have adequate furniture of very high standard and very good design; floors shall have wall-to-wall carpeting; or if the flooring is of high quality (marble, mosaic., etc.), carpets shall be provided and shall be of size proportionate to the size of the rooms; walls shall be well-furnished with well-tailored draperies of very high quality material. Lighting arrangements and fixtures in the rooms and bathrooms shall be so designed as to ensure functional excellence.

Information Materials – Room tariffs shall be prominently displayed in each bedroom plus prominent notice for services offered by the hotel including food and beverage outlets and hour of operation, fire exit guidelines and house rules for guests.

(c)   Front Office/Reception. – There shall be a reception and information counter providing a 24-hour service and staffed by trained and experienced personnel.

Lounge - There shall be a lobby and well-appointed lounge with seating facilities, the size of which is commensurate with the size of the hotel.

Porter Service - There shall be a 24-hour porter service.

Foreign Exchange Counter -- There shall be a licensed and authorized foreign exchange counter.

Mailing Facilities – Mailing facilities including sale at stamps, envelopes or internet access for e-mail, shall be available in the premises.

Long Distance/Overseas Call – Long distance and overseas telephone calls shall be made available in the establishment.

E-mail and Facsimile - There shall be telex-transceiver and facsimile facilities in the establishment.

Reception Amenities:
There shall be a left-luggage room and safety deposit boxes in the establishment.

(d)   Housekeeping. – Housekeeping shall be of high standards.

Linen - There shall be a good supply of all linen, blanket, towel, etc. which shall be of high quality and shall be spotlessly clean. These shall be changed daily.

Laundry/ Dry Cleaning Services – Laundry and dry cleaning services shall be available in the establishment.
Carpeting – All public and private rooms shall have high quality carpeting which shall be well-kept at all times.

(e) Food and Beverage.

Dining Rooms - There shall be a coffee shop and at least one specially dining room which are well-equipped, well-furnished, and well-maintained, serving good quality cuisine and providing entertainment.

Bar – Wherever permissible by law, there shall be an elegant and well-stocked bar with an atmosphere of comfort.

Kitchen – The kitchen, pantry and cold storage shall be professionally designed to ensure efficiency of operation and shall be well-equipped, well-maintained, clean and hygienic. The kitchen shall have an adequate floor area with non-slip flooring and tiled walls and adequate light and ventilation.

Crockery – The crockery shall be of best quality. There shall be adequate supply for it. No piece of crockery in use shall be chipped, cracked or grazed. The silverware shall be kept well-plated and polished at all times.

(f) Recreational Facilities:

Swimming Pool – There shall be a well-designed and properly equipped swimming pool.

Tennis/ Golf/ Squash/ Gym/ Facilities -- There shall be at least one recreational facility or a tie-up with one within the vicinity of the hotel.

(g) Entertainment. Live entertainment shall be provided.

(h) Engineering and Maintenance:

Maintenance — Maintenance of all sections of the hotel (i.e. building, furniture, fixtures, etc.) shall be of very high quality.

Air-conditioning — There shall be centralized air-conditioning for the entire building (except in areas which are at a minimum of 3,000 feet above sea level)

Ventilation - There shall be technologically advanced, efficient and adequate ventilation in all areas at the hotel.

Lighting -- There shall be adequate lighting in all public and private rooms.

Emergency Power -- There shall be high-powered generator capable of providing sufficient lighting for all guest rooms, hallways, public area/rooms, operating elevators, food refrigeration and water services.

Fire Prevention Facilities — The fire prevention facilities shall conform to the requirements of the Fire Code of the Philippines.

(i) General Facilities:

Parking/Valet -- There shall be an adequate parking space and valet service.

Functions/Conference Facilities -- There shall be special rooms for conference/banquet purposes.

Shops -- There shall be a recognized travel agency/tour counter, barber shop beauty parlor and sundries shop.

Security — Adequate security on a 24-hour basis shall be provided on all entrances and exits of the hotel premises.

Medical Service — A medical clinic to service guests and courteous with a registered nurse on a 24-hour basis and a doctor on-call shall be provided.

(j) Service and Staff

Highly qualified, trained, experience, efficient and courteous staff shall be hired. The staff shall be in smart and clean uniforms

(k) Special Facilities. – Facilities for airport transfers shall be provided.

(l) Insurance Coverage -- There shall be an adequate insurance against accident for all guests.

C. Standard Class Hotel

The following are the minimum requirements for the establishments, operation and maintenance of a standard class hotel:

(a) Location. – The locality and environs including approaches shall be suitable for a very good hotel. The architectural features and general construction of the building shall be of very good standard.

(b) Bedroom Facilities and Furnishings:

Size – All single and double rooms shall have a floor area not less than 18 square meters inclusive of bathrooms.

Bathrooms – All rooms shall have bathrooms which shall be equipped with showers and fittings of fitting of good standard with cold running water on a 24-hour basis and hot running water at selected hours.

Telephone - There shall be a telephone in each guest room.

Cold Drinking Water -- There shall be cold drinking water and glasses in each bedroom.

Room Service – Room service shall be provided at selected hours.

Furnishings and Lighting – All guest rooms shall have furniture of every good standard and design; floors shall have good quality carpet; walls shall be well furnished and drapes shall be well-tailored and of goof materials.

Medical Service – A medical clinic to service guests and courteous with a registered nurse on a 24-hour basis and a doctor on-call shall be provided.

(j) Service and Staff
Highly qualified, trained, experience, efficient and courteous staff shall be hired. The staff shall be in smart and clean uniforms

(k) Special Facilities. – Facilities for airport transfers shall be provided.

(l) Insurance Coverage -- There shall be an adequate insurance against accident for all guests.

D. All Class Economy Hotel.

The following are the minimum requirements for the establishment, operation and maintenance of an economy class hotel:

(a) Location. – The locality and environs including approaches shall be such as are suitable for a good hotel. The building shall be well-constructed and in the case of new building, they shall be designed by a competent architect.

(b) Bedroom Facilities and Furnishings. –
Size – All single and double rooms shall have a floor area of not less than 18 square meters inclusive of bathroom.

Bathroom – All rooms shall have bathrooms which shall be equipped with showers and basic fitting of modern sanitation with cold running water on a 24-hour basis and hot running water at selected hours.

Telephone -- There shall be a call bell in each guest room.

Room Service – Shall be provided at selected hours.

Furnishings and Lighting – All guest rooms shall have the basic furniture of good design; floors shall be well-finished. Lighting arrangements and fixtures in all rooms and bathrooms shall be of good standard.

Information materials – Room tariffs shall be prominently displayed in each bedroom plus prominent notices for services offered by the hotel including food and beverage outlets and hours of operation, fire exit guidelines and house rules for guests.

(c)   Front Office/Reception

There shall be a reception and information counter providing a 24-hour service equipped with telephone.

Lounge -There shall be reasonably furnished lounge commensurate with the size of the hotel.

Porter service – Shall be made available upon request.

Mailing Facilities -- There shall be mailing facilities.

Long Distance/Overseas Calls – Shall be made available upon request.

Reception Amenities -- There shall be left-luggage and safe deposit boxes.

Internet Access and Email – Shall be optional.

(d)   Housekeeping - Premises shall be kept clean and tidy.

Linen – Clean, good quality linen/blankets/towels etc. shall be supplied and changed daily.

Laundry and Dry Cleaning Services – Shall be available by arrangement.

(e)   Food and Beverage:

Dining Room – There shall be at least one (1) equipped and maintaining dining room/restaurant serving good, clean and wholesome food.

Kitchen -- There shall be a clean, hygienic and well- equipped and maintained kitchen and pantry. The kitchen shall have an adequate floor area with non-slip flooring and tiled walls and adequate light and ventilation.

Crockery – Shall be of good quality.

(f)   Engineering and Maintenance:

Maintenance – Maintenance of the hotel in all sections shall be of good standard.

Ventilation - There shall be a spare generator for ventilation in all rooms.

Lighting - There shall be adequate lighting in all pubic and private rooms.

Emergency Power – There shall be a spare generator available to provide light and power in emergency cases.

Fire Prevention – Shall conform with the requirements of the Fire Code of the Philippines.

(g)   General Facilities:

Shops - There shall be a sundry shop center.

Security - Adequate security on a 24-hour basis shall be provided on all entrances and exits on the hotel.

Medical Service – The service of a doctor shall be available when needed.

(h)   Service Staff - The staff shall be well-trained, experienced, courteous and efficient.

(i)   Special Facilities – Airport transfers shall be provided upon request.

(j)   Insurance Coverage -- There shall be an adequate insurance against accidents for all guests.

B.   Apartel (Apartment-Hotel)

Apartel is a combination of the term apartment and hotel. It is a kind of accommodation that has the features of both the hotel and an apartment, where the amenities of both are present, i.e., Living, Dining, Bedroom and a kitchen. It may also has the facilities for washing and drying personal apparels. It is designed for long staying guests who may opt to live in a homely atmosphere where they may have the freedom to cook their own food and or opt to dine in an in-house restaurant or coffee shop

The basic requirements for the establishment, operation and maintenance of an apartel:

(a)   Number of Units. – The apartel shall have at least a minimum of 25 lettable apartments.

(b)   Apartment. – Each apartment of the apartel shall be provided with living and dining areas, kitchen and bedroom with attached toilet and bath.

(c)   Living Area. – The living area shall be provided with essential and reasonably comfortable furniture.

(d)   Kitchen. – The kitchen shall be spacious, clean, hygienic and adequately equipped with cooking utensils. It shall also be provided with facilities for storage and refrigeration of foods, for disposal of garbage and for cleaning of dishes and cooking utensils.

(e)   Dining Area. – Shall be spacious and provided with dining table and chairs, including all essential dining facilities such as, but not limited to plates, spoons and forks, drinking glasses, etc.

(f)   Toilet and Bathroom. – Shall always be clean and have adequate sanitation and running water.

(g) Bedroom – Shall be spacious and provided with comfortable bed. These shall also be provided closet and a mirror.

(h) Linen – The apartel shall have sufficient number of good and clean linen.

(i) Ventilation – The apartment shall be sufficiently ventilated.

(j) Lighting. – Lighting arrangements and fixtures in all rooms shall be adequate.

(k) Telephone – There shall be a telephone o a call bell button.

(l) Elevator – An elevator shall be provided for a building of more than three (3) storeys whenever possible.

(m) Staff and Services. – Shall be trained, experienced, courteous and efficient. They shall be provided with smart and clean uniforms.

(n) Medical Facilities – A first aid clinic stocked with appropriate medicines and drugs to service employees and guests shall be provided. Apartels with more than 100 apartments shall hire the services of a physician.

(o) Fire-Fighting Facilities – Shall be in accordance with the Fire Code of the Philippines.

(p) Lounge and Reception Center – There shall be a reasonably furnished lounge commensurate with the size of the apartel. The reception counter shall be attended by trained and experienced staff and shall also be provided with telephone.

(q) Security – Adequate security on a 24-hour basis on all entrances and exits of the apartels premises.

(r) House Rules and Regulations – The apartel shall prescribe reasonable house rules and regulations to govern the use of apartment and other facilities of the apartel.

C.   Tourist Inns

A Tourism Inn is a smaller and lower category of a hotel, basically it has only a bedroom and coffee shop normally for breakfast. Tourist Inn basically offers bed and breakfast type of accommodation only, where the cost of the breakfast is included in the price of the room.

Requirements For Tourist Inns:
The following are the basic requirements for the establishment, operation and maintenance of a tourist inn:

(a)   Location. – The tourist inn, except those directly existing and licensed by the DOT, shall be located along the principal roads and highways or transportation routes and open to business on a 24-hour basis.

(b)   Bedroom Facilities and Furnishings. – All bedrooms shall have attached toilet and bath equipped with 24-hour service of running water. They shall have adequate natural as well as artificial light and ventilation and shall be furnished with comfortable beds and quality furniture (mirror, writing table, chair, closet dresser per room). Wall shall be painted, wall papered or architecturally designed, clean and pleasing to the eyes. Windows shall be furnished with clean and appropriate draperies. Floors shall be good flooring materials. All single bedrooms shall have a floor area of not less than nine (9) square meters and all twin rooms or double rooms shall have a floor area of not less than 16 square meters. There shall be vacuum jugs or thermosplast with drinking water with glasses in each bedroom. There shall be adequate supply of good clean linen, blankets and towels that shall be changed regularly in each occupied room.

(c)   Facilities. – There shall be adequate parking space proportionate to the number of lettable rooms and other public facilities of the inn.

(d)   There shall be a reception and information counter attended by qualified, trained and experienced staff.

(e) There shall be a lobby and well-appointed lounge. There shall be adequate telephone facilities. Services for long distance or overseas telephone calls shall be made available to guest.

(f) There shall be provisions for radio and/or well-maintained dining room restaurant for its guests as well as the public in general.

(g) A kitchen, pantry and cold storage shall be designed and organized to ensure efficiency of operation and shall be well-maintained, clean and hygienic. Washing of cooking utensils, crockery, cutlery, glass wares, etc. shall be sanitarily done.

(h) Adequate security shall be provided to all guests and their belongings. Inns with more than 50 lettable rooms shall have emergency power facilities to light the common areas and emergency exits in case of power failure. Adequate firefighting facilities shall be available as required by the Fire Code of the Philippines.

D. Motel

A Motel is designed for motorist guests, meaning the guest are with their private motor-vehicle on a long distance travel, so that they may opt to pass and stay for few hours, a night or more in a said accommodation facility. Motel is a combination of first syllabus in the word Motorist "Mo" and the last syllabus of the term Hotel "tel", thus, the term is "Motel"

The following are the minimum requirements for the establishment, operation, and maintenance of motels:

(a) Location. – The motel shall be located along or close to the highways or major transportation routes. It shall have at least ten (10) units.

(b) Garage. – The motel shall have an individual garage or a common parking space for the vehicle of its guest.

(c) Bedroom. – Each unit shall be provided with a fully air-conditioned bedroom, or at least, an electric fan, and shall be furnished with comfortable bed/s, clean pillows, linen and bed sheets.

(d) Toilet and Bathroom. – The unit shall be provided with attached toilet and bathroom with cold and hot water, clean towels, tissue paper and soap.

(e) Telephone. - There shall be a telephone or call-bell in each unit.

(f) Staff and Service. – The motel staff shall be trained, experienced, courteous and efficient. They shall wear clean uniforms whole on duty. (g)Medical Services. – Medical services on an emergency basis shall be made available.

(g) Fire-Fighting Facilities. – Adequate fire-fighting facilities shall be provided for each separate unit/building, in accordance with the Fire Code of the Philippines.

(h) Lighting. – Lighting arrangement and fixtures in all units shall be adequate.

(i) Housekeeping. – Efficient housekeeping shall be maintained.

(j) Maintenance. – Efficient maintenance of the motel in all its sections (i.e. building, ground, furniture, fixtures public rooms, air conditioning, etc.) shall be provided on a continuing basis.

(k) Other Facilities. – The motel may, at its portion, serve food and drinks exclusively to its guests, and install such other special facilities necessary for their business.

(l) Signboard. – All motels shall keep and display in a conspicuous place outside the establishment a signboard showing clearly the name of the motel.

No motel is allowed to accept for lodging or accommodation any person below 18 years of age unless accompanied by a parent or guardian. On the departure of guests, the motel clerk shall record in the Registry

Book the date and hour of their departure.

In addition to daily rates, motels may likewise impose wash – up rates. Motels are prohibited to refuse guests who may want to stay on a daily rate basis. The rental rates shall be posted prominently at the reception counter and/or at the door of each room.

E. Home-stay

A Home-Stay is a type of accommodation where guests are accorded with the facilities of a private house where the family owner lives. It is managed by the family and offers very limited rooms to a very select guests.

The following are the minimum requirements for the operation and maintenance of home-stay sites in accordance with the Department's National

Home-stay Program:

(a)   HOMESTAY SITES
(1)   There is prevailing peace and order situation in the area.
(2)   There are existing natural and man-made attractions in the community.
(3)   Site is easily accessible to tourists and with existing transportation services, good road condition and other basic community infrastructures.
(4)   The host community is willing to join the National Homestay Program.
(5)   There is a death of commercial accommodation facilities in the area to service tourists.

(b)   HOME FACILITIES
(1)   Structures are of durable building materials and are in good, presentable condition.

(2) The surroundings are pleasant and helpful.
(3) There shall be at least one (1) adequately furnished guestroom to accommodate paying visitors.
(4) The following shall be available:
-extra bed/s
-adequate lighting system
-running water or if not available, adequate supply of water
-clean and well maintained toilet and bathroom facilities
-meals at reasonable rates
-electric fan or other means of ventilation

(c) TRAINING
Family members shall have completed the special training workshop on Home-stay Program that shall hereinafter be conducted by the Provincial Tourism and Promotion Board (PTPB), or those conducted by Department of Tourism (DOT) duly accredited training centers.

VI. Pension House
Requirements for the Operation of a Pension House
The following are the basic requirements for the establishment, operation and maintenance of pension houses:

(a) Number of Rooms. – A pension shall have at least five (5) lettable rooms.

(b) Bedrooms. – The bedrooms shall be provided with sufficient number of comfortable beds commensurate with the size of the rooms. Each room shall have adequate natural as well as artificial light and ventilation. It shall be provided with at least a writing table, closet, and a water jug with glasses proportionate to the number of beds in the room. Rooms shall be clean and presentable and reasonably furnished to depict the true atmosphere of a Filipino home.

(c) Linen. – The establishment shall provide a toilet and bathroom to be used in common by the guests. There shall be at least one (1) bathroom/shower for every five occupants in all lettable rooms.

(d) Linen. -- There shall be adequate supply of clean linen and towels. Soap and tissue paper shall be provided at all times.

(e) Living Room. – There shall be a reasonably furnished lounge or living room area commensurate to the size of the pension where guests may receive visitors, watch television or read.

(f) Dining Rooms. – The pension shall have a dining room which shall be available for use of its guests.

Restaurant, Cocktail Lounge, Night Club, Training Center & Spa

I. Basic Requirements for Operation and Management

A. Restaurant

The following are the minimum requirements that must be complied with for restaurants:

a) Location. – The locality and environs including approaches shall be pleasant and provided with proper ingress for customers.
b) Parking. - It should be adequate, secured and provided free to customers.
c) Reception. – A reception shall be available to usher in guests. A waiting lounge with a telephone shall also be provided.
d) Dining Room. – Shall be adequate in size with sufficient and well-maintained furniture. Cleaning materials shall be kept clean at all times.
e) Atmosphere – The restaurant shall have a pleasant atmosphere.
f) Cuisine – There shall be a cuisine of good quality and presentation which may be of special interest to tourists available during normal meal hours and served with distinction. Raw food used shall meet minimum government and international standards of grading quality.
g) Menu Book – Shall be presentable, clean and easy to read with the menu items listed in logical sequence. All items shall be made available at all times on a best effort oasis.
h) Linen – All tables shall have clean tablecloth, napkins of good quality, not faded nor with frayed edges and should be changed after every service.
i) Crockery – No piece of crockery, cutlery and tableware in use shall be chipped, cracked or grazed. The silverware shall be kept polished and clean at all times.
j) Service and Staff. – Adequate number of well-trained, well-groomed, experienced, efficient and courteous staff shall be employed. Bar. – The bar shall be well-stocked at all times.

k) Comfort Rooms. – Shall be of good quality fixtures and fittings and provided with running water. The floor and walls shall be covered with impervious materials of good quality workmanship and shall be kept clean and sanitary at all times. Tissue paper, soap, paper towels and/or hand drier shall be provided.

l) Kitchen. – The kitchen pantry and cold storage shall be in good operating condition at all times and shall be well-equipped and hygienic. Equipment necessary to maintain a high standard of sanitation and hygiene shall be installed and used.

m) Lighting. – Adequate lighting arrangement and fixtures shall be installed in the dining rooms, public rooms, comfort rooms, corridors and other public areas.

n) Maintenance. – All sections of the restaurant shall be maintained for all establishments.

o) Fire-Fighting Facilities. – Adequate fire-fighting facilities shall be provided in accordance with the Fire Code of the Philippines.

p) Ventilation. The restaurants should have proper ventilation. An exhaust fan may be necessary to maintain the pleasant air inside the establishment.

B. Bar, Cocktail Lounge, Night Clubs

Operating Requirements for Bar, Cocktail Lounge/Night Clubs
Requirements for the operation are the following :

a) Location – Subject to the provisions of existing law and ordinances, locality and environment including approaches should be pleasant with an atmosphere of comfort. The façade and architectural features of the building shall be appropriately designed.

b) Reception Counter – There shall be a reception counter with a telephone attended by highly qualified, trained and experienced staff. A receptionist shall be available to usher in customers.

c) Engineering and Maintenance:

d) Lighting – Technologically advanced, efficient and adequate lighting arrangement and fixtures shall be installed in all areas of the establishment.

e) Ventilation – The premises shall be well-ventilated.

f) Emergency Power – There should be high-powered generator capable of providing sufficient lighting in all areas of the establishment, including food refrigeration and water services.

g) Maintenance – Shall be of acceptable standard and shall be on a continuing basis, taking into consideration the quality of materials used as well as its upkeep. Regular and hygienic garbage disposal system shall be maintained. Sanitation measures shall be disposal system shall be maintained. Sanitation measures shall be adopted in accordance with the Sanitation Code of the Philippines.
h) Fire-Fighting Facilities – Shall be provided in accordance with the Fire Code of the Philippines.
i) Food and Beverages – Dining Room should be well-equipped, well-furnished and well-maintained, serving a good quality cuisine with good presentation which may be of special interest to tourists. It should be available during normal meal hours and served with distinction. Raw food used shall meet minimum government and international standards of grading and quality. Flooring materials shall be kept clean at all times. Bars should be well-stocked at all times with an atmosphere of comfort.
j) Kitchen/Pantry/Cold Storage – Should be professionally designed to ensure efficiency of operation and should be well-equipped, well-maintained clean and hygienic. Should have an adequate floor area with non-slip flooring and tiled walls and adequate light and ventilation.
k) Crockery. -- Should be best designed, made with good quality and should have adequate supply. No piece of crockery in use should be chipped, cracked or grazed. The silverware should be kept well-plated and polished at all times.
l) Menu/Beverage Book. – Shall be presentable, clean and easy to read with items listed in logical sequence and should be made available at all times on a best effort basis.
m) Linen. – All tables shall have clean table cloths and napkins of good quality. They should not be faded nor with frayed edges and stains and should be changed after every service.
n) Comfort room. – Shall be of good quality fixtures and fittings and provided with running water. The floor and walls shall be covered with impervious materials of good quality workmanship and shall be kept clean and sanitary at all times. Tissue paper, soap, paper towels and/or hand drier shall be provided.
o) Parking Space. – Adequate parking space with security shall be provided free to guests and customers.

p) Entertainment. – Live entertainment should be provided but strictly no lewd, obscene or bold shows as prescribed by law.
q) (Staff and Service. – Adequate number of trained, experienced, courteous and efficient staff shall be employed. They shall wear smart and clean uniforms at all times.
r) Security – adequate security shall be provided on all entrances and exits of the establishments.
s) Employee Facilities. – Adequate and well-maintained locker rooms and bathrooms for male and female employees shall be provided.
t) Posting of "Warning and Precautionary Notices"
u) Management shall post sufficient and visible signs in strategic areas of the cocktail lounge/night clubs/bars to warn and/or inform the guests and customers of the rules and regulations, fire exit guidelines including hours of operation to observe while inside the premises.
v) Littering Prohibited
w) Littering in cocktail lounges, night clubs and bars shall be strictly prohibited. Cocktail lounge, night club and bar owners shall keep their premises clean and shall adopt their own anti-littering measures. Cocktail lounge, night club, and bar owners/operators shall not allow gambling of any form and disorderly conduct of any kind in its premises specifically lewd show. Minors are not allowed to enter the premises. Guests/customers wearing sando and slippers shall not be allowed to enter. Firearms and deadly weapons are strictly prohibited inside the premises.

C. Sports and Recreational Club

The following are the minimum basic requirements for the operation and maintenance of a sports and recreational club:

(a) LOCATION. – The locality and environs including approaches shall be pleasant with proper ingress and egress. The façade and architectural features shall be appropriately designed.
(b) PARKING. – Adequate and secured parking space shall be provided at all times.
(c) SECURITY. – Adequate security shall be provided at all times.

(d) RECEPTION. – A receptionist shall be available to usher in guests. A waiting lounge with telephone shall also be provided.
(e) DINING ROOM. – There shall be a dining outlet adequate in size, with pleasant atmosphere and furnished with appropriate and well- maintained furniture.
(f) SPORTS AND RECREATIONAL EQUIPMENT. – There shall be adequate sports and recreational equipment available for rent.
(g) PUBLIC WASHROOMS. – There shall be provided adequate and accessible toilet facilities separately for male and female. Tissue paper, soap, hand/paper towel shall also be provided.
(h) LOCKER AREA AND FACILITIES. – There shall be adequate number of lockers for male and female. Dressing areas and shower cubicles shall also be provided.

D. Training Center

The following are the minimum requirements for the operation and maintenance of a training center.

(a) Physical Requirements:
  (1) Size of Classroom. – The classrooms shall be able to accommodate a minimum of twenty (20) trainees per class. For purposes of workshop, the floor area shall be at minimum of 1.5 square meters per trainee.
  (2) Lighting and Ventilation. – Lighting and Ventilation fixtures shall be so designed to ensure an atmosphere conducive to training. A stand by generator shall be made available.
  (3) Restrooms. – There shall be separate male and female restrooms.
  (4) Refreshment/Dining Area. – There shall be refreshment/dining area accessible to the trainees.
  (5) Classroom Facilities, Equipment and Supplies. – The center shall be provided with classroom complete with basic facilities, equipment and supplies needed in conducting a training program.

(6) Workshops/on-the-Job Facilities and Equipment – Depending on the training program/s being offered, there shall be adequate supply of the appropriate facilities and equipment.
(7) Reading Room. – There shall be a reading room adequately provided with relevant reference materials, books, journals, magazines and the like.
(8) Other Support Facilities. -- There shall be tool/storage facilities provided.

(b) Training Program:
(1) Relevance – The training program shall respond to the needs of the tourism industry.
(2) Lighting and Ventilation. – Lighting and Ventilation fixtures shall be so designed to ensure an atmosphere conducive to training. A stand by generator shall be made available.
(3) Restrooms. – There shall be separate male and female restrooms.
(4) Refreshment/Dining Area - There shall be refreshment/dining area accessible to the trainees.
(5) Classroom Facilities, Equipment and Supplies. – The center shall be provided with classroom complete with basic facilities, equipment and supplies needed in conducting a training program. Workshop/on-the-Job Facilities and Equipment. Depending on the program/s being offered, there shall be adequate supply of the appropriate facilities and equipment.
(6) Reading Room. -- There shall be a reading room adequately provided with relevant reference materials, books, journals, magazines and the like.
(7) Other Support Facilities - There shall be tool/storage facilities provided.

(c.) Training Program:
(1) Relevance – The training program shall respond to the needs of the tourism industry.
(2) Objectives. – Its objectives shall be clearly defined, realistic and attainable.

(3) Content/Curriculum. – The content/curriculum of the training program shall be in consonance with its objectives. Topics shall be in proper and logical sequence with due consideration to effectiveness of presentation in terms of trainees compensation.
(4) Methodology. -- There shall be an effective, simple, and comprehensive presentation of topics; clear description of examination scheme and test instruments related to course objectives. There shall likewise be a relevant and practical application of theories and concepts.
(5) Minimum Requirements/Qualifications of Participants. – Minimum qualifications of participants shall be based on the standards acceptable to the tourism industry.
(6) Instructional Staff. – The instructional staff shall have thorough experience and knowledge on the subject matter and effective communication skills and teaching style.
(7) Monitoring and Evaluation Procedures. – The training program shall carry effective monitoring and evaluation tools.

E.   SPA
1..   Categories of SPA
Spas are categorized as follows:
(a.)   Day Spa
(b.)   Destination Spa
(c.)   Resort Spa

2.   Requirement for the Operation
The following are the minimum standard requirements for the operation and maintenance of spa:

    (a) LOCATION AND ENVIRONMENT – The Spa shall be situated in a safe and reputable location with clean, calm and relaxing environment.
    (b) LOUNGE AND RECEPTION COUNTER – There shall be a reception counter attended by qualified and trained staff and a reasonably furnished lounge with seating facilities commensurate with the size of the spa.

(c) FOOD BAR - There shall be a well-maintained and well-stocked food bar for clients.
(d) WASHROOMS - There shall be separate clean and adequate washrooms for male and female provided with running water, hand dryer and toiletries.
(e) LOCKER ROOMS - There shall be separate male and female locker rooms for guests.
(f) SHOWER ROOMS - There shall be separate male and female shower and changing rooms.
(g) TREATMENT ROOMS - There shall be separate unlocked treatment rooms for male and female.
(h) SERVICES – The Spa shall provide all of the following services in addition to other spa-related amenities which it may offer:
 1. Massages – Swedish, Lymph Drainage and reflexology, etc.
 2. Steam, Sauna and/or Water Baths; and,
 3. Body Treatments – One or more of the following: body packs and wraps, exfoliation, body toning/contouring, waxing, hand and foot care.
i.) STAFF - There shall be adequate number of well-trained, well-groomed, experienced, courteous and efficient staff. There shall be at least one (1) DOH-registered massage therapist supervising a maximum of twenty (20) massage attendants and the staff shall wear clean, proper and non-transparent uniform at all times.
j.) STEAM, SAUNA AND WATER BATHS. – The baths, sauna and water baths shall be maintained in a level of temperature which will not cause adverse reactions to user. Safety signage shall be provided to include information an allowable maximum temperature, duration of stay and guide in operating temperature regulator.
k.) LINEN - There shall be adequate supply of linen, towels and appropriate garments such as robes or sarongs of good quality which shall be kept clean.
l.) EMPLOYEE FACILITIES - There shall be adequate and well- maintained locker rooms and bathrooms for male and female employees.

m.) PARKING - There shall be adequate, secured parking space provided for free to customers/guests.

n.) EMERGENCY GENERATOR - There shall be high-powered generator capable of providing full power in all areas of the establishment except those spas located in a commercial building with its own emergency generator capable of supplying the power requirements of its tenants.

o.) FIRST AID CABINET - There shall be a well-stocked first aid cabinet available at all times.

p.) FACILITIES FOR DISABLED - There shall be facilities and provisions for the disabled in accordance with Batas Pambansa Blg. 344 promulgated on May 1985, otherwise known as an "Act Enhancing the Mobility of Disabled persons."

q.) MAINTENANCE – Maintenance of all sections of the spa shall be on a continuing basis taking into consideration the quality of equipment and supplies, equipment, robes, sheets, blankets, pillow case, towels or other materials which may come in direct contact with the client's body shall be adopted in accordance with the standards prescribed under Presidential Decree No. 856 otherwise known as the Sanitation Code of 1976.

s.) SIGNBOARDS. – Appropriate sign boards shall be conspicuously displayed outside the establishment showing clearly the name of the spa while safety signages shall be prominently posted in strategic locations inside the spa.

Book 8 - Marketing Tourism & Travel

History And Evolution Of Modern Marketing

I. History of Marketing

In order to understand what marketing is and gain a comprehensive appreciation of its importance in successful enterprises today, it may be well to look backward toward the origins of trading and trace the evolution of modern marketing as the world commerce developed. Most historians agree that business began in the early dawn of man's existence as some form of barter or trading. In an exchange of goods or products for objects of equal or at least comparable value, heavy emphasis was placed on the products themselves. Men traded goods because they needed something. One probably had more than he could use of one article and wished to barter it for something he lacked.

During man's early history, it was comparatively easy for him to measure his needs and the value he obtained by this system of barter or exchange. As civilization progressed, men in increasing numbers migrated from the land to the towns and cities and traded their agricultural pursuits for a variety of handmade products and services which reflected to an increasing degree man's growing knowledge and new-found leisure. He was no longer forced to utilize all his time and energy in the all- consuming task of survival. Life in the city not only created the possibility of leisure, but a growing drive to produce an economic surplus from his work that would permit him to enjoy his nonworking hours.

II. Evolution of Modern Marketing

A. The Development of Two Basic Ideas

There were basic ideas developed which were to have considerable influence during this phase of product emphasis. These are:

1) The growth of product complexity, coupled with continually increasing opportunity for new products and new applications of old products; and,

2) The increasing inability of the buyer to understand the value of the product or service he was receiving and to relate it in some meaningful way to the value of what he was required to give in exchange for it.

This twofold problem reached such proportions in the Middle Ages that for the protection of the community as a whole and the farmer in particular, rigid laws were laid down governing the exchange of products. Of particular interest to us today is the medieval notion of morality in trading. Laws in the Middle Ages forbade charges not directly associated with the production of the product. Included was a ban on what was known as engrossing. This was defined as enlarging the price of a product because of some service associated with its movement or delivery. These are what is termed today as the marketing costs. A punishable offense in the Middle Ages, engrossing was generally held to be morally wrong. Under a feudal system in which tight control was exercised by the lord over his territory, it was possible to enforce a regulation of this type.

B.   The Emergence of New Ideas

As trading routes were opened up and goods were brought from distant places for exchange in the marketplace, a new idea emerged. The precise value of goods was becoming harder and harder to determine and the merchants and the traders set up havens which were outside the control of the feudal lords. These were known as the free towns or free ports. In them the buyer was very much at the mercy of the trader. He went there knowing that the trader would ask whatever he felt he could get. A typical haggling or bargaining session, such as it still is observed today in almost all the market places in North Africa, Asian countries and Arab Bazaars, and the order of the day in free towns in Europe.

The residual effects of this kind of trading is reflected in the attitudes of the modern consumer. Because of the somewhat looser system of controls that prevailed in the free towns, the would-be buyer was constantly warned, both by his feudal lord and by the church authorities, to be wary when he went trading in these free towns. Undoubtedly, he experienced enough cheating and deception at the hands of less scrupulous merchants that eventually he suspected the entire pattern of buying and selling. The prevailing feeling was expressed in a Latin phrase caveat emptor (let the buyer beware).

C. Introduction of Tools and Application of Natural Forces to Power these Tools. (The History of Cotton)

In its simplest terms, the history of trading and the development of products created a very real environment of suspicion. Later, with the introduction of tools and application of natural forces to power these tools, all traditional yardsticks for measuring the value of a product (which had been based largely on personal experience) began to disappear. The history of cotton provides excellent example. Originally, it was possible for a man to hand-clean one pound of cotton per day. With the invention of the hand-operated cotton gin, he turn out fifty pounds a day. With the industrial revolutionand the invention of the steam gin, a man could clean a thousand pounds of cotton in a day. The increase from one to a thousand pounds by the use of power tools upset the basis for comparison to such an extent that it was no longer possible for anyone used to the old yardsticks to make a reliable value of judgment on the new price of cotton. This was equally true to a variety of other areas and products.

D. Technological Progress

The fascination which technological progress has for humans and the consequent lessening of the human skill required in producing products probably came into sharpest focus after the beginning of the industrial revolution in the eighteenth century. Here production for production's sake, with man regarded as a cog in the machine or an expendable element in a production pattern, undoubtedly tended to heighten the emphasis on product to point where man inevitably started to fight back.

In the face of strong feeling that machines were about to take over and run the world, it was inevitable that human values would begin to reassert themselves. In books and periodicals of the 1920s, we constantly come across expressions of wonderment at the technological progress man had made and questions as to how much further he might be able to go. Underlying this wonderment is frequently expressed fear that he might have gone too far. Here we see the beginning of a change in emphasis which slowly during the first half of this century gave rise to what we today characterize as the marketing concept.

E. The Changing Pattern of Man's Need

In order to understand the factors which caused the change in emphasis from product to consumer, we should reexamine the changing patter of man's needs as we have observed it through the course of history. Undoubtedly, the earliest human satisfaction were of basic and necessary bodily needs: eating, sleeping, reproduction, shelter. With the growth of culture and technological improvements in man's condition, needs other than these basic needs were progressively the object of satisfaction. More advanced segments of society came to a stage where all their basic needs were reasonably well satisfied, and with a growing measure of so-called discretionary income, they were in a position to satisfy a great many other needs.

F. Man and his Reaction to Products and Services

Up to this point in time, concentration have been made primarily on the individual and his reaction to products or services which he could obtain. Increasingly, however, life in the towns and cities generated a series of social forces which shaped the choices and priorities of the individual beyond the immediate satisfaction his own physical needs. Eventually these too were affected in that a choice of clothes, food, and other so-called necessities of life added a dimension of style and social acceptability that a way in which companies could obtain worthwhile guidance in streamlining future offerings to meet more precisely the needs of the ultimate user. Psychographic and sociographic measures were substituted for the largely geographic and demographic bases on which the statistical marketing man had relied, and in-depth research began to replace the superficial polls and surveys which had previously been popular.

Chart I

Year	Stage	Basis
1900	Theoretical	History
1910	Theoretical	History
1920		
1930		Geographic
1940	Statistical	
1950		Psychographic
1960	Behavioral	
1970		
1980		
1990	Alternative	Strategy
2000		

MARKETING IN THIS CENTURY

Unfortunately, mounting uncertainties in the late 1960s and early 1970s convinced may marketing men that there was no certain path which could be followed with unswerving dedication that would inevitably lead to a successful product introduction. Increasingly, they began to experiment with alternative approaches, applying both statistical controls and behavioral research in elaborate schemes for test-marketing alternatives, and they were prepared to rapidly withdraw new entries which failed to live up to early expectations. In recent years, the wisdom of this trend has been confirmed by the advent of such totally unanticipated factors as the energy crisis, when companies capable of modifying their marketing patterns or altering their product line within a relatively short period of time were able to make a virtue out of necessity. Others, with more inflexible commitments, had to suffer serious economic disadvantages.

Sophisticated Planning and Viable Alternatives

Today, marketing is characterized as those communication process necessary to create understanding and acceptance of a company and its capabilities in the minds of its customers, and concomitantly, to generate in the minds of all corporate decision-makers an understanding of the needs and wants of the customers which it must satisfy it is to grow and continue to show profit. Sophisticated planning, which proposes a series of viable alternatives, in-depth analysis of present customers and potential markets, careful control over all forms of communication from mass media trough personal contacts, and continuous monitoring of the effectiveness of the process as a whole, offer the best hope that informed corporate decisions can guide the enterprise on its chosen course and utilize resources available to it with the utmost effectiveness.

With the primacy of the customer clearly established, it is now necessary to understand the changes that have taken place in individual and collective behavior throughout the course of this century. Techniques for identifying and defining potential markets can then be understood, and their potential value to the medium- sized or small business objectively assessed.

The Changing Needs And Priorities Of Affluent Society

I. Introduction

Since modern marketing is fundamentally concerned with understanding humans and their purposeful patterns of behavior, it is not surprising that theories of human motivation have played an important part in shaping the thinking of successful practitioners. Dating back to the work of behavioral scientists in the 1930s and 1940s, a very simple model of human behavior can be described as a series of needs which trigger coping or purposeful behavior, which in turn looks for objectives. These, if achieved, can modify or satisfy the needs. Thirst, for example, produces a search for a beverage or liquid which, when consumed, will take the thirst away. While seemingly simple, even a cursory analysis will reveal that the various ways in which the search might be conducted have unlimited possibilities. The types of potables that could satisfy various kinds and levels of thirst are numerous. For this reason modern marketing has concentrated on attempting to understand the relatively limited range of human needs and to focus attention on the genesis of purchasing as a particular pattern of purposeful behavior, rather than attempting to explore all the various ways in which purposeful activity might find satisfactory objective.

II. Development of Purchasing Behavior

Unfortunately, human needs are not as easily identified by the person experiencing the need as one might suppose. Generally accepted theories of purchasing behavior begin with a recognition of a fundamental distinction between needs and wants. Needs are sensations that objects or experiences are missing, the absence of which, communicated to the conscious mind, produces a search for ways or means in which objects or experiences can be found that will supposedly satisfy the need. This wish to find the object or service is described as a want. Unfortunately, here is no guarantee that what one wants will satisfy ones needs.

For this reason, marketing men have developed a sequence of activities which describe a complete cycle of purchasing behavior, beginning chronologically with the needs themselves and ultimately producing resolution of these needs through satisfaction. This is known as the need-want cycle. The various steps are diagrammed in Chart II, which lists the six phases through which the progression normally occurs. It further attempts to visually emphasize the difference between internal experience and external recognition of the experience by dividing various phases of the cycle into experiential and cognitive states.

Chart II
Phases of Progression

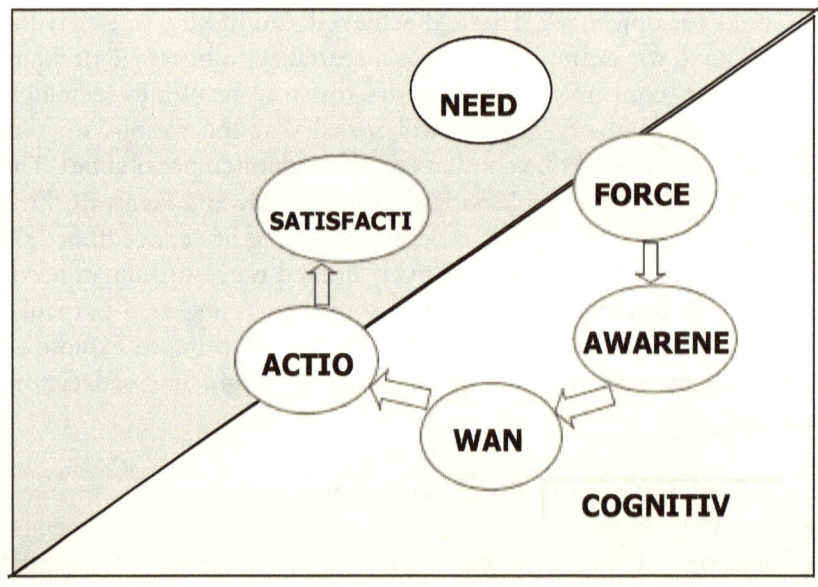

Before exploring any part of the cycle in detail, it may be valuable to describe the various stages of the need-want cycle in forming a successful purchasing pattern. The cycle begins with needs, things or experiences which are missing, either because we once possessed and now lost them or because acquired or innate drives have conditioned us to search for new and potentially satisfying experiences. Many of these forces, may lie dormant until something occurs to awaken us to their existence.

Forces - which awaken our awareness of these needs are either internal or external. Concerned as he is with those areas he can predict and in some measure control, the marketing man has primarily focused his attention on external forces. Chief among these are the social and educational forces which produce a search for physical possessions and a variety of new experiences in a given society. Since different classes of society influence their members to acquire possessions an seek experiences in different ways, the impact of social class on human awareness must be analyzed carefully if we are to predict group trends and obtain early indications of the type of products and services favored by any given group.

Awareness - develops under the pressure of internal and external forces which convert the need into a perceived want. This perception not only includes a vague realization of the existence of a need but also at least a glimmering possibility that some product or service which will eventually meet this need is available and accessible to the would-be purchaser. Now at last marketing man has an opportunity to influence not only the recognition of need but also the specification of the product or service which is most likely to ensure lasting satisfaction of the need itself. Advertising and promotional activities of all types seek to develop this awareness and to mold it into a conscious quest for the product or service of the sponsor.

Wants - are active commitments to the acquisition of a product or service, provided that the terms or conditions under which it can be obtained are acceptable. To ensure this, shopping on the part of the customer and selling on the part of the provider seek to ensure that the transfer of goods and services can be arranged on a mutually agreeable basis.

Action - follows wants can be distinguished clearly from want itself and must include not only those portions of the cycle that involve negotiation and transfer of title to the goods or service but also the subsequent performance of the purchase. Here, realistic structuring of expectation is vital, since the chances of an experience being repeated are directly in proportion to the expectations of the purchaser and the product's or service's ability to meet these expectations. In a highly competitive society, there is an unfortunate tendency to oversell products or services merely to obtain short-term tactical advantage over competition. Unfortunately, subsequent disappointment tends to eliminate any future possibility of repeating the purchasing pattern, and product or service sold in this way runs out of future when it runs out of first-time customers.

Satisfaction - is the feeling of pleasure which occurs when all or a major part of a need complex is eliminated. Satisfaction contains further element of relief since throughout the course of the purchasing pattern there is generally some measure of doubt that a satisfactory solution can be found. Because most products or services enjoy considerable economic advantages from repeat purchasing. The objective in understanding all phases of the cycle and attempting to guide the customer through those which fall within the control of marketing organization is to ensure that maximum satisfaction will be obtained from each purchase. This not only increases the likelihood that the pattern will be repeated but can also significantly lessen the cost incurred by the marketing function.

III. Principal Objectives of Modern Marketing

One of the principal objectives of modern marketing is to build long-term relationships which customers habitually turn toward the company for satisfaction of certain needs. If the entire relationship is handled to the customer's complete satisfaction, the experience not only produces repeat purchases but can create environment in which a given company receives the first opportunity to develop products or services which will meet new need. In this capacity it can increasingly channel its research and development activities along lines which are most likely to yield profitable results. Contrasting the productivity cycle and the need-want cycle, we see that they represent almost diametrically opposed approaches to purchasing behavior. In the first case, the company is looking at its internal capabilities and hopes for future profitability. In the second case, the company looks at the customer needs and adapts all its energies to satisfying these needs in a way best calculated to ensure customer satisfaction.

Having briefly described the various stages of the need-want cycle, it may be valuable to explore in greater depth two aspects of behavior which permit modern marketing to focus more precisely on the individual and on the types of products or services which are most likely to satisfy his individual or collective needs. These areas are the needs themselves and an analysis of the social forces which tend to create awareness of the needs on the part of each purchaser.

While there are various ways of categorizing human needs, the theories of Abraham Maslow developed in the middle of 1950s have not only stood the test of time but have been widely accepted as providing a comprehensive framework within which the priorities of the individual and the varying collective emphases of different groups can be identified and predicted. The theories, distinguish five groups of needs -ranging from physical through self-actualizing needs - and categorizes each as part of developmental process beginning in a predictable sequence and eventually forming a hierarchical pattern which influences every aspect of human behavior.

Physical Needs are apparently created at the moment of birth. In the womb the physical needs of the infant are taken care of on a continuous basis. Nutrition, hygiene, environmental control - all are provided without interruption. Eventually there comes one traumatic moment when the infant loses this continuous care. Fortunately he learns rapidly to utilize his newly acquired ability to cry to restore the lost services. As he experiences various physical needs, his crying draws attention to the fact that he is hungry, wet, or tired, and appropriate action ensures short term satisfaction of his need.

Safety Needs is the product of the undesirable side effect of the Physical needs, as unfortunately crying may cause parental displeasure that can generally create punitive activities which the child rapidly learns to avoid. He learns that purposeful behavior will not only produce desirable responses but can also have undesirable ones. This is the moment, his Safety Needs begin. With each passing year he will become increasingly aware of his own vulnerability, his dependence on others for satisfaction of his physical needs, and his need to conform to the constraints which they place on his behavior.

Social Needs is the effect of the child's incapability of surviving alone when he recognizes at an early age that resolution of potentially dangerous conflicts calls for accommodation with other human beings.

It is a series of slowly developed social needs which calls for the ability on the part of child not only to win social acceptance but also to contribute to the welfare of the group as the price of this own survival.

When he goes to school and increasingly becomes part of a structured society, accommodation with the mores of the group and a willingness to give up personal advantages for the sake of long-term accommodation with group will play an important part in his life.

Esteem Needs comes as safety needs drove him toward the group and forced accommodation with its patterns of behavior, another force, unique apparently to humans, will now start to draw him away from the group. In an effort to retain his own identity, he will consciously compare himself with the group, generally in ways which are favorable to him. They begin with self-esteem, but generally develop into a need to have his superiority in whatever fashion it maybe manifested recognized by the group. This external recognition we term as a desire for status. As satisfaction of physical and social needs becomes more a matter of routine and follows a predictable and consistent pattern, an individual's esteem needs will have a tendency to separate him from the group and may eventually make him relatively independent of the group and its opinions.

Self-Actualizing is the final state in which an individual consciously seeks to develop his own potential and looks for ways in which more of this potential can be developed.

The average man who perceives that he has untapped potential and longs for a chance to express himself is experiencing these needs. Frequently, his occupation or social position may not afford him the opportunities he craves. Put humorously, "Inside every fat man, there is a fatter man trying to get out." This simply indicates that all of us try in some way to be more of whatever we are. When we have reached the limit of our present capacity, we look for new fields to conquer and new ways to express the versatility of the gifts and attributes we possess.

Obviously, a complex need structure exists inside each individual, but he is frequently unaware of the connection between his needs and behavior which seeks in some form to satisfy them. Increasingly, human behavior looks for objective which will simultaneously satisfy more than one need. For example, in the simple act of eating or drinking, we can satisfy more than our physical need for food and drink. By selecting certain types of food, we can show our awareness of health precautions, manner and social poise, and even sufficient knowledge of epicurean delights to satisfy our status needs. We can even satisfy self-actualizing needs by cooking an epicurean delight before a group of friends. This one action can be seen to satisfy all five levels of human needs. It is unlikely that the individual performing this action will be fully aware of his own motives and of the complexity of needs he is seeking to satisfy.

Chart III Illustrates both the direction and the evolution from physical to self- actualizing needs and attempts to analyze varying degrees of emphasis placed by travelers on need satisfaction, depending on whether they travel alone or in a group. The diagram illustrates results of the survey conducted by Communications Research, Inc., of Chicago in which a random sample of individual travelers was contrasted with affiliated groups composed of people with similar occupations or other common interests which led them to travel as an organized group. Predictably the concerns of the individual travelers were most heavily centered around safety and esteem. Most were prepared to put up with a certain amount of physical inconvenience, did not want to get involved with others on the journey, and did not perceive any self-actualizing possibilities in travel itself. In sharp contrast, groups placed heavy emphasis on physical aspects of travel, particularly food and quality of accommodations. They were understandably less concerned about safety, feeling that participation in the group offered an added measure of security.

Chart III
Human Needs (Maslow)

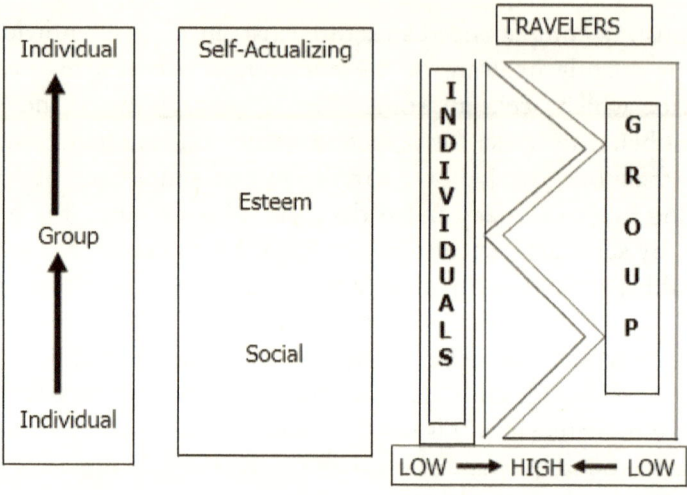

Their social needs were obviously being met by the fact of affiliation in the group. Esteem needs appeared to be low, with greater emphasis on possessions and behavioral characteristics shared in common than those which would tend to differentiate an individual too strongly from the group. In a somewhat surprising development, opportunities for self-actualizing were prized, and the most successful experiences.

Marketing Comes to Retailing

I. Meaning and Role of Marketing

In its simplest terms, marketing is the company function concerned with the needs and wants of its customers. The word concerned at least four separate types of activities:

(1) The company must know what these needs are.
(2) It must shape and focus the forces which work on the needs and wants.
(3) It must provide for the satisfaction of the wants.
(4) It must ensure that this satisfaction is provided on terms pleasing to the customer and favorable to the company.

In its formal definition, Marketing is the specialized function within the company, charged with identifying and defining customer needs, creating a favorable environment for satisfying customers wants, establishing a permanent relationship in which the customer turns to the company for satisfaction of these wants, and providing the product and service at a time and place and in the form best suited to profitably satisfy both needs and wants.

Most modern marketing theory emphasizes the notion that the primary role of marketing department is to make the company meaningful to the customer and the customer meaningful to the company. This process of creating understanding is, of course, communication and as such can be analyzed in communication terms.
The output side of a company's communication is divided into three areas;

1. Those mass communications, such as advertising or sales literature, which are intended by the company and perceived by the recipient as impersonal statements.

4. Personal communications involving contact between two company but are perceived in some personal form by the recipient. These would include instructions or communications carried by the product itself, the way in which it performs, its packaging or convenience.

5. Communications which are intended as impersonal by the company but are perceived in some personal form by the recipient. These would include instructions or communications carried by the product itself, the way in which it performs, its packaging or convenience. The feedback side of communications from a customer to a company tends to take place in both a formal and an informal manner. On the formal level, marketing research, surveys, and other structural ways of gathering information are used by many companies in an informal way, sales, individual contacts with the company, correspondence, complaints, etc., provide feedback on the needs and wants of the customers.

II. Ultimate Objective of Marketing

The management and operation of this communication pattern is entrusted to marketing. The company's ultimate marketing objective is unquestionably to "provide the customer with products or services at a price which is profitable to the company and permanently satisfying to the customer." To build and maintain this permanent relationship, the customer's satisfaction with what the product will do for him must be maintained at all times. Increasingly, companies realize that only a part of this objective can be directly attributed to the marketing department. Design, engineering, production, the overall efficiency of the organization-in short, everything from concept to ultimate replacement-must be carefully controlled and must meet the customer's requirements if the company is to grow and enjoy continued prosperity.

Sensitivity to the effect actions will have on the customer is increasingly described as a marketing attitude. It is generally felt today that unless the marketing attitude is present, the effectiveness of a marketing department is likely to be a little different from that of traditional selling. Only the name has changed, the activities remain the same.

III. The Basic Activities in Marketing
The basic activities in marketing are:

Marketing Research
This identifies and defines the needs of present and potential customers, identifies the forces which shape these needs into wants, and communicates the information to the other departments of the company. Looked at the terms of the need-want cycle, marketing research is uniquely concerned with all elements.

Advertising and Promotion
Advertising and promotion must create and maintain a belief on the part of present and potential customers in the company's willingness and ability to satisfy their needs and wants which the company can profitably satisfy. Advertising should control all those elements of communication which in any sense project an image of the company to the customer. Seen in this way, the activity is much broader than the traditional concept of simply purchasing space to project certain messages to customers. Advertising has the total responsibility for all mass communications, since thee are part of the forces which shape and specify the want that the company ultimately hopes to satisfy.

Sales and Service
The third major activity of marketing is ales and service. Sales and service must convince present and potential customers of the company's willingness and ability to satisfy their wants and must coordinate the satisfaction of these wants in such a way as to establish a permanent and profitable relationship between the company and the customers.

One of the traditional difficulties in marketing has been to differentiate between advertising and selling. They are similar in that both have an effect on persuading a customer that the company has the ability to satisfy his needs. A differentiation in terms of mass communication for advertising and personal communication for selling makes the most sense. This also helps to show how the forces shaped by advertising can be focused on a personal basis through sales personnel.

The second and perhaps increasingly more important element of the sales- service activity is the maintenance of a high level of customer satisfaction. This typically is done not only through personal communication but also by ensuring that a customer's reasonable wants will be satisfied in a form, time, place, and manner suitable to him. This leads us to the fourth activity of marketing, one which, in the light of what we have said, is assuming increasing importance.

Product Selection, Display and Delivery
These must determine the conditions of time, place, and manner under which the highest profitable level of continued customer satisfaction can be achieved and maintained.

The reason for including product selection, display, and delivery under marketing stems from the inescapable connection under with a product is perceived, the form in which it is offered, and the quality condition in which it is received. Combining a company's knowledge of the customer's needs with his determination of the various ways in which his wants can be satisfied, it becomes increasingly important to customize the product while maintaining cost/price advantages associated with many things not formerly in its domain: the units of shipment, the form of packaging (not only to provide the best protection for product but also to appeal emotionally to the customer), type of display, the time and place in which the customer will receive the product, and the various people used in the marketing activity to ensure the satisfaction of the customer. At the same time, marketing must maintain all this within a cost framework which still permits a reasonable profit on the satisfaction of the customer.

This approach provides a logical framework within which the important function of marketing can be examined. The four marketing activities: marketing research; advertising and promotion; sales and service; and, product selection, display, and delivery can each be analyzed in terms of basic techniques.

IV. Retailing in Tourism & Travel Industry

Of all forms of modern retailing, few if any can rival the tourism and travel industry for an attractive ratio of reward to risk. While alleged profits are understandably understated, salary plus benefits, including assisted travel, too frequently fall far short of what comparable effort and investment might produce in other forms of retailing. While the financial risks are substantial, as evidenced by alarming bankruptcies of sizeable enterprises with staggering losses to all concerned, the more serious threat of a total consumer credibility remains of paramount concern in assessing future prospects for the industry.

Traditionally, most forms of retailing marked up goods or services, added their own costs and profit to the manufacturer's and passed to the consumer, who compensated both and expected both to cooperate in ensuring his satisfaction. In the travel and tourism industry uniquely, compensation for the travel agent's or tour operator's services is remitted by the supplier of the services. Because of this, the agent must appear to the thoughtful consumer to be more of a pawn of the supplier than a friend and trusted ally of the would-be-purchaser. Simplistic approaches to selling have relied heavily on the belief that everyone wants something for nothing. However, there is considerable evidence that people value only what they pay for and recognize that there is no such thing as a free lunch. Increasingly, the informed consumer wishes to know who is paying for what and why, and he is suspicious of arrangements which appear to be too good to be true. The mutual cannibalizing of direct selling and independent retailing undoubtedly lessens the effectiveness of both, and the thoughtful consumer perceives that the cost of these duplicate activities must eventually be passed through to him.

Traditionally, anti-trust legislation has recognized the benefit to the consumer of independent retailing and the checks and balances which this form of distribution provides. However, unless the independent retailer is capable of providing the quality of service necessary to meet and stimulate the growing demand, it is unlikely that suppliers will lessen or terminate their direct-selling activities.

Marketing Sophistication a must in Modern Travel and Tourism

Whatever the future holds, the modern travel agents and tour operators must acquire a level of management and marketing sophistication far greater than that required for survival in a more placid era. As a small businessman, he has neither the resources nor the latitude to engage in costly experimentation and must increasingly concentrate his efforts on those market segments he is best equipped to serve. He must find ways of increasing his ability to generate revenue without having to add substantially to overhead. With this in mind, he has learned to identify his marketing objectives clearly. He must know the end-result of each marketing activity and set specific objectives, the accomplishment of which he can measure in each area. While these objectives can be stated in various ways, the following illustrations will provide some guidance in setting individual agency goals.

ADVERTISING To create a growing number of contacts with qualified
DISPLAY To create favorable environment for selling
SELLING To personalize each customer contact
CREDIT To increase individual purchasing power
SERVICES To build long term relationship
RESEARCH To identify the most efficient ways of achieving all the above

While each of the above objectives should be more sharply focused in an individual agency and should include precisely defined standards which will measure accomplishment in every area at any given period of time, it is helpful to begin the marketing process by defining those segments of the travel and tourism market which appear to most accessible to a given enterprise and to understand how marketing processes might vary one social class or one age to the next.

Chart IV., is a summary of the differences in the need-want cycle, with appropriate marketing activities of four contrasting market segments. The upper- middle class, traditionally prime prospects for leisure time travel, is divided into younger and older segments. The lower-middle and upper-middle classes, are treated as separate groups. Of particular interest may be the finding that the younger upper- middle class tends t think of themselves and to purchase in a manner similar to the lower-upper class and to exhibit motivational anomalies which separate them decisively from their parents.

Chart IV
TRAVEL/TOURISM MARKETING SEGMENTATION

CLASS	HIDDEN NEEDS	INTERNAL FORCES	ADVT. PROMOTION	LEVEL OF AWARENESS	SELLING METHOD	CONSCIOUS WANTS	TYPE OF SERVICE	APPROPRIATE ACTION	EVIDENCE OF SATISFACTION
UPPER MIDDLE Younger	Self-Actualizing	Boredom	Oral	Medium	Team	Experience	Deluxe	Tolerance	Repetition
UPPER MIDDLE Older	Esteem	Loneliness	Oral	High	Team	Attention	Deluxe	Deference	Referral
LOWER MIDDLE	Social	Imitation	Written	Medium	Solo	Acceptance	First Class	Conversation	Reminiscing
UPPER LOWER	Safety	Avarice	Pictorial	Low	A/V	Bargain	Standard	Direction	Relief

As with any summary, there is considerable danger of over-simplification. The most effective way to utilize a matrix, such as Chart IV, is to check against past experience in order to validate the correctness of each description. Where considerable discrepancies occur, research in the form of a small number of interviews with prospects can frequently provide necessary clues to either validating the given description or finding a more appropriate way in which to describe the behavior of the group.

A Do-It-Yourself Approach To Marketing

I. Introduction

The metamorphosis of an entrepreneurial venture into an enduring enterprise is not accomplished with considerable unlearning on the part of the leader. Unfortunately, many of the strengths of the entrepreneur may become weakness if allowed to persist in a mature organization. Among these must be numbered the entrepreneur's instinctive feel for the needs of his clients. While it is frequently true that he owes his early success to an intuitive ability to pick people with whom he can work, as the audience for his services broadens, he has too accept a growing need for systematic research and verification of the different and probably changing needs of his clientele and must adapt his recommendations and suggestions to their current needs.

II. The Internal Process

The internal processes necessary to accomplish this are described in various publications on professional management. As a prerequisite for effective marketing, the manager must learn to:

A)   Plan his activities and those of his subordinates in a systematic and comprehensive way;

B)   Organize the work logically and delegate authority to make decisions wherever possible;

C)   Lead his subordinates in a participative way, ensuring both understanding and acceptance of their roles and an opportunity to find maximum personal satisfaction in work that they accomplish;

D)   Further remain flexible, making whatever adjustments may be necessary in the plan as circumstances change and periodically evaluating his own performance and that of his staff in order to establish new objectives and continue the growth and development of the enterprise.

III. The Three Major Areas of Marketing

With awareness of the need for and some commitment to acquiring the skills as described in the preceding, the enterprise is now ready to add the technical advantages of marketing to its list of accomplishments. Reduced to its simplest terms, the medium-sized or small service business should concentrate its marketing efforts in three major areas:

1.) Advertising;
2.) Selling; and,
3.) Research.

Chart V illustrates both the sequence of these activities and a one-word summary of the role of each, with the necessary inclusion of the role of a supplier who must be capable of delivering what the retailer has promised and is committed to. Clearly, to ensure that the cycle will be repeated, the retailer must confirm the promises and commitments have been met.

Chart V

Cycle of Retail Marketing

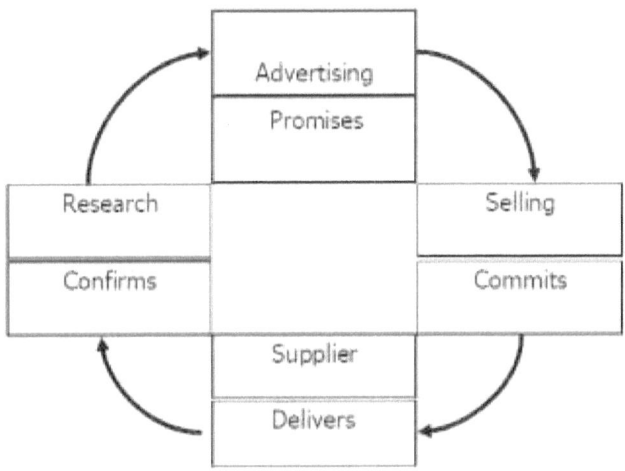

Before discussing in detail how this might be accomplished, it is important to review some of the major conclusions which can be drawn from the findings of modern marketing as we have described them. We will then attempt to apply these conclusions which can be drawn form the findings of modern marketing as we have described them. These conclusions are applied to a recommended sequence of steps in installing a marketing system.

1. Personal Needs must be satisfied if an experience is to be repeated. All purchases include personal and impersonal components of satisfaction. The difference can be clearly seen in buying of a product which meets all reasonable specifications but is solid in such a way that the customer develops a dislike for the salesperson and vows never to purchase anything from him again. Put in other words, the product may meet customer's physical needs, but the way in which it was sold failed to satisfy his need for esteem. Since the probability of an experience increases with its ability to satisfy a broader range of human needs, care must be taken to verify not only the fact but the extent of accomplishment at each step along the way.

2. Wants are expressed in ways which are generally misleading. Most experienced salesmen can recall examples of customers who wanted something they didn't really need, which if sold to them, would inevitably produce dissatisfaction. This apparent ignorance of his own needs on the part of the purchaser can stem from both ignorance of the product and lack of personal insight into his own motivation. Modern marketing must learn to refuse to cooperate in attempts at self-deception.

3. Today's customer is as concerned with "how" as with "what". Education serves to both satisfy and stimulate curiosity. The modern customer expects to be provided with both questions and answers, and he feels that a trusted confidante should show him how to accomplish what he wants to do in the most economic and satisfactory manner possible.

4. Different categories of customers require different strategies. A weakness of traditional selling has been a tendency to treat

customers alike. Clearly differences in age, social class, and other relevant factors must be taken into account as one customizes the approach and the recommended services to the unique needs of each individual. Segmentation of market by social class offers an added benefit in that the most effective media for reaching each group can be isolated and promises can be tailored to create a favorable environment for both contact and deliverable commitment.

5. Comparative values require continuing reeducation in inflationary times. In an age of galloping inflation, the seller of big-ticket items runs into an unusual problem. Since major purchases of this type are intermittent and tend to recur at one or two-year intervals, there is a need to reeducate the would-be purchaser inconspicuously and restructure his value perceptions so that he does not go into economic shock on being informed of the current cost of a proposed service. Though past customers may not currently be shopping, periodic contact to keep them abreast of price increases goes a long way to prevent resistance when they are ready for their next purchase.

6. Competition for the discretionary fund is inter-industry. Competition from others offering the same service in his immediate vicinity understandably makes the retailing entrepreneur nervous. Increasingly, however, marketing men are learning to recognize that major discretionary purchases are compared with one another and that a decision to purchase travel over an automobile, a boat, furniture, or a summer home requires an industry-wide ability to attract the consumer's attention and convince him of he superior benefits to be obtained from purchasing their products rather than someone else's. The success of automobile rows, shopping malls, and furniture warehouses attest to the benefits of size and the need for cooperation on the part of fragmented industry in producing maximum visibility for the products and services it offers.

7. Companies and countries are judged by the people we meet. In a less analytical age, companies were judged by their products and countries, far too often, by the quality and quantity of their plumbing. Expanded travel and increased awareness of the human side of enterprise have diverted attention from the mechanical and focused it

on interpersonal relations to a point where sweeping judgments may be based on a relatively few contacts between people. Required as they are to satisfy esteem needs to an increasing degree and recognizing that only through the recognition of another human being can this be accomplished, everyone associated with an enterprise or an area must be aware of the important role he plays in contributing to the ultimate satisfaction of the purchaser.

8. The seller is held accountable for the performance of the supplier. While most retailers have relatively little control over the physical characteristics of the products they sell, by careful purchasing they can limit their offerings to products they find consistently reliable. In the retailing of services, however, particularly when these services are offered by distant enterprises about which the retailer can have little personal, up-to-date knowledge, the danger of making commitments which the supplier is unwilling or unable to meet cannot be overstated. Generally, the consumer prefers a candid admission of ignorance or guarded statement on pleasant past experiences, coupled with hope of current continuance, to bland reassurances that everything will be fine.

9. Realistic structuring of expectation provides the best protection for both. A safe prescription for effective joint marketing between supplier and retailer is to "under-commit and over-deliver." While there is nothing to be gained from reciting a litany of potential catastrophes, variations in quality of service that occur with any frequency should be factored into a realistic description of what is likely to occur and couched in terms of sufficient caution to convince the would-be purchaser that the retailer is attempting to be completely honest with him about the service he is buying.

10. Technical professionalism cannot exist without management professionalism. A widely observed phenomenon in modern retailing is the tendency on the part of salespeople to treat the customers as they themselves are treated by their superiors. Indecisiveness, unwillingness or inability to communicate, and lack of motivation will invariably be reflected in the performance of the salesperson as he deals with a potential client. Since the goal of professional management is to accomplish results through others pleasantly and effectively as

possible, the internal mechanisms to achieve this must be in place before the full benefits of truly professional marketing can be obtained.

IV. The Fundamental Steps in Modern Marketing

Recognizing that an independent retailer already has a viable selling activity, the development of a minimal marketing effort usually calls for the addition of some research which will provide a factual base on which to both introduce or restructure an advertising effort and reshape the selling activity so that it more precisely meets the needs and wants of present and potential customers. As part of this focusing or refocusing, some enterprises have found it convenient to discontinue present advertising and utilize at least a portion of the resources allocated to that activity to develop the factual base upon which an integrated marketing program can be built. While the following steps are outlined as a do-it-yourself project, larger enterprises may find it advisable to secure the help of competent counsel in areas where this available.

STEP 1. **Define Probable Markets in Behavioral Terms.**

Based on a combination of past experience plus available local data, describe your market as upper-middle, white-collar, or blue-collar, or combination between each of the major groups.

STEP 2. **Rank in Size and Cost of individual Contact.**

Based on past experience, evaluate total size of market within convenient distance of your place of business, segment into leisure, commercial, and other relevant categories, and attempt to assess the cost of services directly associated with developing each new contact. Rank this in descending order of cost.

STEP 3. **Select a median Market for Pilot Effort.**

Pick one or more pilot groups for the experiment, hopefully combing major potential with moderate development costs.

STEP 4. **Identify Cost-Effective Media Mix.**

With appropriate advertising counsel, when available, identify those media which can deliver a major portion of qualified prospects at the lowest unit of cost.

STEP 5. **State Communication Objective and Set Budget**

Beware of attempting to do too much with a singly advertisement.

Simple objectives, such as awareness of your existence and services, are more realistically achievable and can be measured in terms of the number of inquiries they generate. These are preferable to long lists of potential offerings displayed without any clear-cut objectives in mind.

STEP 6. **Test Copy of Graphics on Small Sample.**

A portion of even a modest advertising budget should be devoted to testing the effectiveness of various messages and illustrations prior to embarking on a promotional campaign. A representative sample of as few as 25 individuals from a target group can significantly improve the effectiveness of an individual advertisement.

STEP 7. **Predict Results for Target Market.**

Standards should be clearly indentified in advance which will justify the cost of developing prospects in the target market area. They should identify both the quality and quantity of response but should not be tied to subsequent purchases, since these may result from selling failures rather than ineffectiveness of the promotional effort.

STEP 8. **Conduct Pilot Promotion.**

In an attempt to identify results directly attributable to a given campaign, it is valuable to have discontinued other and previous advertising efforts sufficiently far advance of the promotion that carry-over effect will not obscure the result obtained from it. Further, the promotion itself can be isolated and measured on its independent achievement.

STEP 9. **Evaluate Quality and Quantity of Response Against Predictions.**

Careful evaluation of the number of responses received and the quality of the contacts established should be reviewed before deciding on changes in the promotional activity or attempting alternative approaches.

STEP 10. **Modify or Revise Program,**

Neophytes should guard against early discouragement, since it is unlikely that immediate success will attend every promotional activity. One the other hand, unusual success with the first effort should be regarded with some suspicion until it is clearly established that the results obtained are directly attributable to the promotional activity itself.

STEP 11. **Repeat the Test or Expand with Adaptations.**

If the results have not met expectations, the rest should be modified and repeated. If they have, the program should be expanded, based on funds available and the ability of the enterprise to cope with an expanded rage of services or increased level of activity.

STEP 12. **Evaluate Against objectives and Revise as Needed.**

There is an understandable tendency to ride a winner too long. All marketing activities need frequent revision and need to be constantly upgraded and improved if we wish to ensure steady growth. A total marketing cycle-from advertising and selling through the supplier's ability to deliver on commitments as verified by research-requires constant monitoring if the effectiveness of the enterprise as a whole is to be maintained and improved.

Concluding Notes:

Survival for the medium-sized or small business in an age of giants can only come from utilizing its resources more effectively than its larger competitors. Professional management and professional marketing are tools uniquely designed to achieve this. Modern management leadership can ensure the most effective internal utilization of resources to accomplish desired objective. Modern marketing can add the external dimension of ensuring that every customer becomes both an addict and a missionary perceiving the retailer as his ally and advocate, the accessible guarantor of his satisfaction in whatever activity the retailer recommends.

Marketing In The 21st Century Age Of Digital Information Technology

Strategies in Marketing Tourism

I. Introduction

Every industry and business enterprise sector has its own peculiar characteristics, best practices, and strategies to share a slice of various markets. This is why it's important to look at industries separately when thinking of how to market and expand them. The tourism industry is of not exception, with tourism marketing becoming an imperative in its every day operation.

Techniques and Strategies in Marketing are in fast phased evolution because of the increasing use of technology. In Tourism, travelling tops the popularity in activities. In this Age of Information Technology has allowed digital marketing to provide various kinds of travel information to everyone.

The Information Technology unquestionably demystify the thoughts that travelling is attractive enough on its own, and tourism business are in stiff competition to the top tour marketing company for their destinations, the importance to apply Tourism Marketing to promote the business with distinction from others similarly situate.

II. Marketing Trends in The Tourism Industry

It must be noted that tourism business has different tourism types and changing consumer behaviors and travel trends in the industry. Travel trends in the tourism industry indeed evolved out from the peoples' perception during the early centuries that travelling is a luxury, and that only the influential and wealthy could afford.

.In this age of information technology modernization, everyone is aware that there are available within the fingertips different types or kinds of trips that suit the financial capacity of everyone. From the adventurous individual or small group budget backpackers, middle class professionals, to business owners and executives for the more luxurious fully organized trips with luxury five-star hotel accommodations, people are becoming more aware of their travel needs and choosing their destinations accordingly.

Considering the rapid changes in the industry, tourism key players and front liners in Destination Management Offices (DMOs) need to understand and keep up to date with these developments and trends. They should also aim to adapt their strategies to cater to the ever changing consumer behavior.

III. The Tourism Marketing

Tourism marketing is the term used to describe the different marketing methods and strategies used in the tourism industry.
At its core, tourism marketing refers to a business that aims to attract tourists to a specific location.

The Tourism System is multifaceted, so tourism marketing must include all its components, i.e., airlines, automobile rental services, and hotels and other forms of lodgings and accommodation facilities. Additionally, it covers restaurants, tours, and travel agents to generate awareness, online sales, and increase consumer acquisition.

There are many ways to do this. But first, it's essential to understand that the foundation of a tourism marketing strategy is a well-constructed marketing plan. This marketing plan must outline the techniques, processes, and tools a company intends on using to promote tourism.

The Concept of Tourism Marketing

Tourism marketing is known to flourish in places already considered "hotspots" amongst tourists. But, it can also be used in lesser-known places to attract more visitors. One of the critical aspects of tourism marketing is strategic planning to achieve brand visibility, which ultimately leads to brand awareness.

When an enterprise has successfully created a tourism website, it can focus on achieving brand awareness and targeting potential customers. Through tourism marketing strategies and tools, companies can expand on their tourism market.
A successful marketing mix strategy can even help an entry-level travel business become a monopoly in the travel industry.

Why Marketing Tourism Is Beneficial
An essential part of tourism marketing is adopting the appropriate and relevant marketing strategy. Adopting the right plan could help your company maximize revenue and build awareness.

As one of the world's largest industries, the travel industry is expected to keep growing in the upcoming years. Naturally, because of its demand and expected growth, this industry is highly competitive.
Travel businesses must research, formulate strategies, and think of innovative ways to stand out from their rivals. By using tourism marketing practices and tools, these businesses can promote themselves as the best option for travelers.

The key role is to find a unique selling point and then promote it to reach the masses. But reaching the masses is not enough. Capturing their attention, keeping them engaged (through experiential marketing), and using a content marketing strategy that's relatable is just as crucial.

So, as part of your marketing efforts, you must keep up with the latest trends and adopt a marketing mix strategy that's a perfect blend of the best practices and tools.

Different Types of Tourism Marketing
While there are many types of tourism marketing, here are a few major broad types.

1. Location Marketing
Think of the most popular locations that come to mind when you think of a particular continent or country. For instance, if someone says "Europe", your mind already conjures up images of the UK, Spain,

France, or Italy; and, if you of South East Asia, what comes to mind are the countries of Thailand, Myanmar, Vitnam, Singapore, Malaysia, Indonesia and the Philippines — even if you've never been there.

Why is this so?
Destination (or location) marketing strategies are among the most common forms of marketing in travel and tourism. The focus here is to increase customer attention to a specific place. Destination advertisers will highlight an entire location as a travel destination instead of singling out one attraction or accommodation.

Through this type of marketing, some locations have become so popular worldwide that just the mere mention of their name is enough to elicit a response. For this reason, some travel agencies do, and can, use this type of marketing to remind consumers of these destinations.

2. Activity Marketing

Often, consumers will associate a specific activity with a place that's already famous for that activity. Switzerland is renowned for skiing, France for vineyards, Yellowstone National Park for hiking and camping, and Alaska for Northern Lights. The list goes on and on.

When tourism marketers capitalize (or market) a particular activity in relation to a specific place, it's called "Activity Marketing". This type of marketing has a wide range of different kinds of tourist activities it can cater to; like adventure sports, food tours, and art galleries.

Activity marketing is the type of marketing you should adopt if your goal is to highlight a specific thing to do.

3. Corporate Marketing

It's vital to consider travelers who travel for reasons other than tourism. One of these includes corporate workers who may travel to different places for business purposes.

Imagine a company executive attending a meeting or conference overseas. They wouldn't then be interested in the activities of a destination.

Corporate marketing emerged as a branch of tourism marketing. In this type of tourism marketing, professionals can highlight places where business events can take place. Through this, they can make touristy places more popular and profit off the large number of corporates who would gather at these spots.

IV. Different Methods of Marketing in the Tourism Industry

Most modern tourism marketing strategies make use of multiple channels to attract consumers. Some of these include emails, SMSes, user-generated content, and websites.

If you want your marketing mix strategy to succeed, it's best to use multiple channels and tools. Here are some channels you can use to include in your tourism marketing plan:

1. Digital Marketing

Since we're in the Age of Information and heading towards the Age of Experience, focusing on digital marketing is a must. The travel journey of consumers in this field is centered more on seeking information from trusted sources and experienced travelers.

This is especially true for first-time travelers who plan their trip from thousands of miles away. These travelers will probably spend a couple of hours on each website searching for flight tickets, accommodations, and other touristy things.

Thus, you should focus on building your brand in the digital space to reach your target audience. It's also good to know that most searchers now use their mobile devices for travel information, either on social channels or through website content (for example, a blog post). You should ensure your digital marketing strategy is compatible with mobile devices.

2. Social Media Marketing

A part of the digital marketing strategy mentioned above, social media marketing includes establishing your brand on social media. Influencer marketing and user-generated content are practical parts of social media marketing to make your brand seem credible and trustworthy.

If you're reading this article, chances are you're just as tech-savvy as most Millennials and Gen Zs today. This also means you probably have a social media account where you may enjoy or create content on travelling.

Many tourists and travelers use social media to look for travel inspiration, accommodation and tour reviews, and hot travel tips. So, to keep up to date with the social era, your enterprise should use a robust social media strategy that showcases your travel products and services.

3. Email Marketing

Email marketing in the tourism sector can be used for many purposes, like loyalty programs, weekly newsletters, or lead nurturing. Through email marketing, brands and companies can continuously contact existing and potential customers to build on their relationships.

A form of direct and digital marketing, email marketing can help you send updates to your target market on your latest products and services. You can also use segmented marketing to collect data on your ideal customers' preferences and send out highly personalized content they have a higher chance of liking.

V. Marketing Strategies for Tourism

There are tons of write ups about the importance of marketing strategies, but which strategy to adopt and implement is most effective? The truth is that there's no one-size-fits-all formula when it comes to tourism marketing.

You could take inspiration from other marketing companies, but you'll still have to make some adjustments to the adopted strategy, so it's suitable for your company. Alternatively, you could start from scratch by conducting market research and then selecting the appropriate tools, methods, and marketing activities.

Tourism marketing strategies don't have to be boring; they can be just as exciting as their industry.

Firstly, it's essential to keep up with the latest tourism marketing trends and developments. But that's not enough, also consider the meaning behind these updates and how they'll impact your travel business. Here are some strategies and marketing tips you could use for your company's plan.

1. **Don't Forget Local**

The coronavirus outbreak in 2020 led to governments implementing a lockdown that restricted movements in and around countries. Over the months, lockdown regulations eased, with some countries allowing international travel but mainly sticking to local travel only.

To heal themselves from COVID-19 fatigue, many tourists resorted to touring their own countries. This increased domestic travel, bringing about a new target market.

Destination marketers can then use this to sell the features of their business in such a way that'll appeal to local consumers. Instead of focusing on weather and famous attractions, highlight facilities, one-day trips, and a site's ability to host events.

Additionally, emphasize the best hotels, cafes, and bars in an area as this will appeal to locals who are now more attracted to discovering the best of their town.

2. **Remote Working**

This may sound completely unrelated to tourism marketing, but a result of the pandemic is an increase in remote work.

When many businesses moved to an online working model during the lockdown, the workforce looked for alternate places to serve as their workplace. This created a specific niche of remote workers who turned to hotels and foreign destinations to enjoy work with a different view.

To cater to these business needs, travel marketing companies can create and promote product offerings that appeal to remote workers.

Whether it's a business suite in a 5-star hotel in Dubai or an Airbnb in the forest, the appetite for work-friendly spaces and accommodations is expected to keep growing.

3. Virtual Reality (VR) tours

A part of experiential marketing, Virtual Reality is just one of the many exciting tourism technologies available today. Through VR, tourists and travellers can experience a flight, hotel, restaurant, or attraction from a great distance away.

Easily accessible from a computer or mobile, virtual reality tours provide an opportunity for users to get a sense of an experience that awaits them. By getting a sense of what they can expect, virtual reality tours effectively clear clients' doubts during the booking process and increase their appetite for travel.

4. Voice Search, Chatbots & Other Technologies

Technology just keeps outshining itself, doesn't it? Tour operators can use voice search technology to allow customers to make bookings, seek information, and give feedback just by speaking. This makes it easier for mobile users on the go to use your services.

Chatbots allow for quick responses to customers, even when staff members are not available. Using chatbots on your website allows you to communicate with clients 24/7, in multiple languages, and promote your products and services. This can help increase revenue and improve the customer experience.

Other beneficial technologies include contactless payments, cybersecurity measures, and augmented reality. Or, improving your existing digital content through strategies like on-page SEO optimization and content upgrades to rank higher on search engine result pages.

5. Personalization

Personalization marketing is a branch of marketing that can be used to create more relevant customer offerings.

This type of marketing can be used with email, social media, and other similar marketing tools. Since modern customers have such individualistic personalities and tastes, personalized offerings appeal more to them.

So, through this marketing, travel companies can capture data (for example, from the company's Facebook page or website). And then they can use this data to curate customer profiles and offer personalized offerings and future recommendations.

Final Thoughts on the Marketing of Tourism and Travel
Always remember that customers don't just pay for products and services; they pay for the experience they expect to gain from it. The trick is to find your unique selling point and promote it as a comparatively superior experience in your tourism marketing efforts.
Since so many people love leisure trips, you must aim to make your company or brand stand out as unique compared to other tourism companies in this competitive industry. An effective advertising and marketing strategy can boost brand visibility and awareness for a new audience and the existing customer base.

Book 9 - Asean Mutual Recognition Agreement For Tourism Professionals

Glossary of Words/Terms and Phrases

AADCP - ASEAN Australia Development Cooperation Program;
ACCSTPASEAN – Arrangement between ASEAN Common Competency Standards for Tourism Professionals refers the minimum requirements of competency standards in hotel and travel services which aim to upgrade tourism services and facilitate the development of this Member States;
ASEAN - Association of Southeast Asian Nations;
ASEAN (NTOs) – States; institutions in charge of the tourism sector of ASEAN Member National Tourism Organizations.
ASEC ASEAN Secretariat
Assessee – The person whose performance is being assessed;
ssessment – Refers to the process of appraising the qualification and/or competencies of Tourism Professionals;
Assessment Centre – A location, in the workplace or a vocational or academic institution where assessment takes place;
Assessor – A person qualified to carry out assessment;
ATA – ASEAN Tourism Agreement (2004)
ATFTMD – ASEAN Task Force on Tourism Manpower Development
ATPMC - Tourism Professional Boards (NTPB); ASEAN NTOs and appointed representatives from National ASEAN Tourism Professional Monitoring Committee consists of
ATPRS- ASEAN Tourism Professional Registration System refers to a web- based facility to disseminate details regarding the list of Foreign Tourism Professionals duly certified.
ATQEM – ASEAN Tourism Qualifications Equivalency Matrix; refers to the common curriculum for ASEAN Tourism Professionals as mutually agreed upon by the ASEAN Ministers upon recommendation by the ASEA NTOs.
CATC – Common ASEAN Tourism Curriculum refers to the curriculum for ASEAN Tourism Professionals as mutually agreed upon by the ASEAN Tourism Ministers upon recommendation by the ASEAN NTOs.

CBAMT - Capacity Building for an ASEAN MRA in Tourism;
CBT – Competency Based Training – based on knowledge, skills and attitudes;
CCS - ASEAN Coordinating Committee on Services;
Certification – Refers to the issuance of a certificate to Tourism Professional whose qualification and/or competencies have met the standards specified in ACCSTP;
Child Wise Tourism Program ACCSTP has developed two special units in its curriculum dealing with child protection based on the Child Wise Tourism Program, developed in response to requests for assistance from governments, NGO's and the tourism sector in the ASEAN region to address the growing problem of child sex tourism;
Conformity Assessment – Conformity assessment means systematic examination to determine the extent to which a product, process or service fulfills specified requirements.
Equivalence Assessment – The process of judging the conformity assessment procedures and/or rules of another country to be equivalent to the national procedures.
Professionals Foreign Tourism – Refers to Tourism Professionals who are nationals of any other ASEAN Member States who are certified in an ASEAN Member State;
Host Country = Refers to the ASEAN Member State where a Foreign Tourism Professional applies for recognition to work;
Internal verifier – is an individual who monitors and supervises the operation in the context of vocational qualifications, approved by the awarding body but working for the Approved Centre, the internal verifier of the qualifications awarding scheme;
Mutual Recognition Arrangement – A mutual recognition arrangement (MRA) is an international regulatory agreement designed to promote economic integration and increased trade between nations. This achieved by reducing impediments to the movement of goods and services.
NTPB National Tourism Professional Board refers to a Board for tourism professionals which shall be composed of representatives from the public and private sectors including the academe and other relevant tourism stakeholders, to be determined by the respective ASEAN NTOs;

Performance appraisal – The act of estimating or judging a person's performance; Assessment Performance – The activity of evaluating a person's performance; Indicator Performance – The expected level of desired performance;
RCC – Recognition of Current Competencies;
Recognition – Refers to acceptance by the TPCB of a demonstration of compliance with requirements set out in the ACCSTP;
Registration – Refers to inclusion of duly certified tourism professionals onto ATPRS;
RITS – Roadmap for Integration of Tourism Sector (ASEAN);
RPL – Recognition of Prior Learning;
RQFSRS – Regional Qualifications Framework and Skills Recognition System;
Skills Passport - A Skills Passport may be designed as a typical bound booklet in which verified entries are made or it may exist as a protected on-line portolfio. A Skills Passport can provide individuals with a verified record of their skills, qualifications and achievements, hosted online.
SRA – Skills Recognition Audit.
Standard – he desired level of performance.
Tourism Job Title – refers to a specific job position in the tourism sector as specified in the CATC and ACCSTP Framework.
Tourism Professional – refers to a natural person who holds the nationality of an ASEAN Member State certified by the TCPB-Tourism Professional Certification Board.
TCPB – Tourism Professional Certification Board refers to the government board and/or agency authorized by the government of each ASEAN Member State primarily responsible for the assessment and certification of Tourism Professionals.
TRG – Technical Reference Group
VAP – Vientiane Action Plan

Executive Summary MRA-TP

Mutual Recognition Agreement for Tourism Professionals

I. Background

In 2015, the ASEAN Economic Community will come into being, with one of its key elements being the mutual recognition of professional qualifications within the Community. The ASEAN Mutual Recognition Arrangement on Tourism Professionals (MRA-TP) is one forward-looking initiative designed to enable the mobility of employment for skilled tourism labor within each Member State. The key to this arrangement is recognition of skills and qualifications of working tourism professionals from different ASEAN countries.

In order to function effectively, the MRA - TP requires an infrastructure operating at both the ASEAN and Member State level. The ASEAN Framework Agreement on MRAs (1998) and the ASEAN MRA on Tourism Professionals (2009) provides guidance for these mechanisms, and draws on the experience and expertise available through the development of other MRAs internationally.

This Handbook has been produced as an essential reference to the key policies, processes and implementation guidelines for the MRA – TP, and is provided for National Tourism Organizations in ASEAN. It can be disseminated to staff within NTOs who are responsible for manpower planning, HRD, training and qualifications.

II. Recognition & Eligibility of Foreign Tourism Professionals

The ASEAN MRA on Tourism Professionals will provide a mechanism for agreement on the equivalence of tourism certification procedures and qualifications across ASEAN. When ASEAN nations mutually recognize each other's qualifications this will encourage a free and open market for tourism labor across the region and boost the competitiveness of the tourism sector in each ASEAN nation, while at the same time attracting needed talent to meet local skills shortages. The eligibility to work in a host country will of course be subjected to prevailing domestic laws and regulations of the host country.

In order for a Foreign Tourism Professional to be recognized by other ASEAN Member States and to be eligible to work in a host country, they will need to possess a valid tourism competency certificate in a specific tourism job title as specified in the Common ASEAN Tourism Curriculum (CATC), issued by the Tourism Professional Certification Board (TPCB) in an ASEAN Member State.

It is important to recognize that while the MRA on Tourism Professionals will be active, the application and implementation by the various tourism educational and training providers in each country will be voluntary. This is especially true in terms of quality of instruction, evaluation and standards of curriculum development.

III. The Key MRA Components

The MRA – TP model consists of six mechanisms or components:
The National Tourism Professional Board (NTPB),
The Tourism Professionals Certification Board (TPCB), The Common ASEAN Tourism Curriculum (CATC),
The ASEAN Tourism Professionals Registration System (ATPRS),
The ASEAN Tourism Qualifications Equivalency Matrix (ATQEM), and The ASEAN Tourism Professional Monitoring Committee (ATPMC).

Each component forms part of a connecting infrastructure in support of effective implementation of the MRA - TP system to become operational by 2015. Each part requires a development effort at either ASEAN (regional) level or Member State (national) level.

At national or Member State level two agencies are required – the National Tourism Professional Board and the Tourism Professionals Certification Board. The NTPB has the function of quality control of the education and training system
– the Common ASEAN Tourism Curriculum that delivers the qualifications recognized in the MRA.

The Tourism Professionals Certification Board will apply national competency standards, assess and certify tourism professionals and also support the ASEAN Tourism Professionals Registration System. The ATPRS is a web-based facility designed to disseminate details about qualified tourist professionals in ASEAN Member States and provide a comparative understanding of the scope, content and equivalent value (or status) of a tourism qualification awarded in any one of the ASEAN Member States.

The MRA – TP is challenging because there are no agreed international tourism standards which can act as a basis for conformity assessment for the MRA
- TP. As a result, it is essential to construct an equivalence matrix of tourism qualifications for the AMS – the ASEAN Tourism Qualifications Equivalency Matrix to be used as the basis for conformity assessment. This is an essential supporting mechanism for a robust, reliable and transparent Mutual Recognition Arrangement for Tourism Professionals.

The overall MRA – TP system will be under the oversight of the ASEAN Tourism Professional Monitoring Committee. Each of the six components will be explained herein more detail.

IV.   Conclusions

The MRA on Tourism Professionals is an important driver in raising standards of tourism and improving qualifications of the tourism workforce in the ASEAN region. Member States need to carefully review their MRA status, implementation plans and readiness for the AEC in 2015.

Author's Note

It is hoped that the inclusion of these materials in this book will contribute to the fullest understanding of MRA – TP by the concerned sectors and aid National Training Organizations, Institutions, academe and others in planning and implementing the agreement to contribute in making the tourism sector in the Philippines in particular and the ASEAN region more competitive. It is also envisioned to guide the tourism learners across the ASEAN Member States most specifically the concerned national and local government agencies in the Philippines, with particularity the Local Government Units (LGUs) to fully understand the various benefits of the MRAs, and how it may contribute to their social well-being as frontline innovators in advocating well-meaning initiatives for the continuing development of tourism which benefits shall be shared to future generations of the ASEAN member-states and the whole world.

The Mutual Recognition Agreement For Tourism Professionals

I. Introduction

The tourism industry contributes significantly to the overall ASEAN economy. Based on the ASEAN Travel and Tourism Competitiveness Report 2012, it is estimated that this sector accounts for 4.6 percent of ASEAN GDP. The contribution can be as large as 10.9 percent when all indirect contributions from the sector are taken into account. In addition, it directly employs 9.3 million people, or
3.2 percent of total employment, and indirectly supports some 25 million jobs. The growth of international tourism in ASEAN has been remarkable. In 1991, there were only 20 million international visitor arrivals to ASEAN. After 20 years, the number has grown 4 times, to more than 81 million arrivals in 2011.

II. Rationale

To ensure growth sustainability and greater contribution to the ASEAN economy, the ASEAN tourism attractiveness needs to be accompanied by excellent quality of services provided by the tourism industry within the region. Having high- skilled tourism workers to deliver high-quality services should become normal practice in order to guarantee satisfaction of tourists visiting the region. One of the ways to achieve this goal is through mutual recognition of qualifications of tourism professionals across Member States.

The purpose of this mutual recognition mechanism is to facilitate mobility of tourism professionals within ASEAN based on competence-based tourism qualifications/certificates, and at the same time, improve the quality of services delivered by tourism professionals. There are 32 job titles covered under this MRA, ranging from housekeeping, front office, food and beverages services, and food production for hotel division, to travel agencies and tour operator for travel division.

III. The Mutual Recognition Arrangement

A mutual recognition arrangement (MRA) is an international agreement designed to promote economic integration and increased trade between nations. This is achieved by reducing regulatory impediments to the movement of goods and services. MRAs facilitate trade because they smooth the path in negotiation between nations. Each nation has its own standards, procedures and regulations. If trade is to flow freely between nations then agreement has to be reached on the equivalence – or conformity - between these regulations, standards and procedures. MRAs are the instruments that are used to reach such agreement.

MRAs became important in the field of assessing equivalent standards between partners in the early 1980s. They were formalized by the World Trade Organization under the Agreement on Technical Barriers to Trade (TBT). This agreement has become the guiding basis for all MRAs whether in the public sector (where the majority are found) or in the private sector.

IV. Types of MRAs

While there are a number of types of MRAs, the most common is designed to facilitate agreement on standards. This type of MRA is an agreement between two or more parties to mutually recognize or accept so one or all aspects of one another's conformity assessments. The term is also now applied to agreements on the recognition of professional qualifications.

The early MRAs tended to operate on a bilateral basis, facilitating agreement between two countries wanting to work together. However, as they grew and evolved, MRAs became more complex, dealing with multi-lateral issues of trade, where a number of nations are involved. This is the case in the European Union, APEC, and also in ASEAN where 10 nations are involved. ASEAN now has a variety of MRAs seeking conformance of standards in fields such as nursing, telecommunications and tourism.

V. Benefits of MRAs

For governments, MRAs ensure commitment and agreement to international trade, and encourage the sharing of good practice and information between partners. This can lead to:
Reduced costs;
- Increased competitiveness;
- Increased market access; and
- Freer flow of trade.

For tourism professionals and the industry, MRAs provide the following benefits:
a) Facilitate mobility of tourism professionals based on the tourism competency qualification/ certificate;
b) Enhance conformity of competency based training/education;
c) Recognize skills of tourism professional;
d) Improve the quality of tourism human resources (graduates are ready to work in the industry);
e) Enhance the quality of tourism services.

VI. Purpose of MRA on Tourism Professionals

The ASEAN MRA on Tourism Professionals (MRA-TP) seeks to increase the international mobility of tourism labor across the ASEAN region in line with ASEAN policy. Each ASEAN nation has its own standards, certification and regulations for recognizing the competency of workers in the tourism sector. Therefore, there is a need for an MRA to facilitate agreement on what constitutes equivalent competency to work in tourism by a worker, for example from Indonesia, who is seeking a position in Malaysia. The MRA – TP is therefore designed to:

a) Address the imbalance between supply and demand for tourism jobs across the ASEAN region; and,
b) Establish a mechanism for the free movement of skilled and certified tourism labor across the ASEAN region.

The objectives of MRA – TP are threefold, to:
a) Facilitate mobility of Tourism Professionals;

b) Encourage exchange of information on best practices in competency- based education and training for Tourism Professionals; and,

c) Provide opportunities for cooperation and capacity building across ASEAN Member States.

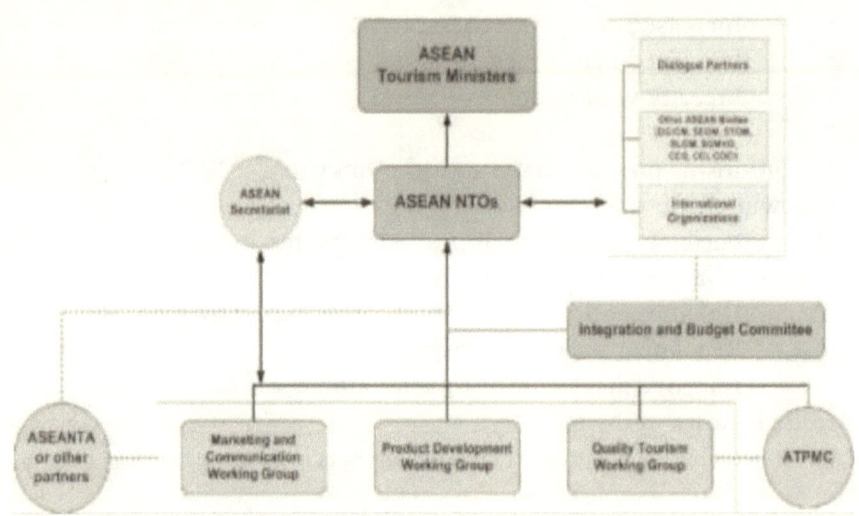

Figure 1-1 ASEAN Tourism Cooperation Organizational Structure

VII. The DEVELOPMENT of MRA – TP Mutual Recognition Agreement for Tourism Professionals

In January 2006 ASEAN Tourism Ministers supported the decision by ASEAN NTOs to establish the ASEAN Task Force on Tourism Manpower Development (ATFTMD) to prepare a Mutual Recognition Arrangement (MRA – TP) for ASEAN Tourism Professionals. The ASEAN MRA on Tourism Professionals was signed by the ASEAN Tourism Ministers in 2009 (See Annex I for the full text). The ATFTMD was one of six tourism task forces formed to assist ASEAN NTOs (National Tourism Organizations) in all matters related to tourism manpower development, especially in the implementation of the Roadmap for Integration of the Tourism sector, the Vientiane Action Program and the ASEAN Tourism Agreement.

The ATFTMD was dissolved in 2010 and the ASEAN Tourism Professional Monitoring Committee (ATPMC) was formally established in June 2010, at Lombok, Indonesia, to take over responsibility for promoting, updating, maintaining and monitoring ACCSTP and CATC, and for disseminating information about MRA – TP. ATPMC will work closely with the Quality Tourism Working Group which is primarily responsible for developing standards and in the implementation of the MRA – TP (see Figure 1.1 for ASEAN Tourism Cooperation Organizational Structure).

The ATPMC's responsibilities in relation to the MRA – TP, are:
a) Create awareness and disseminate information about the MRA on Tourism
b) Professionals within ASEAN;
c) Promote, update, maintain and monitor the ASEAN Common Competency Standards for Tourism Professionals (ACCSTP) and the Common ASEAN Tourism Curriculum (CATC);
d) Notify promptly the concerned Tourism Professional Certification Board (TPCB) upon receipt of feedback from National Tourism Professional Board (NTPB), in case a foreign Tourism Professional is no longer recognized by the host country;
e) Facilitate the exchange of information concerning assessment procedures, criteria, systems, manuals and publications relating to this Arrangement;
f) Report its work progress to the ASEAN NTOs;
g) Formulate and update necessary mechanisms to enable the implementation of the MRA on Tourism Professionals;
h) Such other functions and responsibilities that may be assigned to it by the ASEAN NTOs in the future; and
i) Resolve any differences among ASEAN Member States concerning the interpretation or application of the MRA on Tourism Professionals and to settle them in an amicable manner.

VIII. Key Elements of MRA – TP

The key elements of MRA – TP are listed below and will be expanded upon in the following sections of this Handbook. These elements need to be in place for the system to work fully, and some parts, such as the ASEAN Tourism Professional Registration System (ATPRS), will only be launched in 2015.

- The ASEAN Tourism Professional Monitoring Committee (ATPMC) consists of ASEAN NTOs and appointed representatives from the National Tourism Professional Boards (NTPBs).
- The ASEAN Tourism Professional Registration System (ATPRS) is a web-based facility to disseminate details of certified Foreign Tourism Professionals within ASEAN. This registration system is still under development and will be launched in 2015.
- The National Tourism Professional Board (NTPB) refers to the Board for Tourism Professionals composed of representatives from the public and private sectors (including academia and other relevant tourism stakeholders) to be determined by the respective ASEAN NTOs.
- The Tourism Professional Certification Board (TPCB) refers to the government board and/or agency authorized by the government of each ASEAN Member State primarily responsible for the assessment and certification of Tourism Professionals.
- Tourism Professional refers to a person who holds the nationality of an ASEAN
- Member State certified by the Tourism Professional Certification Board;
- The ASEAN Common Competency Standards for Tourism Professionals (ACCSTP) refers to the minimum requirements of competency standards in hotel and travel services which aim to upgrade tourism services and facilitate the development of MRA between ASEAN Member States.
- The Common ASEAN Tourism Curriculum (CATC) refers to the common curriculum for ASEAN Tourism Professionals as mutually agreed upon by the ASEAN Tourism Ministers upon recommendation by the ASEAN NTOs.
- Assessment refers to the process of appraising the qualification and/or competencies of Tourism Professionals;
- Certification refers to the issuance of a certificate to Tourism Professional whose qualification and/or competencies have met the standards specified in ACCSTP;
- Verification is the means by which a certificate or qualification is checked against ACCSTP to ensure its compatibility and validity. and subject to job offer, a work permit will be provided by the host country.

IX. Principles for Recognition & Eligibility of Foreign Tourism Professionals

An ASEAN MRA on Tourism Professionals will provide a mechanism for agreement on the equivalence of tourism certification procedures and qualifications across ASEAN. Once this is achieved, ASEAN nations will mutually recognize each other's qualifications for tourism. This will encourage a free and open market for tourism labor across the region and boost the competitiveness of the tourism sector in each ASEAN nation.

The qualification of a Foreign Tourism Professional may be recognized by other ASEAN Member States, and if such qualification is recognized, they may be eligible to work in a host country provided that they possess a valid tourism competency certificate in a specific tourism job title as specified in the Common ASEAN Tourism Curriculum (CATC), issued by the Tourism Professional Certification Board (TPCB) in an ASEAN Member State. The eligibility to work in a host country will be subjected to prevailing domestic laws and regulations of the host country.

Most Member States recognize that the free movement of labor will impact on local workers, and there is a growing recognition that there will be a need to protect national interests, especially to ensure local employment is not affected by a flood of unskilled labor, while at the same time attracting needed talent to meet local skills shortages. However, moving from an agreement on mutually recognized qualifications to actually implementing the MRA – TP and getting approval at the national level among Ministries of Labor, Education and Tourism, and then at the regional level, is seen as a process that could take a number of years. There are some areas such as the culinary arts, where mutual recognition would be a distinct advantage in order to facilitate the movement of skilled chefs from one country to another.

X. Implications of MRA for Institutions

It is also important to recognize that while the MRA on Tourism Professionals will be active, the application and implementation by the various tourism educational and training providers in each country will be voluntary. This is especially true in terms of quality of instruction, evaluation and standards of curriculum development. However, should these institutions wish to have the qualifications of their graduates recognized by other ASEAN Member States, then there will need to be a campaign of information to the colleges and educational institutes to ensure they understand the implications of MRA – TP and how they need to modify or align their curricula to meet the requirements of an Common ASEAN Tourism Curriculum (CATC).

XI. Providing Support to Stakeholders

Another area for consideration by NTOs is how to provide support, information and training for national stakeholders. Will there be central training provided? Will there be a need for curriculum and assessment materials? How will the implementation of MRA – TP be implemented and funded?

XII. Readiness of Member States

There are also questions to be asked about the readiness of Member States, and how many will be able to set up a comprehensive MRA – TP system by 2015. In addition there are questions related to implementation especially given the different regulatory frameworks, labour laws and structures within each Member State.

XIII. IMPORTANT ASEAN AGREEMENTS RELATED TO MRA ASEAN Framework Agreement on Services (1995)

(Article V: ASEAN Framework Agreement on Services, signed on 15 December 1995 in Bangkok, Thailand) "Each Member State may recognize the education or experience obtained, requirements met, or licenses or certifications granted in another Member State, for the purpose of licensing or certification of service suppliers. Such recognition may be based upon an agreement or arrangement with the Member State concerned or may be accorded autonomously."

☐ ASEAN Vision 2020 (1997)

(The ASEAN Vision 2020 on Partnership in Dynamic Development, approved 14 June 1997) "The ASEAN Vision 2020 which charted towards the year 2020 for the creation of a stable, prosperous and highly competitive ASEAN Economic Region which would result in:

- free flow of goods, services and investment;
- equitable economic development, and reduced poverty and socio-economic disparities; and enhanced political, economic and social stability;

☐ ASEAN Tourism Agreement (2002)
8th ASEAN Summit (Article VIII of ASEAN Tourism Agreement, signed on 4 November 2002 in Phnom Penh, Kingdom of Cambodia) "Member States shall cooperate in developing human resources in the tourism and travel industry by:

- Formulating non-restrictive arrangements to enable ASEAN Member States to make use of professional tourism experts and skilled workers available within the region on the basis of bilateral arrangements;
- Intensifying the sharing of resources and facilities for tourism education and training programs;
- Upgrading tourism education curricula and skills and formulating competency standards and certification procedures, thus eventually leading to mutual recognition of skills and qualifications in the ASEAN region;
- Strengthening public-private partnerships in human resource development; and Cooperating with other countries, groups of countries and international institutions in developing human resources for tourism."

☐ 2004 ASEAN Sectoral Integration Protocol for Tourism (2004) Adopted by the Economic Ministers at the 10th ASEAN Summit in Vientiane, Laos on 29 November 2004

☐ Mutual Recognition Arrangements for Qualifications (2003) (9th ASEAN Summit & the 7th ASEAN + 3 Summit Bali, Indonesia, 7 October 2003)"Calling for completion of Mutual Recognition Arrangements for qualifications in major professional services by 2008"

☐ Establishment of the ASEAN Community by 2015 (2007)

(Cebu Declaration on the Acceleration of the Establishment of an ASEAN Community by 2015 at 12th ASEAN Summit, 2007) "Agree to accelerate the establishment of an ASEAN Community by 2015 along the lines of ASEAN Vision 2020 and the Declaration of ASEAN Concord II in the three pillars of the ASEAN Security Community, ASEAN Economic Community and ASEAN Socio Cultural Community."

ASEAN Common Competency Standards for Tourism Professionals

I. Introduction

At their eighth summit in November 2002, ASEAN leaders signed the ASEAN Tourism Agreement (ATA) which aimed to create favorable industry conditions in support of ASEAN's vision for a free flow of tourism services before 2020. As part of the agreement, the ASEAN leaders agreed to upgrade tourism education, curricula and skills through the formulation of competency standards and certification procedures, thereby leading to mutual recognition of skills and qualifications in the ASEAN region. In addition, it supported the wider ASEAN agenda of encouraging Member States to adopt national frameworks for qualifications, competencies and training.

II. Rationale for Standards Development

The rationale for development of ASEAN Common Competency Standards was based on the assumption that if a framework of competencies could be compiled, shared and adopted by the ASEAN Member States as a common reference for qualifications, this would lay the foundations and conditions necessary for an MRA to operate. The proposed development and operation of an MRA would then facilitate the free movement of qualified tourism professional staff due to be fully operational by 2015.

III. Priority for Tourism Standards

Tourism is an important economic sector for the Member States of ASEAN.

It provides an important source of export income and is a vital sector for employment particularly for women and small businesses. Not only has the significance of this area of economic development been recognized at the individual state level, but also tourism has been included as a priority sector for economic integration across the ASEAN region.

Human Resources Development

Human resources are a key competitive element of tourism, as destinations increasingly compete on level of service rather than physical or natural assets. In recognition of the imperative to develop a skilled labor force for tourism across the ASEAN region, the ACCSTP project was developed and agreed based upon three general objectives:-

☐ To establish an agreed set of ACCSTP.
☐ To determine the potential for manpower mobility and the establishment of an MRA within ASEAN.
☐ To develop a strategic plan for the regional implementation of ACCSTP and a sustainable network to facilitate the application of an MRA on Tourism Professionals.

IV. **Strategic** Direction

The ASEAN Strategic Plan identified the importance of increasing the quality of services and human resources in the region as a strategic direction, and identified ASEAN tourism standards and implementing the MRA as strategic actions of the plan. Figure 2.1 illustrates these priorities as part of responsible and sustainable tourism development.

Figure 2-1: Vision & Strategic Direction for ASEAN Tourism

V. Basis of the ACCSTP

At the eleventh meeting of the ASEAN Task Force on Tourism Manpower Development, a set of minimum competency standards within a qualifications framework for professionals in retail and wholesale travel companies, housekeeping, front office, and food & beverage service was presented. The standards were based upon the competencies required to perform a set of commonly agreed job titles in retail and wholesale travel companies, housekeeping, front office, and food & beverage service.

VI. Parameters for ACCSTP Framework

In the development of the ACCSTP Framework (2004-2005), ATFTMD helped to identify the minimum competency standards essential for each job title within the following parameters:

☐ The ACCSTP Framework common competency standards matrix must be compatible with best practice to be recognized internationally;
☐ The ACCSTP Framework is the best available common denominator or common language to advance the interests of the ASEAN community;
☐ The ACCSTP Framework would only include competencies that were current, relevant and applicable to member countries.
☐ A 'mainstream approach' has been used in cross-matching the common competencies (among member countries);
☐ Given an agreed ACCSTP Framework, each member country or industry may choose to add (at a later date) additional competencies that may be necessary to suit local requirements.

VII. The Importance of a Competency Framework

The ACCSTP are based on the concept of competency – the knowledge, skills attitudes (KSA) that individuals must have, or must acquire, to perform effectively at work. Competence is all about demonstrable performance outputs and in the case of ACCSTP relates to a system or set of minimum standards required for effective performance at work. A 'competency framework' is a structure that sets out and defines each individual competency (such as problem-solving, checking in hotel guests or managing people) required by individuals working in a tourism organization or part of an organization.

VIII. Structure of the Competency Standards

Competency standards set down the specific knowledge and skills required for successful performance in the workplace and the required standard of performance. They are organized into units, each with a code and title. The standards for hospitality and tourism cover both general areas common to all sectors (e.g. communication, leadership and occupational health and safety), and sector-specific areas.

The ACCSTP Framework lists the minimum common competency standards that should be widely used in the region to allow the skills, knowledge and attitudes (competence) of tourism professionals to be assessed, recognized and equated to comparable qualifications in other ASEAN countries in order for an MRA to function.

IX. Common Labor Divisions

The ACCSTP are arranged as sets of competencies required by qualified professionals who seek to work in the various divisions of labor that are common across various sectors of tourism in ASEAN Member States.

2.7.1 Minimal Competencies

Compliance with these "minimal" competencies will be an essential reference or benchmark for anyone wishing to apply for a position in another ASEAN Member State. The terms minimum or minimal simply refer to the essential basic skills required for a particular job description. It is useful in setting a basic benchmark or standard in professional performance. In the ACCSTP Framework, the minimal competencies required are arranged on a framework using common divisions of labor as illustrated in Table 2.1:

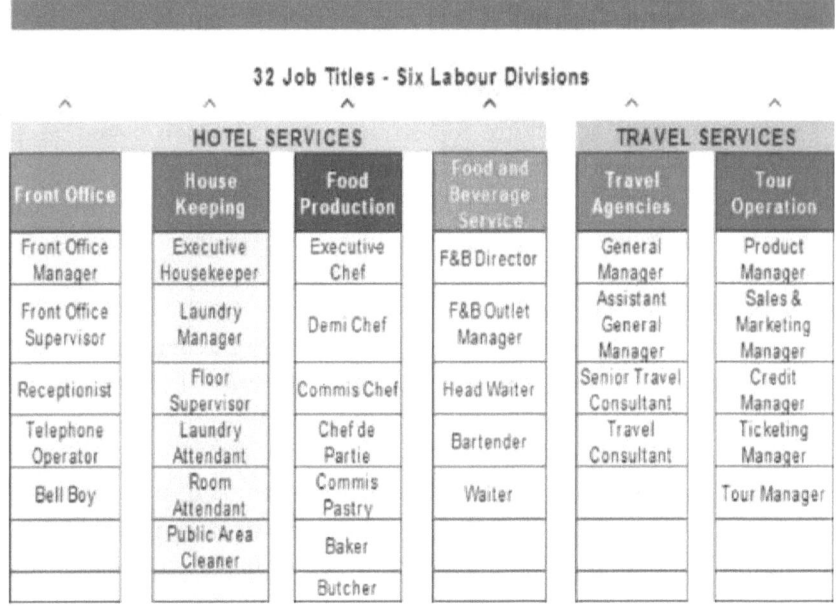

Table 2-1: 32 Job Titles & Six Common Labor Divisions

The positions listed under each labor division are of varying levels of sophistication and responsibility, some of which might require extensive vocational training whereas others might only require short-term training of one to two weeks or on-the-job training.

X. Setting Job Positions

The principle for setting job positions is that for some positions it is entirely possible that someone can carry out a series of responsibilities in a highly professional manner without any formal education. This is certainly the case within the industry where some managers have little formal education but a great deal of life and industry experience. This is not to say that formal education at the higher managerial levels is not important but clearly industry experience needs to be recognized in any hiring process.

XI. Divisions of Labor

The term labor division might be slightly misleading in that some of the tasks are operational in nature and labor intensive, but many of the position classifications are clearly supervisory or managerial.

XII. Core, Generic and Functional Competencies

The competency standards for tourism professionals listed in the ACCSTP Framework are the minimum acceptable common competency standards required by industry and employers to enable the standard of a qualified person's skills to be recognized and assessed equitably in ASEAN countries. This is an essential mechanism required for the effective operation of an MRA.

In the ACCSTP Framework, the Competencies are graded into three related groups of skills: Core, Generic and Functional Competencies.

XIII. Core Competencies

Competencies that industry has agreed are essential to be achieved if a person is to be accepted as competent in a particular primary division of labor. They are directly linked to key occupational tasks and include units such as 'Work effectively with colleagues and customers, and Implement occupational health and safety procedures.'

XIV. Generic Competencies

Competencies that industry has agreed are essential to be achieved if a person is to be accepted as competent at particular secondary division of labor. The name 'life skills' is sometimes used to describe these competencies and they include units such as: 'Use common business tools and technology,' and 'Manage and resolve conflict situations.'

XV. Functional Competencies

Functional Competencies are specific to roles or jobs within the labor division, and include the specific skills and knowledge (know-how) to perform effectively, such as 'Receive and process reservations, Provide housekeeping services to guests, and Operate a bar facility.' These competencies could be generic to a Labor Division as a whole, or be specific to roles, levels or jobs within the Labor Division.

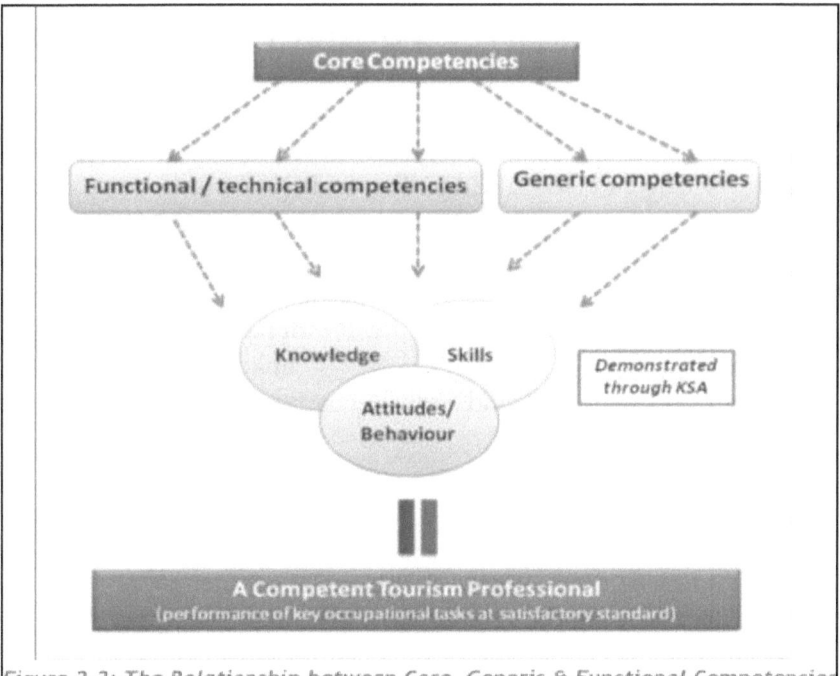

Figure 2-2: The Relationship between Core, Generic & Functional Competencies

XVI. Future Developments

As part of the ongoing work of ASEAN, the following activities will take place:

- ☐ Development of a Regional Qualifications Framework and Skills Recognition System (RQFSRS)
- ☐ Development of 242 Toolboxes for each Competency Standard in the 6 Labor Divisions (Housekeeping Division has already been completed)
- ☐ Training of Trainer Program for Master Trainer and Master Assessor for Front Office, Food and Beverage Services, Food Production, Travel Agents, and Tour Operators
- ☐ Establishment of a Regional Secretariat for ASEAN Tourism Professionals.

Common ASEAN Tourism Curriculum

I. Introduction

The Common ASEAN Tourism Curriculum (CATC) is the approved common curriculum for ASEAN Tourism Professionals as mutually agreed upon by the ASEAN Tourism Ministers upon recommendation by the ASEAN NTOs. The concept is founded upon a number of initiatives, including the Vientiane Action Plan (VAP), ASEAN Tourism Agreement (ATA) and the Roadmap for Integration of Tourism Sector (RITS). The CATC is linked to the Regional Qualifications Framework and Skills Recognition System (RQFSRS)

II. Design Principles

The curriculum was designed to be industry based, well-structured and flexible, in order to meet varying local requirements of the Member States. It is based on the agreed Competencies adopted by all Countries in ASEAN, and using the agreed ACCSTP Units of Competence aims at making qualifications relevant and useful to both students and the tourism industry.

III. Common ASEAN Tourism Curriculum

The CATC is founded upon six labor divisions: Front Office, Housekeeping, Food Production, Food & Beverage Service, Travel Agencies and Tour Operations. CATC & RQFSRS go hand in hand. CATC supports and contributes to the development of a harmonized tourism education and training framework within the ASEAN region, while the RQFSRS supports and contributes to the implementation of the MRA - TP which ultimately will facilitate skilled labor mobility, contributing to economic integration of the region.

IV. Rationale for CATC

CATC is founded on the Competency Based Training (CBT) approach that is recognized worldwide as being the most effective means of delivering vocational training. CBT is training that provides trainees with skills, knowledge and attitudes necessary to demonstrate competence against prescribed and endorsed Industry Competency Standards. This concept is especially applicable to Tourism where 'attitude' is an extremely vital element of all customer-contact and service situations.

V. CATC Framework

CATC aims at providing an efficient and practical model for the delivery of vocational training which can be expected to prove popular with industry, students and training providers. The model is straightforward and consistent across all Secondary Labor Divisions of Travel Agencies, Tour Operation, Housekeeping, Front Office, Food and Beverage Service, and Food Production. It offers qualifications in each of the labor divisions from Certificate II level to Advanced Diploma level. The framework is:

☐ Industry-based – the units of competency and the content for each one has been set by industry: qualifications will match industry need in order to make qualifications relevant and useful to both students and industry;

☐ Flexible – allowing students, industry and training providers the highest level of flexibility in the selection of units for each qualification stakeholders can individually determine on a case-by-case basis the actual mix of units that will combine to fulfill the packaging requirements for a qualification;

☐ Well-structured – there is a logical flow between qualifications: this facilitates advancement through qualifications, enables movement between streams and enables students to gain higher level managerial qualifications while still retaining a practical and operational focus.

VI. Structure of CATC

CATC consists of five qualification levels across all six Labor Divisions providing vocational streams within each Labor Division that reflect the stated needs of AMS and the needs of industry. In all cases Certificate II incorporates Certificate I on the advice of participating countries. Table 3.1 gives an overview of the level at which each of the five qualifications in the Framework is set.

Table 3.1: CATC Six Level of Qualifications

Framework Level	Level Indicator
Level 5 - Advanced Diploma	Sophisticated, broad and specialized competence with senior management skills
	Technical, creative, conceptual or managerial applicationsbuilt around competencies of either a broad or specializedbase and related to a broader organizational focus.
Level 4 - Diploma	Specialized competence with managerial skills
	Assumes a greater theoretical base and consists of specialized technical or managerial competencies used toplan, carry out and evaluate work of self and/or team.
Level 3 Certificate IV	Greater technical competence with supervisory skills
	More sophisticated technical applications involving competencies requiring increased theoretical knowledge, applied in a non-routine environment and which may involve team leadership and management and increased responsibility for outcomes.
Level 2 Certificate III	Broad range of skills in more varied context and team leader responsibilities
	Skilled operator who applies a broad range of competencies within a more varied work context, possibly providing technical advice and support to a teamincluding having team leader responsibilities.
Level 1 - Certificate II	Basic, routine skills in a defined context
	A base operational qualification that encompasses a rangeof functions/activities requiring fundamental operational knowledge and limited practical skills in a defined context.

In summary, fifty two qualifications across six labor divisions were packaged for CATC & RQFSRS, see Table 3.2 below:

Table 3.2: 52 Qualifications Across 6 Labor

	Cert. II	Cert. III	Cert. IV	Diploma	Advanced Diploma	Sub-Total
Food & Beverage	2	2	3	1	1	9
Food Production	2	3	3	1	1	10
Front Office	1	1	1	1	1	5
Housekeeping	1	1	1	1	1	5
Tour Operation (Management)	2	3	4	2	1	12
Travel Agencies	3	3	3	1	1	11
TOTAL						52

VII. Career Progression

CATC is based upon the vocational training model with the concept of 'qualifications rather than courses'. No two hospitality/tourism properties are identical and no two hospitality/tourism properties have training (or any other) needs that are the same. Therefore CATC is designed for different working environments and based around unique qualifications for local needs rather than standard training courses.

VIII. Flexibility and Choice

The Framework requires students to undertake industry-based core and generic units of competency but allows flexibility for the functional units that complete the requirements for each qualification. This will enable students to:

- select functional units to suit their workplace needs and/or personal career aspirations
- pick an industry stream most relevant to employer needs which will deliver targeted training appropriate to workplace requirements
- move easily between streams most relevant to their changing or emerging professional and workplace needs
- engage only in vocational training that is directly relevant to identified industry and personal imperatives.

IX. Flexible Pathways

Participants can also enter – or leave - the qualification Framework at any level: there is no obligation to complete, for example, Certificate II before undertaking Certificate III or higher. For example:

1. A student enters the Tour Operation field unsure of what their final career might be.

⬇

2. The student elects to enrol in a Certificate II in Tour Operation (Guiding), an entry/base-level qualification in the Secondary Labour Division of Tour Operation.

⬇

3. The student is required to take five Core and Generic competencies plus six additional functional competencies from Tour Operations or Tour Guide Services.

⬇

4. The student can select competencies to steer them in the direction of their anticipated career and/or to reflect the current needs of their workplace, but the final choice is theirs.

X. Building on Existing Qualifications

Reflect the blend of functional competencies they wish to attain and as previous units count towards their new qualification additional units are included to add the new competencies.

Enrolling in a higher level qualification enables the student to use and build on the previous units they have studied. Their unit selection will again demanded by industry. The extent to which the student varies the functional competency clusters from which they select will depend on their career goal and industry need. This can also work over lifetimes by enabling employees to take additional modules and thus to 'grow' into new jobs.

XI. Practical and Progressive

This approach has produced qualifications that represent a blend of industry- identified competencies that enable practical workplace application as well as providing the basis for promotion and continued learning, and the ability for trainees to move between labor divisions as the need or opportunity arises.

XII. Industry-Based Content & Units of Competency

The qualifications listed in the proposed Framework are based on units of competency developed by industry making the training content relevant and responsive to industry need. As the qualifications rise through the levels (Certificate II to Advanced Diploma), so the choices of units of competency that exist within the packaging rules vary to respond to the changing workplace nature of the tasks that need to be completed.

XIII. A Blend of Competencies

These changes to selection options reflect the required functional competencies identified by industry as being necessary for the various job titles that have been classified. Every qualification requires participants to undertake a blend of mandatory core and generic competencies as well as elective functional competencies.

Each of the qualifications has been designed holistically with a focus on essential core and generic units of competency together with the ability for trainees to select the most appropriate functional competencies to support their workplace needs or aspirations.

XIV. Life-long Learning

The key to this capability lies in the freedom of people to choose units of competency from functional competency clusters that best suit their individual workplace and training needs, and yet still be credited with (some) previous units they have already studied. In this way, this framework actively supports the concept of life-long learning by encouraging further study through acknowledgment of workplace learning and recognition of past study.

XV. Accumulation of Skills and Knowledge

The underpinning intention of this approach is to provide a vocational education and training system that enables trainees to accumulate skills and knowledge as they move through the system and study to gain higher qualifications. This will facilitate movement between qualifications, streams and labor divisions for trainees thereby providing a system that meets and can respond quickly to changing employer demand and one that maximizes trainee choice of units of competency, streams and labor divisions.

XVI. Robust Framework

While providing freedom and flexibility the educational integrity and robustness of the framework, it is guaranteed by the need for trainees to complete the designated number of units at each qualification level before a complete certificate can be issued.

XVII. Portability of Qualifications

The flexible structure of CATC will enhance the portability of qualifications between industries and countries and the intended audit requirements that will be imposed on all training providers will assure provider integrity, reliability and commitment.

XVIII. Recognition of Attainment

It will be a requirement that any statement of attainment issued by any training provider must be recognized for the purposes of 'prior standing' by every other training provider within the system regardless of where that training provider is located and regardless of the perceived reputation of that organization. This can be gained in the classroom (Recognition of Prior Learning - RPL) or in the workplace (Recognition of Current Competence – RCC).

XIX. Mobility of Career Pathways

This means that trainees can readily move from (for example) Housekeeping to Front Office or Food and Beverage service, and can move readily from Tour Operations to Travel Agencies. The structure also enables trainees to move easily into supervisory or managerial qualifications, or retain an operational role within the industry while gaining additional skills.

XX. Contextualization

It is recommended that each Member State adopts and agrees on a common, regional framework both in curriculum and qualifications as the first step before considering how to integrate CATC with its existing vocational tourism training arrangements.

XXI. Customized by Member States

CATC can be tailored to suit the individual needs of different Member States through the way the curriculum is written and interpreted by those who use it. In practice, each country can use their own regulations, legislation, codes of practice, rules, etc., because of the way the curriculum is written. They can also make reference to their own authorities, bodies, agencies and organizations.

Providers within each Member State can also tailor units of competency to suit their specific industry, country or other needs and are free to add their own 'extra content' within any unit they deliver as well as to add extra non-accredited units they deem appropriate or necessary.

XXII. Local Additions and Amendments

Contextualization could involve additions or amendments to the unit of competency to suit particular delivery methods, learner profiles, specific enterprise equipment requirements, or to otherwise meet local needs. However, the integrity of the overall intended outcome of the unit of competency must be maintained.

XXIII. Boundaries of Contextualization

Any contextualization of units of competency can be done but within the following boundaries so that providers may:

☐ Add specific industry terminology to performance criteria where this does not distort or narrow the competency outcomes;

☐ Make amendments and additions to the range statement as long as such changes do not diminish the breadth of application of the competency and reduce its portability;

☐ Add detail to the evidence guide in areas such as the critical aspects of evidence or resources and infrastructure required where these expand the breadth of the competency but do not limit its use;

☐ Not remove or add to the number and content of elements and performance criteria.

XXIV. Important Note

The key to contextualization is that the rigor and structure of each unit remain, but that the content can be varied to suit the needs of the user, provided the four 'rules' (see above) are complied with.

XXV. Localized Units of Competence

ASEAN NTOs identified the need to include the two additional units of competence from the Child Wise Tourism Program (http://www.childwise.net) into the curriculum and qualifications framework. Two units of competence have been added to CATC – one unit at the Certificate entry level, 'Perform Child Protection Duties relevant to the Tourism Industry' and the other unit at the Diploma level, 'Develop Protective Environments for Children in Tourism Destinations.'

Challenges in Implementing CATC

I. Orientation and Training
There will be a need for orientation and training to fully understand how the qualifications are structured and implemented, especially for users unfamiliar with Competence-based Training, ACCSTP and the qualifications under CATC. NTOs should consider how to promote, inform, and provide training and orientation on country-by-country basis but perhaps with common, shared resources.

II. Bridging Programs
Consideration of the development of 'Bridging Programs' to facilitate movement of students currently studying, or having recently completed, existing qualifications into the revised framework.

III. Recognition of Current Competence
Systems should be developed to assist those with experience but no formal qualifications to have this experienced formally recognized and facilitate their movement into the formal vocational training system.

IV. Credit Transfer Process
NTOs should consider the development of a formal Credit Transfer process to enable those with existing qualifications to have these recognized for the purposes of gaining standing within the new system

V. Articulation Agreements
Development of appropriate articulation pathways that students can take to move from Advanced Diploma into tertiary study and qualifications, along with agreements with providers of higher education.

VI. Quality Assurance
An independent third party auditing process should be developed for providers to ensure minimum standards in relation to trainers, resources, training facilities, training, assessment, general levels of professionalism etc., and other compliance requirements are being met.

References: Technical Report on Final Common ASEAN Tourism Curriculum & Regional Qualifications & Skills Recognitions Systems

Assessment of Competence

I. Introduction

Competence-based Training (CBT) and Competence-based Assessment (CBA) focus on what a worker can do or is required to do at work. Competency refers to the ability to perform particular tasks and duties to the standard of performance expected in the workplace. ASEAN has adopted the CBT/CBA training system to enable member countries to produce the type of worker that industry is looking for and this therefore increases trainees' chances of obtaining employment. CBA involves collecting evidence and making a judgment of the extent to which a worker can perform his/her duties at the required competency standard.

II. Competency

Competency requires the application of specified knowledge, skills and attitudes relevant to effective participation, consistently over time and in the workplace environment. The essential skills and knowledge are either identified separately or combined.

- Knowledge identifies what a person needs to know to perform the work in an informed and effective manner.
- Skills describe the application of knowledge to situations where understanding is converted into a workplace outcome.
- Attitude describes the founding reasons behind the need for certain knowledge or why skills are performed in a specified manner.

Competency covers all aspects of workplace performance and involves:
- Performing individual tasks
- Managing a range of different tasks
- Responding to contingencies or breakdowns Dealing with the responsibilities of the workplace
- Working with others.

III. Unit of Competency

All qualifications or programs include a range of topics that focus on the
ability of the trainee to perform a task or job in a specific work area and with particular responsibilities or job functions. For purposes of assessment, ACCSTP uses the unit of competency that applies in the tourism workplace. Each unit of competency identifies a discrete workplace requirement and includes:
- Knowledge and skills that underpin competency
- Language, literacy and numeracy
- Occupational health and safety requirements.

Each unit of competency must be adhered to in training and assessment to ensure consistency of outcomes.

IV. Element of Competency

An element of competency describes the essential outcomes within a unit of competency. The elements of competency are the basic building blocks of the unit of competency. They describe in terms of outcomes the significant functions and tasks that make up the competency.

V. Performance criteria

Performance criteria indicate the standard of performance that is required to demonstrate achievement within an element of competency. The standards reflect identified industry skill needs. Performance criteria will be made up of certain specified skills, knowledge and attitudes. Figure 4.3 which compares competency standards with curriculum and shows the linkages between both methods of learning and assessment.

VI. Competency Based Assessment (CBA)

CBA is the strategy of assessing the competency of a trainee or worker. Assessment utilizes a range of assessment strategies to ensure that trainees are assessed in a manner that demonstrates validity, fairness, reliability, flexibility and fairness of assessment processes.

Assessment can be completed in a variety of ways:
- On-the-job – in the workplace
- Off-the-job – at an educational institution or dedicated training environment
- As a combination of these two options.

No longer is it necessary for trainees to be absent from the workplace for long periods of time in order to obtain recognized and accredited qualifications.

VII. Principles of Competency Based Assessment (CBA)

Competency based assessment is aimed at compiling a list of evidence that shows that a person is competent in a particular unit of competency. Competencies are gained in many ways including:

- Training and development programs

- Formal education
- Life experience
- Apprenticeships On-the-job experience
- Self-help programs.

In CBA, assessors and participants work together, through the 'collection of evidence' in determining overall competence. This evidence can be collected using different formats, supported by different people in the workplace or in the training institution, and collected over a period of time.

The assessor, who is ideally someone with considerable experience in the area being assessed, reviews the evidence and verifies the person as being competent or not.

VIII. Flexibility in Assessment

The Toolkits developed for each ACCSTP Competence Unit are very comprehensive and provide Trainers and Assessors with a range of methods and tools to aid in the assessment process. For all assessments, suitable alternate assessment tools may be used, according to the requirements of the participant.

The assessment needs to be equitable for all participants, taking into account their cultural and linguistic needs. Competency must be proven regardless of:

- Language
- Delivery Method
- Assessment Method.

IX. Assessment Objectives

The assessment tools used for ACCSTP are designed to determine competency against the 'elements of competency' and their associated 'performance criteria'. The assessment tools are used to identify sufficient:

a) knowledge, including underpinning knowledge
b) skills and,
c) attitudes.

Assessment tools are activities that trainees are required to undertake to prove competency. All assessments must be completed satisfactorily for participants to obtain competence for the units submitted for assessment and it is possible that in some cases several assessment items may be combined and assessed together.

X. Types of Assessment

A number of assessment tools can be used to determine competency, and these are suggested in the AACSTP Standards. Assessment methods can include: work projects, written questions, oral questions, third party reports, observation checklists etc. Instructions on how assessors should conduct these assessment methods are explained in the Assessment Manuals and Toolkits.

XI. Alternative Assessment Tools

The assessor can also use different assessment methods to measure the competency of a participant. Evidence is simply proof that the assessor gathers to show participants can actually do what they are required to do and whilst there is a distinct requirement for participants to demonstrate competency, there are many and diverse sources of evidence available to the assessor.

Ongoing performance at work, as verified by a supervisor or physical evidence, can count towards assessment. Additionally, the assessor can talk to customers or work colleagues to gather evidence about performance.

- On-the-job – in the workplace
- Off-the-job – at an educational institution or dedicated training environment
- As a combination of these two options.

No longer is it necessary for trainees to be absent from the workplace for long periods of time in order to obtain recognized and accredited qualifications.

XII. Principles of Competency Based Assessment (CBA)

Competency based assessment is aimed at compiling a list of evidence that shows that a person is competent in a particular unit of competency. Competencies are gained in many ways including:

- Training and development programs
- Formal education
- Life experience
- Apprenticeships On-the-job experience
- Self-help programs.

In CBA, assessors and participants work together, through the 'collection of evidence' in determining overall competence. This evidence can be collected using different formats, supported by different people in the workplace or in the training institution, and collected over a period of time.

The assessor, who is ideally someone with considerable experience in the area being assessed, reviews the evidence and verifies the person as being competent or not.

XIII. Flexibility in Assessment

The Toolkits developed for each ACCSTP Competence Unit are very comprehensive and provide Trainers and Assessors with a range of methods and tools to aid in the assessment process. For all assessments, suitable alternate assessment tools may be used, according to the requirements of the participant.

The assessment needs to be equitable for all participants, taking into account their cultural and linguistic needs. Competency must be proven regardless of:

- Language
- Delivery Method
- Assessment Method.

XIV. Assessment Objectives

The assessment tools used for ACCSTP are designed to determine competency against the 'elements of competency' and their associated 'performance criteria'. The assessment tools are used to identify sufficient:

- knowledge, including underpinning knowledge;
- skills; and,
- attitudes.

Assessment tools are activities that trainees are required to undertake to prove competency. All assessments must be completed satisfactorily for participants to obtain competence for the units submitted for assessment and it is possible that in some cases several assessment items may be combined and assessed together.

XV. Types of Assessment

A number of assessment tools can be used to determine competency, and these are suggested in the AACSTP Standards. Assessment methods can include: work projects, written questions, oral questions, third party reports, observation checklists etc. Instructions on how assessors should conduct these assessment methods are explained in the Assessment Manuals and Toolkits.

XVI. Alternative Assessment Tools

The assessor can also use different assessment methods to measure the competency of a participant. Evidence is simply proof that the assessor gathers to show participants can actually do what they are required to do and whilst there is a distinct requirement for participants to demonstrate competency, there are many and diverse sources of evidence available to the assessor.

Ongoing performance at work, as verified by a supervisor or physical evidence, can count towards assessment. Additionally, the assessor can talk to customers or work colleagues to gather evidence about performance.

A range of assessment methods to assess competency include: practical demonstrations at work or in simulated work conditions, problem solving, portfolios of evidence, critical incident reports, journals, oral presentations, interviews, videos, visuals: slides, audio tapes, case studies, log books, projects, role plays, group projects, group discussions and examinations.

XVII. The Process of Assessment

Conducting assessments against the ACCSTP competency standards and CATC qualifications involves collecting evidence through various assessment methods including observing work, interviewing, conducting oral and written tests and practical testing, and making a judgment that the person can perform work in accordance with the competency standard.

The following process may be used in conducting competency based assessments.

Step 1. The assessor
- establishes the context and purpose of the assessment
- identifies the competency standards, assessment guidelines and qualifications
- identifies the Toolkit that has been developed to facilitate the assessment process (if available)
- interprets the competency standards and identifies the evidence requirements

Step 2 - Prepare the candidate
The assessor meets with the candidate to:
- explain the context and purpose of the assessment and the assessment
- process
- explain the competency standards to be assessed and the evidence to be collected
- outline the assessment procedure, the preparation which the candidate should undertake and answer any questions
- assess the needs of the candidate and establish any allowable adjustments in the assessment procedure
- seek feedback regarding the candidate's understanding of the competency standards, evidence requirements and assessment process
- determine if the candidate is ready for assessment and decide on the time and place of the assessment
- develop an assessment plan.

Step 3 – Collect and Judge Evidence
The assessor must:
- establish a plan for gathering sufficient and quality evidence about the candidate's performance in order to make the assessment decision
- source or develop assessment materials to assist the evidence gathering process

- organize equipment or resources required to support the evidence gathering process
- coordinate and brief other personnel involved in the evidence gathering process.
- establish and oversee the evidence gathering process to ensure its validity, reliability, fairness and flexibility
- collect appropriate evidence and match compatibility to the elements, performance criteria, range of variables and Evidence Guide in the relevant units of competency
- incorporate specified allowable adjustments to the assessment procedure, where appropriate

Step 4 – Record Assessment
The assessor will:
- evaluate the evidence in terms of validity, consistency, currency, equity, authenticity and sufficiency
- consult and work with other staff, assessment panel members or technical experts involved in the assessment process
- record details of evidence collected
- make a judgment about the candidate's competence based on the evidence and the relevant unit(s) of competency.

Step 5 - Provide Feedback on the Assessment
The assessor must provide advice to the candidate about the outcomes of the assessment process. This includes providing the candidate with:
- clear and constructive feedback on the assessment decision
- information on ways of overcoming any identified gaps in competency revealed by the assessment
- the opportunity to discuss the assessment process and outcome information on reassessment and appeals processes.

Step 6 - Record and Report the Result
The assessor must:
- record the assessment outcome according to the approved policies and procedures
- maintain records of the assessment procedure, evidence collected and the outcome according to the approved policies and procedure

☐ maintain the confidentiality of the assessment outcome
☐ organize the issuance of qualifications and/or Statements of Attainment according to the approved policies and procedures

XVIII. Review the Assessment Process

Feedback on the assessment process will be helpful to the assessment center, so a review the assessment process by the assessor is valuable. The assessor should be encouraged to report on the positive and negative features of the assessment to those responsible for the assessment procedures and make suggestions on improving the assessment procedures to appropriate personnel in the TCPB.

In addition, the assessor may be involved in providing feedback and counseling to the candidate, if required, regarding the assessment outcome or process and to provide the candidate with information on the reassessment and appeals process. The assessor should report any assessment decision that is disputed by the candidate to the appropriate personnel in the TCPB and participate in the reassessment or appeal according to the approved policies and procedures.

XIX.   Recognition of Current Competency

Recognition of Prior Learning is the process that gives current industry professionals who do not have a formal qualification, the opportunity to benchmark their extensive skills and experience against the standards set out in each unit of competency/subject.

Also known as a Skills Recognition Audit (SRA), this process is a learning and assessment pathway which encompasses: Recognition of Current Competencies (RCC) Skills auditing Gap analysis and training Credit transfer.

Recognition of Prior Learning (RPL) is a similar process to RCC that recognizes previous study or learning which can be mapped against competency standards.

XX.   Assessing Competence

As mentioned earlier, assessment is the process of identifying a participant's current knowledge, skills and attitudes against all elements of competency within a unit of competency. Traditionally in education, grades or marks were given to participants, dependent on how many questions the participant successfully answered in an assessment tool

Competency based assessment does not award grades, but simply identifies if the participant has the knowledge, skills and attitudes to undertake the required task to the specified standard. Therefore, when assessing competency, an assessor has two possible results that can be awarded: Pass Competent (PC) or Not Yet Competent (NYC).

If the participant is able to successfully answer or demonstrate what is required, to the expected standards of the performance criteria, they will be deemed as 'Pass Competent' (PC). The assessor will award a 'Pass Competent' (PC) if they feel the participant has the necessary knowledge, skills and attitudes in all assessment tasks for a unit.

If the participant is unable to answer or demonstrate competency to the desired standard, they will be deemed to be 'Not Yet Competent' (NYC). This does not mean the participant will need to complete all the assessment tasks again. The focus will be on the specific assessment tasks that were not performed to the expected standards. The participant may be required to:
- Undertake further training or instruction
- Undertake the assessment task again until they are deemed to be 'Pass' Competent Table 4.2 below shows an example of a Unit of Competence and how the performance criteria are assessed.

XXI. Competency covers all aspects of workplace performance and involves
- Performing individual tasks
- Managing a range of different tasks
- Responding to contingencies or breakdowns
- Dealing with the responsibilities of the workplace
- Working with others

XXII. Unit of Competency
All qualifications or programs include a range of topics that focus on the ability of the trainee to perform a task or job in a specific work area and with particular responsibilities or job functions. For purposes of assessment, ACCSTP uses the unit of competency that applies in the tourism workplace. Each unit of competency identifies a discrete workplace requirement and includes:

- Knowledge and skills that underpin competency

- Language, literacy and numeracy
- Occupational health and safety requirements

Unit Code: _____	Unit Title: _____
Unit Descriptor: _____	
Element: _____	Performance Criteria:
Range of Variable: _____	
Evidence Guide : Underpinning Skills and Knowledge •Context of Assessment •Critical Aspects of Assessment •Linkages to Other Units	
Key Competency	

Figure 4-2 : Structure of a Unit of Competency

Each unit of competency must be adhered to in training and assessment to ensure consistency of outcomes

XXIII. Element of Competency

An element of competency describes the essential outcomes within a unit of competency. The elements of competency are the basic building blocks of the unit of competency. They describe in terms of outcomes the significant functions and tasks that make up the competency.

XXIV. Performance Criteria

Performance criteria indicate the standard of performance that is required to demonstrate achievement within an element of competency. The standards reflect identified industry skill needs. Performance criteria will be made up of certain specified skills, knowledge and attitudes. Figure 4.3 which compares competency standards with curriculum and shows the linkages between both methods of learning and assessment.

XXV. Performance Criteria

CBA is the strategy of assessing the competency of a trainee or worker. Assessment utilizes a range of assessment strategies to ensure that trainees are assessed in a manner that demonstrates validity, fairness, reliability, flexibility and fairness of assessment processes.

Assessment can be completed in a variety of ways:
- On-the-job – in the workplace
- Off-the-job – at an educational institution or dedicated training environment
- As a combination of these two options.

No longer is it necessary for trainees to be absent from the workplace for long periods of time in order to obtain recognized and accredited qualifications.

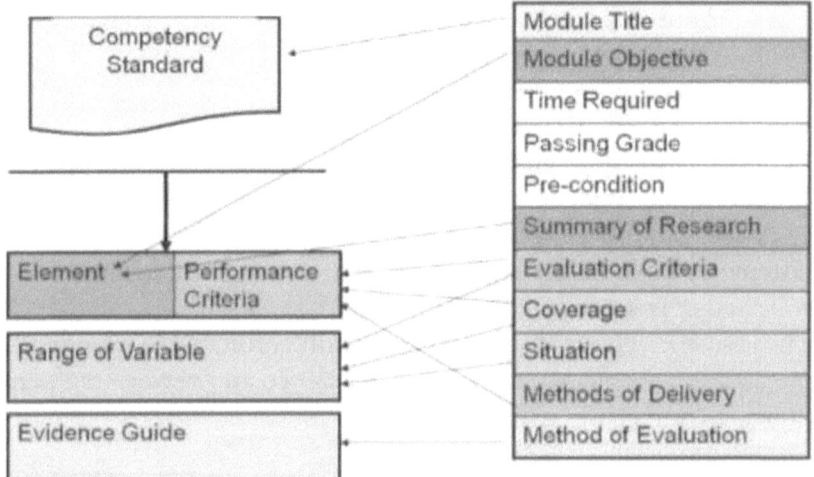

XXVI. Principles of Competency Based Assessment (CBA)

Competency based assessment is aimed at compiling a list of evidence that shows that a person is competent in a particular unit of competency. Competencies are gained in many ways including:

- Training and development programs

- Off-the-job – at an educational institution or dedicated training environment
- As a combination of these two options.

No longer is it necessary for trainees to be absent from the workplace for long periods of time in order to obtain recognized and accredited qualifications.

XXVII. Principles of Competency Based Assessment (CBA)

Competency based assessment is aimed at compiling a list of evidence that shows that a person is competent in a particular unit of competency. Competencies are gained in many ways including:

- Training and development programs
- Formal education
- Life experience
- Apprenticeships
- On-the-job experience
- Self-help programs.

In CBA, assessors and participants work together, through the 'collection of evidence' in determining overall competence. This evidence can be collected using different formats, supported by different people in the workplace or in the training institution, and collected over a period of time.

The assessor, who is ideally someone with considerable experience in the area being assessed, reviews the evidence and verifies the person as being competent or not.

XXVIII. Flexibility in Assessment

The Toolkits developed for each ACCSTP Competence Unit are very comprehensive and provide Trainers and Assessors with a range of methods and tools to aid in the assessment process. For all assessments, suitable alternate assessment tools may be used, according to the requirements of the participant.

The assessment needs to be equitable for all participants, taking into account their cultural and linguistic needs. Competency must be proven regardless of:

☐   Language
☐   Delivery Method
☐   Assessment Method.

XXIX. Assessment Objectives

The assessment tools used for ACCSTP are designed to determine competency against the 'elements of competency' and their associated 'performance criteria'. The assessment tools are used to identify sufficient a) knowledge, including underpinning knowledge, b) skills and c) attitudes.

Assessment tools are activities that trainees are required to undertake to prove competency. All assessments must be completed satisfactorily for participants to obtain competence for the units submitted for assessment and it is possible that in some cases several assessment items may be combined and assessed together.

XXX. Types of Assessment

A number of assessment tools can be used to determine competency, and these are suggested in the AACSTP Standards. Assessment methods can include: work projects, written questions, oral questions, third party reports, observation checklists etc. Instructions on how assessors should conduct these assessment methods are explained in the Assessment Manuals and Toolkits.

XXXI. Alternative Assessment Tools

The assessor can also use different assessment methods to measure the competency of a participant. Evidence is simply proof that the assessor gathers to show participants can actually do what they are required to do and while there is a distinct requirement for participants to demonstrate competency, there are many and diverse sources of evidence available to the assessor.

Ongoing performance at work, as verified by a supervisor or physical evidence, can count towards assessment. Additionally, the assessor can talk to customers or work colleagues to gather evidence about performance.

A range of assessment methods to assess competency include: practical demonstrations at work or in simulated work conditions, problem solving, portfolios of evidence, critical incident reports, journals, oral presentations, interviews, videos, visuals: slides, audio tapes, case studies, log books, projects, role plays, group projects, group discussions and examinations.

XXXII. The Assessment Process

Conducting assessments against the ACCSTP competency standards and CATC qualifications involves collecting evidence through various assessment methods including observing work, interviewing, conducting oral and written tests and practical testing, and making a judgment that the person can perform work in accordance with the competency standard.

The following process may be used in conducting competency based assessments.

Step 1. The assessor:

☐ establishes the context and purpose of the assessment
☐ identifies the competency standards, assessment guidelines and qualifications
☐ identifies the Toolkit that has been developed to facilitate the assessment process (if available)
☐ interprets the competency standards and identifies the evidence requirements

Step 2 - Prepare the candidate

The assessor meets with the candidate to:

☐ explain the context and purpose of the assessment and the assessment process
☐ explain the competency standards to be assessed and the evidence to be collected
☐ outline the assessment procedure, the preparation which the candidate should undertake and answer any questions
☐ assess the needs of the candidate and establish any allowable adjustments in the assessment procedure

- seek feedback regarding the candidate's understanding of the competency standards, evidence requirements and assessment process
- determine if the candidate is ready for assessment and decide on the time and place of the assessment
- develop an assessment plan.

Step 3 – Collect and Judge Evidence
The assessor must:
- establish a plan for gathering sufficient and quality evidence about the candidate's performance in order to make the assessment decision
- source or develop assessment materials to assist the evidence gathering process
- organize equipment or resources required to support the evidence gathering process
- coordinate and brief other personnel involved in the evidence gathering process.
- establish and oversee the evidence gathering process to ensure its validity, reliability, fairness and flexibility
- collect appropriate evidence and match compatibility to the elements, performance
- criteria, range of variables and Evidence Guide in the relevant units of competency
- incorporate specified allowable adjustments to the assessment procedure, where appropriate

Step 4 – Record Assessment
The assessor will:
- evaluate the evidence in terms of validity, consistency, currency, equity, authenticity and sufficiency
- consult and work with other staff, assessment panel members or technical experts involved in the assessment process
- record details of evidence collected
- make a judgment about the candidate's competence based on the evidence and the relevant unit(s) of competency.

Step 5 - Provide Feedback on the Assessment
The assessor must provide advice to the candidate about the outcomes of the assessment process. This includes providing the candidate with:

- clear and constructive feedback on the assessment decision
- information on ways of overcoming any identified gaps in competency revealed by the assessment
- the opportunity to discuss the assessment process and outcome• information on reassessment and appeals processes.

Step 6 - Record and Report the Result
The assessor must:
- record the assessment outcome according to the approved policies and procedures
- maintain records of the assessment procedure, evidence collected and the outcome according to the approved policies and procedure
- maintain the confidentiality of the assessment outcome
- organize the issuance of qualifications and/or Statements of Attainment according to the approved policies and procedures

XXXIII. Review the Assessment Process
Feedback on the assessment process will be helpful to the assessment center, so a review the assessment process by the assessor is valuable. The assessor should be encouraged to report on the positive and negative features of the assessment to those responsible for the assessment procedures and make suggestions on improving the assessment procedures to appropriate personnel in the TCPB.

In addition, the assessor may be involved in providing feedback and counseling to the candidate, if required, regarding the assessment outcome or process and to provide the candidate with information on the reassessment and appeals process. The assessor should report any assessment decision that is disputed by the candidate to the appropriate personnel in the TCPB and participate in the reassessment or appeal according to the approved policies and procedures.

XXXIV. Recognition of Current Competency
Recognition of Prior Learning is the process that gives current industry professionals who do not have who do Ongoing performance at work, as verified by a supervisor or physical evidence, can count towards assessment. Additionally, the assessor can talk to customers or work colleagues to gather evidence about performance.

A range of assessment methods to assess competency include: practical demonstrations at work or in simulated work conditions, problem solving, portfolios of evidence, critical incident reports, journals, oral presentations, interviews, videos, visuals: slides, audio tapes, case studies, log books, projects, role plays, group projects, group discussions and examinations.

XXXV. The Process of Assessment

Conducting assessments against the ACCSTP competency standards and CATC qualifications involves collecting evidence through various assessment methods including observing work, interviewing, conducting oral and written tests and practical testing, and making a judgment that the person can perform work in accordance with the competency standard.

The following process may be used in conducting competency based assessments:

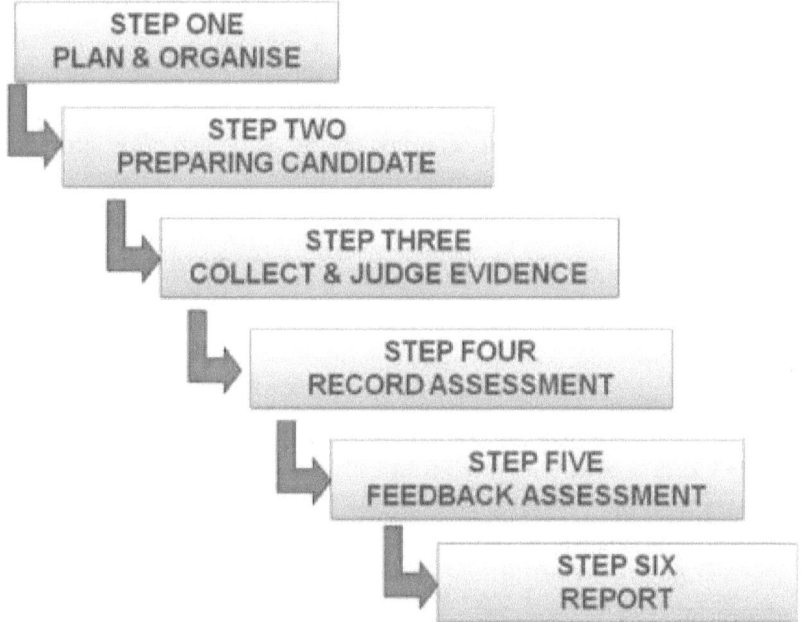

Figure 4.-4: The Assessment Process

Step 1 – Plan and Organize
The assessor:
- establishes the context and purpose of the assessment
- identifies the competency standards, assessment guidelines and qualifications
- identifies the Toolkit that has been developed to facilitate the assessment process (if available)
- interprets the competency standards and identifies the evidence requirements

Step 2 - Prepare the candidate
The assessor meets with the candidate to:
- explain the context and purpose of the assessment and the assessment process
- explain the competency standards to be assessed and the evidence to be collected
- outline the assessment procedure, the preparation which the candidate should undertake and answer any questions
- assess the needs of the candidate and establish any allowable adjustments in the assessment procedure
- seek feedback regarding the candidate's understanding of the competency standards, evidence requirements and assessment process
- determine if the candidate is ready for assessment and decide on the time and place of the assessment.
- develop the assessment plan

Step 3 – Collect and Judge Evidence
The assessor must:
- establish a plan for gathering sufficient and quality evidence about the candidate's performance in order to make the assessment decision;
- source or develop assessment materials to assist the evidence gathering process;

- organize equipment or resources required to support the evidence gathering process;
- coordinate and brief other personnel involved in the evidence gathering process;
- establish and oversee the evidence gathering process to ensure its validity, reliability, fairness and flexibility;
- collect appropriate evidence and match compatibility to the elements, performance criteria, range of variables and Evidence Guide in the relevant units of competency;
- incorporate specified allowable adjustments to the assessment procedure, where appropriate.

Step 4 – Record Assessment
The assessor will:
- evaluate the evidence in terms of validity, consistency, currency, equity, authenticity and sufficiency
- consult and work with other staff, assessment panel members or technical experts involved in the assessment process
- record details of evidence collected
- make a judgment about the candidate's competence based on the evidence and the relevant unit(s) of competency.

Step 5 - Provide Feedback on the Assessment
The assessor must provide advice to the candidate about the outcomes of the assessment process. This includes providing the candidate with:
- clear and constructive feedback on the assessment decision
- information on ways of overcoming any identified gaps in competency revealed by the assessment
- the opportunity to discuss the assessment process and outcome• information on reassessment and appeals processes.

Step 6 - Record and Report the Result
The assessor must:
- record the assessment outcome according to the approved policies and procedures
- maintain records of the assessment procedure, evidence collected and the outcome according to the approved policies and procedure
- maintain the confidentiality of the assessment outcome

☐ organize the issuance of qualifications and/or Statements of Attainment according to the approved policies and procedures

Review the Assessment Process
Feedback on the assessment process will be helpful to the assessment center, so a review the assessment process by the assessor is valuable. The assessor should be encouraged to report on the positive and negative features of the assessment to those responsible for the assessment procedures and make suggestions on improving the assessment procedures to appropriate personnel in the TCPB.

In addition, the assessor may be involved in providing feedback and counseling to the candidate, if required, regarding the assessment outcome or process and to provide the candidate with information on the reassessment and appeals process. The assessor should report any assessment decision that is disputed by the candidate to the appropriate personnel in the TCPB and participate in the reassessment or appeal according to the approved policies and procedures.

Recognition of Current Competency
Recognition of Prior Learning is the process that gives current industry professionals who do not have a formal qualification, the opportunity to benchmark their extensive skills and experience against the standards set out in each unit of competency/subject.

Also known as a Skills Recognition Audit (SRA), this process is a learning and assessment pathway which encompasses: Recognition of Current Competencies (RCC) Skills auditing Gap analysis and training Credit transfer.

Recognition of Prior Learning (RPL) is a similar process to RCC that recognizes previous study or learning which can be mapped against competency standards.

Assessing Competence
As mentioned earlier, assessment is the process of identifying a participant's current knowledge, skills and attitudes against all elements

of competency within a unit of competency. Traditionally in education, grades or marks were given to participants, dependent on how many questions the participant successfully answered in an assessment tool. Competency based assessment does not award grades, but simply identifies if the participant has the knowledge, skills and attitudes to undertake the required task to the specified standard. Therefore, when assessing competency, an assessor has two possible results that can be awarded: Pass Competent (PC) or Not Yet Competent (NYC).

If the participant is able to successfully answer or demonstrate what is required, to the expected standards of the performance criteria, they will be deemed as 'Pass Competent' (PC). The assessor will award a 'Pass Competent' (PC) if they feel the participant has the necessary knowledge, skills and attitudes in all assessment tasks for a unit.

If the participant is unable to answer or demonstrate competency to the desired standard, they will be deemed to be 'Not Yet Competent' (NYC). This does not mean the participant will need to complete all the assessment tasks again.

The focus will be on the specific assessment tasks that were not performed to the expected standards. The participant may be required to:

☐ Undertake further training or instruction
☐ Undertake the assessment task again until they are deemed to be 'Pass Competent Table 4.1 below shows an example of a Unit of Competence and how the performance criteria are assessed.

Table 4-1 : Example of Unit of Competence & its Key Components

Unit Variables
The Unit Variables provide advice to interpret the scope and context of this unit of competence, allowing for differences between enterprises and workplaces. It relates to the unit as a whole and facilitates holistic assessment.

This unit applies to the delivery of housekeeping services in an industry sector that provides accommodation facility to guests within the labour divisions of the hotel and travel industries and may include:
1. Housekeeping

Services delivered by a room attendant may be related to:
- routine housekeeping and room servicing/cleaning duties
- rotational cleaning duties
- special area cleaning, such as sauna, steam room, nominated outside areas and nominated inside areas/rooms which may include private offices and public areas
- turn down services

- Describe grooming and personal presentation standards for a room attendant
- Interpret enterprise policies and procedures for the provision of housekeeping services
- Identify and explain the role of communication in the provision of housekeeping services

Element 2: Prepare for cleaning duties
2.1 Replenish linen room supplies
2.2 Load housekeeping trolley with supplies for service
2.3 Check housekeeping trolley prior to use
2.4 Identify rooms to be cleaned for the shift
2.5 Access and enter guest room appropriately

Element 3: Make beds
3.1 Strip and re-make bed with fresh bed linen
3.2 Re-make bed using existing bed linen

Element 4: Clean bathroom
4.1 Clean bath and shower area
4.2 Clean toilets

The Mechanisms Supporting MRA for Tourism Professionals

I. Introduction

Since the signing of the ASEAN Framework Agreement on Services (Article V) on 15 December 1995 in Bangkok, Thailand there has been steady progress towards realization of a full MRA for Tourism Professionals by all Member States for implementation in 2015. The key statement confirms, "Each Member State may recognize the education or experience obtained, requirements met, or licenses or certifications granted in another Member State, for the purpose of licensing or certification of service suppliers. Such recognition may be based upon an agreement or arrangement with the Member State concerned or may be accorded autonomously." In order to function effectively, the MRA - TP will require an infrastructure operating at both the ASEAN and Member State levels. The ASEAN Framework Agreement on MRAs (1998) provides guidance for these mechanisms, recognizing also the experience and expertise available through the development of other MRAs internationally. This chapter of the Handbook will explain the key mechanisms and components required for effective implementation of the MRA.

The Key MRA Components

The MRA – TP model consists of six mechanisms or components:

a) The National Tourism Professional Board (NTPB), B) The Tourism Professionals Certification Board (TPCB),
- The Common ASEAN Tourism Curriculum (CATC),
- The ASEAN Tourism Professionals Registration System (ATPRS),
- The ASEAN Tourism Qualifications Equivalency Matrix (ATQEM), and
- The ASEAN Tourism Professional Monitoring Committee (ATPMC).

Each component forms part of a connecting infrastructure in support of effective implementation of the MRA - TP system to become operational by 2015. Each part requires a development effort at either ASEAN (regional) level or Member State (national) level.

At national or Member State level two agencies are required – the National Tourism Professional Board (NTPB) and the Tourism Professionals Certification Board (TPCB). The NTPB has the function of quality control of the education and training system that delivers the qualifications utilized in the MRA. The TPCB will apply national competency standards and assess and certify tourism professionals and will also support the (ATPRS). Each of these will be explained in more detail in this Handbook.

III. National Tourism Professional Boards (NTPB)

The NTPB of each ASEAN Member State shall have the following responsibilities:

- Create awareness and disseminate information about this the MRA – TP;
- Promote, update, maintain, and monitor the ACCSTP and the CATC;
- Facilitate the exchange of information concerning assessment procedures, criteria, systems, manuals and publications relating to this MRA – TP;
- Report its work progress to the ASEAN NTOs, including actions taken on cases referred to it by the TPCB and/or ATPMC;
- Formulate and update necessary mechanisms to enable implementation of this MRA;
- Facilitate the exchange of best practices and prevailing developments in tourism sector with the view to harmonizing and updating regional and/or international tourism competencies and curricula; and
- Such other functions and responsibilities that may be assigned to it by the ASEAN NTOs in the future.

IV. Tourism Professional Certification Boards (TPCB)

Each Member State will establish a Tourism Professional Certification Board (TPCB). Most will already have an established national qualifications accreditation agency that would take on the role as TPCB. The TPCB would function in support of the ATPRS by providing in-country qualification endorsements on existing professional qualifications by applying the template established by the CATC Regional Qualifications Framework. In some countries, a TPCB or equivalent already exists and this development presents a further indicator of the country's readiness to proceed. For example, the Government of Viet Nam with assistance from the EU established a working TPCB named the Vietnam Tourism Certification Board which functions in support of the Viet Nam National Authority on Tourism.

V. Composition of TPCB

The composition of each TPCB will vary by Member Country, as it will be dependent upon existing government structures and private sector involvement. It may also be the case that the NTPB and the TPCB can be separate arms of the same agency.

VI. Responsibilities of the TPCB

Each Member Country will require the services of a Tourism Professionals Certification Board. The TPCB will apply national competency standards and assess and certify tourism professionals with an accredited qualification in order that they can be registered on the ATPRS. One of the primary functions of the TPCB is to manage the day-to-day operation of the ATPRS. The TPCB is rooted firmly at the Member County level.

VII. Terms of Reference of TPCBs

- Assess qualifications and/or competencies of tourism professionals as specified in the ACCSTP;
- Issue certificates to tourism professionals whose qualifications and/or competencies have met the standards specified in the ACCSTP;

- Develop, process and maintain a register of certified tourism professionals and job opportunities onto the ATPRS; and
- Notify the NTPB promptly in case foreign tourism professionals are no longer qualified to provide a particular service or have violated technical, professional or ethical standards.
- Providing information to other Member Countries TPCBs.

VIII. ASEAN Tourism Professional Monitoring Committee (ATPMC)

The ATFTMD and the CBAMT agreed on a need for a monitoring body to be established to oversee the effective operation of the MRA – TP mechanism and to adjudicate on any operational disputes. A QA/QC mechanism will be established to ensure that the ATPRS and its supporting parts are enabled to function in the manner intended and with transparency.

IX. ATPMC Responsibilities

The committee has the overall responsibility for the operation of the MRA, including monitoring of on-going performance of the mechanism. In practice the committee would become a component part of the greater MRA mechanism. The ATPMC will review, adjudicate and resolve disputes, as well as monitor the operation of the TPCBs and the conformity equivalents being issued.

X. ATPMC Terms of reference

The ATPMC is funded by Member States and supported by the ASEAN Secretariat. It is comprised of members of the NTOs and other (co-opted) nominees of individual Member Countries. Its terms of reference are as follows:
- Create awareness and disseminate information about MRA on tourism professionals within ASEAN
- Promote, update, maintain and monitor ACCSTP
- Upon receipt of feedback from NTPBs, to notify promptly the concerned TPCB in case foreign tourism professionals are no longer qualified to provide a particular service or have violated technical, professional or ethical standards
- Facilitate exchange of information concerning assessment procedures, criteria, systems, manuals and publications

- Report its progress of work to the ASEAN NTOs
- Formulate and update necessary mechanisms to enable the implementation of this MRA
- Other functions and responsibilities that may be assigned to it in the future.

XI. ASEAN Tourism Professionals Registration System (ATPRS)

Of the four component parts of the support mechanism for the MRA - TP, the ATPRS is the device most essential to the effective operation of the MRA concept. It will perform two functions in parallel and will underpin the MRA in tourism in terms of regional best practice and efficient use of resources.

XII. ATPRS Purpose

There are two aims of the ATPRS:
- To compile the records of applicants (tourism professionals) in a format compliant with an agreed model and procedure. By this procedure, tourism professionals will be registered and thus formally identified for recognition by industry as a registered professional, and,
- Further to a satisfactory registration process, the ATPRS would provide a database system on which the data on applicants could be appraised by licensed employers or agencies. The process would indicate expressions of interest from registered professionals in seeking employment on an industry-approved contract in another AMS.

XIII. ATPRS Ethos

ATPRS will be established to provide affordable access, (equitable) to meet the needs of suitably qualified job-seekers irrespective of where they live in the ASEAN region.

It will be a well-defined reference mechanism, linked to the standards of the ACCSTP Framework. Most importantly, ATPRS will be managed in an environment conducive to the MRA goals and in a competent manner that would engender confidence in its operation and potential outcomes.

XIV. ATPRS Design

The MRA mechanism must be technologically current and sustainable, with a web-based registration system suitable to enable eligible applicants to lodge a formal expression of interest in seeking work in a relevant industry sector and in a foreign ASEAN member country. The design would:

- It would allow for applications to be registered through multiple portals in each Member State and thus access would not be limited to only one or two locations in each country;
- The initiative of applying to become a registered job-seeker would not impose a heavy cost burden on those the system is most designed to serve and with a minimal capacity to pay;
- The basis of operation would remain "industry-driven", (because employers would still be the ones responsible and authorized to initiate proceedings) but with a much clearer emphasis on the qualifications of the job-seeker it delivers a more equitable system;
- With appropriate accessibility, the ATPRS would have additional potential to assist qualified job-seekers in more rural areas to seek skilled employment in a safe local environment;
- Through wider accessibility, the ATPRS would have additional potential to assist qualified women to seek out appropriate skilled employment in a safe local environment.

ATPRS Features

The ATPRS is still under development and will be launched in readiness for the MRA in 2015 with the following features:

- A regional mechanism and a central feature of the MRA support system.
- A web-based database facility.
- A system that operates in real time.
- Accessible to licensed users only. This would apply equally to inputs of data from qualified applicants as well as for access by job placement agencies, companies and industry employer organizations.

☐ Equipped to maintain a profile of appropriate users, to be developed for licensing to protect the system from risks of malpractice in the early phase of operation.
☐ Owned by the ATPMC Regional Secretariat with the day-to-day management, maintenance and operation out-sourced to an appropriate IT services provider.

XVI. Monitoring and Reporting

The monitoring of the MRA will be through monthly reports from the ATPRS. The ATPRS database should facilitate generation of monthly reports automatically as required by the ATPMC. The data should support the evaluation of the MRA operation through the following reports:
☐ Volume of registrations on the ATPRS;
☐ Timings/seasonality of registrations on the ATPRS;
☐ Types of qualifications registered on the ATPRS;
☐ The nationality, gender and other characteristics of registrations, and
☐ Other variables as required by AMS and the ATPMC.
Through these reports, both the ATPMC and Member States (via the NTPBs) will be able to review the effectiveness of the MRA according to its established objective

XVII Reporting Responsibilities

The automatic monthly reporting procedures from the ATPRS will be agreed with variables determined in consultation with Member States and the ATPMC.
☐ The ATPMC should monitor the reports on a six monthly basis.
☐ The NTPB in each AMS should monitor the data for their own AMS on a quarterly basis and report concerns to the ATPMC, and
☐ ATPMC should report on their monitoring findings annually to the NTOs.
While the monitoring and evaluation of the MRA would initially be based on data drawn from the ATPRS, there will be other data available at both national and international levels that relates to the tourism labour market in ASEAN. This could be used to supplement material from the ATPRS and would also allow for the monitoring of

movements into and out of the ASEAN region and provide a broader contextual setting for the ATPRS data.

XV. Challenges to MRA Sustainability

The design of the MRA for Tourism Professionals is dependent upon three entities that will require the commitment of experienced personnel – the ATPMC (a regional committee) and the NTPB and TPCB bodies (both national bodies).

Recognition of Tourism Professional Qualifications

I. Introduction
For the MRA for Tourism Professionals to function effectively across ASEAN Member States there needs to be a system of recognition of tourism professional qualifications. Countries that import tourism labour must accept and comply with the regulatory requirements of the exporting country. Likewise, countries that export tourism labour must ensure they conform to the requirements of the importing country by validating the local tourism qualifications of the employees wishing to work in another ASEAN member country.

II. Recognition of Tourism Professionals
The ASEAN Mutual Recognition Arrangement states,
 A foreign tourism professional may be recognized as eligible for a certain tourism job title in the labour divisions as specified in APPENDIX III in a host country provided that he/she possesses tourism competency qualification/certificate in a specific tourism job title as specified in the ACCSTP, issued by the TPCB in an ASEAN Member Country, provided further that he/she shall comply with the prevailing domestic laws and regulations of the host country."

III. Conformity Assessment
According to the ASEAN Framework Agreement on Mutual Recognition Agreements: 'Conformity Assessment means systematic examination to determine the extent to which a product, process or service fulfils specified requirements'. For international arrangements, cross-border conformance can occur in two ways:
1. Countries can accept the results of other country's conformance assessment as the basis for their own conformity assessment decisions. This is useful as it does not need extensive promotional campaigns, but it does less to reduce redundancy in assessment; or,

2. They can promote the direct acceptance of the conformance assessment results of the other countries by customers in their own country. This needs considerable promotional activity, but eliminates most of the redundancy in the system. This is the most common arrangement and the one recommended for the ASEAN MRA in tourism.

Countries therefore mutually accept each other's conformity assessment in terms of tourism qualifications. This acceptance relates to the process of conformity assessment. It is important to note that this does not imply harmonization where the exporting country checks the regulations of the importing country before export. The purpose of an ASEAN MRA – TP is therefore to ensure that all ten ASEAN countries accept the conformity assessment relating to tourism competency qualifications produced in any single ASEAN Member State.

IV. Rationale for the Approach

In order to achieve conformity, each of the ten ASEAN countries will need to have their tourism qualification system evaluated against the requirements established under the MRA – TP to demonstrate their competence to be part of the MRA. This arrangement will involve the comparison of tourism qualifications across the ten ASEAN countries.

V. Equivalence Assessment

Here, the key process is equivalence assessment – the process of judging the conformity assessment procedures and/or rules of another country to be equivalent to national conformity assessment procedures and/or rules. If the MRA – TP is to be a robust arrangement then this equivalence assessment needs to take place.

The reason that the equivalence assessment process is so pivotal to this MRA relates to the fact that tourism is comprised of non-regulated occupations:

☐ A regulated occupation is one that is controlled and governed by a professional organization or regulatory body. The regulatory body governing the profession or trade has the authority to set entry requirements and standards of practice, to assess applicants' qualifications and credentials, to certify, register, or license qualified applicants, and to discipline members of the profession/trade.

☐ Requirements for entry, which may vary from one country to another, usually consist of such components as examinations, a specified period of supervised work experience, and language competency.
☐ However, there are agreed standards across the profession, which can be built into an MRA. Examples of sectors that comprise regulated occupations include medicine, engineering or law.
☐ A non-regulated occupation is a profession or trade for which there is no legal requirement or restriction on practice with regard to licenses,
☐ Certificates, or registration.
Tourism falls into this category and as a result, the design of an MRA for tourism professionals is more challenging.

VI. Equivalence Matrix of Tourism Qualifications

The MRA – TP is challenging because there are no agreed international tourism standards which can act as a basis for conformity assessment for the MRA
- TP. As a result, it is essential to construct an equivalence matrix of tourism qualifications for the AMS to be used as the basis for conformity assessment. This is an essential supporting mechanism for a robust, reliable and transparent Mutual Recognition Arrangement for Tourism Professionals.

VII. Registration of Tourism Professionals onto ATPRS

The TPCB will be responsible for the registration of applicants onto the ASEAN Tourism Professionals Registration System (ATPRS). The ATPRS is a web-based facility designed to disseminate details about qualified tourist professionals in ASEAN Member States.
award structures and given an equivalent weighting or value.
The ATQEM output assessment code places a value on the suitability of a qualification for a specific purpose in employment in circumstances where that applicant and qualification are derived from a foreign source and system.
The ATQEM device will function electronically to provide a licensed user with a comparative weighting expressed either as an indexed number (e.g., 7.8 on a 10-point scale) or as a band on a scale that informs the user of the quality of a particular applicant's qualification

in simple terms. This could be described as 'a qualifications matching system' that provides a comparison with an accepted ASEAN benchmark based on the ACCSTP Framework and the CATC (see Figure 6.2).

Although ATQEM is still under development, the planned essential features are as follows:

☐ Records for AMSs can be built over time. Inputs or changes can only be made by licensed national TPCB bodies
☐ A sub-database allocated to each Member State would provide a storage option. The TPCB is responsible to manage whatever award data is stored
☐ An automated electronic function that will indicate the status of an award on the basis of CATC
☐ Scope of awards / qualifications listed will have to comply with ASEAN specifications (CATC)
☐ Able to respond to simultaneous input and reading functions. Integrated with the ATPRS
☐ Ownership of the ATQEM will be tied to ownership and location of ATPRS
☐ Available to licensed industry associations, and licensed employers or agencies
☐ For validity and reliability, the ATQEM system must operate in real time and be designed to run on a shared-cost basis associated with the function of the parent ATPRS mechanism
☐ Input data must be in English
☐ Restricted access to licensed or approved users for security reasons.

VIII. Importance of the ATQEM

From 2015 tourism professionals from ten different and highly variable academic systems and accreditation standards will be able to apply for tourism and hospitality jobs in other ASEAN countries through the MRA – TP.

The ATQEM will assist applicants and employers (end users) to interpret (electronically and automatically) the status of tourism qualifications. Employers need to be confident in their ability to ascertain the relevance of the candidate's certificate or diploma, the accrediting authority and date, status and quality of a qualification for purposes of (a) registration of an applicant, and (b) appraisal by an employer or his/her appointed agency of the suitability of an applicant for a particular job vacancy.

Most AMS have a National Qualification Framework which provides coherence for national qualifications. ASEAN is also exploring the possibility of a Regional Qualification Framework to aid in the harmonization and recognition of national qualifications between Member States (see Figure 6.3).

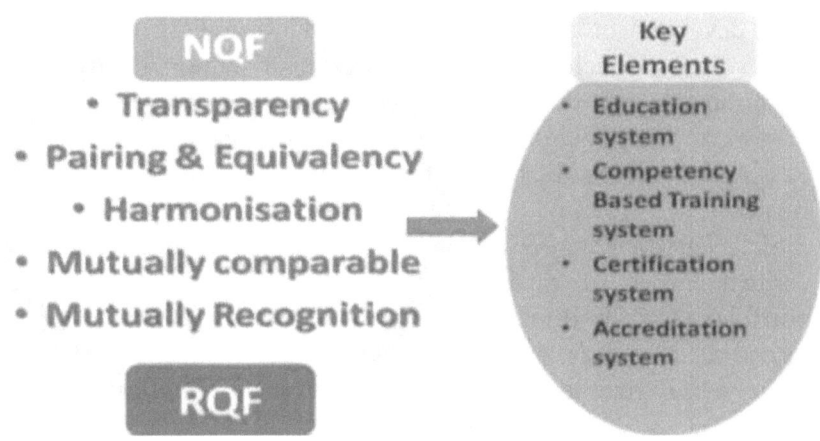

Figure 6-3: Harmonization of National Qualifications Frameworks with Regional Qualification Frameworks

IX. Features of the ATQEM

The development of the ATQEM is part of the ATPRS. The key features of the system are:

☐ The electronic database system – the ATPRS - to facilitate the registration of qualified tourism professionals through approved portals, including the national TCPB and approved industry associations in Member States.

☐ Guidelines for the registration of tourism professionals in accordance with the regulations associated with the approved ASEAN MRA on tourism (2008).

☐   An electronic mechanism, to be integrated with the ATPRS – the ATQEM
- to facilitate automatic cross-referencing and matching of qualifications registered by applicants against accepted and existing ASEAN benchmarks, specifically the CATC.

X.   Skills Passbook

In the hospitality and tourism industry, and specifically in the ASEAN region, it is common to find demand for labor outstripping the supply of well-qualified professionals to fill job vacancies. One particular challenge that employers face is how to reliably track the training and skills development undertaken by qualified job applicants.

One solution which has enjoyed widespread support in the United Kingdom, Canada and the European Union, is the concept of a Skills Passbook. One example of an ASEAN skills passport is the Skills Passbook developed by the EU for the Vietnam Tourism Certification Board.

A Skills Passbook may be designed as a typical bound booklet in which verified entries are made, or it may exist as a protected on-line portfolio. A Skills Passbook can provide individuals with a verified record of their skills, qualifications and achievements, hosted online.
Figure 6-3: Extract from VTCB Vietnam Tourism Certification Board.

INTRODUCTION TO YOUR SKILLS PASSBOOK

This is your Skills Passbook. Please keep it in a safe place and ask your trainer(s) to keep it up to date. It records your ability to do the job under normal working conditions. You will need to produce it as evidence before obtaining your final certificate. The Passbook is your property and you should take it with you if you transfer to another employer. It will provide your new employer with evidence of the skills you possess to date.

How to use your Skills Passbook

The purpose of the Skills Passbook is to record your progress as you develop competence when you are being trained by your employer. Each trainee/employee registered with VTCB will automatically receive his/her own Skills Passbook. You will normally be trained and coached at work (or at an institute) under the supervision of a qualified trainer.

On the following pages are your personal details together with the details of tasks for which you will receive training. Your trainer will agree the training program with you (based on the applicable VTOS standard) until workplace competence is achieved. When this occurs your trainer will 'sign you off'. If you are already competent because of your experience to date, you could be 'signed off' without further training. Training will normally take place at the workplace, however it may take place elsewhere, for example at a training institute.

Vietnam Tourism Certification Board

A skills passbook can be issued by an employer, a training provider, a vocational college or another organization registered for the purpose. This method has many benefits for the tourism professional, especially those seeking work overseas as it is suitability for record keeping and has some of the features of the planned ATPRS.

XI. Conclusion

The mutual recognition of tourism qualifications is at the heart of the MRA process. The key mechanisms to ensure this is managed efficiently and professionally are through the ATPRS and the ATQEM systems. The ASEAN Tourism Professional Monitoring Committee will continue to support member NTOs by developing the various mechanisms, disseminating information and providing training and development opportunities.

References:

Technical Report on Final Common ASEAN Tourism Curriculum & Regional Qualifications & Skills Recognitions Systems

The ASEAN Framework Agreement on Mutual Recognition Agreements

Conclusion and Roadmap

I. Introduction

The MRA for tourism professionals has been a coordinated and managed process since 1999 when the ATFTMD was formed and has taken a logical approach to development.

Figure 7-1 : Process of MRA – TP Development 2005-2015

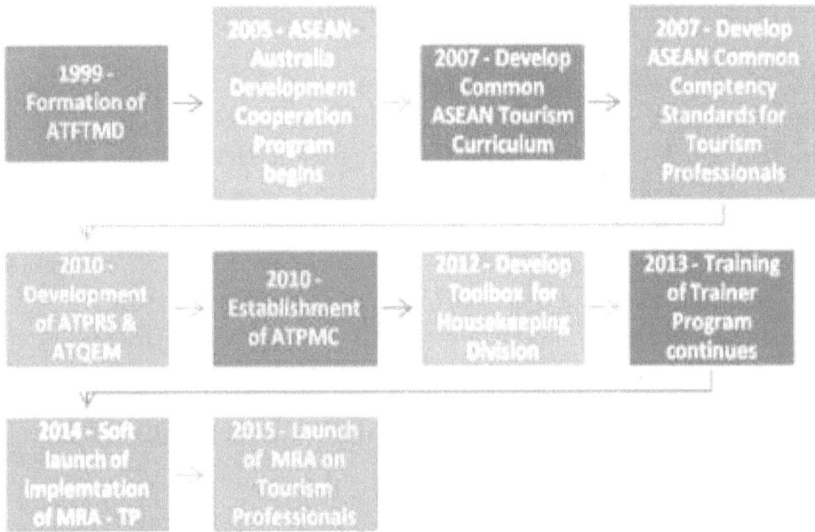

The 13th ASEAN Tourism Ministers' Meeting in January 2010 endorsed "MRA Follow-up Implementation Requirements" including capacity development for members of related organizations under the MRA at regional and national levels.

II. Training & Assessment Toolboxes

ASEAN Member States agreed to develop training toolboxes for common competencies for the six identified labor divisions (housekeeping, food production, food and beverages services, front office, tour operation and travel agencies) and additional toolboxes for the specific housekeeping division's competencies.

III. Housekeeping Division

The housekeeping division was identified as a priority due to significant employment opportunities in the region. The toolboxes will be used by tourism training and education institutions in ASEAN Countries (Certificate II to Advanced Diploma levels), as a reference to deliver a standardized competency-based training system for the housekeeping division. It will also be used to conduct professional certification programs for the housekeeping division.

IV. Implementation of Toolboxes

The Tourism Professional Certification Boards (TPCB) and National Tourism Professional Boards (NTPB) of respective ASEAN Member States are involved in the development and implementation of the toolboxes. NTPBs will be given the ownership of the developed toolboxes and entrusted with the responsibility to ensure systematic implementation of the toolboxes in their respective countries.

The overall project will contribute to efforts to strengthen the tourism sector, a priority integration sector within the AEC Blueprint, by supporting efforts to build the skills of workers in the tourism industry. It will do so by developing training materials for selected competencies in the tourism industry.

V. Project Phases

This project has followed two phases. The first has been to develop training toolboxes for common and generic competencies for all six tourism labor divisions and selected toolboxes for housekeeping division competencies.

The second phase, begun in 2012, is to develop a pool of ASEAN Master Assessors and Trainers, provide Training of Trainers and support limited piloting testing of the toolboxes.

VI. Progress of Implementation of MRA Work Plan

The progress of the Implementation of MRA Work Plan is shown in the hereunder Table.

	Work Plan	Status	Target dates
1	Establishment of ATPMC	Done	2010
2	Review of ACCSTP Framework & CATC	On-going	Implemented continuously
3	Development of Training Toolbox for Housekeeping	Done	2011-2012
4	Development of ATPRS including ASEAN Tourism Qualifications Equivalent Matrix (ATQEM)	Project on "Gap Analysis on the Implementation of MRA on Tourism Professionals" is now on-going, funded by AADCP II. The Development of ATPRS would be conducted through a separate project in 2013	2012
5	Feasibility Study for development of regional secretariat to implement MRA of Tourism Professional	On-going, funded by AADCP II	2012
6	Development of training toolbox (functional competencies: Front Office, Food and Beverage Services, and Food Production	On-going, funded by AADCP II	2012-2013
7	Training Program for ASEAN Master Trainer and Master Assessor for Housekeeping Division	Funding for this activity from AADCP II has been secured for implementation after toolboxes for housekeeping are completed	2012-2013
8	Development of training toolbox (functional competencies: Travel Agents and Tour Operators)	Funding for this activity from AADCP II has been secured.	2013
9	Training of Trainer Program for Master Trainer and Master Assessor for Front Office, Food and Beverage Services, Food Production, Travel Agents, and Tour Operators	To be implemented after toolbox of respective division is finalized	2013
10	Implementation of CATC for 6 tourism labor division	To be implemented after toolbox of respective division is implemented	2013
11	Establishment of Regional Secretariat for ATPMC	Some Member States had indicated its readiness to host the Regional Secretariat	2013
12	Soft Launching of the Implementation of MRA on Tourism Professionals		2014
13	Assistance to Least Developed Countries in Implementing MRA		2014
14	Grand Launching of the Implementation of MRA - TP		2015

VII. Roadmap for MRA –TP

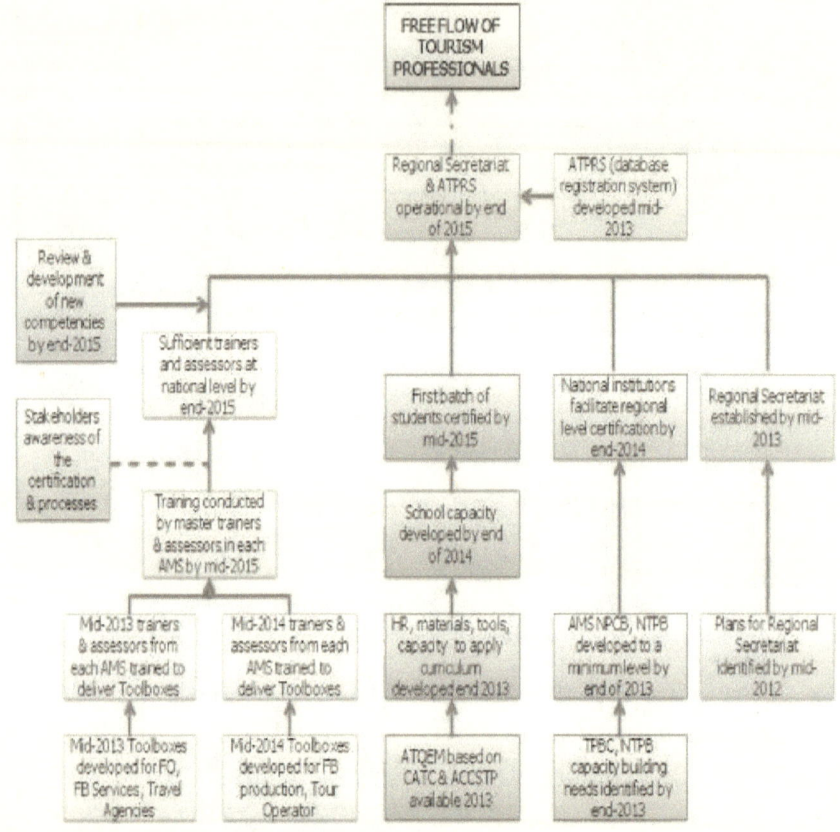

Figure 7-2 Roadmap for MRA – TP

VIII. Conclusions

The MRA on Tourism Professionals is an important driver in raising standards of tourism and improving qualifications of the tourism workforce in the ASEAN region. Member States need to carefully review their MRA status, implementation plans and readiness for the AEC in 2015.

It is hoped that this Handbook will contribute to understanding of MRA – TP and aid NTOs and others in planning and implementing the arrangement.

The ATMPC are willing to support and advise on the process and help those NTOs with any challenges or needs. Regional and country workshops and seminars will continue to be held over the next period to inform, assist and train master assessors, trainers and other key staff involved in implementing the MRA – TP. For further help and support please contact the ATPMC.

References
ASEAN Tourism Marketing Strategy (ATMS) 2012-2015 ASEAN Tourism Strategic Plan 2011 – 2015
ASEAN–Australia Development Cooperation Program Regional Partnerships Scheme. Capacity Building for an ASEAN MRA in Tourism – Revised Strategic Plan 2008A

ASEAN MRA-Mutual Recognition Agreement Guide Book for Tourism Education and Training Providers

INTRODUCTION

In 2015, the ASEAN Economic Community (AEC) will come into being, with one of its features being the mutual recognition of professional qualifications within the Community. The ASEAN Mutual Recognition Arrangement on Tourism Professionals (MRA-TP) is designed to enable the mobility of employment for skilled tourism labor within each Member State and to recognize the skills and qualifications of working tourism professionals from different ASEAN countries. This means that qualified tourism professionals can apply for jobs in other ASEAN member countries, and tourism companies can search for qualified personnel from the Community to meet their staffing needs.

This Guidebook has been included as an essential reference for tourism professionals, employers and training organizations in preparing for the launch of the ASEAN Economic Community in 2015. The Guidebook will try to answer questions about how MRA – TP works, and the requirements and implications for tourism employees and employers.

This GUIDE is for Education and training providers to review their curriculum and qualifications to ensure it matches or can be mapped to the Common Asian Tourism Curriculum in order to provide relevant qualifications to their students or trainees.

A discussion with your National Tourism Professional Certification Board should take place to review how your existing qualifications or programs need to be adapted or changed to meet the requirements of ASEAN for mutual recognition of tourism qualifications.

1. **What is the Mutual Recognition Arrangement on Tourism Professionals (MRA – TP)?**

The MRA – TP aims to facilitate mobility of tourism professionals within ASEAN based on competence-based tourism qualifications/certificates, and at the same time, improve the quality of services delivered by tourism professionals.

The ASEAN MRA – TP provides a mechanism for agreement on the equivalence of tourism certification procedures and qualifications across ASEAN. When ASEAN nations mutually recognize each other's qualifications this will encourage a free and open market for tourism labour across the region and boost the competitiveness of the tourism sector in each ASEAN nation, while at the same time attracting needed talent to meet local skills shortages. The eligibility to work in a host country will of course be subjected to prevailing domestic laws and regulations of the host country.

In order for a Foreign Tourism Professional to be recognized by other ASEAN Member States and to be eligible to work in a host country, they will need to possess a valid tourism competency certificate in a specific tourism job title as specified in the Common ASEAN Tourism Curriculum (CATC), issued by the Tourism Professional Certification Board (TPCB) in an ASEAN Member State. There are 32 job titles covered under this MRA, ranging from housekeeping, front office, food and beverages services, and food production for hotel division, to travel agencies and tour operator for travel division.

The MRA on Tourism Professionals is an important driver in raising standards of tourism and improving qualifications of the tourism workforce in the ASEAN region. Tourism and hospitality professionals are encouraged to review their existing qualifications if they wish to consider working overseas in the AEC.

Further questions on MRA – TP can be directed to the ASEAN Tourism Professional Monitoring Committee at the email address here: eddy@asean.org

2.   What is the purpose of MRA for Tourism Professionals?

The ASEAN MRA on Tourism Professionals (MRA-TP) seeks to increase the international mobility of tourism labor across the ASEAN region in line with ASEAN policy. Each ASEAN nation has its own standards, certification and regulations for recognizing the competency of workers in the tourism sector.

Therefore, there is a need for an MRA to facilitate agreement on what constitutes equivalent competency to work in tourism by a worker, for

example from Indonesia, who is seeking a position in Malaysia. The MRA – TP is therefore designed to:
- Address the imbalance between supply and demand for tourism jobs across the ASEAN region; and
- Establish a mechanism for the free movement of skilled and certified tourism labor across the ASEAN region.

The objectives of MRA – TP are threefold, to:
- Facilitate mobility of Tourism Professionals;
- Encourage exchange of information on best practices in competency- based education and training for Tourism Professionals; and,
- Provide opportunities for cooperation and capacity building across ASEAN Member States.

3. What are the benefits of MRAs?

For governments, MRAs ensure commitment and agreement to international trade, and encourage the sharing of good practice and information between partners. This can lead to:
- Reduced costs;
- Increased competitiveness; • Increased market access; and
- Freer flow of trade.

For tourism professionals and the industry, MRAs provide the following benefits:
- Facilitate mobility of tourism professionals based on the tourism competency qualification/ certificate
- Enhance conformity of competency based training/education
- Recognize skills of tourism professionals
- Improve the quality of tourism human resources (graduates are ready to work in the industry)
- Enhance the quality of tourism services.

For education and training providers, MRAs provide the following benefits:
- A clear set of standards for development of training programs
- A competency-based training and assessment system for preparing trainees for the tourism industry

☐   A range of job-based tourism qualifications based on common labour divisions

☐   An opportunity to become one of the preferred education and training providers for the range of ACCSTP qualifications.

4.   What are the key elements of MRA – TP?

The key elements of MRA – TP are shown below:

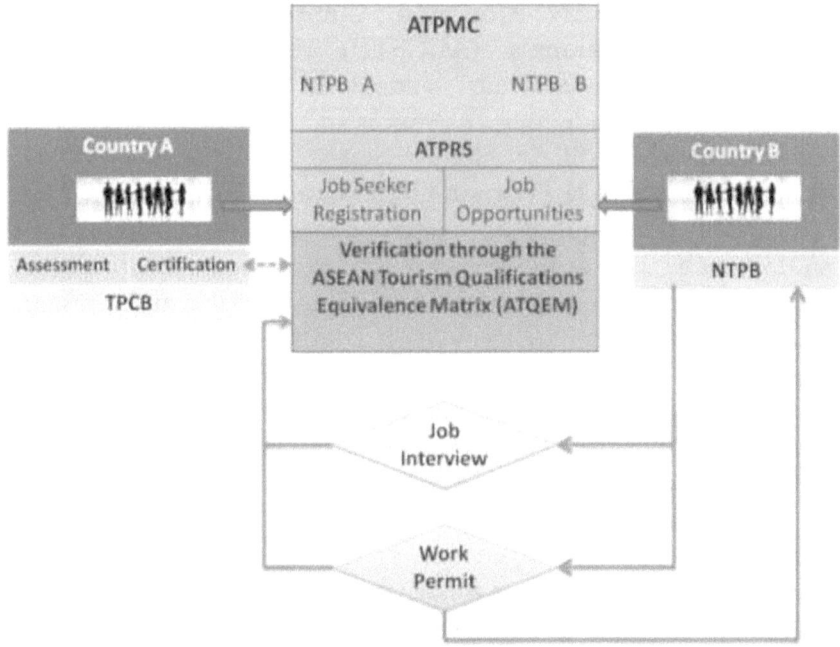

a)   **The ASEAN Tourism Professional Monitoring Committee (ATPMC)** consists of ASEAN NTOs and appointed representatives from the National Tourism Professional Boards (NTPBs);

b)   **The ASEAN Tourism Professional Registration System (ATPRS)** is a web- based facility to disseminate details of certified Foreign Tourism Professionals within ASEAN. This registration system is still under development and will be launched in 2015;

c)   **The National Tourism Professional Board (NTPB)** refers to the Board for Tourism Professionals composed of representatives from the public and private sectors (including academia and other relevant tourism stakeholders) to be determined by the respective ASEAN NTOs;

d) **The Tourism Professional Certification Board (TPCB)** refers to the government board and/or agency authorized by the government of each ASEAN Member State;

e) **Tourism Professional** refers to a person who holds the nationality of an ASEAN Member State certified by the Tourism Professional Certification Board;

f) **The ASEAN Common Competency Standards for Tourism Professionals (ACCSTP)** refers to the minimum requirements of competency standards in hotel and travel services which aim to upgrade tourism services and facilitate the development of MRA between ASEAN Member States;

g) **The ASEAN Tourism Qualifications Equivalency Matrix (ATQEM)** is an equivalence matrix of tourism qualifications for the AMS – to be used as the basis for conformity assessment. This is an essential supporting mechanism for a robust, reliable and transparent Mutual Recognition Arrangement on Tourism Professionals.

h) **The Common ASEAN Tourism Curriculum (CATC)** refers to the common curriculum for ASEAN Tourism Professionals as mutually agreed upon by the ASEAN Tourism Ministers upon recommendation by the ASEAN NTOs;

i) **Assessment** refers to the process of appraising the qualification and/or competencies of Tourism Professionals;

j) **Certification** refers to the issuance of a certificate to Tourism Professional whose qualification and/or competencies have met the standards specified in ACCSTP.

5. How will MRA - TP benefit my education or training organization?

The 2002 ASEAN Tourism Agreement (ATA) pledged to upgrade tourism education, curricula and skills through the formulation of competency standards and certification procedures, thereby leading to mutual recognition of skills and qualifications in the ASEAN region. In addition, it supported the wider ASEAN agenda of encouraging member states to adopt national frameworks for qualifications, competencies and training.

The ASEAN MRA on Tourism Professionals will provide a mechanism for agreement on the equivalence of tourism certification procedures and qualifications across ASEAN. Once this is achieved, ASEAN nations will mutually recognize each other's qualifications for tourism. This will encourage a free and open market for tourism labor across the region and boost the competitiveness of the tourism sector in each ASEAN nation.

From 2015 the qualification of a Foreign Tourism Professional may be recognized by other ASEAN Member States, and if such qualification is recognized, they may be eligible to work in a host country provided that they possess a valid tourism competency certificate in a specific tourism job title as specified in the Common ASEAN Tourism Curriculum (CATC), issued by the Tourism Professional Certification Board (TPCB) in an ASEAN Member State.

The eligibility to work in a host country will be subjected to prevailing domestic laws and regulations of the host country.
Education and training providers should review their training programs and qualifications to ensure these can be recognized by ASEAN. A discussion with your National Tourism Professional Certification Board should take place to review how your existing qualifications or programs need to be adapted or changed to meet the requirements of ASEAN for mutual recognition of tourism qualifications.

You may wish to have some of your teachers/trainers undertake a training program to become assessors or trainers for the new ASEAN Common Competency Standards for Tourism Professionals. This could lead to new business opportunities for your organization as the MRA – TP comes into force in 2015.

6. **How do I have my qualifications recognized?**
In order to satisfy the ASEAN 'Conformity Assessment' requirements, an ASEAN Tourism Qualifications Equivalence Matrix (ATQEM) will be developed using the Common Asian Tourism Curriculum qualification framework.

From the introduction of MRA – TP in 2015, applicants will be required to exhibit their local qualifications weighted for conformity by the TPCB in their home country through the ATPRS. The pre-requisite for this is completion of the ATQEM.

Your existing tourism qualifications can be submitted to your National Tourism Professional Board (NTPB) and evaluated on the ASEAN Tourism Qualification Equivalency Matrix (ATQEM). This will help identify if you need to gain a tourism They also sign a consent form agreeing to their information being available to the system, enabling the registration board in the importing country to check their details and after this checking process, allow industry bodies in the importing country to access their details on competency certificate under the Common ASEAN Tourism Curriculum.

The ATQEM is designed to provide an "at a glance" interpretation (weighting) of a registered applicant's qualification in a relevant field of professional performance in tourism, but derived from another country's system of accredited academic awards. It should function as a fast and reliable electronic cross- referencing matrix whereby similar qualifications coming from somewhat similar award structures accredited in another ASEAN country can be appraised against established ASEAN award structures and given an equivalent weighting or value.

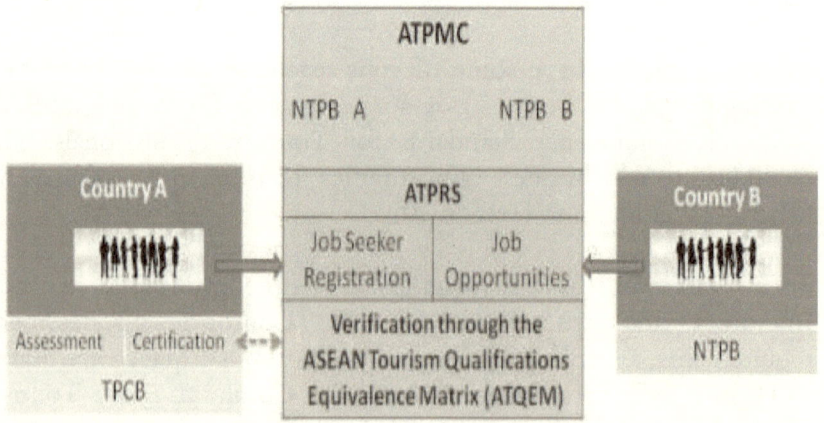

Figure: The ATPRS showing how verification is completed through the ATQEM

The ATQEM will assist applicants and employers to interpret (electronically and automatically) the status of tourism qualifications. Employers need to be confident in their ability to ascertain the relevance of the candidate's certificate or diploma, the accrediting authority and date, status and quality of a qualification for purposes of (a) registration of an applicant, and (b) appraisal by an employer or his/her appointed agency of the suitability of an applicant for a particular job vacancy.

Registration on to the ATPRS

The TPCB in each ASEAN country will oversee the management of the ASEAN Tourism Professionals Registration System (ATPRS) in their country. It will be the responsibility of the TPCB to ensure reliable means of recording, securing and storing relevant information about applicants.

Tourism Professionals can apply for registration under mutual recognition, by forwarding their details to their home registration board for posting on the ATPRS the database.

It is recommended that in order to be eligible to be entered on the ATPRS an applicant must as a minimum:

☐ Demonstrate a qualification delivered and accredited by a recognized institution in any ASEAN member country; or

☐ Demonstrate a qualification accredited by a body independent of the education authority in the ASEAN country (such as an overseas college or industry body operating in that country) providing that it has been endorsed by the TPCB and included on the approved list.

In addition, the TPCB may wish to include and monitor other professional information such as:

☐ Years spent in the industry.
☐ Evidence that the applicant has kept their professional development up to date.
☐ The applicant has agreed to a professional code of conduct.
☐ Involvement in any disciplinary matters.

Other issues:

☐ Normally, the checking of the applicant's qualifications will be done automatically using the qualifications equivalence matrix.

☐ However, in the case of a dispute or a non-standard application, the TPCB will be responsible for making a decision as to an applicant's eligibility and it is normal to allow up to one month for a decision.

☐ Short-notice applications can normally be handled by making specific exemptions. For example, the short-notice need for a specialist chef to accompany a VIP on an overseas visit can be handled by exempting the chef from registration providing the chef only cooks for that one VIP.

Find your NTPB by going to your national tourism organization website.

7. How do employees register on the ASEAN Tourism Professionals Registration System (ATPRS)?

Each Member State will establish a Tourism Professional Certification Board (TPCB). Most will already have an established national qualifications accreditation agency that would take on the role as TPCB. The TPCB would function in support of the ASEAN Tourism Professionals Registration System (ATPRS) by applying national competency standards and assessing and certifying tourism professionals
with an accredited qualification in order that they can be registered on the ATPRS. The TPCB will also provide in-country qualification endorsements on existing professional qualifications by applying the CATC Regional Qualifications Framework.

One example from the Government of Viet Nam, who with assistance from the EU, established a working TPCB named the Vietnam Tourism Certification Board which functions in support of the Viet Nam National Administration of Tourism.

The Tourism Professional Certification Board (TPCB) in each ASEAN Member State will be responsible for the registration of applicants onto the ASEAN Tourism Professionals Registration System (ATPRS). The ATPRS is a web-based facility designed to disseminate details about qualified tourist professionals in ASEAN Member States.

The steps to registration on the ATPRS include:
The NTPB will design an application form for registration onto the ATPRS.
- To apply for registration under mutual recognition, individuals forward their details to their home registration board for posting on the ATPRS.
- Individuals also sign a consent form agreeing to their information being available to the system, enabling the registration board in the importing country to check their details and after this checking process, allow industry bodies in the importing country to access their details on the database.
- The web based system will allow an applicant's relevant information to be easily accessible by registration boards in all AMS.
- It is recommended that in order to be eligible to be entered on the ATPRS an applicant must as a minimum:
- Demonstrate a qualification delivered and accredited by a recognised institution in any AMS; or
- Demonstrate a qualification accredited by a body independent of the education authority in the AMS (such as an overseas college or industry body operating in that country) providing that it has been endorsed by the NTPB and included on the approved list.
- In addition, the NTPB may wish to include and monitor other professional information such as:
- Years spent in the industry.
- Evidence that the applicant has kept their professional development up to date.
- The applicant has agreed to a professional code of conduct.
- Involvement in any disciplinary matters. primarily responsible for the assessment and certification of Tourism Professionals;

Tourism Professional refers to a person who holds the nationality of an ASEAN Member State certified by the Tourism Professional Certification Board;

The ASEAN Common Competency Standards for Tourism Professionals (ACCSTP) refers to the minimum requirements of competency standards in hotel and travel services which aim to upgrade tourism services and facilitate the development of MRA between ASEAN Member States;

The ASEAN Tourism Qualifications Equivalency Matrix (ATQEM) is an equivalence matrix of tourism qualifications for the AMS – to be used as the basis for conformity assessment. This is an essential supporting mechanism for a robust, reliable and transparent Mutual Recognition Arrangement on Tourism Professionals.

The Common ASEAN Tourism Curriculum (CATC) refers to the common curriculum for ASEAN Tourism Professionals as mutually agreed upon by the ASEAN Tourism Ministers upon recommendation by the ASEAN NTOs;

Assessment refers to the process of appraising the qualification and/or competencies of Tourism Professionals;

Certification refers to the issuance of a certificate to Tourism Professional whose qualification and/or competencies have met the standards specified in ACCSTP.

8. How will MRA - TP benefit my education or training organization?

The 2002 ASEAN Tourism Agreement (ATA) pledged to upgrade tourism education, curricula and skills through the formulation of competency standards and certification procedures, thereby leading to mutual recognition of skills and qualifications in the ASEAN region. In addition, it supported the wider ASEAN agenda of encouraging member states to adopt national frameworks for qualifications, competencies and training.

The ASEAN MRA on Tourism Professionals will provide a mechanism for agreement on the equivalence of tourism certification procedures and qualifications across ASEAN. Once this is achieved, ASEAN nations will mutually recognize each other's qualifications for tourism. This will encourage a free and open market for tourism labor across the region and boost the competitiveness of the tourism sector in each ASEAN nation.

From 2015 the qualification of a Foreign Tourism Professional may be recognized by other ASEAN Member States, and if such qualification is recognized, they may be eligible to work in a host country provided that they possess a valid tourism competency certificate in a specific tourism job title as specified in the Common ASEAN Tourism Curriculum (CATC), issued by the Tourism Professional Certification Board (TPCB) in an ASEAN Member State.

The eligibility to work in a host country will be subjected to prevailing domestic laws and regulations of the host country.

Education and training providers should review their training programs and qualifications to ensure these can be recognized by ASEAN. A discussion with your National Tourism Professional Certification Board should take place to review how your existing qualifications or programs need to be adapted or changed to meet the requirements of ASEAN for mutual recognition of tourism qualifications.

You may wish to have some of your teachers/trainers undertake a training program to become assessors or trainers for the new ASEAN Common Competency Standards for Tourism Professionals. This could lead to new business opportunities for your organization as the MRA – TP comes into force in 2015.

9. How do I have my qualifications recognized?

In order to satisfy the ASEAN 'Conformity Assessment' requirements, an ASEAN Tourism Qualifications Equivalence Matrix (ATQEM) will be developed using the Common Asian Tourism Curriculum qualification framework.

From the introduction of MRA – TP in 2015, applicants will be required to exhibit their local qualifications weighted for conformity by the TPCB in their home country through the ATPRS. The prerequisite for this is completion of the ATQEM.

Your existing tourism qualifications can be submitted to your National Tourism Professional Board (NTPB) and evaluated on the ASEAN Tourism Qualification Equivalency Matrix (ATQEM). This will help identify if you need to gain a tourism competency certificate under the Common ASEAN Tourism Curriculum.

The ATQEM is designed to provide an "at a glance" interpretation (weighting) of a registered applicant's qualification in a relevant field of professional performance in tourism, but derived from another country's system of accredited academic awards. It should function as a fast and reliable electronic cross- referencing matrix whereby similar qualifications coming from somewhat similar award structures accredited in another ASEAN country can be appraised against established ASEAN award structures and given an equivalent weighting or value.

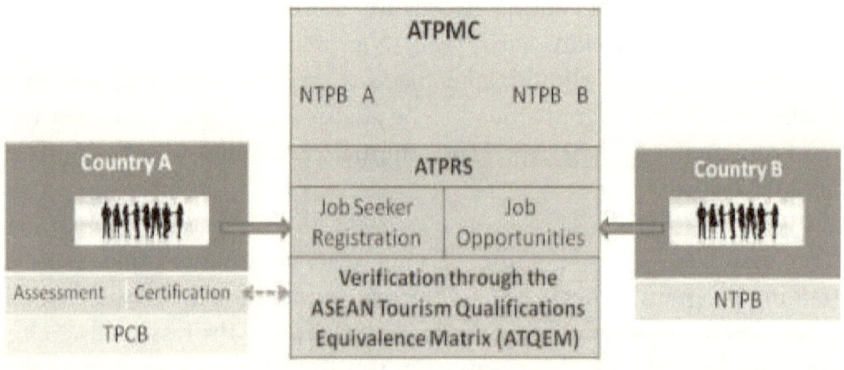

Figure: The ATPRS showing how verification is completed through the ATQEM

The ATQEM will assist applicants and employers to interpret (electronically and automatically) the status of tourism qualifications. Employers need to be confident in their ability to ascertain the relevance of the candidate's certificate or diploma, the accrediting authority and date, status and quality of a qualification for purposes of (a) registration of an applicant, and (b) appraisal by an employer or his/her appointed agency of the suitability of an applicant for a particular job vacancy.

Registration onto the ATPRS

The TPCB in each ASEAN country will oversee the management of the ASEAN Tourism Professionals Registration System (ATPRS) in their country. It will be the responsibility of the TPCB to ensure reliable means of recording, securing and storing relevant information about applicants.

Tourism Professionals can apply for registration under mutual recognition, by forwarding their details to their home registration board for posting on the ATPRS.

They also sign a consent form agreeing to their information being available to the system, enabling the registration board in the importing country to check their details and after this checking process, allow industry bodies in the importing country to access their details on the database.

It is recommended that in order to be eligible to be entered on the ATPRS an applicant must as a minimum:

- Demonstrate a qualification delivered and accredited by a recognized institution in any ASEAN member country; or
- Demonstrate a qualification accredited by a body independent of the education authority in the ASEAN country (such as an overseas college or industry body operating in that country) providing that it has been endorsed by the TPCB and included on the approved list.

In addition, the TPCB may wish to include and monitor other professional information such as:

- Years spent in the industry.
- Evidence that the applicant has kept their professional development up to date.
- The applicant has agreed to a professional code of conduct.
- Involvement in any disciplinary matters.

Other issues:

- Normally, the checking of the applicant's qualifications will be done automatically using the qualifications equivalence matrix.

☐ However, in the case of a dispute or a non-standard application, the TPCB will be responsible for making a decision as to an applicant's eligibility and it is normal to allow up to one month for a decision.

☐ Short-notice applications can normally be handled by making specific exemptions. For example, the short-notice need for a specialist chef to accompany a VIP on an overseas visit can be handled by exempting the chef from registration providing the chef only cooks for that one VIP.

Find your NTPB by going to your national tourism organization website.

8. How do employees register on the ASEAN Tourism Professionals Registration System (ATPRS)?

Each Member State will establish a Tourism Professional Certification Board (TPCB). Most will already have an established national qualifications accreditation agency that would take on the role as TPCB. The TPCB would function in support of the ASEAN Tourism Professionals Registration System (ATPRS) by applying national competency standards and assessing and certifying tourism professionals with an accredited qualification in order that they can be registered on the ATPRS. The TPCB will also provide in-country qualification endorsements on existing professional qualifications by applying the CATC Regional Qualifications Framework.

One example from the Government of Viet Nam, who with assistance from the EU, established a working TPCB named the Vietnam Tourism Certification Board which functions in support of the Viet Nam National Administration of Tourism.

The Tourism Professional Certification Board (TPCB) in each ASEAN Member State will be responsible for the registration of applicants onto the ASEAN Tourism Professionals Registration System (ATPRS). The ATPRS is a web-based facility designed to disseminate details about qualified tourist professionals in ASEAN Member States.

9. What do employees need to do in order to qualify for a job in the AEC?

The Tourism Professional whose qualification and/or competencies have met the standards specified in ACCSTP will be issued a Certificate by the Tourism Professional Certification Board (TPCB) in their home country, and this information will be entered onto the ASEAN Tourism Professionals Registration System (ATPRS). See the diagram below:

Contact the National Tourism Professional Board in your home country by going to your national tourism organization website.

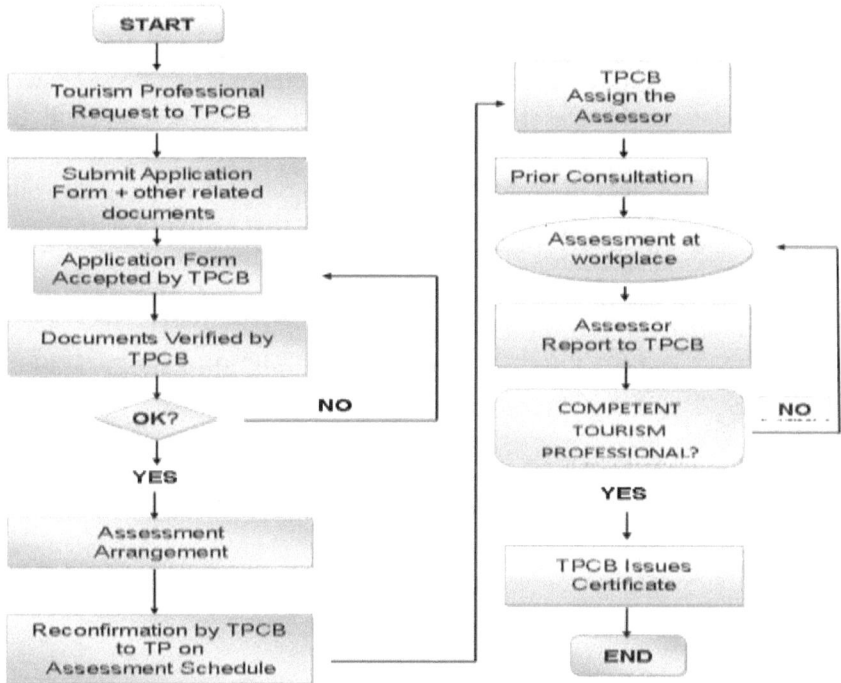

10. How can employees get Recognition for their Prior Learning or Current Competence?

Recognition of Prior Learning or Current Competence is the process that gives current industry professionals who do not have a formal qualification, the opportunity to benchmark their extensive skills and experience against the standards set out in each unit of competency of the ASEAN Common Curriculum Standards for Tourism Professionals (ACCSTP).

Assessing Competence
Assessment is the process of identifying a participant's current knowledge, skills and attitudes against all elements of competency within a unit of competency of the ACCSTP. Traditionally in education, grades or marks were given to participants, dependent on how many questions the participant successfully answered in an assessment tool.

Competency based assessment does not award grades, but simply identifies if the participant has the knowledge, skills and attitudes to undertake the required task to the If the participant is unable to answer or demonstrate competency to the desired standard, they will be deemed to be 'Not Yet Competent'. This does not mean the participant will need to complete all the assessment tasks again. The focus will be on the specific assessment tasks that were not performed to the expected standards. The participant may be required to:

- Undertake further training or instruction
- Undertake the assessment task again until they are deemed to be 'Pass Competent

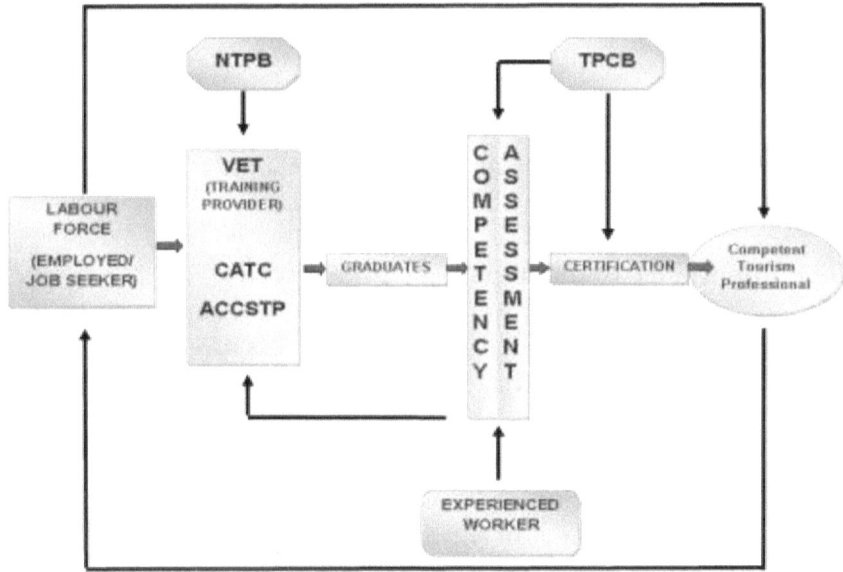

Certification

On satisfactory assessment, the Tourism Professional whose qualification and/or competencies have met the standards specified in ACCSTP will be issued a Certificate by the National Tourism Professional Certification Board (TPCB) and this will information will be entered onto the ASEAN Tourism Professionals Registration System (ATPRS).

10. What are the ASEAN Common Competency Standards for Tourism Professionals?

The ASEAN Task Force on Tourism Manpower Development developed a set of minimum competency standards for tourism professionals. The standards were based upon the competencies required to perform a set of commonly agreed job titles in retail and wholesale travel companies, housekeeping, front office, and food & beverage service.

The minimum competency standards essential for each job title were decided on the following basis:

- Should be compatible with best practice to be recognized internationally;

- Should be the best available common denominator or common language to advance the interests of the ASEAN community;
- Would only include competencies that were current, relevant and applicable to member countries;
- Each member country or industry may choose to add additional competencies that may be necessary to suit local requirements.

The Importance of a Competency Framework

The ACCSTP are based on the concept of competency – the knowledge, skills attitudes (KSA) that individuals must have, or must acquire, to perform effectively at work.

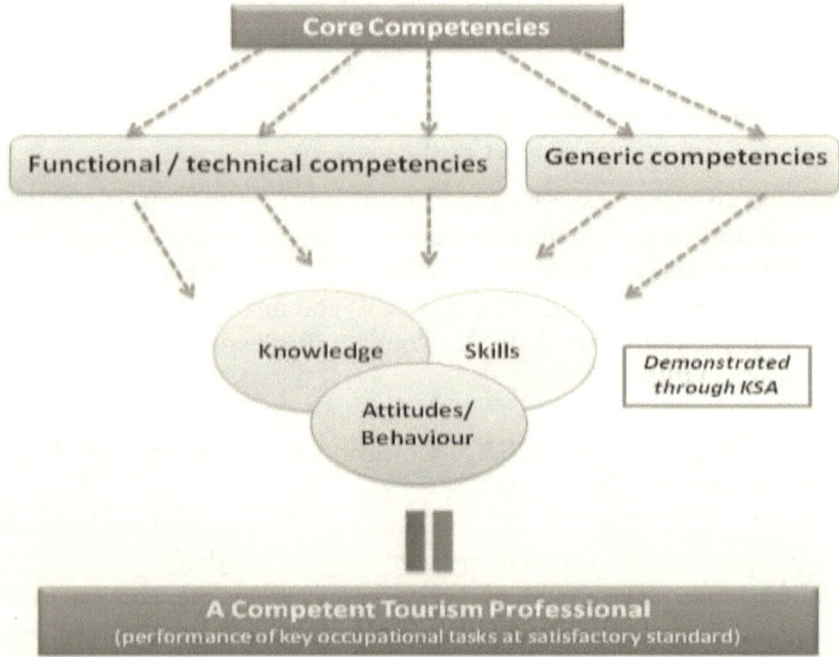

Competence is all about demonstrable performance outputs and in the case of ACCSTP relates to a system or set of minimum standards required for effective performance at work. A 'competency framework' is a structure that sets out and defines each individual competency (such as problem-solving, checking in hotel guests or managing people) required by individuals working in a tourism organization or part of an organization.

Structure of the Competency Standards
Competency standards set down the specific knowledge and skills required for successful performance in the workplace and the required standard of performance. They are organized into units, each with a code and title. The standards for hospitality and tourism cover both general areas common to all sectors (e.g. communication, leadership and occupational health and safety), and sector-specific areas.

The ACCSTP Framework lists the minimum common competency standards that should be widely used in the region to allow the skills, knowledge and attitudes (competence) of tourism professionals to be assessed, recognized and equated to comparable qualifications in other ASEAN countries in order for an MRA to function.

Common Labor Divisions
The ACCSTP are arranged as sets of competencies required by qualified professionals who seek to work in the various divisions of labor that are common across various sectors of tourism in ASEAN Member States.

Minimal Competencies
Compliance with these "minimal" competencies will be an essential reference or benchmark for anyone wishing to apply for a position in another ASEAN Member State. The terms minimum or minimal simply refer to the essential basic skills required for a particular job description. It is useful in setting a basic benchmark or standard in professional performance. In the ACCSTP Framework, the minimal competencies required are arranged on a framework using common divisions of labor as illustrated in the Table below:

32 Job Titles - Six Labour Divisions

HOTEL SERVICES				TRAVEL SERVICES	
Front Office	**House Keeping**	**Food Production**	**Food and Beverage Service**	**Travel Agencies**	**Tour Operation**
Front Office Manager	Executive Housekeeper	Executive Chef	F&B Director	General Manager	Product Manager
Front Office Supervisor	Laundry Manager	Demi Chef	F&B Outlet Manager	Assistant General Manager	Sales & Marketing Manager
Receptionist	Floor Supervisor	Commis Chef	Head Waiter	Senior Travel Consultant	Credit Manager
Telephone Operator	Laundry Attendant	Chef de Partie	Bartender	Travel Consultant	Ticketing Manager
Bell Boy	Room Attendant	Commis Pastry	Waiter		Tour Manager
	Public Area Cleaner	Baker			
		Butcher			

The positions listed under each labor division are of varying levels of sophistication and responsibility, some of which might require extensive vocational training whereas others might only require short-term training of one to two weeks or on-the-job training.

Setting Job Positions

The principle for setting job positions is that for some positions it is entirely possible that someone can carry out a series of responsibilities in a highly professional manner without any formal education. This is certainly the case within the industry where some managers have little formal education but a great deal of life and industry experience. This is not to say that formal education at the higher managerial levels is not important but clearly industry experience needs to be recognized in any hiring process.

The Labor Division
The term labor division might be slightly misleading in that some of the tasks are operational in nature and labor intensive, but many of the position classifications are clearly supervisory or managerial.

Core, Generic and Functional Competencies
The competency standards for tourism professionals listed in the ACCSTP Framework are the minimum acceptable common competency standards required by industry and employers to enable the standard of a qualified person's skills to be recognized and assessed equitably in ASEAN countries. This is an essential mechanism required for the effective operation of an MRA.

In the ACCSTP Framework, the Competencies are graded into three related groups of skills: Core, Generic and Functional Competencies.

Core Competencies
Competencies that industry has agreed are essential to be achieved if a person is to be accepted as competent in a particular primary division of labor. They are directly linked to key occupational tasks and include units such as 'Work effectively with colleagues and customers, and Implement occupational health and safety procedures.'

Generic Competencies
Competencies that industry has agreed are essential to be achieved if a person is to be accepted as competent at particular secondary division of labor. The name 'life skills' is sometimes used to describe these competencies and they include units such as: 'Use common business tools and technology,' and 'Manage and resolve conflict situations.'

Functional Competencies
Functional Competencies are specific to roles or jobs within the labour division, and include the specific skills and knowledge (know-how) to perform effectively, such as 'Receive and process reservations, Provide housekeeping services to guests, and Operate a bar facility.' These competencies could be generic to a Labor Division as a whole, or be specific to roles, levels or jobs within the Labor Division.

11. What is the ASEAN Common Tourism Curriculum?

The Common ASEAN Tourism Curriculum (CATC) is the approved common curriculum for ASEAN Tourism Professionals as mutually agreed upon by the ASEAN Tourism Ministers upon recommendation by the ASEAN NTOs. The concept is founded upon a number of initiatives, including the Vientiane Action Plan (VAP), ASEAN Tourism Agreement (ATA) and the Roadmap for Integration of Tourism Sector (RITS). The CATC is linked to the Regional Qualifications Framework and Skills Recognition System (RQFSRS).

Design Principles

The curriculum was designed to be industry based, well-structured and flexible, in order to meet varying local requirements of the Member States. It is based on the agreed Competencies adopted by all Countries in ASEAN, and using the agreed ACCSTP Units of Competence aims at making qualifications relevant and useful to both students and the tourism industry.

Common ASEAN Tourism Curriculum

The CATC is founded upon six labor divisions: Front Office, Housekeeping, Food Production, Food & Beverage Service, Travel Agencies and Tour Operations. CATC & RQFSRS go hand in hand. CATC supports and contributes to the development of a harmonized tourism education and training framework within the ASEAN region, while the RQFSRS supports and contributes to the implementation of the MRA - TP which ultimately will facilitate skilled labor mobility, contributing to economic integration of the region.

Rationale for CATC

CATC is founded on the Competency Based Training (CBT) approach that is recognized worldwide as being the most effective means of delivering vocational training. CBT is training that provides trainees with skills, knowledge and attitudes necessary to demonstrate competence against prescribed and endorsed Industry Competency Standards. This concept is especially applicable to Tourism where 'attitude' is an extremely vital element of all customer-contact and service situations.

Figure: Components of Competence-based Training

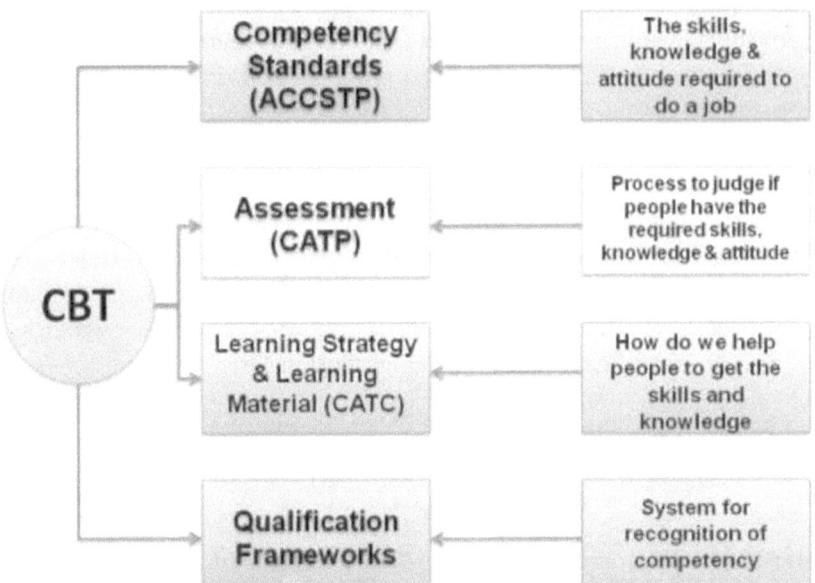

CATC Framework

CATC aims at providing an efficient and practical model for the delivery of vocational training which can be expected to prove popular with industry, students and training providers. The model is straightforward and consistent across all Secondary Labor Divisions of Travel Agencies, Tour Operation, Housekeeping, Front Office, Food and Beverage Service, and Food Production. It offers qualifications in each of the labor divisions from Certificate II level to Advanced Diploma level. The framework is:

☐ Industry-based – the units of competency and the content for each one has been set by industry: qualifications will match industry need in order to make qualifications relevant and useful to both students and industry

☐ Flexible – allowing students, industry and training providers the highest level of flexibility in the selection of units for each qualification:

☐ stakeholders can individually determine on a case-by-case basis the actual mix of units that will combine to fulfil the packaging requirements for a qualification

☐ Well-structured – there is a logical flow between qualifications: this facilitates advancement through qualifications, enables movement between streams and enables students to gain higher level managerial qualifications while still retaining a practical and operational focus.

Structure of CATC

CATC consists of five qualification levels across all six Labor Divisions providing vocational streams within each Labor Division that reflect the stated needs of AMS and the needs of industry. In all cases Certificate II incorporates Certificate I on the advice of participating countries. The table below gives an overview of the level at which each of the five qualifications in the Framework is set.

Framework Level Indicator
Level 5 - Advanced Diploma — Sophisticated, broad and specialized competence with senior management skills
Technical, creative, conceptual or managerial applications built aroundcompetencies of either a broad or specialized base and related to a broader organizational focus.
Level 4 - Diploma — Specialized competence with managerial skills
Assumes a greater theoretical base and consists of specialized, technical or managerial competencies used to plan, carry out and evaluate work of self and/orteam.
Level 3 - Greater technical competence with supervisory skills **CertificateIV**
More sophisticated technical applications involving competencies requiring increased theoretical knowledge, applied in a non-routine environment and which may involve team leadership and management and increased responsibility for outcomes.
Level 2 Certificate III — **Broad range of skills in more varied context and team leader** responsibilities

Skilled operator who applies a broad range of competencies within a more varied work context, possibly providing technical advice and support to a team including having team leader responsibilities.
Level 1 - Basic, routine skills in a defined context **Certificate II**
A base operational qualification that encompasses a range of functions/activities requiring fundamental operational knowledge and limited practical skills in a defined context.

Table: Qualification & Description of the Competencies used at each Level I found in the next page.

Gives Flexible Pathways for Career Development

Participants can also enter – or leave - the qualification Framework at any level: there is no obligation to complete, for example, Certificate II before undertaking Certificate III or higher. For example:

1. A student enters the Tour Operation field unsure of what their final career might be.

2. The student elects to enrol in a Certificate II in Tour Operation (Guiding), an entry/base-level qualification in the Secondary Labour Division of Tour Operation.

3. The student is required to take five Core and Generic competencies plus six additional functional competencies from Tour Operations or Tour Guide Services.

4. The student can select competencies to steer them in the direction of their anticipated career and/or to reflect the current needs of their workplace, but the final choice is theirs.

Figure: Progression possibilities

Enables Tourism Professionals to Build on Existing Qualifications

Enrolling in a higher level qualification enables the student to use and build on the previous units they have studied. Their unit selection will again reflect the blend of functional competencies they wish to attain and as previous units count towards their new qualification additional units are included to add the new competencies demanded by industry. The extent to which the student varies the functional competency clusters from which they select will depend on their career goal and industry need. This can also work over lifetimes by enabling employees to take additional modules and thus to 'grow' into new jobs.

Practical and Progressive

This approach has produced qualifications that represent a blend of industry identified competencies that enable practical workplace application as well as providing the basis for promotion and continued learning, and the ability for trainees to move between labor divisions as the need or opportunity arises.

Industry-Based Content and Units of Competency
The qualifications listed in the proposed Framework are based on units of competency developed by industry making the training content relevant and responsive to industry need. As the qualifications rise through the levels (Certificate II to Advanced Diploma), so too do the choices of Units of Competency that exist within the packaging rules vary to respond to the changing workplace nature of the tasks that need to be completed.

A Blend of Competencies
These changes to selection options reflect the required Functional Competencies identified by industry as being necessary for the various job titles that have been classified. Every qualification requires participants to undertake a blend of mandatory Core and Generic competencies as well as elective Functional competencies.

Each of the qualifications has been holistically designed with a focus on essential Core and Generic units of competency together with the ability for trainees to select the most appropriate Functional Competencies to support their workplace needs or aspirations.

Encourages Life-long Learning
The key to this capability lies in the freedom of people to choose units of competency from Functional Competency clusters that best suit their individual workplace and training needs, and yet still be credited with (some) previous units they have already studied. In this way, this framework actively supports the concept of life-long learning by encouraging further study through acknowledgment and recognition of past study.

Enables Accumulation of Skills and Knowledge
The underpinning intention of this approach is to provide a vocational education and training system that enables trainees to accumulate skills and knowledge as they move through the system and study to gain higher qualifications. This will facilitate movement between

qualifications, streams and Labor Divisions for trainees thereby providing a system that meets and can respond quickly to changing employer demand and one that maximizes trainee choice of units of competency, streams and Labor Divisions.

A Robust Framework

While providing freedom and flexibility the educational integrity and robustness of the framework is guaranteed by the need for trainees to complete the designated number of units at each qualification level before a complete credential can be issued.

Enables Portability of Qualifications

The flexible structure of CATC will enhance the portability of qualifications between industries and countries and the intended audit requirements that will be imposed on all training providers will assure provider integrity, reliability and commitment.

Provides Recognition of Attainment

It will be a requirement that any statement of attainment issued by any training provider must be recognized for the purposes of 'prior standing' by every other training provider within the system regardless of where that training provider is located and regardless of the perceived reputation of that organization.

Enables Mobility of Career Pathways

This means that trainees can readily move from (for example) Housekeeping to Front Office or Food and Beverage service and can move readily from Tour Operations to Travel Agencies. The structure also enables trainees to move easily into supervisory or managerial qualifications, or retain an operational role within the industry while gaining additional skills.

13. What are Competency-based Qualifications?

Competency

Competency requires the application of specified knowledge, skills and attitudes relevant to effective participation, consistently over time and in the workplace environment. The essential skills and knowledge are either identified separately or combined.

☐ Knowledge identifies what a person needs to know to perform the work in an informed and effective manner.
☐ Skills describe the application of knowledge to situations where understanding is converted into a workplace outcome.
☐ Attitude describes the founding reasons behind the need for certain knowledge or
☐ why skills are performed in a specified manner.

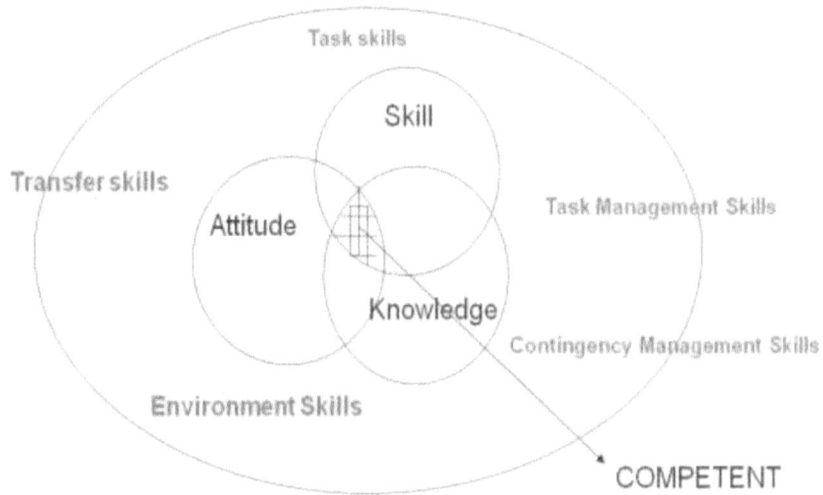

Figure: A Competent Worker

Competency covers all aspects of workplace performance and involves:
☐ Performing individual tasks
☐ Managing a range of different tasks
☐ Responding to contingencies or breakdowns
☐ Dealing with the responsibilities of the workplace
☐ Working with others.

Unit of Competency

All qualifications or programs include a range of topics that focus on the ability of the trainee to perform a task or job in a specific work area and with particular responsibilities or job functions. For purposes of assessment, ACCSTP uses the unit of competency that applies in the tourism workplace. Each unit of competency identifies a discrete workplace requirement and includes:

- Knowledge and skills that underpin competency
- Language, literacy and numeracy
- Occupational health and safety requirements.

Each unit of competency must be adhered to in training and assessment to ensure consistency of outcomes.

Figure: Structure of a Unit of Competency

Unit Code:	Unit Title:
Unit Descriptor:	
Element:	Performance Criteria:
Range of Variable:	
Evidence Guide : Underpinning Skills and Knowledge •Context of Assessment •Critical Aspects of Assessment •Linkages to Other Units	
Key Competency	

Element of Competency

An element of competency describes the essential outcomes within a unit of competency. The elements of competency are the basic building blocks of the unit of competency. They describe in terms of outcomes the significant functions and tasks that make up the competency.

Performance criteria

Performance criteria indicate the standard of performance that is required to demonstrate achievement within an element of competency. The standards reflect identified industry skill needs Performance criteria will be made up of certain specified skills, knowledge and attitudes. Figure 4.3 which compares competency standards with curriculum and shows the linkages between both. methods of learning and assessment.

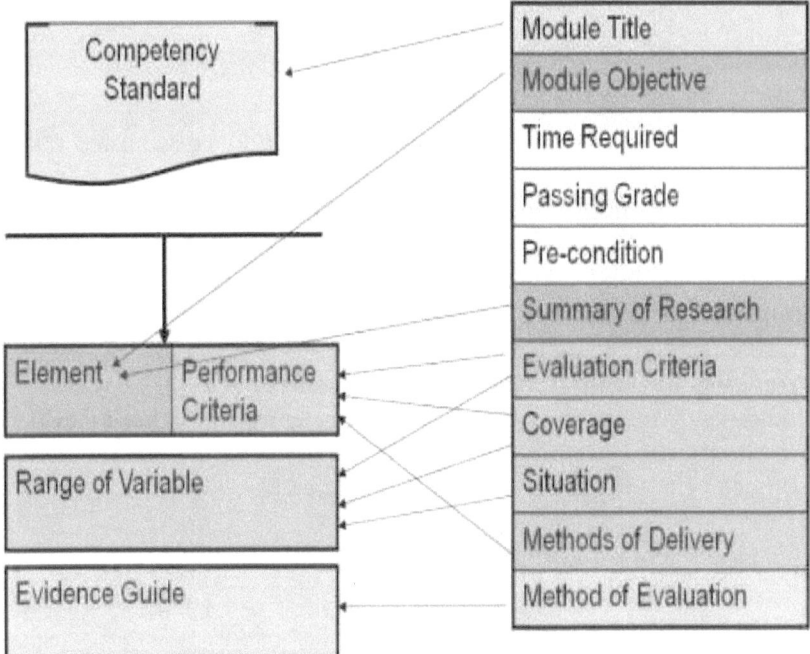

Figure: Competency Standards versus Curriculum

14. How is competency assessed?

Introduction
Competence-based Training (CBT) and Competence-based Assessment (CBA) focus on what a worker can do or is required to do at work. Competency refers to the ability to perform particular tasks and duties to the standard of performance expected in the workplace. ASEAN has adopted the CBT/CBA training system to enable member countries to produce the type of worker that industry is looking for and this therefore increases trainees' chances of obtaining employment. CBA involves collecting evidence and making a judgment of the extent to which a worker can perform his/her duties at the required competency standard.

Competency Based Assessment (CBA)
CBA is the strategy of assessing the competency of a trainee or worker. Assessment utilizes a range of assessment strategies to ensure that trainees are assessed in a manner that demonstrates validity, fairness, reliability,

flexibility and fairness of assessment processes. Assessment can be completed in a variety of ways:

- On-the-job – in the workplace
- Off-the-job – at an educational institution or dedicated training environment
- As a combination of these two options.
- No longer is it necessary for trainees to be absent from the workplace for long periods of time in order to obtain recognized and accredited qualifications.

Principles of Competency Based Assessment (CBA)
Competency based assessment is aimed at compiling a list of evidence that shows that a person is competent in a particular unit of competency. Competencies are gained in many ways including:

- Training and development programs
- Formal education
- Life experience
- Apprenticeships
- On-the-job experience
- Self-help programs.

In CBA, assessors and participants work together, through the 'collection of evidence' in determining overall competence. This evidence can be collected using different formats, supported by different people in the workplace or in the training institution, and collected over a period of time.
The assessor, who is ideally someone with considerable experience in the area being assessed, reviews the evidence and verifies the person as being competent or not.

Flexibility in Assessment
The Toolkits developed for each ACCSTP Competence Unit are very comprehensive and provide Trainers and Assessors with a range of methods and tools to aid in the assessment process. For all assessments, suitable alternate assessment tools may be used, according to the requirements of the participant.

The assessment needs to be equitable for all participants, taking into account their cultural and linguistic needs. Competency must be proven regardless of:

- Language
- Delivery Method
- Assessment Method.

Assessment Objectives

The assessment tools used for ACCSTP are designed to determine competency against the 'elements of competency' and their associated 'performance criteria'. The assessment tools are used to identify sufficient a) knowledge, including underpinning knowledge, b) skills and c) attitudes.

Assessment tools are activities that trainees are required to undertake to prove competency. All assessments must be completed satisfactorily for participants to obtain competence for the units submitted for assessment and it is possible that in some cases several assessment items may be combined and assessed together.

Types of Assessment

A number of assessment tools can be used to determine competency, and these are suggested in the AACSTP Standards. Assessment methods can include: work projects, written questions, oral questions, third party reports, observation checklists etc. Instructions on how assessors should conduct these assessment methods are explained in the Assessment Manuals and Toolkits.

Alternative Assessment Tools

The assessor can also use different assessment methods to measure the competency of a participant. Evidence is simply proof that the assessor gathers to show participants can actually do what they are required to do and whilst there is a distinct requirement for participants to demonstrate competency, there are many and diverse sources of evidence available to the assessor.

Ongoing performance at work, as verified by a supervisor or physical evidence, can count towards assessment. Additionally, the assessor can talk to customers or work colleagues to gather evidence about performance.

A range of assessment methods to assess competency include: practical demonstrations at work or in simulated work conditions, problem solving, portfolios of evidence, critical incident reports, journals, oral presentations, interviews, videos, visuals: slides, audio tapes, case studies, log books, projects, role plays, group projects, group discussions and examinations.

The Process of Assessment

Conducting assessments against the ACCSTP competency standards and CATC qualifications involves collecting evidence through various assessment methods including observing work, interviewing, conducting oral and written tests and practical testing, and making a judgment that the person can perform work in accordance with the competency standard.

Recognition of Current Competency

Recognition of Prior Learning is the process that gives current industry professionals who do not have a formal qualification, the opportunity to benchmark their extensive skills and experience against the standards set out in each unit of competency/subject.

Also known as a Skills Recognition Audit (SRA), this process is a learning and assessment pathway which encompasses: Recognition of Current Competencies (RCC) Skills auditing Gap analysis and training Credit transfer.

Recognition of Prior Learning (RPL) is a similar process to RCC that recognizes previous study or learning which can be mapped against competency standards.

Assessing Competence

As mentioned earlier, assessment is the process of identifying a participant's current knowledge, skills and attitudes against all elements of competency within a unit of competency. Traditionally in education, grades or marks were given to participants, dependent on how many questions the participant successfully answered in an assessment tool.

Competency based assessment does not award grades, but simply identifies if the participant has the knowledge, skills and attitudes to undertake the required task to the specified standard. Therefore, when assessing competency, an assessor has two possible results that can be awarded: Pass Competent (PC) or Not Yet Competent (NYC).

If the participant is able to successfully answer or demonstrate what is required, to the expected standards of the performance criteria, they will be deemed as 'Pass Competent' (PC). The assessor will award a 'Pass Competent' (PC) if they feel the participant has the necessary knowledge, skills and attitudes in all assessment tasks for a unit.

If the participant is unable to answer or demonstrate competency to the desired standard, they will be deemed to be 'Not Yet Competent' (NYC). This does not mean the participant will need to complete all the assessment tasks again. The focus will be on the specific assessment tasks that were not performed to the expected standards. The participant may be required to:

Undertake further training or instruction

Undertake the assessment task again until they are deemed to be 'Pass Competent

15. What is the ASEAN Tourism Qualifications Equivalency Matrix
 Conformity Assessment ?

According to the ASEAN Framework Agreement on Mutual Recognition Agreements: 'Conformity assessment means systematic examination to determine the extent to which a product, process or service fulfill specified requirements'. For international arrangements, cross-border conformance can occur in two ways:

Countries can accept the results of other country's conformance assessment as the basis for their own conformity assessment decisions. This is useful as it does not need extensive promotional campaigns, but it does less to reduce redundancy in assessment; or,

They can promote the direct acceptance of the conformance assessment results of the other countries by customers in their own country. This needs considerable promotional activity, but eliminates most of the redundancy in the system. This is the most common arrangement and the one recommended for the ASEAN MRA in tourism.

Countries therefore mutually accept each other's conformity assessment in terms of tourism qualifications. This acceptance relates to the process of conformity assessment.

It is important to note that this does not imply harmonization where the exporting country checks the regulations of the importing country before export.

The purpose of an ASEAN MRA – TP is therefore to ensure that all ten ASEAN countries accept the conformity assessment relating to tourism competency qualifications produced in any single ASEAN country.

Rationale for the Approach
In order to achieve conformity, each of the ten ASEAN countries will need to have their tourism qualification system evaluated against the requirements established under the MRA – TP to demonstrate their competence to be part of the MRA. This arrangement will involve the comparison of tourism qualifications across the ten ASEAN countries.

Equivalence Assessment
Here, the key process is equivalence assessment – the process of judging the conformity assessment procedures and/or rules of another country to be equivalent to national conformity assessment procedures and/or rules. If the MRA – TP is to be a robust arrangement then this equivalence assessment needs to take place.

The reason that the equivalence assessment process is so pivotal to this MRA relates to the fact that tourism is comprised of non-regulated occupations.

16. What is the role of the Tourism Professional Certification Board (TPCB) ? Tourism Professional Certification Boards (TPCB)
Each Member State will establish a Tourism Professional Certification Board (TPCB). Most will already have an established national qualifications accreditation agency that would take on the role as TPCB. The TPCB would function in support of the ATPRS by providing in-country qualification endorsements on existing professional qualifications by applying the template established by the CATC Regional Qualifications Framework.

In some countries, a TPCB or equivalent already exists and this development presents a further indicator of the country's readiness to proceed. For example, the Government of Viet Nam with assistance from the EU established a working TPCB named the Vietnam Tourism

Certification Board which functions in support of the Viet Nam National Authority on Tourism.

Composition of TPCB
The composition of each TPCB will vary by Member Country, as it will be dependent upon existing government structures and private sector involvement. It may also be the case that the NTPB and the TPCB can be separate arms of the same agency.

Responsibilities of the TPCB
Each Member Country will require the services of a Tourism Professionals Certification Board. The TPCB will apply national competency standards and assess and certify tourism professionals with an accredited qualification in order that they can be registered on the ATPRS. One of the primary functions of the TPCB is to manage the day-to-day operation of the ATPRS. The TPCB is rooted firmly at the Member County level.

Terms of Reference of TPCBs
☐ Assess qualifications and/or competencies of tourism professionals as specified in the ACCSTP;
☐ Issue certificates to tourism professionals whose qualifications and/or competencies
☐ have met the standards specified in the ACCSTP;
☐ Develop, process and maintain a register of certified tourism professionals and job opportunities onto the ATPRS; and
☐ Notify the NTPB promptly in case foreign tourism professionals are no longer qualified to provide a particular service or have violated technical, professional or ethical standards.
☐ Providing information to other Member Countries TPCBs.

17. The National Tourism Professional Board (NTPB)
National Tourism Professional Board
The National Tourism Professional Board (NTPB) refers to the Board for Tourism Professionals composed of representatives from the public and private sectors (including academia and other relevant tourism stakeholders) to be determined by the respective ASEAN NTOs.

Responsibilities of the NTPB

According to the ASEAN Framework Agreement on Mutual Recognition Agreements the member states need to designate a body to be responsible for monitoring the assessment standards:

'A designating body means a body appointed by a member state to a sectoral MRA, with the responsibility to identify and monitor conformity assessment bodies. A conformity assessment body means a body whose activities and expertise include performance of all, or any stage of the conformity assessment process, except for accreditation'.

Terms of Reference of NTPBs

The NTPB of each ASEAN Member State shall have the following responsibilities:

☐ Create awareness and disseminate information about this Arrangement;

☐ Promote, update, maintain, and monitor the ACCSTP and the CATC;

☐ Facilitate the exchange of information concerning assessment procedures, criteria, systems, manuals and publications relating to this Arrangement;

☐ Report its work progress to the ASEAN NTOs, including actions taken on cases referred to it by the TPCB and/or ATPMC;

☐ Formulate and update necessary mechanisms to enable implementation of this Arrangement;

☐ Facilitate the exchange of best practices and prevailing developments in tourism sector with the view to harmonizing and updating regional and/or international tourism competencies and curricula; and

☐ Such other functions and responsibilities that may be assigned to it by the ASEAN NTOs in the future.

18. Local Contextualization of new ASEAN Qualifications

It is recommended that each Member State adopts and agrees on a common, regional framework both in curriculum and qualifications as the first step before considering how to integrate CATC with its existing vocational tourism training arrangements.

Customized by Member States

CATC can be tailored to suit the individual needs of different Member States through the way the curriculum is written and interpreted by those who use it. In practice, each country can use their own regulations, legislation, codes of practice, rules, etc., because of the way the curriculum is written. They can also make reference to their own authorities, bodies, agencies and organizations.

Providers within each Member State can also tailor units of competency to suit their specific industry, country or other needs and are free to add their own 'extra content' within any unit they deliver as well as to add extra non-accredited units they deem appropriate or necessary.

Local Additions and Amendments
Contextualization could involve additions or amendments to the unit of competency to suit particular delivery methods, learner profiles, specific enterprise equipment requirements, or to otherwise meet local needs. However, the integrity of the overall intended outcome of the unit of competency must be maintained.

Boundaries of Contextualization
Any contextualization of units of competency can be done but within the following boundaries. Providers may:
- Add specific industry terminology to performance criteria where this does not distort or narrow the competency outcomes
- Make amendments and additions to the range statement as long as such changes do not diminish the breadth of application of the competency and reduce its portability
- Add detail to the evidence guide in areas such as the critical aspects of evidence or resources and infrastructure required where these expand the breadth of the competency but do not limit its use.
- Not remove or add to the number and content of elements and performance criteria.

Important **Note**
The key to contextualization is that the rigor and structure of each unit remain, but that the content can be varied to suit the needs of the user, provided the four 'rules' (see above) are complied with.

Localized Units of Competence
ASEAN NTOs identified the need to include the two additional units of competence from the Child Wise Tourism Program (http://www.childwise.net) into the curriculum and qualifications

framework. Two units of competence have been added to CATC – one unit at the Certificate entry level, "Perform Child Protection Duties relevant to the Tourism Industry" and the other unit at the Diploma level, "Develop Protective Environments for Children in Tourism Destinations."

19. Challenges in Implementing the Common ASEAN Tourism Curriculum

Orientation and Training

There will be a need for orientation and training to fully understand how the qualifications are structured and implemented, especially for users unfamiliar with Competence-based Training, ACCSTP and the qualifications under CATC. NTOs should consider how to promote, inform, and provide training and orientation on country-by-country basis but perhaps with common, shared resources.

Bridging Programs

Consideration of the development of 'Bridging programs' to facilitate movement of students currently studying, or having recently completed, existing qualifications into the revised framework

Recognition of Prior Learning

Systems should be developed for Recognition of Prior Learning (RPL) process to assist those with experience but no formal qualifications to have this experienced formally recognized and facilitate their movement into the formal vocational training system.

Credit Transfer Process

NTOs should consider the development of a formal Credit Transfer process to enable those with existing qualifications to have these recognized for the purposes of gaining standing within the new system.

Articulation Agreements

Development of appropriate articulation pathways that students can take to move from Advanced Diploma into tertiary study and qualifications, along with agreements with providers of higher education.

Quality Assurance

An independent third party auditing process should be developed for providers to ensure minimum standards in relation to trainers, resources, training facilities, training, assessment, general levels of professionalism etc and other compliance requirements are being met.

20. The Assessment Process

The following process may be used in conducting competency based assessments.

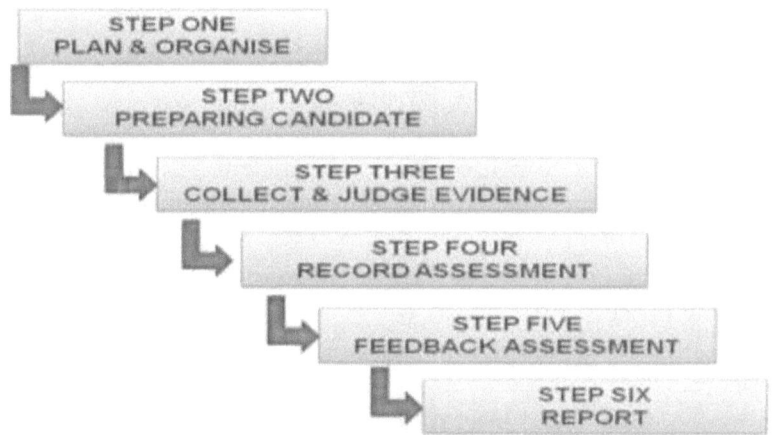

Figure: The Assessment Process

Step 1 – Plan and Organize
The assessor:
- establishes the context and purpose of the assessment
- identifies the competency standards, assessment guidelines and qualifications
- identifies the Toolkit that has been developed to facilitate the assessment process (if available)
- interprets the competency standards and identifies the evidence requirements

Step 2 - Prepare the candidate
The assessor meets with the candidate to:
- explain the context and purpose of the assessment and the assessment process
- explain the competency standards to be assessed and the evidence to be collected

- outline the assessment procedure, the preparation which the candidate should undertake and answer any questions
- assess the needs of the candidate and establish any allowable adjustments in the assessment procedure
- seek feedback regarding the candidate's understanding of the competency standards, evidence requirements and assessment process
- determine if the candidate is ready for assessment and decide on the time and place of the assessment
- develop an assessment plan.

Step 3 – Collect and Judge Evidence
The assessor must:
- establish a plan for gathering sufficient and quality evidence about the candidate's performance in order to make the assessment decision
- source or develop assessment materials to assist the evidence gathering process
- organic equipment or resources required to support the evidence gathering process
- coordinate and brief other personnel involved in the evidence gathering process.
- establish and oversee the evidence gathering process to ensure its validity, reliability, fairness and flexibility

- collect appropriate evidence and match compatibility to the elements, performance criteria, range of variables and Evidence Guide in the relevant units of competency
- incorporate specified allowable adjustments to the assessment procedure, where appropriate

Step 4 – Record Assessment
The assessor will:
- evaluate the evidence in terms of validity, consistency, currency, equity, authenticity and sufficiency
- consult and work with other staff, assessment panel members or technical experts involved in the assessment process
- record details of evidence collected

☐ make a judgment about the candidate's competence based on the evidence and the relevant unit(s) of competency.

Step 5 - Provide Feedback on the Assessment
The assessor must provide advice to the candidate about the outcomes of the assessment process. This includes providing the candidate with:
☐ clear and constructive feedback on the assessment decision
☐ information on ways of overcoming any identified gaps in competency revealed by the assessment
☐ the opportunity to discuss the assessment process and outcome
☐ information on reassessment and appeals processes.

Step 6 - Record and Report the Result The assessor must:
☐ record the assessment outcome according to the approved policies and procedures
☐ maintain records of the assessment procedure, evidence collected and the outcome according to the approved policies and procedures
☐ maintain the confidentiality of the assessment outcome
☐ organize the issuance of qualifications and/or Statements of Attainment according to the approved policies and procedures

Review the Assessment Process
Feedback on the assessment process will be helpful to the assessment center, so a review the assessment process by the assessor is valuable. The assessor should be encouraged to report on the positive and negative features of the assessment to those responsible for the assessment procedures and make suggestions on improving the assessment procedures to appropriate personnel in the TCPB.
In addition, the assessor may be involved in providing feedback and counseling to the candidate, if required, regarding the assessment outcome or process and to provide the candidate with information on the reassessment and appeals process. The assessor should report any assessment decision that is disputed by the candidate to the appropriate personnel in the TCPB and participate in the reassessment or appeal according to the approved policies and procedures

21. Who do I contact if I have any questions?

Please contact your National Tourism Professional Board through your The ASEAN Tourism Qualification Equivalence Matrix

The tables in the next pages show the Qualification Level of Competencies with the corresponding Focus of Qualifications and Job Titles.

Qualification & Level	Focus of Qualification	Job titles at this level may include but are not restricted to:
FUNCTIONAL COMPETENCIES – FOOD & BEVERAGE SERVICE QUALIFICATIONS		
Certificate II in Food and Beverage Services (Waiting) - incorporating Certificate I	Designed to reflect the role of individuals who perform mainly routine guest service tasks in the Secondary Labor Division of Food and Beverage Service and work under direct supervision.	Busboy; Trainee Waiter; Trainee Server; Restaurant and Bar Service Agent.
Certificate II in Food and Beverage Service (Beverages) - incorporating Certificate I	Designed to reflect the role of individuals who perform mainly routine guest service tasks in the Secondary Labor Division of Food and Beverage Service and work under direct supervision.	Busboy; Trainee Waiter; Trainee Server; Restaurant and Bar Service Agent
Certificate III in Food and Beverage Service (Waiting)	Designed to reflect the role of individuals who perform a range of skilled guest service tasks in the Secondary Labor Division of Food and Beverage Service using discretion and judgment and having the ability to select, adapt and transfer skills to different situations.	Waiter; Server; Restaurant Steward; Wait Person; Restaurant and Bar Service Agent.

Certificate III in Food and Beverage Service (Beverages)	Designed to reflect the role of individuals who perform a range of skilled guest service tasks in the Secondary Labor Division of Food and Beverage Service using discretion and judgment and having the ability to select, adapt and transfer skills to different situations.	Bar Tender; Bar Attendant; Bar Person; Restaurant and Bar Service Agent
Certificate IV in Food and Beverage Service (Waiting)	Designed to reflect the role of individuals who perform a broad range of guest service tasks in the Secondary Labor Division of Food and Beverage Service including evaluation and planning, and providing leadership and guidance to others with some responsibility for group outcomes.	Head Food Waiter; Assistant Restaurant Manager; Shift Leader; Team Leader; Restaurant and Bar Service Supervisor
Certificate IV in Food and Beverage Service (Beverages)	Designed to reflect the role of individuals who perform a broad range of guest service tasks in the Secondary Labor Division of Food and Beverage Service including evaluation and planning, and providing leadership and guidance to others with some responsibility for group outcomes.	Head Bar Attendant; Cellar Person; Cocktail Bar Attendant; Beverage Manager; Head Waiter; Assistant Restaurant Manager; Shift Leader; Team Leader; Restaurant and Bar Service Supervisor

Certificate IV in Food and Beverage Service (Supervision)	Designed to reflect the role of individuals who perform a broad range of guest service tasks in the Secondary Labor Division of Food and Beverage Service including evaluation and planning, and providing leadership and guidance to others with some responsibility for group outcomes.	Restaurant\ Supervisor; Food and Beverage Outlet Manager; Restaurant Manager; Outlet Manager; Assistant Manager; Restaurant and Bar Service Supervisor
Diploma of Food And Beverage Service (Supervision and Administration)	Designed to reflect the role of a supervisor or assistant manager in the Secondary Labor Division of Food and Beverage Service.	Food and Beverage Manager; Assistant Food and Beverage Director; Assistant Outlet Manager
Advanced Diploma of Food and Beverage Service (Management)	Designed to reflect the role of an owner-operator or manager in the Secondary Labor Division of Food and Beverage Service,	General Manager; Food and Beverage Director; Outlet Manager
Incorporating Certificate I	Food Production and work under direct supervision.	
The Certificate II in Food Production (Patisserie) - Incorporating Certificate I	Designed to reflect the role of individuals who perform mainly routine guest service tasks in the Secondary Labor Division of Food Production and work under direct supervision.	Kitchen Hand; Commis Pastry
The Certificate III in Food Production (Cookery)	Designed to reflect the role of individuals who perform a range of skilled guest service tasks in the Secondary Labor Division of Food	Commis Chef

	Production using discretion and judgment and having the ability to select, adapt and transfer skills to different situations.	
The Certificate III in Food Production (Operations)	Designed to reflect the role of individuals who perform a range of skilled guest service tasks in the Secondary Labor Division of Food Production using discretion and judgment and having the ability to select, adapt and transfer skills to different situations.	Assistant Catering Manager
The Certificate III in Food Production (Patisserie)	Designed to reflect the role of individuals who perform a range of skilled guest service tasks in the Secondary Labor Division of Food Production using discretion and judgment and having the ability to select, adapt and transfer skills to different situations.	Assistant Pastry Chef
The Certificate IV in Food Production (Cookery)	Designed to reflect the role of individuals who perform a broad range of guest service tasks in the Secondary Labor Division of Food Production including evaluation and planning, and providing leadership and guidance to others with some responsibility for group outcomes.	Second Chef; Demi Chef; Assistant Head Chef
The Certificate IV in Food Production (Operations)	Designed to reflect the role of individuals who perform a broad range of guest service tasks in the Secondary Labor Division of Food Production including evaluation	Catering Manager

	and planning, and providing leadership and guidance to others with some responsibility for group outcomes.	
The Certificate IV in Food Production (Patisserie)	Designed to reflect the role of individuals who perform a broad range of guest service tasks in the Secondary Labor Division of Food Production including evaluation and planning, and providing leadership and guidance to others with some responsibility for group outcomes	Chef de Partie; Pastry Chef
The Diploma of Food Production (Supervision and Administration)	Designed to reflect the role of a supervisor or assistant manager in the Secondary Labor Division of Food Production.	Head Chef; Assistant to the Executive Chef
The Advanced Diploma of Food Production (Management)	Designed to reflect the role of an owner-operator or manager in the Secondary Labor Division of Food Production.	Executive Chef

FUNCTIONAL COMPETENCIES – FOOD QUALIFICATIONS PRODUCTION		
Qualification & Level	Focus of Qualification	Job titles at this level may include but are not restricted to:
The Certificate IIin Food Production (Cookery) -	Designed to reflect the role of individuals who perform mainly routine guest service tasks in the Secondary Labor Division of	Kitchen Hand; Butcher; Baker

The Certificate IV in Food Production (Operations)	Designed to reflect the role of individuals who perform a broad range of guest service tasks in the Secondary Labor Division of Food Production including evaluation and planning, and providing leadership and guidance to others with some responsibility for group outcomes.	Catering Manager
The Certificate IV in Food Production (Patisserie)	Designed to reflect the role of individuals who perform a broad range of guest service tasks in the Secondary Labor Division of Food Production including evaluation and planning, and providing leadership and guidance to others with some responsibility for group outcomes.	Chef de Partie; Pastry Chef
The Diploma of Food Production (Supervision and Administration)	Designed to reflect the role of a supervisor or assistant manager in the Secondary Labor Division of Food Production.	Head Chef; Assistant to the Executive Chef
The Advanced Diploma of Food Production (Management)	Designed to reflect the role of an owner-operator or manager in the Secondary Labor Division of Food Production.	Executive Chef

FUNCTIONAL COMPETENCIES–FRONT OFFICE		
Qualification & Level	Focus of Qualification	Job titles at this level may include but are not restricted to:

The Certificate II in Front Office – Incorporating Certificate I	Designed to reflect the role of individuals who perform mainly routine guest service tasks in the Secondary Labor Division of Front Office and work under direct supervision.	Junior Bell Boy; Assistant Porter; Bell Boy; Porter; Bellhop
The Certificate III in Front Office	Designed to reflect the role of individuals who perform a range of skilled guest service tasks in the Secondary Labor Division of Front Office using discretion and judgment and having the ability to select, adapt and transfer skills to different situations.	Front Office Attendant; Assistant Receptionist; Relief Receptionist; Telephone Operator; Telephonist; Switchboard Operator
The Certificate IV in Front Office (Guest Services Supervision)	Designed to reflect the role of individuals who perform a broad range of guest service tasks in the Secondary Labor Division of Front Office including evaluation and planning, and providing leadership and guidance to others with some responsibility for group outcomes.	Front Office Receptionist; Manager – Guest Relations; Concierge; Front Office Team leader; Night Auditor; Front Office Shift Captain.
The Diploma of Front Office (Supervision and Administration)	Designed to reflect the role of a supervisor or assistant manager in the Secondary Labor Division of Front Office.	Front Office Supervisor
The Advanced Diploma of Front Office (Management)	owner-operator or manager in the Secondary Labour Division of Front Office.	Front Office Manager

FUNCTIONAL COMPETENCIES FOR HOUSEKEEPING QUALIFICATIONS		
Qualification & Level	Focus of Qualification	Job titles at this level may include but are not restricted to:
The Certificate II in Housekeeping - Incorporating Certificate I	Designed to reflect the role of individuals who perform mainly routine guest service tasks in the Secondary Labor Division of Housekeeping and work under direct supervision.	Junior Cleaner; Assistant Cleaner; Assistant Public Area Cleaner; Cleaner; Public Area Cleaner; Attendant; Room Maid; PA Attendant
The Certificate III in Housekeeping	Designed to reflect the role of individuals who perform arange of skilled guest service tasks in the Secondary Labor Division of Housekeeping using discretion and judgment and having the ability to select, adapt and transfer skills to different situations.	Room Attendant; Housekeeping Attendant; Room Assistant; Laundry Attendant; Room Maid; Public Area Attendant; Linen Attendant; Florist Attendant; Gardener Attendant
The Certificate IV in Housekeeping (Guest Services Supervision)	Designed to reflect the role of individuals who perform abroad range of guest servicetasks in the Secondary Labor Division of Housekeeping including evaluation and planning, and providingleadership and guidance to others with some responsibility for group outcomes	Room Inspector; Shift Leader: Floor Supervisor; Housekeeping Supervisor; Senior staff; Florist Supervisor;Linen Supervisor; Public Area Supervisor; Floor Butler; Housekeeping Coordinator
The Diploma of Housekeeping (Supervision and Administration)	Designed to reflect the role of a supervisor or assistant manager in the Secondary Labor Division ofHousekeeping	Laundry Manager; Head Housekeeper; Assistant ExecutiveHousekeeper; Assistant; Assistant Housekeeper Administrator

The Advanced Diploma of Housekeeping (Management)	Designed to reflect the role of an owner-operator or manager in the Secondary Labor Division of Housekeeping.	Executive Housekeeper; Housekeeping Manager; Manager – Rooms Division; Manager

FUNCTIONAL COMPETENCIES FOR TOUR OPERATIONS QUALIFICATIONS		
Qualification & Level	Focus of Qualification	Job titles at this level may include but are not restricted to:
The Certificate II in Tour Operation (Reservations and Ticketing) -Incorporating Certificate I	Designed to reflect the role of individuals who perform mainly routine reservations and ticketing tasks in the Secondary Labor Division of Tour Operation and work under direct supervision.	Trainee Ticketing Officer; Trainee Reservations Clerk; Trainee Ticketing Clerk; Clerk
The Certificate II in Tour Operation (Guiding) - Incorporating Certificate I	Designed to reflect the role of individuals who perform mainly routine guiding tasks in the Secondary Labor Division of Tour Operation and work under direct supervision.	Camp Assistant; Assistant Camp Cook; Assistant Guide; Porter; Trainee Tour Guide; Trainee Tour Leader; Trainee Local Guide; Trainee Eco-Tour Guide; Trainee Driver Guide

The Certificate III in Tour Operation (Reservations and Ticketing)	Designed to reflect the role of individuals who perform a range of skilled reservations and ticketing tasks in the Secondary Labor Division of Tour Operation using discretion and judgment and having the ability to select, adapt and transfer skills to different situations.	Trainee Ticketing Officer; Trainee Reservations Clerk; Trainee Clerk; Ticketing Ticketing Officer; Reservations Clerk; Ticketing Clerk; Clerk.
The Certificate III in Tour Operation (Guiding)	Designed to reflect the role of individuals who perform a range of skilled guiding tasks in the Secondary Labor Division of Tour Operation using discretion and judgment and having the ability to select, adapt and transfer skills to different situations	Tour Guide; Tour Leader; Local Guide; Eco-Tour Guide; DriverGuide; Supervisor
The Certificate III in Tour Operation (Sales and Finance)	individuals who perform a range of skilled sales and finance tasks in the Secondary Labor Division of Tour Operation using discretion and judgment and having the ability to select, adapt and transfer skills to different situations	Assistant Reservations Manager; Assistants Sales Manager; Assistant Contracts Manager; Asssistant Promotions Manager; Supervisor
The Certificate IV in Tour Operation (Reservations	Designed to reflect the role of individuals who perform a broad range of reservations and ticketing tasks in the Secondary Labor Division of Tour	Ticketing Supervisor; Reservations Manager; Manager

and Ticketing)	Operation including evaluation and planning, and providing leadership and guidance to others with some responsibility for group outcomes.	
The Certificate IV in Tour Operation (Guiding)	Designed to reflect the role of individuals who perform a broad range of guiding tasks in the Secondary Labor Division of Tour Operation including evaluation and planning, and providing leadership and guidance to others with some responsibility for roup outcomes.	Senior Tour Guide; Tour Leader; Resort Representatives; Guide Captain; Tour Manager; Manager.
The Certificate IV in Tour Operation (Sales and Finance)	Designed to reflect the role of individuals who perform a broad range of sales and finance tasks in the Secondary Labor Division of Tour Operation including evaluation and planning, and providing leadership and guidance to others with some responsibility for group outcomes.	Sales Manager; Credit Controller; Marketing Manager; Sales Manager; Promotions Manager; Manager.
The Certificate IV in Tour Operation (Eco Tours)	Designed to reflect the role of individuals who perform a broad range of eco tour tasks in the Secondary Labor Division of Tour Operation including evaluation and planning, and providing leadership and guidance to others with some responsibility for group outcomes.	Eco-Tour Senior Guide. Driver; Eco-Tour

FUNCTIONAL COMPETENCIES FOR TRAVEL AGENCIES QUALIFICATIONS		
Qualificatio & Level	Focus of Qualification	Job titles at this level may include but are not restricted to:

The Certificate II in Travel Agencies (Reservations and Ticketing) Incorporating -Certificate I	Designed to reflect the role of individuals who perform mainly routine reservations and ticketing tasks in the Secondary Labor Division of Travel Agencies and work under direct supervision.	Junior Office Assistant; Trainee Ticketing Officer; Trainee Reservations Clerk; Trainee Ticketing Clerk.
The Certificate II in Travel Agencies (Sales and Service) Incorporating Certificate I	Designed to reflect the role of individuals who perform mainly routine sales and customer service tasks in the Secondary Labor Division of Travel Agencies and work Under direct supervision.	Trainee Travel Advisor; Trainee Domestic Travel Consultant; Trainee Domestic International Consultant; Trainee Corporate Travel Consultant.
The Certificate II in Travel Agencies (Operations) - Incorporating Certificate I	Designed to reflect the role of individuals who perform mainly routine operational tasks in the Secondary Labor Division of Travel Agencies and work under direct supervision.	Trainee Travel Advisor; Trainee Domestic Travel Consultant; Trainee Domestic International Consultant; Trainee Corporate Travel Consultant; Trainee Ticketing Officer; Trainee Reservations Clerk; Trainee Ticketing Clerk.
The Certificate III in Travel Agencies (Reservations and Ticketing	Designed to reflect the role of individuals who perform a range of skilled reservations and ticketing tasks in the Secondary Labour	Ticketing Officer; Reservations Clerk; Ticketing Clerk; Inbound Tour

Book 10 - ASEAN Mutual Recognition Agreement For Tourism Professionals (MRA-TP)

Guide Book for Assessors

Competency Based Assessment (CBA) – An introduction for assessors
Assessment is the process of identifying a participants current knowledge, skills and attitudes sets against all elements of competency within a unit of competency.

Suggested Assessment Methods
For each unit of competency a number of assessment tools have been identified including:
- Work Projects
- Oral Questions
- Written Questions
- Third Party statements
- Observation Checklists.
- Instructions and Evidence Recording Sheets have been identified in this Assessment Manual for use by Assessors.

Alternative Assessment Methods
While the above mentioned assessment methods are suggested assessment methods, the assessor may use an alternate method of assessment taking into account:

- The nature of the unit
- The strengths of participants
- The number of participants in the class
- Time required to complete assessments
- Time dedicated to assessment
- Equipment and resources required.
- Alternate assessment methods include:
- Practical demonstrations
- Practical demonstrations in simulated work conditions
- Problem solving
- Portfolios of evidence
- Critical incident reports
- Journals

- Oral presentations
- Interviews
- Videos
- Visuals/slides/audio tapes
- Case studies
- Log books
- Projects and Role plays
- Group projects
- Recognition of Prior Learning.

While there is no specific instruction or evidence collection documents for all the alternative assessment methods, assessors can record competency in the "Other" section within the „Competency Recording Sheet".

Selection of Assessment Methods
Each assessor will determine the combination of Assessment Methods to be used to determine Competency for each Competency Unit on a student by student basis. "Sufficient" evidence to support the "Competent"/"Not Yet Competent" decision must be captured.

In practice this means a minimum of two - three Assessment Methods for each candidate for each Competency Element is suggested.
At least one method should provide evidence of practical demonstration of competence.

The following assessment methods deemed to provide evidence of practical demonstration of competence include:

- Practical Work Projects

- Third Party Statement
- Observation Checklist.

Assessing Competency

Competency based assessment does not award grades, but simply identifies if the participant has the knowledge, skills and attitudes to undertake the required task to the specified standard.
Therefore, when assessing competency, an assessor has two possible results that can be awarded:

"Pass Competent" (PC)
"Not Yet Competent" (NYC).
Pass Competent (PC)

If the participant is able to successfully answer or demonstrate what is required, to the expected standards of the performance criteria, they will be deemed as „Pass Competent" (PC).
The assessor will award a "Pass Competent" (PC) if they feel the participant has the necessary knowledge, skills and attitudes in all assessment tasks for a unit.
Not Yet Competent' (NYC)
If the participant is unable to answer or demonstrate competency to the desired standard, they will be deemed to be "Not Yet Competent" (NYC).
This does not mean the participant will need to complete all the assessment tasks again. The focus will be on the specific assessment tasks that were not performed to the expected standards.

The participant may be required to:
- Undertake further training or instruction
- Undertake the assessment task again until they are deemed to be „Pass Competent".

Regional Qualifications Framework and Skills Recognition System

The "Regional Qualifications Framework and Skills Recognition System", also known as the "RQFSRS" is the overriding educational framework for the ASEAN region. The purpose of this framework is to provide:

- A standardized teaching and assessment framework
- Mutual recognition of participant achievement across the ASEAN region. This includes achievement in individual Units of Competency or qualifications as a whole.

The role of the "RQFSRS" is to provide, ensure and maintain „quality assurance" across all countries and educational providers across the ASEAN region.

Recognition of Prior Learning

Recognition of Prior Learning is the process that gives current industry professionals who do not have a formal qualification, the opportunity to benchmark their extensive skills and experience against the standards set out in each unit of competency/subject.

- This process is a learning and assessment pathway which encompasses:
- Recognition of Current Competencies (RCC)
- Skills auditing
- Gap analysis and training
- Credit transfer.

Code of practice for assessors

This Code of Practice provides:

- Assessors with direction on the standard of practice expected of them
- Candidates with assurance of the standards of practice expected of assessors
- Employers with assurance of the standards maintained in the conduct of assessment.

The Code detailed below is based on the International Code of Ethics and Practice (The National Council for Measurement in Education [NCME]).

- The differing needs and requirements of the person being assessed, the local enterprise and/or industry are identified and handled with sensitivity
- Potential forms of conflict of interest in the assessment process and/or outcomes are identified and appropriate referrals are made, if necessary

☐ All forms of harassment are avoided throughout the planning, conducting, reviewing and reporting of the assessment outcomes
☐ The rights of the candidate are protected during and after the assessment
☐ Personal and interpersonal factors that are not relevant to the assessment of competency must not influence the assessment outcomes
☐ The candidate is made aware of rights and process of appeal
☐ Evidence that is gathered during the assessment is verified for validity, reliability, authenticity, sufficiency and currency
☐ Assessment decisions are based on available evidence that can be produced and verified by another assessor
☐ Assessments are conducted within the boundaries of the assessment system policies and procedures
☐ Formal agreement is obtained from both the candidate and the assessor that the assessment was carried out in accordance with agreed procedures
☐ The candidate is informed of all assessment reporting processes prior to the assessment
☐ The candidate is informed of all known potential consequences of decisions arising from an assessment, prior to the assessment
☐ Confidentiality is maintained regarding assessment results
☐ The assessment results are used consistently with the purposes explained to the candidate
☐ Opportunities are created for technical assistance in planning, conducting and reviewing assessment procedures and outcomes.

Instructions and checklist for assessors
Instructions
General instructions for the assessment
☐ Assessment should be conducted at a scheduled time that has been notified to the candidate
☐ Facilitators must ensure participants are made aware of the need to complete assessments and attend assessment sessions
☐ If a participant is unable to attend a scheduled session, they must make arrangements with the Assessor to undertake the assessment at an alternative time

☐ At the end of the assessment the Assessor must give feedback and advise the participant on their C/NYC status
☐ Complete the relevant documentation and submit to the appropriate department.

Preparation
☐ Gain familiarity with the Unit of Competency, Elements of Competency and the Performance Criteria expected
☐ Study details assessment documentation and requirements
☐ Brief candidate regarding all assessment criteria and requirements.

Briefing Checklist
Begin the assessment by implementing the following checklist and then invite the candidate to proceed with assessment.

Competency Based Assessment (CBA) An introduction for assessors
Assessment is the process of identifying a participant's current knowledge, skills and attitudes sets against all elements of competency within a unit of competency.

Suggested Assessment Methods
For each unit of competency a number of assessment tools have been identified including:
☐ Work Projects
☐ Oral Questions
☐ Written Questions
☐ Third Party statements
☐ Observation Checklists.
☐ Instructions and Evidence Recording Sheets have been identified in this Assessment Manual for use by Assessors.

Alternative Assessment Methods
While the above mentioned assessment methods are suggested assessment methods, the assessor may use an alternate method of assessment taking into account:
☐ The nature of the unit

- The strengths of participants
- The number of participants in the class
- Time required to complete assessments
- Time dedicated to assessment
- Equipment and resources required.
- Alternate assessment methods include:
- Practical demonstrations
- Practical demonstrations in simulated work conditions
- Problem solving
- Portfolios of evidence
- Critical incident reports
- Journals
- Oral presentations
- Interviews
- Videos
- Visuals/slides/audio tapes
- Case studies
- Log books
- Projects and Role plays
- Group projects
- Recognition of Prior Learning.

While there is no specific instruction or evidence collection documents for all the alternative assessment methods, assessors can record competency in the
„Other" section within the „Competency Recording Sheet".

Selection of Assessment Methods

Each assessor will determine the combination of Assessment Methods to be used to determine Competency for each Competency Unit on a student by student basis. "Sufficient" evidence to support the "Competent"/"Not Yet Competent" decision must be captured.

In practice this means a minimum of two - three Assessment Methods for each candidate for each Competency Element is suggested.

At least one method should provide evidence of practical demonstration of competence.

The following assessment methods deemed to provide evidence of practical demonstration of competence include:

- Practical Work Projects
- Third Party Statement
- Observation Checklist.

Assessing Competency

Competency based assessment does not award grades, but simply identifies if the participant has the knowledge, skills and attitudes to undertake the required task to the specified standard.

Therefore, when assessing competency, an assessor has two possible results that can be awarded:

- "'Pass Competent" (PC)
- "Not Yet Competent" (NYC).

Pass Competent (PC)

If the participant is able to successfully answer or demonstrate what is required, to the expected standards of the performance criteria, they will be deemed as "Pass Competent" (PC).

The assessor will award a „Pass Competent" (PC) if they feel the participant has the necessary knowledge, skills and attitudes in all assessment tasks for a unit.

"Not Yet Competent" (NYC)

If the participant is unable to answer or demonstrate competency to the desired standard, they will be deemed to be "Not Yet Competent" (NYC).

This does not mean the participant will need to complete all the assessment tasks again. The focus will be on the specific assessment tasks that were not performed to the expected standards.

The participant may be required to:

- Undertake further training or instruction
- Undertake the assessment task again until they are deemed to be "Pass Competent".

Regional Qualifications Framework and Skills Recognition System

The "Regional Qualifications Framework and Skills Recognition System", also known as „RQFSRS" is the overriding educational framework for the ASEAN region. The purpose of this framework is to provide:

- A standardized teaching and assessment framework
- Mutual recognition of participant achievement across the ASEAN region. This includes achievement in individual Units of Competency or qualifications as a whole.
- The role of the "RQFSRS" is to provide, ensure and maintain „quality assurance" across all countries and educational providers across the ASEAN region.

Recognition of Prior Learning

Recognition of Prior Learning is the process that gives current industry professionals who do not have a formal qualification, the opportunity to benchmark their extensive skills and experience against the standards set out in each unit of competency/subject.

This process is a learning and assessment pathway which encompasses:

- Recognition of Current Competencies (RCC)
- Skills auditing
- Gap analysis and training
- Credit transfer.

Code of practice for assessors
This Code of Practice provides:

- Assessors with direction on the standard of practice expected of them
- Candidates with assurance of the standards of practice expected of assessors
- Employers with assurance of the standards maintained in the conduct of assessment.

The Code detailed below is based on the International Code of Ethics and Practice (The National Council for Measurement in Education [NCME]).

- The differing needs and requirements of the person being assessed, the local enterprise and/or industry are identified and handled with sensitivity
- Potential forms of conflict of interest in the assessment process and/or outcomes are identified and appropriate referrals are made, if necessary
- All forms of harassment are avoided throughout the planning, conducting, reviewing and reporting of the assessment outcomes
- The rights of the candidate are protected during and after the assessment
- Personal and interpersonal factors that are not relevant to the assessment of competency must not influence the assessment outcomes
- The candidate is made aware of rights and process of appeal
- Evidence that is gathered during the assessment is verified for validity, reliability, authenticity, sufficiency and currency
- Assessment decisions are based on available evidence that can be produced and verified by another assessor
- Assessments are conducted within the boundaries of the assessment system policies and procedures
- Formal agreement is obtained from both the candidate and the assessor that the assessment was carried out in accordance with agreed procedures
- The candidate is informed of all assessment reporting processes prior to the assessment
- The candidate is informed of all known potential consequences of decisions arising from an assessment, prior to the assessment
- Confidentiality is maintained regarding assessment results
- The assessment results are used consistently with the purposes explained to the candidate
- Opportunities are created for technical assistance in planning, conducting and reviewing assessment procedures and outcomes.

Instructions and checklist for assessors
Instructions
General instructions for the assessment
- ☐ Assessment should be conducted at a scheduled time that has been notified to the candidate
- ☐ Facilitators must ensure participants are made aware of the need to complete assessments and attend assessment sessions
- ☐ If a participant is unable to attend a scheduled session, they must make arrangements with the Assessor to undertake the assessment at an alternative time
- ☐ At the end of the assessment the Assessor must give feedback and advise the participant on their C/NYC status
- ☐ Complete the relevant documentation and submit to the appropriate department.

Preparation
- ☐ Gain familiarity with the Unit of Competency, Elements of Competency and the Performance Criteria expected
- ☐ Study details assessment documentation and requirements
- ☐ Brief candidate regarding all assessment criteria and requirements.

Briefing Checklist
Begin the assessment by implementing the following checklist and then invite the candidate to proceed with assessment.

Checklist for Assessors

Prior to the assessment I have:	Tick (ü)	Remarks
Ensured the candidate is informed about the venue and schedule of assessment.		
Received current copies of the performance criteria to be assessed, assessment plan, evidence gathering plan, assessment checklist, appeal form and the company's standard operating procedures (SOP).		

Reviewed the performance criteria and evidence plan to ensure I clearly understood the instructions and the requirements of the assessment process.		
Identified and accommodated any special needs of the candidate.		
Checked the set-up and resources for the assessment.		

During the assessment I have:		
Introduced myself and confirmed identities of candidates.		
Put candidates at ease by being friendly and helpful.		
Explained to candidates the purpose, context and benefits of the assessment.		
Ensured candidates understood the assessment process and all attendant procedures.		
Provided candidates with an overview of performance criteria to be assessed.		
Explained the results reporting procedure.		
Encouraged candidates to seek clarifications if in doubt.		
Asked candidates for feedback on the assessment.		
Explained legal, safety and ethical issues, if applicable.		
After the assessment I have:		
Ensured candidate is given constructive feedback.		
Completed and signed the assessment record.		
Thanked candidate for participating in the assessment.		

Instructions for recording competency

Specifications for Recording Competency

The following specifications apply to the preparation of Evidence Gathering Plans:

- A Competency Recording Sheet must be prepared for each candidate to ensure and demonstrate all Performance Criteria and Competency Elements are appropriately assessed. This Sheet indicates how the Assessor will gather evidence during their assessment of each candidate
- This Competency Recording Sheet is located at the end of the Assessment Plan
- It is the overriding document to record competency
- Assessor may vary the Competency Recording Sheet to accommodate practical and individual candidate and/or workplace needs
- Assessor must place a tick (ü) in the „Assessment Method" columns to identify the methods of assessment to be used for each candidate
- Multiple Competency Elements/Performance Criteria may be assessed at the one time, where appropriate
- The assessor and participant should sign and date the Competency Recording Sheet, when all forms of evidence and assessment have been completed
- The assessor may provide and feedback or clarify questions which the participant may have in regards to the assessment grade or findings
- All documents used to capture evidence must be retained, and attached to the Competency Recording Sheet for each candidate for each Competency Unit.

Instructions for different assessment methods Specifications for Work Project Assessment

- These guidelines concern the use of work projects.
- The work projects identified in the Training Manuals involve a range of tasks, to be performed at the discretion of the Assessor.
- Work project tasks can be completed through any form of assessment as identified in the Trainer and Trainee Manuals and stated at the start of this section.
- Assessors should follow these guidelines:

- [ ] Review the Work Projects at the end of each „Element of Competency" in the Trainee Manual to ensure you understand the content and what is expected
- [ ] Prepare sufficient resources for the completion of work activities including:
- [ ] Time – whether in scheduled delivery hours or suggested time participants to spend outside of class hours
- [ ] Resources – this may involve technical equipment, computer, internet access, stationery and other supplementary materials and documents
- [ ] Prepare assessment location (if done in class) making it conducive to assessment
- [ ] Explain Work Projects assessment to candidate, at the start of each Element of Competency. This ensures that participants are aware of what is expected and can collate information as delivery takes place.
- [ ] Assessors can use the following phrase as a guide (where an "X" is identified, please input appropriate information):
- [ ] "At the end of each Element of Competency there are Work Projects which must be completed. These projects require different tasks that must be completed.
- [ ] These work projects are part of the formal assessment for the unit of competency titled X.
- [ ] You are required to complete these activities:
- [ ] Using the 'X' method of assessment.
- [ ] At 'X' location
- [ ] You will have 'X time period' for this assessment.
- [ ] You are required to compile information in a format that you feel is appropriate to the assessment.
- [ ] Do you have any questions about this assessment?"
- [ ] Commence Work Project assessment:
- [ ] The assessor may give time for participants to review the questions at this time to ensure they understand the nature of the questions. The assessor may need to clarify questions.
- [ ] Participants complete work projects in the most appropriate format
- [ ] Participants must submit Work Project evidence to the assessor before the scheduled due date

☐ Assessor must assess the participant's evidence against the competency standards specified in each Element of Competency and their own understanding. The assessor can determine if the participant has provided evidence to a „competent" standard.
☐ Transcribe results/details to Competency Recording Sheet
☐ Forward/file assessment record.

Specifications for Oral Question Assessment
These guidelines concern the use of oral questioning.
Assessors should follow these guidelines.

• Prepare Assessment Record for Oral Questioning. One record for each candidate:
☐ Enter Student name
☐ Enter Assessor name
☐ Enter Location
• Familiarize self with Questions to be asked
• Prepare assessment location (table and chairs) making it conducive to assessment
• Explain Oral Questioning assessment to candidate, using the following phrase as a guide (where a „X" is identified, please input appropriate information):

"These oral questions are part of the formal assessment for the unit of competency titled X.
There are X questions and you are required to answer all of them to the best of your ability and I will record whether or not you have answered correctly.

We have 60 minutes for this assessment.
☐ I will give you feedback at the end of the assessment.
☐ Do you have any questions about this assessment?"
• Commence Oral Questioning assessment:
• Complete Assessment Record for the Oral Questioning by:
☐ Ticking C or NYC, as appropriate
☐ Entering "Remarks" as required
☐ Completing Oral Questioning within 60 minutes
• Complete Oral Questioning and provide feedback to candidate

- Transcribe results/details to Competency Recording Sheet
- Forward/file assessment record.

Specifications for Written Question Assessment
These guidelines concern the use of written questioning.
Assessors should follow these guidelines.
- Familiarize self with Questions and Answers provided.
- Print and distribute copies of „Written Questions" for participants. Ideally this should take place with adequate time for participants to answer all questions before the expected due date.
- Explain Written Questioning assessment to candidate, using the following phrase as a guide (where a „X" is identified, please input appropriate information):
- "These written questions are part of the formal assessment for the unit of competency titled X.
- There are X questions and you are required to answer all of them to the best of your ability.
- You may refer to your subject materials, however where possible try to utilize your existing knowledge when answering questions.
- Where you are unsure of questions, please ask the Assessor for further instruction. This may be answering the question orally or asking the assessor to redefine the question.
- We have X time for this assessment.
- The due date for completion of this assessment is X
- On this date you must forward the completed questions to the assessor by X time on the date of X
- Do you have any questions about this assessment?"
- The assessor may give time for participants to review the questions at this time to ensure they understand the nature of the questions. The assessor may need to clarify questions.
- Participants may record written answers (where possible)
- Participants must submit the written answers to the assessor before the scheduled due date
- Assessor must assess the participant's written answers against the model answers provided as a guide, or their own

understanding. The assessor can determine if the participant has answered the questions to a "competent" standard.
- ☐ Transcribe results/details to Competency Recording Sheet
- ☐ Forward/file assessment record.

Specifications for Observation Checklist

These specifications apply to the use of the Observation Checklist in determining competency for candidates.

Only an approved assessor is authorized to complete the Observation Checklist.

The assessor is required to observe the participant, ideally in a simulated environment or their practical workplace setting and record their performance (or otherwise) of the competencies listed on the Observation Checklist for the Competency Unit.

To complete the Observation Checklist the Assessor must:
- ☐ Insert name of candidate
- ☐ Insert assessor name
- ☐ Insert identify of location where observations are being undertaken
- ☐ Insert date/s of observations – may be single date or multiple dates
- ☐ Place a tick in either the „Yes" or „No" box for each listed Performance Criteria to indicate the candidate has demonstrated/not demonstrated that skill
- ☐ Provide written (and verbal) feedback to candidate – as/if appropriate
- ☐ Sign and date the form
- ☐ Present form to candidate for them to sign and date
- ☐ Transcribe results/details to Competency Recording Sheet for candidate
- ☐ Forward/file Observation Checklist.
- ☐ This source of evidence combines with other forms of assessment to assist in determining the "Competent" or "Not Yet Competent" decision for the participant.

Specifications for Third Party Statement

These specifications relate to the use of a relevant workplace person to assist in determining competency for candidates.

The Third Party Statement is to be supplied by the assessor to a person in the workplace who supervises and/or works closely with the participant.

This may be their Supervisor, the venue manager, the Department Manager or similar.

The Third Party Statement asks the Supervisor to record what they believe to be the competencies of the participant based on their workplace experience of the participant. This experience may be gained through observation of their workplace performance, feedback from others, inspection of candidate's work etc.

A meeting must take place between the Assessor and the Third Party to explain and demonstrate the use of the Third Party Statement.

To complete the Third Party Verification Statement the Assessor must:
- ☐ Insert candidate name
- ☐ Insert name and contact details of the Third Party
- ☐ Tick the box to indicate the relationship of the Third Party to the candidate
- ☐ Present the partially completed form to the Third Party for them to finalize
- ☐ Collect the completed form from the Third Party
- ☐ Transcribe results/details to Competency Recording Sheet for candidate
- ☐ Forward/file Third Party Statement.

The Third Party must:

Record their belief regarding candidate ability/competency as either:
- Competent = Yes
- Not Yet Competent = No
- Unsure about whether candidate is competent or not = Not Sure
- Meet briefly with the assessor to discuss and/or clarify the form.

This source of evidence combines with other forms of assessment to assist in determining the "Competent" or "Not Yet Competent" decision for the candidate.

A separate Third Party Statement is required for each Competency Unit undertaken by the candidate.

Competency Standard

UNIT TITLE: ACCESS AND RETRIEVE COMPUTER-BASED DATA	NOMINAL HOURS: 25 hours
UNIT NUMBER: D1.HRS.CL1.01; D1.HOT.CL1.06; D2.TCC.CL1.10	
UNIT DESCRIPTOR: This unit deals with the skills and knowledge requiredto access and retrieve computer-based data in the hotel and travel industries workplace context.	
ELEMENTS AND PERFORMANCE CRITERIA	**UNIT VARIABLE AND ASSESSMENT GUIDE**
Element 1: Open file **1.1** Turn on/access computersystem correctly **1.2** Select or load appropriatesoftware **1.3** Identify and open correctfile **Element 2: Access computer-based data** **2.1** Use computer features toaccess a range of data or information **2.2** Retrieve data using prescribed systems, sequencesand appropriate keyboard techniques	**Unit Variables** The Unit Variables provide advice to interpret the scope and context of this unit of competence, allowing for differences between enterprises and workplaces. It relates to the unit as a whole and facilitates holistic assessment. This unit applies to accessing and retrieving computer-based data within the labor divisions of the hotel and travel industries andmay include: • Front Office • Housekeeping • Food and Beverage • Travel Agencies • Tour Operation *Computer system* will vary depending on the enterprise, and may include: • Windows

2.3 Access data stored on a variety of data storage mediums, private computer networks and the Internet **2.4** Use searches and queries to find desired Information	• Mac • Portable computers

Element 3: Retrieve computer-based data **3.1** Locate data to be retrieved **3.2** Check that data meets requirements **3.3** Print or transfer file to data storage medium as required.	• Stand-alone computers • Networked computers. *Data or information* may include: • Costs • Availability, e.g. room, tour, seats, etc • Product information • Industry information • Customer information • Time • Timetables • Reservation data. *Retrieve data* may relate to: • Finding document data • Saving changes made to the document • Finding document. *Data Storage mediums* include: Compact Disks – (CDR); Digital Video Disks (DVDR); Floppy disks; Flash Drives; Portable harddrives; External hard drives; Local hard drives;

	Network drives. *Locate data to be retrieved* may relate to data stored on: Compact Disks – (CD); Digital Video Disks (DVD); BluRay Disks; Floppy disks; Flash Drives; Portable hard drives; External hard drives; Local Drives; Network Drives **Assessment Guide** The following skills and knowledge must be assessed aspart of this unit:<ul><li>Knowledge of enterprise policies and proceduresin regard to using the computer system to</li><li>Access and retrieve computer-based data</li><li>Ability to apply basic principles of computersearches and/or queries</li><li>Ability to undertake administrative proceduresrelated to accessing requested data.</li></ul>
	Linkages To Other Units This is a core unit that underpins effective performance inall other units; combined training and assessment may be appropriate **Critical Aspects of Assessment** Evidence of the following is essential:<ul><li>Demonstrated ability to access enterprisecomputer system</li></ul>

- Demonstrated ability to access and retrieve computer-based data within accepted timeframe
- Demonstrated ability to apply knowledge of basic computer operations.

Context of Assessment

This unit may be assessed on or off the job Assessment should include practical demonstration of
accessing and retrieving computer- Based data either in the workplace or through a simulation activity, supported by a range of

- Methods to assess underpinning knowledge
- Assessment must relate to the individual's work area, job role and area of responsibility.

Resource Implications

Training and assessment to include access to a real or simulated workplace; and access to workplace standards, procedures, policies, guidelines, tools and equipment.

Assessment Methods

The following methods may be used to assess competency for this unit:
Case studies
Observation of practical candidate performance
Oral and written questions Portfolio evidence
Problem solving Role plays
Third party reports completed by a supervisor Project and assignment work.

Key Competencies in this Unit
Level 1 = competence to undertake tasks effectively
Level 2 = competence to manage tasks
Level 3 = competence to use concepts for evaluating

Key Competencies	Level	Examples
Collecting, organizing and analyzing information	1	Compare sources of information anddata; retrieve data in a format that is useful
Communicating ideas and information	1	Use searches andqueries to find information
Planning and organizing activities	1	Prioritize actions
Working with others and in teams	0	
Using mathematical ideas and techniques	0	
Solving problems	1	Use computer to find information to resolve complaints
Using technology	1	Use computer to access and retrieve data

Oral Questions

Student name	
Assessor name	
Location/venue	
Unit of competency	Access and retrieve computer-based data D1.HRS.CL1.01; D1.HOT.CL1.06; D2.TCC.CL1.10
Instructions	• Ask student questions from the attached list toconfirm knowledge, as necessary • Place tick in boxes to reflect student achievement (Competent „C" or Not Yet Competent „NYC") • Write short-form student answer in the spaceprovided for each question.

Questions	Response	
	C	NYC
1. Tell me how you turn on your computer at work.	q	q

Questions	Response	
	C	NYC
2. What different software is available on your workplace computer and how do you switch from one to another when you need to use different programs?	q	q
3. What arrangement of folders, sub-folders and files exists onyour workplace computer to help you identify and open required files?	q	q
4. What features does the software on your workplace have?What things do they allow/enable you to achieve?	q	q

Questions	Response	
	C	NYC
5. Tell me how you retrieve data from your workplacecomputer.	q	q
6. Where and how is electronic data stored in your workplace in a way it can be accessed using your computer?	q	q

Questions	Response	
	C	NYC
7. A person has asked you to identify and retrieve a file containing the phrase „It has come to our attention": how would you find the files containing this phrase?	q	q
8. When you have a file opened on the screen of your workplace computer, how can you identify the name of thatfile?	q	q
9. How would you verify the data you have accessed and retrieved meets the requirements of the person who requestedthe data?	q	q
10. You have been asked to provide a hard copy of the document open on your computer: tell me how you do this.	q	q

Written Questions for Trainers as the Basis on Testing the Knowledge and Competency of Tourism Workers

Access and retrieve computer-based data – D1.HRS.CL1.01; D1.HOT.CL1.06; D2.TCC.CL1.10
Student Name:

Answer all the following questions and submit to your Trainer.
1. What is the difference between a username and a password?

___

2. Why do computer have usernames and password?

___

3. When considering a computer program, what does sort mean?

___

4. What is a query?

___

5. What is the naming system given to storage medium in a Windows computer?
_____
___

6. How does a user commence a file search?
_____
___

7. When printing, what does collated mean?
_____
___

8. Explain what the filter process does in a table in Excel.
_____
___

9. Are searches case sensitive?
_____
___

10. What is a multi-level sort?
_____
___

11. What is a quick sort?
_____
___

12. Which program creates a spreadsheet?
_____
___

13. What is a table in Access?
_____
___

14. When considering page setup, what factors should be considered?

———

15. Describe the operation of a search engine?

———

16. Which program stores data in fields?

———

Answers to Written Questions
Access and retrieve computer-based data – D1.HRS.CL1.01; D1.HOT.CL1.06; D2.TCC.CL1.10

The following are model answers only – Trainers/Assessors must use discretion when determining whether or not an answer provided by a Student is acceptable or not.

- **What is the difference between a username and a password?**
  ☐ username is a name created by the system administrator to distinguish each user from the other user. A password is a set of characters to prove the person is the user.
- **Why do computer have usernames and password?**
  ☐ They are used to maintain the security and ensure that only approved users are allowed to access the data. They also ensure that correct permissions are allocated to the correct user.
- **When considering a computer program, what does sort mean?**
  ☐ The process of sorting reorders the data into a more meaningful order to make the information more usable.
- **What is a query?**

- query is the process of accepting or rejecting records for inclusion by using an identifiable set of criteria.
- **What is the naming system given to storage medium in a Windows computer.**
- Each storage medium is given a letter and a colon, ":". So a drive may be G:.
- **How does a user commence a file search?**
- search can be commenced by clicking on start and then entering the search criteria in the Start Search box.
- Entering the search criteria into the top window located on the top right in an Explorer window.
- **When printing, what does collated mean?**
- The term relates to situations where there a multiple copies of the same document produced. A collated print produces an entire copy of the document before printing another copy. An uncollected document would print the total number of a page and then print the total number of the next page.
- **Explain what the filter process does in a table in Excel.**
- filter hides records that do not meet a specified criterion.
- **Are searches case sensitive?**
- There are usually options in the search box that indicates where the search should be case sensitive or not.
- **What is a multi-level sort?**
- multi-level sort is where a sort uses more than one key or level so that a secondary sort occurs, and this is especially true when considering records that have duplicate criteria that is the key of the first search. For example, customers may be sorted on surname and, the secondary sort, then on given names to assist in finding the correct record.
- **What is a quick sort?**
- This is a sort using a previously defined set of criteria. Especially useful when re-sorting a table using the same keys after a new record has been added or a row edited.
- **Which program creates a spreadsheet?**
- Excel is the most common program to create a spreadsheet.
- **What is a table in Access?**
- Access is the most common program to create a spreadsheet.

- **When considering page setup, what factors should be considered?**
  - Page setup factors cover the orientation of the paper, margins which determine where printing will start and stop on a page, number of copies, and collation requirements.
- **Describe the operation of a search engine.**
  - It is a program that searches a database of website information to find matches to criteria supplied by the user and presents the results in the form of a webpage.
- **Which program stores data in fields?**
  - Access stores data in records which presents a complete picture about the object in the record. A record may be a customer. A field is a group of data elements that make up the record. E.g. Given name, surname, street, etc.

Student name	
Assessor name	
Location/venue	
Unit of competency	Access and retrieve computer-based data D1.HRS.CL1.01; D1.HOT.CL1.06; D2.TCC.CL1.10
Dates of observation	
Instructions	<ul><li>Over a period of time observe the student completing each of the following tasks: a) Open file b) Access computer-based data c) Retrieve computer-based data</li><li>Enter the date on which the tasks were undertaken</li><li>Place a tick in the box to show they completed each aspect of the task to the standard expected in the enterprise</li><li>Complete the feedback sections of the form, if required.</li></ul>

Observation checklist

Did the candidate…..	Yes	No
Element 1: Open file		
Turn on/access computer system correctly	q	q
Select or load appropriate software	q	q
Identify and open correct file	q	q
Element 2: Access computer-based data		
Use computer features to access a range of data or information	q	q
Retrieve data using prescribed systems, sequences and appropriate keyboard techniques	q	q
Access data stored on a variety of data storage mediums, private computer networks and the Internet	q	q
Use searches and queries to find desired information	q	q
Did the candidate…..	Yes	No
Element 3: Retrieve computer-based data		
Locate data to be retrieved	q	q
Check that data meets requirements	q	q
Print or transfer file to data storage medium as required	q	q
Did the student's overall performance meet the standard?	q	q
Feedback to student and trainer/assessor		
Strengths:		
Improvements needed:		
General comments:		
Candidate signature	Date	
Assessor signature	Date	

Third Party Statement

Studentname:			
Name of third party:		Contact no	
Relationshipto student:	q Employer q Supervisor q Colleague q Other *Please specify:* _____ *Please do not complete the form if you are a relative, close friend or have a conflict of interest]*		
Unit of competency:	Access and retrieve computer-based data D1.HRS.CL1.01; D1.HOT.CL1.06; D2.TCC.CL1.10		
The student is being assessed against industry competency standards and we areseeking your support in the judgment of their competence. Please answer these questions as a record of their performance while workingwith you. Thank you for your time.			

Do you believe the trainee has demonstrated thefollowing skills? *(tick the correct response]*	Yes	No	Not sure
Turns on/accesses computer system and selects/loads required software correctly	q	q	q
Identifies and opens correct files	q	q	q
Uses computer features to access a range of data or information	q	q	q
Retrieves data	q	q	q
Accesses data stored on a variety of data storage mediums, private computer networks and the Internet	q	q	q
Uses searches and queries to find desired information	q	q	q
Locates and checks data to be retrieved	q	q	q
Prints and/or transfers file to data storage medium	q	q	q

Third Party Statement

Comments/feedback from Third Party to Trainer/Assessor:	
Third party signature: end to:	Date:

Competency Student Recording

Name of Student		
Name of Assessor/s		
Unit of Competency	Access and retrieve computer-based data	D1.HRS.CL1.01; D1.HOT.CL1.06; D2.TCC.CL1.10
Date assessment commenced	Competent / NotYet Competent (Circle one)	
Date assessment finalized		
Assessment decision		
Follow up action required		
(Insert additional work and assessment required to achieve competency)		
Comments/observations by assessor/s		

Element & Performance Criteria	Observation of skills	3rd Party Statement	Oral Questions	Written Questions	Work Projects	Other
Element 1: Open file						
Turn on/access computer system correctly						
Select or load appropriate software						
Identify and open correct file						
Element 2: Access computer-based data						
Use computer features to access a range of data or information						

Retrieve data using prescribed systems, sequences and appropriate keyboard techniques							
Access data stored on a variety of data storage mediums, private computer networks and the Internet							
Use searches and queries to find desired information							
Element 3: Retrieve computer-based data							
Locate data to be retrieved							
Check that data meets							

requirements						
Print or transfer file to data storage medium as required						

Review Guide to Update Industry Knowledge In Preparation for Competency Assessment
ASEAN MRP-Mutual Recognition Agreement Tourism Professionals Competency Based Assessment

A. Tourism Industry Concerns

1. Meanings and Definitions of the term TOURISM
Please refer to Book ONE, Chapter One, No. II of this book. Any of the meanings as therein stated may do.

2. Composition of Tourism as a System with which it evolves
Please refer to Book TWO, Chapter 1.

3. Elements of a Tourist Worthy Destination.
Refer to Book FIVE, Chapter ONE, No. III.

4. Factors that Influence the Tourism Industry.
Demand - is the major factor that influence the Tourism Industry. Demand increases for the following:

Reasons for the Increase of Tourism Industry Demand
1. Necessity Employment
2. Inflation
3. Disposable income
4. Costs of goods and services
5. Opportunity costs Basic needs and wants
6. Marketing and promotions.

5. Sources of Economic and Political Issues?
1. Local government websites
2. Internet research.
3. Local community and council meetings
4. Economic and business websites
5. Legal journals
6. Industry publications

7. Newspapers

6. Resource Information Relating to Tourism Industry Statistics and Trends
1. Trade magazines
2. Hotel School Publications
3. Newsletters
4. Brochures
5. Advertisements
6. Reference books.

7. The Major Tourism Industry Statistics for Tourism Executives
There are endless statistics that can be researched, some of these include: Types of tourism businesses
Types and demographics of customers Top destinations
Hotel occupancy percentages Reasons for stays
Current industry information Destination countries Departure months
Length of stay
Type of organization for the trip Transport mode
 Accommodation type Expenditure
Popular tourist attractions.

8. The Businesses in the Community that Tourism Professionals should Know
Local attractions Shopping and retail areas Events and festivals
Eateries Supermarkets Local transport Activities
Places of worship.

9. What are two ways you can find out information about businesses in the local community?
Visiting local businesses and finding out what they provide Talking to management and staff of local businesses Collecting and reading brochures
Keeping up with local media including radio stations, television, newsletters or newspapers
Visiting the local Tourist Information Centre Attending town meetings
Looking at notice boards in shopping centers.

10. The Major Market Segments for Tourism Business
Leisure:
FIT (Free Independent Travellers) who arrange their own accommodation

Tours / coach groups Honeymooners Families
Elderly Religious Sporting.
Meetings, Incentive, Conventions and Exhibits
- Health and Wellness

11. Formal Methods for Information Gathering on Suitable Market Segments?

Customer comment cards
General Manager cocktail parties Interviews and follow up calls
Meetings
Performance.

12. Close Business Relationship with other Industries

is Indispensably Necessary in Tourism. Every industry is contributory to tourism development. A Tourism Professional i

13. What Tourism Professionals should know about other businesses?

Opening and closing times Key features and benefits Costs
Summary information about the business.

14. The Tourism Industry Sectors

Accommodation Attractions and theme parks Tour operators
Inbound tour wholesaler Outbound tour wholesaler Congress Organizers
Tourism & Hospitality Training Centers

15. **Tourist Information Center** is the ultimate source of information for Tourism Businesses (Hotels, Resorts, Restaurants, Tours and Transports, Attractions and Schedules of Special Events.

16. Sustainable tourism?

"Sustainable tourism" is based on the principles of sustainable development. It is based on minimizing adverse impacts on local communities, heritage, landscapes, water resources, habitats and species while supporting social and economic development. Taking care of the environment means taking care of the visitor and local community.", or.

"The management of all resources that meet the needs of tourists and host regions while protecting the opportunities for the future, in such a way that economic, social and aesthetic needs can be fulfilled while maintaining cultural integrity, essential ecological processes, biological diversity and life support systems." -- or -

"The sustainable development approach implies that the natural, cultural and other resources of tourism are conserved for continuous use in the future, while still bringing benefits to the present society."

17. The Ways How to Undertake Sustainable Tourism

Proper planning for tourism development with due regards to the environmental protection and preservation.

Institutionalization of the Culture of Tourism in Governance, Academe and the local community.

Cooperation rather than competition in the delivery of tourism products to the tourists.

Carrying capacity of the destination must be given due regards.

18. What is Tourism Development Plan

Refer to Book FIVE, Chapter II, No. IV.

19. The Importance of Tourism Development Planning

Refer to Book FIVE, Chapter II, No. III

20. What are the Steps in most effective Tourism Development Planning?

Refer to Book FIVE, Chapter II, No. III.

21. The Basic Steps for Seeking a Career in Tourism Industry

Understand the industry – research the industry to gain a sound understanding of what the industry involves and current information and trends

Understand the roles in the industry – unless you know what types of jobs there are, you won"t know which one will be of interest for you. In addition, managers often ask applicants about what they know about the job they are applying for

Education – educate yourself with the necessary knowledge or skills to be able to undertake the position you are seeking. This may be undertaking research activities, short courses through to tourism related qualifications

Develop a resume – develop a concise resume which clearly articulates your personal information and your skills sets

Look at recruitment vacancies - these may be advertisements in newspaper, advertised in the businesses themselves, through recruitment companies, on local notice boards, in shop windows, through word of mouth, recruitment days or internet searches

Familiarize yourself with businesses – conduct research on the business you are trying to seek employment with whether through personal visits or internet research

Make yourself known - visit businesses personally and try to introduce yourself to key recruitment contacts, whether Human Resources or departmental managers and supervisors.

22. Steps for Employed in Tourism to Improve Chances for Promotion

Confer with management and Human Resources to identify:

The knowledge, skills, education or experience required to progress to a higher position

What further training opportunities are present

Likely vacancies within the business, be it in the local organization or in the chain

The job roles and duties of higher positions.

Gain an understanding of what you need to not only successfully get a higher position, but to be able to perform fully well once given the opportunity

Express your desire for progression:

Unless your manager knows you want to move to a higher position, you may be overlooked. It is good to be pro-active and plant the seed in the mind of management

Ask your manager for additional responsibilities or tasks to improve your skill set to demonstrate your motivation towards promotion.

23. The Most Important Things to Do to Update Knowledge what is Happening in Tourism.

Special events Weather

VIP and customer activities Emergencies

Legal requirements

Local attractions, festivals and events. Tourist facilities

Transportation schedules and equipment

24. Ways to Improve Time Management?

Preparing a list of all activities to be performed

Identifying tasks by "1,2,3" or "a,b,c" to indicate their importance

Prioritizing and completing important tasks first

Breaking time into small management chunks Use of a timer when completing activities Identifying and reducing time wasters

Having the ability to say no to people or tasks that are not a priority.

21. Quality Determination

In Tourism, "Quality" is always determined by the Customer not by the any tourism business.

22. The Concept of 'quality assurance' and how it is Achieved.

"Quality assurance" (QA). This is a term used to systematically measure and compare aspects of operations within a business against operational standards of performance.

In essence these concepts have the same aim: to look at every aspect of a business's operation and see how it can be improved to improve the product or service provided to the customer.

23. The Importance and Purposes of Information technology in the tourism industry

Streamline and speed up access and delivery of tourism services
Improve management and profitability of tourism operations
Enhance marketing of the industry as a whole and the businesses within it Improve the relationships between tourism businesses and its customers.

24. The Uses of Information Technology to Improve tourism

Standardized set of XML messages for the distribution of tour and activity data
Short-term, purely spontaneous travel specials Dedicated travel apps
Sharing of traveller's personal information to simplify bookings Advanced travel search engines
Travellers to find activities and local content in a mobile optimized environment
Small business owners to access the business travel market
Hotels and resorts to communicate with guest through on property mobile before, during, and after their visit to the property.
Hotels manage their online reputation and social media Friends to collaborate and plan trips together
Travellers research and decide where to go, where to stay and what to do.

25. The Employer Responsibilities under the Laws?

Employer responsibilities include:
Complying with occupational health and safety regulations Providing equal and fair services to all people in accordance with
EO legislation

Paying relevant taxes and fees associated with the operation of the business

Ensuring appropriate insurance is taken out to cover workers

Offering products and services that conform to what is advertised

Being a responsible corporate citizen and community member.

Observing the Best Practice in complying Corporate Social Responsibilities

26. The Employee's Responsibilities under the Laws

Employee responsibilities extend to, though are not restricted to: Undertaking duties as they apply to their employment category Not acting in a discriminatory manner towards their employer, colleagues or customers

Adhering to the regulations set out in the OH&S Act Representing the best interests of the business Working to the best of their ability Keeping commercial information in confidence

Being responsible and accountable for all money received on behalf of the business

Obeying all lawful instructions from management.

27. Ethics in Tourism

Although Ethical Issues may or may not be enforced by laws or regulation governing the tourism sector, it is always necessary that there must be written Code of Ethical Standards that defines the parameters in the practice and exercise of the delivery for their products and services to instill orderliness and avoid destructive competition. It is about doing something "morally" right.

28. Ethical Behavior that Concerns the Tourism Business

Personnel Piracy

Cut-Throat Competition in Rate Offerings

Baseless and Malicious Propaganda to destroy the image of others

Untruthful Advertising

29. The Areas covering "Industrial Relations" activity?

Recruitment & Retention Termination of staff Workplace health and safety Workplace agreements Harassment & Discrimination Conflict in the workplace.

30. The Department Information on 'industrial relations'?

Human Resources.

31. Causes for concern in the Tourism Industry

The state of the economy – interest rates, currency exchange levels, level of employment
Environmental considerations and concerns Terrorism
Customer confidence Eco-tourism Sustainable tourism
Impact of development in tourism Climate change
Visa restrictions & tourism Cultural tourism
Weather
Technological and legislative changes that impact on the industry.

32. The labor issues in a tourism business
Pay rates
The ability to recruit sufficient and properly trained or experienced staff
Working conditions Training
Mandatory licensing and certification requirements Superannuation / Insurance
 Disciplinary and dismissal procedur

33. The ways for communication with colleagues
Conversations Staff briefings
E-mails and Telephone calls.

34. The most common way to communication with customers
Verbally is best, as it provides the opportunity to provide further explanation, body language, provide examples and answer questions the customer may have.

35. The best ways to ensure you complete allocated tasks
Work quickly
Practice being interrupted Practice tact and diplomacy
Take a minute to plan and prioritize Ask for help where required.

36. Tasks should be prioritized as each task is as important as each other.
While all tasks assigned to the position are as important as each other, priority must always be accorded with those that require immediate and proper action

37. How Incorporate knowledge and information into day to day operations

Working in accordance with new or revised requirements Using new knowledge to modify personal work practices Updating printed materials

•Supplying information to customers that incorporates the new knowledge.

38. The Importance of Information Sharing with people in the workplace

Information sharing is an indispensable part in a team to achieve the desired goals in a common workplace. It is also necessary to avoid contradicting opinions that normally cooperation and inability to perform well in a work place.

39. How to incorporate knowledge and information into day to day operations

Working in accordance with new or revised requirements Using new knowledge to modify personal work practices Updating printed materials

Supplying information to customers that incorporates the new knowledge.

B. Fundamentals in the Use of Computer

1. The Username and Password

- Username is a name created by the system administrator to distinguish each user from the other user.
- Password is a set of characters to prove the person is the user.

2. Purpose of Usernames and Password

Both are used to maintain the security and ensure that only approved users are allowed to access the data. They also ensure that correct permissions are allocated to the correct user.

3. Sort in Consideration of Computer Program

It is process of sorting or reorders the data into a more meaningful order to make the information more usable.

4. What is a query

Query is the process of accepting or rejecting records for inclusion by using an identifiable set of criteria.

5. The naming system given to storage medium in a Windows computer.

Each storage medium is given a letter and a colon, ":". So a drive may be

G:.
6. **How User may commence search?**
Search can be commenced by clicking on start and then entering the search criteria in the Start Search box.
 Entering the search criteria into the top window located on the top right in an   Explorer window.
7. **The Collated Printing**
The term relates to situations where there are multiple copies of the same document produced. A collated print produces an entire copy of the document before printing another copy. An uncollected document would print the total number of a page and then print the total number of the next page.
8. **The filter process does in a table in Excel.**
Filter hides records that do not meet a specified criterion.
9. **The Searches case.**
There are usually options in the search box that indicates where the search should be case sensitive or not.
10. **The multi-level sort**
Multi-level sort is where a sort uses more than one key or level so that a secondary sort occurs, and this is especially true when considering records that have duplicate criteria that is the key of the first search. For example, customers may be sorted on surname and, the secondary sort, then on given names to assist in finding the correct record.
11. **The quick sort**
This is a sort using a previously defined set of criteria. Especially useful when re-sorting a table using the same keys after a new record has been added or a row edited.
12. **The Program that creates a spreadsheet**
Excel is the most common program to create a spreadsheet.
13. **The Table in Access**
Access is the most common program to create a spreadsheet.
14. **Factors considered in Page Set-Up**
 Page setup factors cover the orientation of the paper, margins which determine where printing will start and stop on a page, number of copies, and collation requirements.
15. **The Program in Operation of a Search Engine.**

It is a program that searches a database of website information to find matches to criteria supplied by the user and presents the results in the form of a webpage.

16. The Program stores Data in Fields

Access stores data in records which presents a complete picture about the object in the record. A record may be a customer. A field is a group of data elements that make up the record. E.g. Given name, surname, street, etc.

Book 11 - Asean Mutual Recognition Agreement On Tourism Professionals

Preamble

The Governments of Brunei Darussalam, the Kingdom of Cambodia, the Republic of Indonesia, the Lao People's Democratic Republic, Malaysia, the Union of Myanmar, the Republic of the Philippines, the Republic of Singapore, the Kingdom of Thailand, and the Socialist Republic of Viet Nam, Member States of the Association of South East Asian Nations (hereinafter collectively referred to as "ASEAN" or "ASEAN Member States" and singularly as "ASEAN Member State");

RECOGNISING the objectives of the ASEAN Framework Agreement on Services (hereinafter referred to as "AFAS"), which are to enhance cooperation in services amongst ASEAN Member States in order to improve efficiency and competitiveness, diversify production capacity and supply and distribution of services of their services suppliers within and outside ASEAN; to eliminate substantially the restrictions to trade in services amongst ASEAN Member States; and to liberalize trade in services by expanding the depth and scope of liberalization beyond those undertaken by ASEAN Member States under the General Agreement on Trade in Services (hereinafter referred to as "GATS") with the aim to realizing free trade in services;

RECOGNISING the ASEAN Vision 2020 on Partnership in Dynamic Development, approved on 14 June 1997, which charted towards the year 2020 for the creation of a stable, prosperous and highly competitive ASEAN Economic Region which would result in: free flow of goods, services and investment;

equitable economic development, and reduced poverty and socio-economic disparities; and

enhanced political, economic and social stability;

RECOGNISING the objectives of the ASEAN Tourism Agreement (hereinafter referred to as "ATA"), which are to cooperate in facilitating travel into and within ASEAN; to enhance cooperation in the tourism industry among ASEAN Member States in order to improve its efficiency and competitiveness; to substantially reduce restrictions to trade in tourism and travel services among ASEAN Member States; to enhance the development and promotion of ASEAN as a single tourism destination with world-class standards, facilities and attractions; to enhance mutual assistance in human resource development and strengthen cooperation to develop, upgrade and expand tourism and travel facilities and services in ASEAN; and to create favorable conditions for the public and private sectors to engage more deeply in tourism development, intra-ASEAN travel and investment in tourism services and facilities;

RECOGNISING the Cebu Declaration on the Establishment of the ASEAN Community by 2015 adopted at the 12th ASEAN Summit that agreed to accelerate the establishment of an ASEAN Community by 2015 along the lines of ASEAN Vision 2020 and the Declaration of ASEAN Concord II in the three pillars of the ASEAN Security Community, ASEAN Economic Community and ASEAN Socio-Cultural Community;

NOTING the decision of the Bali Concord II adopted at the Ninth ASEAN Summit held in 2003 in Bali, Indonesia calling for completion of Mutual Recognition Arrangements for qualifications in major professional services by 2008; and

NOTING that the ASEAN Framework for the Integration of Priority Sectors (2004) recognizes the priority for the creation of a single economic area for ASEAN and the importance of close partnerships with the private sector,

HAVE AGREED on this ASEAN Mutual Recognition Arrangement on Tourism Professionals (hereinafter referred to as "this Arrangement") as follows:

ARTICLE I: OBJECTIVES

The objectives of this Arrangement are:

1.1 To facilitate mobility of Tourism Professionals; and

1.2 To exchange information on best practices in competency-based education and training for Tourism Professionals and to provide opportunities for cooperation and capacity building across ASEAN Member States.

ARTICLE II: DEFINITIONS AND SCOPE

In this Arrangement, unless the context otherwise states,

2.1 **ASEAN Common Competency Standards for Tourism Professionals (ACCSTP)** refers to the minimum requirements of competency standards in hotel and travel services as listed in the APPENDIX which aim to upgrade tourism services and facilitate the development of this Arrangement between ASEAN Member States;

2.2 ASEAN National Tourism Organizations (ASEAN NTOs) refers to the government institutions in charge of the tourism sector of ASEAN Member States;

2.3 ASEAN Tourism Professional Monitoring Committee (ATPMC) consists of ASEAN NTOs and appointed representatives from the National Tourism Professional Boards (NTPBs);

2.4 ASEAN Tourism Professional Registration System (ATPRS) refers to a web-based facility to disseminate details regarding the list of Foreign Tourism Professionals duly certified in accordance with Articles 2.10 and 2.14;

2.5 Assessment refers to the process of appraising the qualification and/or competencies of Tourism Professionals;

2.6 Certification refers to the issuance of a certificate to Tourism Professional whose qualification and/or competencies have met the standards specified in ACCSTP;

2.7 Common ASEAN Tourism Curriculum (CATC) refers to the common curriculum for ASEAN Tourism Professionals as mutually agreed upon by the ASEAN Tourism Ministers upon recommendation by the ASEAN NTOs;

2.8 Foreign Tourism Professionals refer to Tourism Professionals who are nationals of any other ASEAN Member States who are certified in an ASEAN Member State;

2.9 Host Country refers to the ASEAN Member State where a Foreign Tourism Professional applies for recognition to work in accordance with ARTICLE III;

2.10 National Tourism Professional Board (NTPB) refers to the Board for Tourism Professionals which shall be composed of representatives from the public and private sectors including the academia and other relevant tourism stakeholders, to be determined by the respective ASEAN NTOs;

2.11 Recognition refers to acceptance by the TPCB of a demonstration of compliance with requirements set out in the ACCSTP;

2.12 Tourism Job Title refers to a specific job position in the tourism sector as specified in the ACCSTP;

2.13 Tourism Professional refers to a natural person who holds the nationality of an ASEAN Member State certified by the Tourism Professional Certification Board; and

2.14 **Tourism Professional Certification Board (TPCB)** refers to the government board and/or agency authorised by the government of each ASEAN Member State primarily responsible for the assessment and certification of Tourism Professionals.

ARTICLE III: RECOGNITION AND ELIGIBILITY OF FOREIGN TOURISM PROFESSIONALS

The qualification of a Foreign Tourism Professional may be recognized by other ASEAN Member States, and if such qualification is recognized, he/she may be eligible to work in a host country provided that he/she possesses a valid tourism competency certificate in a specific tourism job title as specified in the ACCSTP, issued by the TPCB in an ASEAN Member State. The eligibility to work in a host country will be subjected to prevailing domestic laws and regulations of the host country.

ARTICLE IV: BASIS OF RECOGNITION AND QUALIFICATIONS

4.1 The ASEAN Member States recognize that competencies based on qualification, education, training and/or experiences shall be the principal elements considered in granting mutual recognition of Foreign Tourism Professional; and

4.2 The ASEAN Member States are encouraged to apply the ACCSTP and CATC.

ARTICLE V: RESPONSIBILITIES

5.1 National Tourism Professional Board (NTPB)

5.1.1 The NTPB of each ASEAN Member State shall have the following responsibilities:

5.1.2 Create awareness and disseminate information about this Arrangement;

5.1.3 Promote, update, maintain, and monitor the ACCSTP and the CATC;

5.1.4 Facilitate the exchange of information concerning assessment procedures, criteria, systems, manuals and publications relating to this Arrangement;

5.1.5 Report its work progress to the ASEAN NTOs, including actions taken on cases referred to it by the TPCB and/or ATPMC;

5.1.6 Formulate and update necessary mechanisms to enable implementation of this Arrangement ;

5.1.7 Facilitate the exchange of best practices and prevailing developments in tourism sector with the view to harmonizing and updating regional and/or international tourism competencies and curricula; and

5.1.8 Such other functions and responsibilities that may be assigned to it by the ASEAN NTOs in the future.

5.2 The Tourism Professional Certification Board (TPCB)

The TPCB of each ASEAN Member State shall have the following responsibilities:

5.2.1 Assess qualifications and/or competencies of Tourism Professionals as specified in ACCSTP;

5.2.2 Issue certificates to Tourism Professionals whose qualifications and/or competencies have met the standards specified in ACCSTP;

5.2.3 Develop, process and maintain a registry of certified Tourism Professionals and job opportunities on the ATPRS; and

5.2.4 Notify the NTPB promptly in the event that foreign Tourism Professionals are no longer qualified to provide a particular service or have violated technical, professional or ethical standards;

5.3 ASEAN Tourism Professional Monitoring Committee (ATPMC)

The ATPMC shall have the following responsibilities:

5.3.1 Create awareness and disseminate information about this Arrangement on Tourism Professionals within ASEAN;

5.3.2 Promote, update, maintain and monitor the ACCSTP and the CATC;

5.3.3 Notify promptly the concerned TPCB upon receipt of feedback from NTPBs, in case a foreign Tourism Professional is no longer recognised by the host country;

5.3.4 Facilitate the exchange of information concerning assessment procedures, criteria, systems, manuals and publications relating to this Arrangement;

5.3.5 Report its work progress to the ASEAN NTOs;

5.3.6 Formulate and update necessary mechanisms to enable the implementation of this Arrangement; and

5.3.7 Such other functions and responsibilities that may be assigned to it by the ASEAN NTOs in the future.

ARTICLE VI: RIGHT TO REGULATE
This Arrangement shall not reduce, eliminate or modify the rights, powers and authority of each ASEAN Member State. ASEAN Member States, however, shall undertake to exercise their regulatory powers responsibly and in good faith without creating any unnecessary barriers towards each other.

ARTICLE VII: DISPUTE SETTLEMENT
7.1   ASEAN Member States shall at all times endeavour to agree on the interpretation and application of this Arrangement and shall make every attempt through communication, dialogue, consultation and cooperation to arrive at a mutually satisfactory resolution of any matter that might affect the implementation of this Arrangement.
7.2   The provision of the ASEAN Protocol on Enhanced Dispute Settlement Mechanism, done at Vientiane, Lao PDR on 29 November 2004, shall apply to disputes concerning the interpretation, implementation, and/or application of any of the provisions under this Arrangement.

ARTICLE VIII: AMENDMENT
8.1   The provisions of this Arrangement may only be modified through amendments mutually agreed upon in writing by all ASEAN Member States.
8.2   Any revision, modification or amendments agreed to by the ASEAN Member States shall be reduced into writing and shall form part of this Arrangement.
8.3   Notwithstanding Article 8.1 above, the APPENDIX may be amended administratively by the ASEAN Secretary General upon notification by ATPMC.
8.4   Such revision, modification or amendment shall come into force on such date as may be determined by the ASEAN Member States.
8.5   Any revision, modification, or amendment shall not prejudice the rights and obligations arising from or based on this Arrangement prior or up to the date of such revision, modification, or amendment.

ARTICLE IX: FINAL PROVISIONS

9.1 Subject to Article 9.2, this Arrangement shall enter into force after all ASEAN Member States have completed and For the Republic of Indonesia: JERO WACIK Minister of Culture and Tourism
For Lao People's Democratic Republic: established the TPCB and NTPB or their equivalent bodies and notified the Secretary-General of ASEAN within one hundred and eighty (180) days from the date of its signing.

9.2 In the event that any ASEAN Member State has not completed and established the TPCB and NTPB or their equivalent bodies within one hundred and eighty (180) days from the date of signing, this Arrangement shall enter into force for that ASEAN Member State upon the date of notification in writing to the Secretary General of ASEAN of the completion and establishment of the TPCB and NTPB or their equivalent bodies.

9.3 This Arrangement shall be deposited with the Secretary-General of ASEAN, who shall promptly furnish a certified copy thereof to each ASEAN Member State.

9.4 This Arrangement or any part thereof shall only be terminated upon mutual agreement of the ASEAN Tourism Ministers upon recommendation of the ASEAN NTOs.

IN WITNESS WHEREOF, the undersigned, being duly authorized by their respective governments, have signed the ASEAN Mutual Recognition Arrangement on Tourism Professionals.

For Brunei Darussalam:

PEHIN DATO YAHYA
Minister of Industry and Primary Resources For the Kingdom of Cambodia:

DR. THONG KHON
Minister of Tourism

SOMPHONG MONGKHONVILAY
Minister, Chairman of Lao National Tourism Administration

For Malaysia:

DATO' SRI AZALINA DATO' OTHMAN SAID

Maximino P. Zurbito, Jr.
Minister of Tourism

For Union of Myanmar:

BRIG GENERAL AYE MYINT KYU
Deputy Minister, Ministry of Hotels and Tourism

For the Republic of the Philippines:

JOSEPH H. DURANO
Secretary, Department of Tourism

For the Republic of Singapore:

.S. ISWARAN
Senior Minister of State for Trade and Industry

For the Kingdom of Thailand:

CHUMPOL SILAPA-ARCHA
Deputy Prime Minister & Minister of Tourism and Sports For the

Socialist Republic of Viet Nam:

HOANG TUAN ANH
Minister of Culture, Sports and Tourism

References

___/Republic Act 9593, National Tourism Policy Act, Republic of the Philippines;

___/ASEAN Economic Integration Mutual Recognition Agreements on Tourism Professionals Handbook ISBN 978-xxxxxx(to be added using ESRT ISBNs)Incorporated as per Express Permission /Approval hereunder:"The text of this publication may be freely quoted or reprinted with proper acknowledgement. "Copyright: Association of Southeast Asian Nations (ASEAN) 2013 www.asean-tourism.com

___/Official Gazette, 1985 Edition

___/Maximiliano Korstanje, Etymological Study on the Origin and Meaning of Tourism, , e-Review of Tourism Research (eRTR), Vol. 5, No. 5, 2007);

___/ Wekipedia

___/ Extension Bulletin E-2004 Cooperative Extension Service November 1990Michigan State University;

___/IAPCO-International Association of Professional Congress Organizers Seminar on Congress Management, Tagaytay City, Philippines

___/WATA-World Association of Travel Agencies, WATA Master Key, Geneva, Switzerland, 1982;

___/Maximino P. Zurbito, Jr., Final Report Scholar's Account on Experience and Investigative Research on International Tourism conducted during the WATA 1980 International Tourism Traveling Scholarship in 21 cities of 14 countries and states in Asia and Europe

___/Msximiino P. Zurbito, Jr., Winning Essays: "Why I Have Chosen the Profession of a Travel Agen"t, and "Mass Tourism-Saturation of Sites, Monuments and Historical Museums", 1979;

___/How to Focus Your Marketing Efforts, Monthly Bulletin ASTA-American Society of Travel Agencies, November 1981;

About the Author

Maximino P. Zurbito, Jr.

A post graduate is Juris Doctor with a professional title of Ph.D., Doctor of Philosophy and enrolled in the Roll of Tourism Experts in Development Panning, Education and Training by the ILO International Labour Office Technical Cooperation for Developing Countries, Geneva, Switzerland. The author has extensive hands-on work experience of more than Three Decades in the tourism sector, particularly in destination management including among others Travel and Tours Agency, Meetings, Incentives, Conference and Exhibits (MICE); and Accommodation service systems. He has participated in varopis domestic and international tourism-related conventions, conferences and exhibits; the First in Asia and the only Filipino awarded with the WATA World Association of Travel Agencies Daniel V, Dedina International Tourism Travel Scholarship Grant, that brought him to 27 cities of 21 countries in Asia and Europe where he conducted an investigative research in travel and tourism planning, development, operation, education, and management. Among his Work Experience includes: Founder and Senior Associate, MPZ Consult & Associates. He Formulated/Authored Tourism development related Documents including among others the following:2019: Development Concept, Project TREASURE Tourism Reinvented for Eco Agri Stimulus of the Unproductive to Rejuvenate Economy, which major program component is the conduct of 'Continuing Education-Key to Institutionalization Culture of Tourism' thru the creation of CREATED Center for Rural Eco Agri Tourism Education and Development that shall focus on tourism-related acadenuc and and technical training programs, that is likewise adopted into its system by the Association of Northern Iloilo Tourism Oriented Services, a local Non-Government Organization as a continuing flagship project, and the Northern Iloilo State University thru the latter's Board of Trustees.

www.ingramcontent.com/pod-product-compliance
Lightning Source LLC
LaVergne TN
LVHW091611070526
838199LV00044B/756